Hollywood's African American Films

Hollywood's African American Films

The Transition to Sound

Ryan Jay Friedman

RUTGERS UNIVERSITY PRESS
NEW BRUNSWICK, NEW JERSEY, AND LONDON

Library of Congress Cataloging-in-Publication Data

Friedman, Ryan Jay.

Hollywood's African American films : the transition to sound / Ryan Jay Friedman.

p. cm.

Includes bibliographical references and index.

ISBN 978-0-8135-5048-0 (hardcover : alk. paper) — ISBN 978-0-8135-5049-7 (pbk. : alk. paper)

1. African Americans in motion pictures. 2. African Americans in the motion picture industry. 3. Race in motion pictures. 4. Motion pictures—United States—History—20th century. I. Title.

PN1995.9.N4F75 2011

791.43'652996073—dc22 2010041969

A British Cataloging-in-Publication record for this book is available from the British Library.

Visit our Web site: http://rutgerspress.rutgers.edu

Manufactured in the United States of America

For Ruth

Contents

Acknowledgments

In bringing this book to completion, I am struck by the extent to which its existence depends on the encouragement, insights, and examples offered by supportive teachers, colleagues, friends, and family. Although it is difficult to do so adequately or comprehensively, I would like to express my gratitude for these many gifts.

I was fortunate to have encountered such rigorous, challenging, inspiring, and kind teachers and mentors while a graduate student at Northwestern University. I would like to thank especially Kevin Bell, Betsy Erkkila, Christine Froula, Jay Grossman, Chris Lane, Susan Manning, and Jeffrey Masten. Chuck Kleinhans deserves special thanks for a series of early conversations that helped me to navigate the then-unfamiliar terrain of film studies. Perhaps the single most important influence on this project and my critical sensibility more broadly has been Julia Stern, whose sharp analytical eye and rhetorical acumen continue to provide models for my own work. An ideal mentor, Julia devoted an extraordinary amount of time and effort to reading and discussing my writing with me and provided professional guidance and emotional support throughout my time at Northwestern.

I must also thank several bodies within the Northwestern community for providing financial support essential to the progress of my work: the Weinberg College of Arts and Sciences for awarding me a fellowship (2002–2003), the Kaplan Center for the Humanities for making me a graduate affiliate (2003–2004), and the Department of English for hiring me as a visiting assistant professor (2004–2005). I thank the faculty and staff of the Department of English at Rice University, who were extremely welcoming and generous in helping me to learn the ropes during my year there as a visiting assistant professor. Thanks in particular to Caroline Levander and Susan Wood.

I am most grateful to my colleagues in the Department of English and on the Interdisciplinary Film Studies Committee at The Ohio State University

(OSU) for the range of support they have given me, from feedback on drafts, to advice on placing my manuscript, to answers to teaching questions, to intellectual community, to general encouragement and goodwill. I want to thank in particular Chad Allen, Mark Conroy, Tommy Davis, Alan Farmer, Steve Fink, Harvey Graff, Ron Green, John Hellman, Beth Hewitt, Pranav Jani, Ethan Knapp, Manny Martinez, Linda Mizejewski, Sean O'Sullivan, Jim Phelan, Joe Ponce, Elizabeth Renker, Rebecca Wanzo, and Andrea Williams. For their general support, I am indebted to my department chairs and program directors at OSU, John Davidson, Richard Dutton, and Valerie Lee. I owe a particular debt of gratitude to two colleagues and good friends, Jared Gardner and Koritha Mitchell. In addition to devoting long hours to reading and offering sharp feedback on my work, Jared has been my guide in all things professional and all things institutional at OSU. Koritha has been a true intellectual collaborator, providing a great example and inspiration with her own work and insightful responses to mine.

This book attests to the encouragement and criticism offered (in its myriad forms, small and large) by a range of peers in the field, some of them old friends, others of brief or more recent acquaintance. While it would be impossible to name all of these people here, I would like to express thanks to Katy Chiles, Lisa Collins, Marcy Dinius, Thomas Doherty, David Gerstner, James Grossman, Hunt Howell, Coleman Hutchison, Peter Jaros, Dwight McBride, and Judith Weisenfeld.

In researching and writing this book, I have benefited greatly from the assistance of interested, knowledgeable archivists and librarians. I want to recognize the staffs of the following institutions for making materials available and helping me to navigate their collections: the Margaret Herrick Library of the Academy of Motion Picture Arts and Sciences (especially Jenny Romero and Kristine Krueger), the Warner Bros. archive at the University of Southern California (especially Sandra Joy Lee), the Film and Television Archive at the University of California, Los Angeles (UCLA) (especially Mark Quigley), Special Collections and Performing Arts Special Collections at UCLA (especially Lauren Buisson), the Wisconsin Center for Film and Theater Research (especially Dorinda Hartmann), the Black Film Center/Archive at Indiana University (especially Mary Huelsbeck), the Celeste Bartos International Film Study Center at the Museum of Modern Art (especially Charles Silver), the Periodicals Department and Special Collections at Northwestern University Library, the Kelvin Smith Library at Case Western Reserve University, and the University Libraries system at OSU. Thanks also to Ashley, Gayle, and Jesse Byock for opening their home to me during an extended research trip in the Los Angeles area.

My deepest thanks go to Rutgers University Press for bringing this book into print. I have benefited immensely from the support and guidance of Editor in

Chief Leslie Mitchner. Thanks also to Katie Keeran for kind, helpful answers to my many questions. I am most appreciative of Arthur Knight for his extremely careful, fair, and incisive reading of and response to my manuscript.

Finally, I give fond thanks to my family: my parents, Jim and Kathy, and my siblings, Scott, Andrea, and Sean. It would be impossible for me to do justice to the many ways in which their constant love and friendship have helped and continue to help to sustain me in my endeavors. I am also blessed with extremely supportive in-laws in the Williams family. With many a thoughtful gift of books or videos, Reba has offered particular encouragement. The person who has been most centrally involved in the day-to-day labor of writing this book is my wife, Ruth, to whom my greatest thanks are due. With her love, imagination, and humor, Ruth graces my life in every way. There is certainly no way to imagine the completion of this book without her involvement—from long hours spent discussing main ideas, to keen editorial assistance, to countless, less tangible forms of sharing in this project. The book is dedicated to her.

Hollywood's African American Films

Introduction

NEGRO TALKING PICTURES

Speaking outside the Lafayette Theater on 20 August 1929, Congressman Oscar DePriest announced: "We are standing on the threshold of civil and cultural emancipation in America. Tonight we have seen how far our race has progressed culturally and artistically since the Emancipation Proclamation."[1] With these remarks, DePriest bore witness to an unprecedented event: the premier screening of *Hallelujah*, an African American–cast feature film by a Hollywood studio (MGM), at a race theater in Harlem.[2] Representing the First Congressional District of Illinois, which covered Chicago's predominantly African American South Side, DePriest himself had recently achieved the unprecedented. In March 1929, DePriest became the first African American politician from a northern state to serve in the national legislature and the first African American politician from any state to do so in the twentieth century.[3]

Placing the *Hallelujah* premier in a typological framework of emancipation events, DePriest used a strategy of historical interpretation that had shaped discussions of the most significant event in the preceding fifteen years of African American social history, the Great Migration. To call the Great Migration, the movement of roughly one and a half million African Americans from the South to northern cities between 1916 and 1929, a "second emancipation" was to view this mass movement "within a historical context anchored by the first emancipation and as a similarly transforming event."[4] A migrant himself in the late nineteenth century, DePriest had moved with his family from Florence, Alabama, to Salina, Kansas, to Dayton, Ohio, and on his own to Chicago.[5] DePriest became the first African American alderman in Chicago in 1915, and his career in politics unfolded in tandem with the transformation of the South Side by the first wave of the Great Migration.[6] The South Side's emergence as a major African American metropolis rivaling Harlem occasioned DePriest's involvement with the production and promotion of *Hallelujah*. As a piece in the black weekly *California Eagle* explained, DePriest's praise of the film carried the authority of "one who is the recognized leader and . . . chosen representative ['of an entire race']."[7]

Perhaps recognizing DePriest's unique, representative stature, MGM had invited him to visit the Culver City, California, soundstage where some scenes of *Hallelujah* were produced. The *New York Amsterdam News* published a studio lot photograph of DePriest with *Hallelujah*'s white director, King Vidor, and one of the film's stars, Nina Mae McKinney.[8] The *Eagle* later reprinted the text of a wire DePriest sent to MGM upon *Hallelujah*'s release: "Accept my congratulations on production of Hallelujah. You have opened up a new field of motion picture entertainment. The scenes are realistic, music the best I have heard, photography and directing superb, and work of actors truly remarkable."[9]

Daniel Haynes, the actor who played *Hallelujah*'s main character, Zeke Johnson, published his own testimony on the film's historical significance in the African American press. In "What 'Hallelujah' Means to the Negro Race," Haynes, like DePriest, constructed an analogy between the work of African American actors in the Hollywood cinema and the "always upward" movement of black collective struggle: "Slowly rising from 'atmosphere' to small 'bits' and parts in which he proved his worth and ability, the Negro has finally broken through the shell of apathy and indifference and emerged in the light on the screen."[10] With this analogy, Haynes traced a movement from virtual nonexistence to "articulate" presence on screen, effectively conflating the capacity for cinematic self-expression with the larger struggle of "the Negro . . . to express the thought in his heart" in American society.[11]

Haynes also envisioned a path-breaking role for his own generation of African American film actors. Having "broken through the shell of apathy and indifference" on screen and in the cinema industry, these actors carry "one and only thought in [their] hearts": "to make it possible for other members of our race to follow in our footsteps. It is not what the picture will do for me or anyone else in the cast that has been thought of at all—for what we have in mind is far bigger than our own individual successes. We are trying to pave the way for others of our people to follow on our trail."[12]

The "way" that Haynes envisioned was not just a path into the cinema but also a larger exodus or emancipatory movement, making the film an anchoring point for collective hopes: "'Hallelujah' will, as Moses led his people from the wilderness, lead ours from the wilderness of misunderstanding and apathy."[13] Oddly personifying the film, Haynes portrayed *Hallelujah* as bringing African Americans to the cinema screen and, in turn, promising to liberate an entire people from social stigma. In this last move, Haynes appeared to equate screen presence with social and cultural legitimacy and power. To "emerge" into the "light" of the screen was to claim a space of official, sanctioned self-representation. This representational space, or "new field" as

DePriest called it, seems to have represented for both men a means to broader social recognition for African Americans; the cinema appeared to be nothing less than a national mirror, legitimating as American subjects the social groups whose images it captured.

DePriest's and Haynes's claims about *Hallelujah* exemplify the enthusiasm with which many African American journalists, film critics, and cinephiles greeted the exhibition of *Hallelujah* and *Hearts in Dixie*, another feature-length African American–cast musical that was released by Fox just a few months before the MGM film. Publishing largely in the black press but also, in two important cases, in a film journal and an anthology dedicated to the study of folklore, these writers celebrated the advent of "talking pictures," films with recorded, synchronized sound and dialogue, as a new area of opportunity for African American performers in the white-owned and -operated Hollywood studios.

For instance, the editors of the widely circulating African American weekly the *Pittsburgh Courier* addressed "The Value of the Talkies" in June 1929, claiming, "The Talking Pictures ought to contribute considerably toward bettering race relations in the United States. Not only have two sympathetic Negro plays been produced, one of which [*Hearts in Dixie*] has received wide acclaim, even in the South, but a number of Negro acts, singing and dancing have gone into the most remote sections."[14] For the *Courier* editors, the mere fact of the national circulation of "Negro films" amounted to a traversal of social barriers. Using rhetoric similar to Haynes's, they concluded their commentary by suggesting that, while the "Negro plays and acts so far to appear on the talking screen have not been all that the Negroes desired . . . they are paving the way for something better."[15]

Like DePriest, many African American observers argued that the talkies opened "a new field to actors of our group," highlighting the possibilities afforded by the experimental phase of sound-film production, in which the studios appeared open to forms of entertainment they previously had not considered.[16] Geraldyn Dismond published an important essay in a 1929 issue of the British avant-garde film journal *Close Up* dedicated especially to the subject of "Negro Film." In "The Negro Actor and the American Movies," she traces the history of black screen roles through the dominant U.S. and race (or black independent) cinemas of the silent era. Dismond identifies the transition to sound with a sudden change in the "attitude of the white producer toward Negro talent," a new form of recognition by the dominant film industry.[17]

After surveying changing ideologies about African Americans as expressed in literature, drama, and film, Dismond states that, in the 1920s, "the white dilettante, exhausted with trying to find new thrills, stumbled over the Negro and exclaimed, 'See what we have overlooked! These beloved vagabonds! Our own Negroes, right here at home!' And voila!—Black became the fad."[18] Dismond's tone is layered here: she is appropriately sarcastic about the voyeuristic and patronizing nature of the "white dilettante's" interest in African American culture. At the same time, she understands this cultural fad's "influence" on what she calls the "development of the Negro as part of the moving picture game."[19] As an anonymous writer in Monroe Work's *Negro Yearbook* put it, what was happening in Hollywood recapitulated the Harlem Renaissance moment when (to use Langston Hughes's phrase) "the Negro was in vogue": "Negro films are becoming a field in themselves in Hollywood. The popularity of the Negro plays and dancers and musicians that originated in New York finds an echo in film production."[20] Indeed, writers in the white trade press had begun to make similar claims starting in late 1928.

While the occasion for Dismond's piece is the production of *Hearts in Dixie* and *Hallelujah*, which she terms "all-Negro talking pictures," she observes a larger shift, a "slow recognition of the Negro as movie material."[21] Because her essay focuses on the state of African American actors in the movies, she finds evidence of this shift in places far beyond "all-Negro talking pictures." For instance, Dismond makes reference to employment opportunities for African American extras in a section of Eric von Stroheim's *Queen Kelly* (an otherwise white-cast silent film with one section set in colonial East Africa), which was being shot at the time of her writing. Additionally, Dismond sees "Negro film corporations," like Oscar Micheaux's, as part of this larger shift. She cites Micheaux's 1929 *The Wages of Sin* (nonextant) specifically, even though the transition to sound responsible for "all-Negro talking pictures" would effectively put Micheaux out of business for a couple of years.[22]

Hollywood's African American Films: The Transition to Sound delineates an archive that is broader than the specific genre category of "all-Negro talking pictures" but still narrower than the one that Dismond ultimately suggests. Under the guise of tracing a significant shift, Dismond effectively lumps together all films being produced around 1929 that feature African American actors in any kind of role, including in roles codified in earlier periods of film history. By contrast, this book focuses on the two "all-Negro talking pictures" and on films less clearly defined in terms of genre or casting structure, which also demonstrably "echo" the "popularity of the Negro plays and dancers and musicians that originated in New York." In other words, all of the films that this book examines feature African American performers in contemporary settings, working in the styles of music and dance popularized during the 1920s in black nightclubs, on the concert stage, and on phonograph recordings. As such, all of these films are "all-talkies," or films with synchronized sound throughout.

As what Dismond calls "Negro all-talkers," *Hearts in Dixie* and *Hallelujah* best illustrate the cinematic "echo" of these other cultural media; yet these films should, I argue, be situated on a continuum with a series of other films from this period that showcase African American performers in similar ways. Dismond herself suggests this continuum through the attention that she gives to the African American–cast musical shorts and comedy shorts that were made during the transitional period. Dismond mentions Warner Bros.' featuring of popular African American blues, jazz, and vaudeville musicians in Vitaphone shorts. And she refers to the small Christie studio's production of two-reel comedies adapted from Octavus Roy Cohen's comedic dialect stories of black middle-class life in Birmingham, Alabama. With the exception of the Christie-Cohen shorts, I include this range of films in my archive, looking in depth at short musicals like the visual translation of James P. Johnson's *Yamekraw* (Warner Bros., 1930); Dudley Murphy's avant-garde rendering of Duke Ellington and His Orchestra's nightclub performance, *Black and Tan* (RKO, 1929); as well as the Ethel Waters vehicle *Rufus Jones for President* (Warner Bros., 1933).[23]

My archive includes another crucial category of film: otherwise white-cast features containing African American musical sequences, like *On With the Show*, a 1929 backstage musical by Warner Bros. featuring Ethel Waters and other African American singers and dancers in a series of "specialty" numbers within the intradiegetic show; and *Safe in Hell*, a 1931 First National melodrama in which Nina Mae McKinney has a substantial dramatic role and entertains a group of white men during a crucial set piece. Perhaps the most complex and interesting of these films, RKO's 1930 prestige production *Check and Double Check*, features the Ellington orchestra performing at a party for wealthy white socialites—this in a film that is ostensibly a cinematic adaptation of the popular *Amos 'n' Andy* radio serial. In the film, the two white comedians who voiced the characters, Freeman Gosden and Charles Correll, play Amos and Andy in blackface for the duration of the film.

Although film historians have tended to include films containing white blackface performance in historical studies of the formation of the "black image" in American movies, I otherwise avoid these films. In this regard, I take my cue from Dismond and other African American observers of the black film fad who, anticipating Michael Rogin's argument, understand that such films effectively foreclose opportunities for African American performers while pretending to showcase "black" performance.[24] The musical set piece in *Check and Double Check*, coupled with the film's unique gambit of using white actors in blackface to dramatize diegetically "black" characters for the duration of the film—as opposed to having white actors "black up" during the film for embedded scenes of performance—makes it an exceptional case meriting attention here: a film of "Negro" life that keeps African American performers on the margins.

Given the relatively sparse, inconsistent nature of the studios' output, the talk of a "Negro film" fad in the African American press subsides rather quickly after the initial period of enthusiasm that led critics like Dismond to prognosticate a major shift in cinematic production. By late 1931, just as the sound-film production becomes "standardized" and as the "classical" style of film narrative developed in the silent era becomes dominant again, the discourse of a new "field" or new opportunities largely subsides.[25] As substantial parts for African American actors in feature films seem to evaporate following 1930 and 1931, such talk ceases in trade magazines like *Variety* and *Motion Picture News*. Yet I am compelled to include as the latest film in my archive the United Artists–distributed adaptation of Eugene O'Neill's *The Emperor Jones* (1933). This production brings to the screen what is, especially for white critics writing in the trade press, something like the ur-text of white "highbrow" exploitation of African American "primitivism." The O'Neill play is a frequent point of reference in attempts by these writers to explain the potential white-audience appeal of films like *Hearts in Dixie* and *Hallelujah*. Thus, the film adaptation, which also acts like a compendium of the thematic concerns and formal strategies elaborated in the earlier films, provides an ideal bookend to my archive, despite the later date of its production.

One of this book's goals is to demonstrate that the range of films assembled here, despite being produced by different studios and according to a variety of genre and casting conventions, comprises a coherent corpus, which merits being studied as such. Abiding by the spirit if not the letter of Dismond's essay, the book refers to these films, collectively, as "Negro talking pictures," to emphasize the centrality of African American musical performance as refracted through period conceptions of "the Negro" and determined by the American cinema's transition to sound. I argue that these films are shaped by three interrelated determinants, which I examine in depth in the next chapter: the "echo" of the wider black-cultural "fad" in film, the mythology of the African American voice as ideally suited to recording on the new apparatus, and the studios' identification of so-called highbrow white audiences as a privileged sector of the aggregate film audience.

Exodus and Exorbitance

From a contemporary perspective, Haynes's, DePriest's, and other African American commentators' claims about the "value of the talkies" can seem excessive or inflated, even exorbitant. Envisioning transformative effects for early sound-era "Negro films," these commentators seem to overestimate their value, imagining a payoff for them that is too high. In light of these seeming excesses, critics of African American representation in the Hollywood cinema have conventionally dismissed African American cinephiles' enthusiastic response to the arrival of sound. The films, these critics argue, did not bring about "something better" in the Hollywood cinema, nor did they contribute to "bettering race relations" on a large scale. From this point of view, early sound-era "Negro films" are, predictably, failures.

For Daniel Leab, who foregrounds white blackface performance in early sound film, the transitional period saw "mostly the same old dross," with sound simply adding another register in which the stereotyped "screen image of the black" could be reinforced.[26] According to Leab's narrative of the unchanging stereotype, "Blacks gained little from the introduction of sound": "performers . . . who could sing, dance, or play jazz" got some "additional work" but achieved very "limited distinction" in the industry.[27] Likewise, Thomas Cripps sees the brief "flash[ing] on screen" of African Americans in the late 1920s and early 1930s as inflating the hopes of black critics and audiences only to dash them immediately.[28] He even charges the early all-African American–cast musicals with "once and for all dragg[ing] serious black critics away from the 'race movies' and toward Hollywood as a final source of black aesthetic redemption."[29]

Parting ways with this conventional verdict, *Hollywood's African American Films* reevaluates the seeming exorbitance of African American press discourse on the talkies. This study takes seriously, instead of dismissing, these apparent overestimations in order to pose the question of what is valuable (from a contemporary critical perspective) in "Negro talking pictures" and to theorize new ways of evaluating them. Rather than following the predictable course of reading the films as simply more of the same in classical Hollywood cinema, the book highlights the exorbitance of this period of film history relative to those that immediately precede and follow it. Likewise, the readings contained in *Hollywood's African American Films* privilege the moments at which the films themselves become exorbitant—those points at which they literally deviate from or run out of their designated tracks.[30] As a change of trajectory or destination, exorbitance is structurally analogous with the exodus trope that looms so large in this period's African American press discourse about the cinema. Rooted in ongoing historical struggles, the exodus trope speaks to African Americans' symbolic deviation from assigned social and cultural ambits and provides a powerful means of theorizing how "Negro talking pictures" both assign places or pathways to African American characters and register the possibility of their movement outside of these places and pathways.

To properly pose and address the question of what is valuable in "Negro talking pictures," it becomes necessary to historicize value in the Hollywood cinema during the transition to sound. A series of questions arise here. What value does African American musical performance accrue as a commodity, such that the Hollywood studios become interested in showcasing it at this moment? In what specific ideologies and relations of power is this form of value rooted? How might we construct an alternative, critical form of valuation, adopting a perspective sympathetic to period struggles for African American social and cultural emancipation? This critical strategy would necessarily be dynamic and dialectical, approaching the historical form of value employed by the Hollywood studios as the horizon against which exorbitant cinematic phenomena—phenomena that are outside of or opposed to this form of value—become visible as such.

This strategy would, likewise, contest the idealist assumption that underlies canonical American film history and, to a degree, troubles the claims made by African American partisans of the talkies about the cinema's ability to "show the way" for American society: the assumption that the cinema is an ideologically neutral apparatus whose very structure necessarily and automatically promotes social inclusion and equality. As I have argued elsewhere, this particular understanding of the cinema as a national "Mirror Screen" dates back to the earliest critical accounts of film as an American institution.[31] The white poet and journalist Vachel Lindsay coined the phrase "Mirror Screen" in his 1915 *The Art of the Moving Picture*, the text that inaugurated American film criticism as a scholarly enterprise.[32] From Lindsay's vantage point, the American population was a budding but not fully unified "people" composed of multiple groups ("nations" or "races"). As a social "panorama," the cinema seemed capable of carrying out the important civic project of forging a unified "people." The "Mirror Screen" could "[show] the entire American population its own face."[33] Lindsay does not mean that every single American will appear in a film but rather that images of group representatives will work, mimetically, to capture the full heterogeneity of the population, and, prophetically, to demonstrate an essential unity of groups—to prefigure a utopian, posthistorical, human coexistence without martial or political strife.

As Lindsay's pronouncements make clear, the imaginary social "panoramas" created by visual technologies like cinema offer a means to popular representation in which the relations of production that actually structure society come to seem untouchable. The "Mirror Screen" serves to enshrine these relations as sacred. Illustrating this point, Lindsay offers a program toward the end of *The Art of the Moving Picture* for engineering a utopia of "the people" without concrete economic reforms. Lindsay believes that the United States is capable of achieving a sense of its own perfection by "visualizing" itself in the proper light, even "if it is not possible to bring in the New Jerusalem to-day, by public act, with every citizen eating bread and honey under his vine and fig-tree, owning forty acres and a mule."[34] Lindsay's sarcastic reference to the failed project of Radical Reconstruction—to set the African American freedmen on stable economic footing through a just redistribution of property—illustrates his sympathy with the bourgeoning model of the "democracy of consumers," a model that pretends to offer social equality while obviating any changes to the existing relations of production (or of race).

By the time *Hallelujah* was released in 1929, the "Mirror Screen" model had achieved the status of an official ideology for the Hollywood cinema, which increasingly linked itself to the American democracy of consumers.[35] Consider the account of "The Genesis of the Motion Picture" given by Will Hays, director of the Motion Picture Producers and Distributors of America (MPPDA), in his 1929 treatise *See and Hear.* Here Hays articulates his own version of the "Mirror Screen," drawing on (without explicitly citing) Lindsay's work. At the beginning of the chapter, Hays imagines a solitary observer "stand[ing] on a high mountain and see[ing] long lines of men, women, and children moving slowly forward."[36] The moving crowd includes people of all ages, people from rural and urban locales, as well as people from every social class. This is an Exodus tableau of sorts (despite the overt reference to Genesis), and what the crowd seeks, of course, is "the motion picture." The motion picture theater provides them with a "place to dream," and they see an image of "that which they desire" in the theater's "flickering shadows."[37] Remarkably, all of these people "desire" the same thing despite the social, geographical, and other differences among them.

A romanticized image of the actual national film audience, Hays's moving crowd has the same relationship to the screen as the audience depicted in formative film-historical texts from Lindsay's *The Art of the Moving Picture* to Terry Ramsaye's *A Million and One Nights*, a reflexive one. The crowd seems to see itself in an ideal light, or as it desires to be, in the "flickering shadows" of the screen. Regardless of the precise content of the images thrown up on the screen, the cinema forges disparate individuals into a single mass and provides them with a shared sense of desire, purpose, or destiny. Anyone can go to the movies, and anything may appear on the screen.[38]

Without a doubt, DePriest's and Haynes's accounts of "what *Hallelujah* means" draw on this ideological discourse of motion pictures as a national mirror. They predict that, once African Americans "emerge in the light of the screen" through the opportunities opened up by talking pictures, they will stake a claim to national belonging, to symbolic inclusion in Hays's moving crowd. However, the fact that Haynes and DePriest use this exodus rhetoric to describe an emancipatory movement of African Americans over and against white racist attitudes and institutions serves to point out the ideological limitations of the "Mirror Screen" model. Their comments remind us that there is no reason to assume that, when Hays stresses that his crowd includes "men and women of every race and of every tongue, moving slowly forward," he has African Americans in mind.[39] While this claim requires further elaboration, suffice it to say that the Hollywood cinema, as a cluster of large corporations producing, distributing, and retailing cultural commodities, shared what Robert Weems has identified as the dominant view of "early twentieth-century white enterprises," that they could "ignore and disrespect African American consumers with impunity."[40]

This point is crucial, not only because it gives the lie to Hays's inclusive rhetoric but also because it points out the irony in his use of tropes of movement or exodus in the first place. The crowd he depicts is narcissistically captivated by its own image as made sacred in the ideal light of the screen, moving in what amounts to a circle. Offering a fantasy compensation, the screen palliates the hard and/or unremunerative work to which the passage frequently refers in descriptions like "women with hands reddened and coarsened by work."[41] The screen gives the group the sense of having achieved its "dreams" or "desires" without having to actually redress the underlying conditions of labor. In contrast to Hays's vision of a circular movement, DePriest's and Haynes's allusions to African American "exodus"—in the form of mass migration—point to a history of emancipatory movement that would be, from Hays's perspective, exorbitant.

Two years before describing the cinema as a national mirror, Hays offered a more honest, revealing analogy: the film screen as shop window. In 1927, Hays proclaimed, "No longer does the girl in Sullivan, Indiana, guess what the styles are going to be in three months. She knows because she sees them on the screen," going on to detail a range of cases in which spectator-consumers will encounter a new product and then go "down . . . to the dealers to ask for the new goods."[42] According to Lary May's seminal study *Screening Out the Past: The Birth of Mass Culture and the Motion Picture Industry*, the convergence of cinema and consumerism in the 1920s marks the full formation of American mass culture.[43] As the film industry openly embraces its role as a venue for mass-marketing particular goods, for stimulating consumer desire, and for transforming purchasing habits, it adopts the commodity form as its main form of valuing and selecting particular subjects for exhibition.

In his rich, anecdotal history, Charles Eckert has demonstrated how manufacturers and advertisers sought in the 1920s and 1930s to capitalize upon an emergent mode of consumerist spectatorship by forging commercial relationships with the major studios.[44] For example, clothing companies developed Hollywood-centered clothing lines (and, in one case, a chain of stores selling "Cinema Fashions"), employing film stars to endorse the clothes in print advertisements and in-store displays. Through advertisements in movie fan magazines and other mass-circulation periodicals, female stars, in particular, modeled the new fashions in which they would soon appear on screen, simultaneously promoting the merchandise and the upcoming film release. These relationships also included more elaborate product "tie-ups," in which manufacturers (of automobiles, appliances, and foodstuffs) paid the studios to display their brands, to incorporate references to them in the dialogue of feature films, and even to produce short films that were unabashedly advertisements.[45]

In addition to raising capital directly through such tie-ups, the studios benefited, May suggests, by embracing this secondary function of films as product showcases. The cultural relevance and visual pleasure afforded by films were enhanced through their participation in the realm of fashion and consumerist emulation. May emphasizes two representative instances of how the film industry embraced its function as an arbiter of taste and "stimulant to trade." While highly illustrative, these examples demand to be reread according to their obscured racial dynamics. In one chapter, May shows how the prolific director Cecil B. DeMille, in collaboration with his set designers, crafted an opulent, commodity-studded mise-en-scène that added aesthetic and spectacular interest—an aura of "richness" and "modernity"—to narrative film.[46] In another chapter, May illustrates how theater chains owned by the major studios invested in lavish "movie palaces" in an effort to embed the experience of moviegoing in commodified opulence and thus to restyle that activity as a paradigm of the new "democratic" culture of consumption. Offering sumptuous decor and personalized services, these theaters themselves became "high-class" spaces (nominally) accessible to all who could purchase a ticket, spaces enabling simulated status mobility and a kind of consumerist "sovereignty."

At the most basic level, mass culture involves the production and distribution of entertainment media (movies, radio, phonograph recordings, magazines) on a national or international scale. In the early twentieth century, the technologies and organizational structures of industrial manufacturing come to serve this process, making "standard products" available at "countless locations."[47] For Max Horkheimer and Theodor Adorno, mass-entertainment media craft their products according to considerations of use—of their "suitability" as commodities.[48] Structured according to their "marketability," films are, in essence, "what they are used for": as the means of a transaction between an alienated worker (in the guise of the consumer) and as an instrument of finance capital.[49] For Adorno, mass culture "veils" its own commodity character by offering an immediacy of experience, a "ghastly" parody of utopian longings.[50] Where Hollywood cinema is concerned, these universal-democratic and utopian elements are conceived in a way that is not only self-negating but also exclusive. Racial exclusions historically define the "mass" in mass culture as a white collective, creating a specific form of social privilege within an ostensibly democratic realm. Although May does not focus on issues of race, this point becomes clear in the cases of the DeMille comedies and of movie palaces.

Made in the late teens and early 1920s, the DeMille comedies that May examines—films set in a high-society milieu and typically working in the vein of what Stanley Cavell calls "the comedy of remarriage"—include African Americans as uniformed domestic servants. In particular, African American women appear as maids for young white women, attending to them at dressing tables, where the white characters don the trappings of desirable consumer selfhood. Similar black characters appear in DeMille's *Old Wives for New* (Paramount, 1918), *Don't Change Your Husband* (Paramount, 1919), *Why Change Your Wife?* (Paramount, 1920), and *The Clinging Vine* (DeMille Pictures Corporation, 1926).

Don't Change Your Husband includes a striking fantasy sequence, which revealingly exaggerates the basic fantasy of white consumer sovereignty that these films disseminate. Schuyler Van Sutphen (Lew Cody), the younger suitor of a bored, married woman, Leila Porter (Gloria Swanson), begins to express his feelings for her in veiled terms. Having shown Leila his costume for a medieval court–themed masquerade ball, Schuyler begins to wax poetic about what he would do for her if he "were king": "I'd bring you three priceless Gifts: 'Pleasure'—'Wealth' and 'Love'—and the first should be '*Pleasure*'!" This litany prompts three fantasy tableaux. In the "Wealth" tableau, black male servants (slaves?) clad only in loincloths proceed into a faux-Turkish set, carrying chests full of jewels and bowing on their way out. Meanwhile, Leila sits on a lacquered slab supported by two crouching servants whose skin appears to be oiled—as if to gleam like the smooth floor below—while another's prostrate body provides her with a footrest.

Acting as a *mise en abyme* for the film's broader dynamics of race and consumption, this tableau links white pleasure in material objects with black servitude. African Americans provide the physical support for the commodity, while the exposed skin of their laboring bodies becomes another signifier of opulence. The tableau highlights Leila's position of total ownership and provides the spectator with an eroticized object of visual consumption. This is a scene of white consumption unbound. Here, the film goes beyond the dynamics of employer-servant on view in the rest of *Don't Change Your Husband* and the other contemporary DeMille comedies, conjuring a position of aristocratic and colonial power for the white female consumer. Interestingly, this screen image of consumer pleasure and racial mastery finds subtle echoes in the history of the movie palace as an exhibition space.

Often featuring ornate, Orientalist decor, movie palaces provided a fantasy space of sovereign consumption within a putatively egalitarian setting. Profiling the chain of Chicago palaces opened by pioneering exhibitors Barney and A. J. Balaban and Sam Katz, a magazine writer in 1929 summed up this paradox of royal democracy: "in the 'de luxe' house every man is a king and every woman a queen. Most of these cinema palaces sell all their seats at the same price,—and get it; the rich man stands in line with the poor; and usually tipping is forbidden. In this suave atmosphere, the differences of cunning, charm, and wealth, that determine our lives outside are forgotten. All men enter these portals equal, and thus the movies are perhaps a symbol of democracy. Let us take heart from this, and not be downcast because our democratic nation prudently reserves its democracy for the temple of daydreams."[51] According to this writer, the radically "democratic" aspect of the movie palace lies not so much in the uniform price of admission or in the equal treatment that patrons receive but in the extreme opulence that even the most humble consumer may enjoy while occupying the theater. As in DeMille's filmic tableau of wealth, extreme

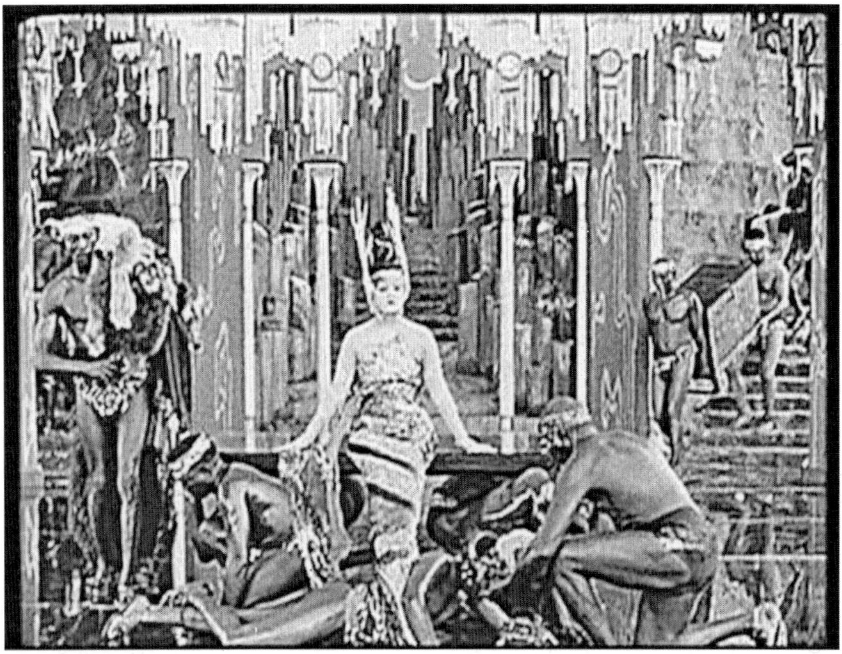

Figure 1. White "wealth" and black servitude in *Don't Change Your Husband* (Artcraft Pictures, 1919).

opulence and calculated references to "exotic" scenes of social inequality make the space of consumption a "palace" and the consumer—prototypically a woman in the article—a "queen." Strikingly, this writer even concedes that the democracy of consumers is a kind of fantasy consolation, "reserve[d]" for such escapist venues.

If the milieu for consumer democracy is already restricted, then this milieu is itself structured around exclusions and markings of the racial "other." Again, the DeMille tableau and the space of the movie palace echo one another. Racial difference is the one form of socially determining distinction that cannot be "forgotten" in the passage through the "portal" into the "temple of daydreams." The official manuals of the Balaban & Katz chain specified certain restricted roles for African American employees and identified ideal physiological "types" for those employees. Citing *The Fundamental Principles of Balaban & Katz Theatre Management* (1926), Lizabeth Cohen describes these racial aesthetics of service. Ushers had to be white, and the theaters hired African Americans only "in stereotyped roles, as front door footmen ('approaching the old Southern coachman type'), as messenger boys ('of slight and slender build, well formed in good proportions, not markedly of the negro type with heavy features'), and as maids and porters in the washrooms."[52]

While the same manuals advocated an admissions policy that did not discriminate by "race, class, nationality, or creed," Cohen alludes to anecdotal evidence suggesting that Balaban & Katz palaces may have practiced de facto segregation, denying access to African American patrons or seating them only in balconies or in the least "conspicuous" positions at the extreme edges of the theater floor.[53] Film trade magazines routinely commented in this period on civil rights cases stemming from allegations of Jim Crow seating practices. The most striking such piece of evidence that I have encountered in my own research comes from a court decision announced in 1925 in *Variety*: Dr. Leon M. Headen, an African American dentist, sued the management of Balaban & Katz's Tivoli theater, alleging assault and discrimination. According to the article, "Headen alleged he had been set upon and beaten by ushers two years ago, when he objected against accepting inferior seats." A jury in the Superior Court of Illinois found the defendant guilty of the assault charge (awarding Headen $2,000 damages) but not guilty of discrimination.[54]

These two cases from the history of American mass culture illustrate the context in which, during the transition to sound, African American musical performance comes into fashion ("vogue") and acquires new value as a commodity for the Hollywood studios. Even as what Adorno would call the "considerations of marketability" for black performance shift, the studios do not suddenly change their stance relative to African American consumers or adopt a new racial-political viewpoint. Rather, popular African American musical styles enter into the cinema's particular commodity form in a context in which African Americans appear as supports for or ornaments to white pleasure but are stigmatized or even excluded as an audience. While the new value accorded to African American performers themselves during this transition changes these dynamics, such a change cannot be construed as an instance of group "inclusion" via the cinematic mirror in any simple way.

The ideology of the screen as a mechanism of national self-portraiture coexists with the Hollywood cinema's investment in a particular model of consumer spectatorship—a particular relationship to corporate capitalism. Thus, African American performance as commodity is incorporated into film and marketed to potential audiences in ways that are consistent with this model and that serve definite relations of production. Even as the studios package black performance as something that exists for white consumption, their products emerge from a productive context shaped and mediated by racial categories. American racism expresses itself during this period not only in social barriers (like Jim Crow and unsanctioned, de facto segregation practices) and forced political inequality but also in economic deprivations like pervasive landlessness, lack of property and access to capital, exploitation, and wage discrimination.

According to the Marxian analytic tradition in which Horkheimer and Adorno write, this complex nexus of social relations is encoded in commodities like films. As a "social hieroglyphic," the commodity is a seemingly ordinary thing in which the "social character of men's labor" appears in the distorted guise of an objective property or substance, value. Creating a "fantastic relation between things" separate from the labor that produces them, value "converts every product into a social hieroglyphic," inscribing (or "stamping") it with an enigmatic though legible expression. Marx, thus, compares commodities to language: not a language of self-explanatory "labels," but a coded language that must be "deciphered," its "secret" liberated.[55] Hence, the Marxian analytic of the commodity provides a means to charting how relations of production (within the film industry and American society at large) register in "Negro talking pictures," despite the films' efforts to mystify or distort these relations.

The commodity form can be seen as both controlling and failing to control the meanings of these films. And those failures by the commodity form to control meaning become the basis in this study for defining what might be valuable about "Negro talking pictures" from a contemporary critical perspective—value that is exorbitant in the terms afforded by period African American press discourse. These moments of exorbitant value arise, then, in those signifying structures in the films that have no role in supporting their dominant ideological projects, that point out the social character of labor rather than disguising it as a set of relations between things, or that make the symbolism of migration as exodus legible.

Interiors and Fault Lines

In histories of African American representation in Hollywood, the period between D. W. Griffith's vitriolic racist *The Birth of a Nation* and the arrival of sound is characterized as one of relative stagnation for black performers, a period in which roles were few and limited in scope. Leab's chapter on this period suggestively describes the "freezing of an image": the reduction of the African American screen presence to a set of stock gestures and character types.[56] Emphasizing the rise of the white star system and the cinema's concomitant preference for "prestigious" subject matter, Cripps demonstrates that African Americans were effectively barred from leading roles, cast only as menials, as comic buffoons, or in "atmospheric" roles in "jungle" films.[57] Cripps further attributes the studios' refusal to "[depict] black despair, poverty, neglect, outrage, caste, or discrimination" to their overall conservatism in terms of issues of class and social mobility. During a time in which the MPPDA was attempting to garner public approval for the industry—to establish an image of "pious rectitude"—the studios clung to "the American success" myth and were loathe to point out "stratification along lines of wealth" or "segregation of the races."[58]

The "frozen" image of African Americans on view in classical silent film, then, was an effect of the cinema's effort to disseminate a certain image of white social mobility while tacitly sanctioning racial segregation in American life. A pair of 1920s films with strong genealogical links to the archive assembled here help to illustrate this point: *Manslaughter* (Paramount, 1922), one of DeMille's iconic mass-cultural fantasy films, and *The Crowd* (MGM, 1926), a King Vidor melodrama containing what might be seen as a character sketch for Zeke Johnson, the protagonist of *Hallelujah*. These films are pertinent for the ways in which they use minor black figures to chart the shifting social status of white characters. Moreover, they are distinguished by their relatively ambivalent (for this period) views of social privilege and aspirations toward wealth. Thus, they serve to complicate Cripps's claim about class politics somewhat, while illustrating the constraints within which the transition to sound's disruptive un-"freezing" of black roles occurs.

Like Leila in *Don't Change Your Husband*, the white protagonist of *Manslaughter*, Lydia Thorne (Leatrice Joy), features in an exotic tableau of wealth unbound. In this case, however, the scene is framed from an ostensibly critical perspective. Surveying the scene at an uproarious high-society New Year's Eve party, replete with alcohol, gambling, jazz, and feverish dancing, the upstanding district attorney, Daniel O'Bannon (Thomas Meighan), compares the proceedings to a Roman "Feast of Bacchus." O'Bannon is in love with Lydia but worries that the young woman, who has money and a fast car but no parents, has too much freedom; he even predicts that Lydia's "mad young set of wasters" will lead the nation to ruin (as in the case of the fall of the Roman Empire). As O'Bannon explains the analogy to Lydia's chaperone, the shot of the dancing crowd dissolves into a graphically similar shot of a Roman bacchanal. In this first of several Roman scenes, Lydia sits on an elevated throne, flanked by soldiers in armor, who are white, with shirtless black servant or slave characters posed sculpturally behind her. Here, as in *Don't Change Your Husband*, subject black bodies serve to highlight white wealth and "license."

After Lydia's reckless driving causes the death of a police patrol officer and she is sentenced to prison, *Manslaughter* again uses marginal African American figures to chart her social status. For Lydia, the prospect of incarceration is most terrifying because it represents a loss of the privileges associated with wealth. The film represents her being entered into the penal system as a literal and figurative stripping off of these privileges. Moreover, being incarcerated means that Lydia now occupies the same position as her disgraced former maid, a white woman who stole jewelry from Lydia in order to try to secure money to pay for her sick son's medical care.

Manslaughter uses anonymous African American women in the first prison scenes to triangulate the relationship between the two white women and to underscore Lydia's swift downward social trajectory. The film alternates shots of one of the jailers forcibly examining Lydia—taking her fingerprints, measuring her head with calipers, looking inside her mouth and ears—with shots of an

African American inmate undergoing similar treatment. Intended to illustrate the extent to which this experience is degrading and upsetting for Lydia, the parallel editing suggests, by contrast, that the jailers' treatment is more natural or fitting for the African American convict. As Lydia begins to put on her uniform, a group of older, disheveled-looking inmates, including one African American woman, taunt her through the bars on her cell door. Here again, the film uses an African American figure as shorthand for a lack of social status; the mere proximity of white and black women in a social space where no racial segregation or hierarchy is in force carries a threatening charge.

African American women in the prison scenes, like the men in the Roman fantasy scenes, occupy a fixed position against which white mobility may be gauged. While Lydia will return to her position of wealth and power after she serves her sentence—and after she undergoes an extreme moral reformation—African American characters throughout the film are constant in their menial position. Tellingly, once Lydia begins to repent of her crime and earns a supervisory role in the prison kitchen, she is shown bantering with an older black woman in a kind of plantation mistress-mammy tableau. In a film preoccupied with the pleasures and dangers of mobility (and the moral license that goes along with it), the question of African American social change or movement is never at issue.

The same dynamics hold in Vidor's *The Crowd*, which deals with an idealistic young white man's (James Murray) attempts to distinguish himself from the great mass of New Yorkers, gaining money and prestige. *The Crowd* uses a series of brief vignettes to introduce the character, aligning him with the nationalistic fantasy of individual success that drives him (or that causes his discontent, the film seems to suggest). The protagonist, Johnny, is born in a small town on 4 July 1900, prompting comparisons between his birth and the signing of the Declaration of Independence. In light of this propitious date, his father makes the bold statement to the doctor, "There's a little man the world is going to hear from all right." The intertitles also jokingly align his youthful activities with those of Washington and Lincoln.

Skipping ahead, the film shows a twelve-year-old Johnny seated on a post-and-rail fence, with a group of other boys. As they discuss their aspirations for the future, a white boy asks the only African American boy in the group what he intends to be when he grows up. The boy, whom, in an attempt at irony, the film names Whitey, answers, "I detend to be a preacher man! Hallelujah!" Judging by the other boys' reactions, Whitey's declaration is meant to provide comic relief; he acts as a foil for Johnny, whose grandiose aspirations the film takes quite seriously. A moment later, Johnny, looking into the distance, proclaims that he will be somebody "big." Whether or not Whitey could actually become a minister (a position entailing some degree of social standing) is not at issue here. Rather, his malapropism and naive enthusiasm indicate that he has no prospect of entering the realm of social aspiration and competition in which the film will situate the adult Johnny.

The relatively unregulated context of childhood interactions in a small town allows Whitey to exist on more or less equal footing with the white children, but, even at this early point, his marking as a comic foil signals that he occupies a fixed social position outside of the realm that boys like Johnny will soon enter. The only other African American character with lines of dialogue is a porter whom Johnny encounters on a train during his honeymoon. The porter's speech is also marked as dialect on the intertitles, and his appearance in a service role works primarily to throw into relief the dreams of suburban comfort that Johnny and his wife are discussing just before he appears.

Limited to brief screen appearances, which establish visual and symbolic social counterpoint, African American characters in both of these films are primarily fixed points of reference in relation to which the trajectories of white characters can be gauged. Hence, it stands to reason that the basic redistribution of screen space and time entailed by early "Negro films" would disrupt this carefully codified ("frozen") formula of symbolic social relations. What would happen if the studios started to make films focused entirely or even in part on characters like the anonymous prison inmate in *Manslaughter*, the train porter in *The Crowd*, or even Whitey? And what if these films made white figures the social points of reference for these protagonists, or altogether omitted white characters, giving this role to other African American figures? In broad terms, these questions speak to the novelty of "Negro talking pictures" relative to late silent Hollywood films. Haynes's Zeke Johnson character from *Hallelujah* does endeavor to make himself "a preacher man," and, as if to mark the connection, Vidor takes as the film's title Whitey's expression of exuberance. Later, Dudley Murphy's *The Emperor Jones*, indeed, features an African American train porter as its protagonist.

Yet, as I have begun to suggest, the brief reevaluation of black performance as a production feature that occurs during the transition to sound does not cause or follow from a concomitant change in the studios' racial politics. Zeke Johnson and Brutus Jones come to the screen independent of any project on the studios' part to "[depict] black despair, poverty, neglect, outrage, caste, or discrimination." Hence, this film corpus is best conceptualized in negative terms: as *not* an experiment in making films that call for social recognition or inclusion of African Americans. With these films, the studios set out *not* to make racially inclusive images of "what we want" or "where we are going," or films that would, as Haynes describes, "show the way."[59] The studios even seek to mitigate against any suggestion that "Negro talking pictures" have "a mission or a problem to solve."[60]

Therefore, "Negro talking pictures" emerge from a contradictory situation. They rearrange the diegetic positions codified in earlier Hollywood films without initiating a corresponding shift in the cinema's racial imaginary. In films that show African American protagonists moving physically (within the frame and within fictional geographic space), willing things to happen, and acting on desires but that symbolize these gestures as instances of black social stasis and immobility, a deep structural contradiction is at work. The force of this contradiction manifests itself in the films, I argue, in the form of an expressive distortion of their narratives and mise-en-scène. The formal aspects of the films bear the imprint of a logical tension that, in turn, makes legible the overtly unrepresentable social underpinnings of these films. A film that both elevates its African American protagonist to tremendous heights and reduces him to a totally abject position (one coded in explicitly racialist terms), *The Emperor Jones* provides a particularly illustrative case study in these contradictions.

Unlike O'Neill's 1920 play, which is set entirely on an unnamed "island in the West Indies," Murphy's film adaptation of *The Emperor Jones* begins somewhere in South Carolina. The first thirty minutes of the film trace Brutus Jones's (Paul Robeson) rise from Pullman porter to "Emperor" of the island, dramatizing and embellishing crucial events that the play establishes as antecedent action through dialogue. In the opening scene of Murphy's *The Emperor Jones*, the African American townspeople hold a nighttime service during which they pray for Jones's success in his new job and a preacher praises his virtuous and humble character. Cutting back and forth between the preacher delivering his praise and Jones admiring his new Pullman uniform in the mirror, the film ironically undermines the preacher's remarks, intimating that Jones possesses a certain vanity and lust for power. As Jones prepares for his departure, he paints a glorious picture of his future in the wider world for his girlfriend, Dolly (Ruby Elzy).

The dialogue between Jones and Dolly establishes his character's interest in upward mobility—in wealth and recognition as a national subject. He describes a fantastic encounter in the shadow of "the Capitol buildin,' lookin' like a palace on de hill." The president of the United States, "marching down de avenue, wid a band before and a band behind," stops to "compliment" Jones on "landin' the job" with the Pullman Company, calling him "much of a man." But, as this ironic juxtaposition of his words to the minister's begins to suggest, the film frames Jones's self-important discourse as in part premeditated and strategic—as a kind of bluff he uses to overawe less worldly people—and in part delusional—as an effect of his hubris. While Dolly listens interestedly to his narrative, Jones's next girlfriend, a Harlem sophisticate named Undine (Fredi Washington), will seek to deflate his ego, taunting him about his claims to have met the president. At the same time, Jones will use an aura of authority and importance to win power over Smithers (Dudley Digges), the white British trader, and over the inhabitants of the unnamed island.

Figure 2. Brutus Jones (Paul Robeson) inspecting his Pullman uniform in *The Emperor Jones* (United Artists, 1933).

Coupled with the brevity of Jones's reign, his excessive, theatrical gesture of naming himself "Emperor"—he rejects "President" as too prosaic—works to expose the character as a fantasist. His desire for power in a "civilized" context is, the film finally wants to say, delusional. He is, as Smithers repeatedly says in the original play, constantly putting on "high and mighty airs." Driven into the island's "jungle" by the threat of revolt and by his own fears, Jones gradually sheds these "airs" over the remainder of the film; he is transmuted from a position of fictitious authority and control to a "natural" position of abject fear and irrationality. In both the play and the film, this decline is presented as a process of atavistic "regression." Jones falls backward into the original or "primitive" condition dictated by his racial "heritage."[61] Within this context, the film's heavy use of mirrors in the mise-en-scène—a motif of the filmmakers' own invention—becomes highly significant. The fact that Jones admires himself in a mirror each time he has donned the next, more impressive type of attire, shows his conceit and weak grasp on reality. He is involved in an ongoing masquerade, which will be cut short once he flees into the "primeval" forest, his gradual stripping off of his emperor's costume highlighting his reverse transformation.

In a crucial way, though, *The Emperor Jones* is not about Jones's social mobility or achievement of national-symbolic identity. The film responds to the negative demand cited above, offering an exaggerated version of what Jones will not and cannot secure in its imagined meeting between him and the American president—recognition as a national subject. *The Emperor Jones*, like the other films discussed in this book, uses a range of formal strategies to disavow the work associated with the Mirror Screen understanding of cinema—a sort of work that is, in the first place, imaginary. Recall how the moving crowd in Hays's text moves with great satisfaction toward its own image with no change in the underlying conditions of its members' existences. *The Emperor Jones*'s many diegetic mirrors offer just one example of such formal strategies—strategies for giving African American characters what I call a "surplus grounding" in the film diegesis. Doubling Jones's image in the frame, these mirrors magnify the character's physical presence and highlight his envelopment in the physical interior of the scene. The film's jungle sequence offers another, still more striking case of grounding and envelopment. In these shots, photographed on blue-tinted film stock, Jones almost always appears in a clearing or niche defined by walls and canopies of vegetation: tree trunks and masses of leaves surround him and, in some cases, form a lattice mediating between his figure and the camera. Low-key, high-contrast lighting further emphasizes the sense of oppressive gloom in these scenes, surrounding Jones's figure with shadows and dark corners of the frame.

The film, drawing heavily on O'Neill's original directions, stages the jungle as a space of extreme "blackness." In the directions that open scene 2, O'Neill writes, "In the rear the forest is a wall of darkness dividing the world. Only when the eye becomes accustomed to the gloom can the outlines of separate trunks of the nearest trees be made out, enormous pillars of deeper blackness. A somber monotone of wind lost in the leaves moans in the air. Yet this sound serves but to intensify the impression of the forest's relentless immobility, to form a background throwing into relief its brooding, implacable silence."[62]

According to Carme Manuel, O'Neill employed detailed stage directions in the play in an attempt to use setting to convey a precise "emotional expression."[63] O'Neill's vision of the settings for *The Emperor Jones* "drew inspiration," specifically, from contemporary developments in European expressionism. In theatrical and cinematic expressionism, "formal distortion[s]" within the plastic realm—comprised of sets, costumes, and actors' gestures and motions—serve to "exteriorize" complex subjective states and, in particular, agitated or disturbed minds—like Jones's succumbing to "primal" fears.[64] As Manuel's work further demonstrates, O'Neill's viewing of the German expressionist film *The Cabinet of Dr. Caligari* (dir. Robert Wiene, 1920) shaped his experiments with expressive "stagecraft and decor" and made him immediately interested in the possibility of film adaptation.[65]

Figure 3. The jungle "interior" in *The Emperor Jones* (United Artists, 1933).

Although produced some thirteen years after O'Neill's play debuted, Murphy's film brings out the script's expressionist elements, seeking to create what Siegfried Kracauer would call a "scenery of the soul" for Jones's tragic demise.[66] Yet the film, like the play, posits a particularly *racialized* interiority, in which "atavism" is integral to Jones's psyche. As realized on screen, the "immobile" and "implacable" enclosure of the jungle gives concrete physical form—"deeper blackness"—to the black-primitive chaos toward which the drama inexorably drives Jones.[67] In a 1933 newspaper interview, Murphy attributed his interest in "doing Negro things"—working on African American–cast projects like his earlier shorts *Black and Tan* and *St. Louis Blues*—to the "chance for mood and fantasy and camera angles" these subjects offered.[68] Expressionist formal distortion and phantasmagoria were, for Murphy, particularly suited to the treatment of African American subjects, as if there existed a distinct black-primitive interiority that could only be represented through an unconventional cinematic language.

Typifying the visual strategies that "Negro talking pictures" use to represent African American social immobility without linking that immobility to concrete practices of oppression, *The Emperor Jones* constructs a striking diegetic "interior" for its protagonist. The film's soundtrack further heightens the sense of enclosure and interiority, by picking up on the sonic cues from O'Neill's script. The jungle scene's initial silence is broken by a "tom-tom" beat, gradually rising in intensity along with Jones's terror.[69] Jones's visitation by "ha'nts" from his past and the collective "racial" past, made all the more uncanny through the possibilities of double exposure offered by film, further turn the jungle into a racial phantasmagoria—what I would call a "camera obscura," a "dark" room where Jones becomes a captive viewer of projected images.

As in the examples just cited, conventionally expressionist elements like mirrors and high-contrast or chiaroscuro lighting offer a graphic illustration of how mise-en-scène may be used to create an interior space that envelops and confines. Indeed, several of the "Negro talking pictures" examined in this book rely on such scenic effects, making the language of cinematic expressionism an important unifying thread. At the same time, strategies of interiorization take multiple forms throughout these films: from narrative strategies of enframing and enveloping, to repetitions and circular plot devices, to doubled characters, to the embedding of black performers in "specialty" numbers, to audiovisual constructions of black excess embodiment, to the very diegetic universe of the all–African American–cast film. As figurative containments of African American subjectivity, such forms are analogous to the forms of inscribing sexual difference that Kaja Silverman traces in her landmark, psychoanalytic, feminist study of classic Hollywood film, *The Acoustic Mirror: The Female Voice in Psychoanalysis and Cinema*.

Silverman identifies a wide range of classic cinematic strategies that serve to confine "woman" to a "recessed space within the [diegesis]," while linking "man" with the "elements of the story that seem in one way or another to frame that recessed space."[70] Hence, classic cinema's "situating [of] the female voice within a hyperbolically diegetic context" works to attribute to a women a condition of "interiority." This condition "has a very different status in classic cinema from the one that it enjoys in the literary and philosophical tradition which Derrida critiques."[71] (In this Western metaphysical tradition, the voice, emanating from the human interior, is believed to represent full presence and authentic expression.) "Far from being a privileged condition, synonymous with soul, spirit, or consciousness," Silverman writes, "interiority in Hollywood films implies linguistic constraint and physical confinement—confinement to the body, to claustral spaces, and to inner narratives."[72] In an analogous manner, "Negro talking pictures" ensconce African American characters in a condition of interiority, which serves to signify their stasis, fixity, or immobility. These tropes figuratively illustrate African Americans' nonparticipation in the nation or in the full prerogatives of social life, explaining this as an effect of some inherent disposition or limited capacity, rather than as an effect of deliberate oppression.[73] Thus, these tropes participate in the ideological work of primitivism as conventionally theorized. Nevertheless, by disavowing a symbolic inclusion that has not been asserted, these tropes have a highly disruptive effect and, as such, are legible in two opposing directions.

To claim that "Negro talking pictures" are shaped by an imperative not to take up social missions or to propagandize is not to say that they are simply devoid of socially significant content. Strategies of surplus diegetic grounding like the ones I have been highlighting here—*The Emperor Jones*'s use of mirrors, creation of a "dark" interior space, and circular and regressive plot—draw attention to the very realms that Hollywood films, according to the ideological imperatives of the Mirror Screen, conventionally bracket off: the realm of economic production, which the Mirror Screen model rejects as insignificant to the utopian striving for "what we want" as a nation, and the realm of class division or struggle, which the Mirror Screen model rejects as irrelevant to the historical existence of "the people."

What is visible in the films is a kind of disavowal of the sort theorized by Freud: an excessive or even gratuitous gesture of denial that serves to limn, in negative fashion, within the conscious mind a thought otherwise relegated to the unconscious stratum.[74] As long as we assume that historical African American oppression is not, in the first place, a question of deficient "inclusion" within the media spectacle—and thus that the solution to historical oppression does not lie, reflexively, in a compensatory gesture by this same spectacle—we are able to observe the paradoxical effect of these films' collective refusal to question the racial-political status quo. "Negro talking pictures" ultimately draw attention to the realms of social struggle that the Mirror Screen would not otherwise recognize.[75]

Consider the narrative transitions that the film *The Emperor Jones* uses prior to the island section, which function, rhetorically, in a very similar way to the film's many mirrors. In shifting from one scene to another, the film relies heavily on dissolves that establish graphic matches. For instance, a shot of an African American Pullman porter's hands rhythmically buffing the toe of a passenger's shoe dissolves into a shot of an African American pianist's hands working the keyboard at a Harlem cabaret. These dissolves provide a sense of continuity between disparate scenes, spaces, and activities—a continuity that is explicitly racialized in the film's first such transition. The opening credits of the film appear over a series of shots of a group of shirtless black drummers and dancers wearing feathered headdresses and carrying shields and spears. In the last of these shots, the camera takes in a group of dancers moving in a circle from a high angle. At this point, the film dissolves into the opening shot of the church scene, where the worshippers form a graphically similar ring.

Given that the figures in the credit sequence are not located in space and time, the film posits at the outset a sort of timeless primitive state of black cultural expression, against which the church scene can be viewed as a thinly disguised reenactment. Thus, the film encourages the viewer to read these match-dissolve transitions in reverse. While the narrative trajectory of the opening scenes traces a movement toward cultural sophistication—from the country to the city, from humble beginnings to great power—such a trajectory, the film hints, is an illusion. These opening scenes instead set the stage for Jones's immanent "regression." What appears like progress in the first sections of the narrative is, at best, the constant repetition of the same, or, at worst, incipient regression—the accumulation of false trappings of "civilization" that will collapse under the pressure of Jones's flight from his pursuers. Either way, the film uses the dissolve to suture together totally unlike things, using the logic of "race history" and atavism to envelop Jones's story within a narrative context of immobility and stasis.

Like the film's many mirrors, these transitions work to double or reiterate what has already been shown or said. And yet these narrative transitions can be read, like the mirrors themselves, as signs of disavowed white complicity in African American social immobility. Both strategies seem intended to naturalize black social immobility by making stasis or entrapment appear natural; at the same time, they draw attention to the sorts of social tensions and hierarchies that are otherwise invisible in the film.

Each of the film's transitions prior to the island sequences relocates Jones in space and time. He goes from South Carolina to Harlem, from Harlem to a series of destinations along the East Coast and back. Along these routes, Jones does gain wealth and social standing. He invests money in a "merger" scheme hatched by a rich white passenger on the train and briefly seems to realize his stated goal of becoming involved in "trade." The precise nature of this business deal and of Jones's success is not clear to the viewer because the film very blatantly leaves out the events that follow Jones's initial conversation with the white financier; a quick wipe shifts the scene to Jones trying on his tuxedo in Undine's room. From this interpretive perspective, the timing and placement of the film's transitions draw attention to all of the logistical details that it omits—details always related to Jones's quest for the sort of success and social recognition he describes in his imagined meeting with the president.

In the same manner, the ways in which the film frames the church scenes—by projecting them onto a static, "primitive" cultural backdrop and by interrupting them with the shots of Jones's self-admiration—draw attention to key points of otherwise obscure context. Comprised of members of the Hall Johnson Choir, the congregation sings portions of three traditional African American spirituals, "Oh, I Want Two Wings," "Now Let Me Fly," and "Same Train." The African American composer J. Rosamond Johnson, brother of James Weldon Johnson, provided "Vocal Arrangements" for the film. Because the songs all appear in book collections that Johnson edited or for which he supplied arrangements, we can also infer that he selected them. Featured most prominently, the first two spirituals ostensibly use the motif of flight to describe heavenly ascension following death. The lyrics of "Oh, I Want Two Wings" implore the Lord for two wings with which to "fly away" to meet Jesus, while "Now Let Me Fly" envisions an ascent to "Mount Zion" and "the promised land." But, in a fashion consistent with the historical role of African American religious music (beginning with slave insurrections and the Underground Railroad), the lyrics of both also convey a desire for physical translation to a more welcoming place, signifying this-worldly redemption.[76]

By virtue of Johnson's selection and arrangement of music for the film, the scene in the South Carolina church highlights the film's migration subtext. The congregants express their hope for the well-being of one of their members who is about to leave a condition of evident poverty in search of more stable material footing—who is about to join the mass of African American migrants leaving the rural, southern United States in an attempt to escape Jim Crow, political disenfranchisement, peonage, and racial vigilantism.

The fact that Jones's path of upward mobility begins with his move to Harlem is highly suggestive. Whereas O'Neill, writing in 1920, would likely not have been aware of African American mass migration as a social phenomenon, for the filmmakers, working in the early 1930s, migration offers a logical and timely point of reference for depicting such mobility. Indeed, considering its handling of the church, nightclub, and chain-gang settings, as well as its use of the motif of train travel, the narrative prologue that Murphy has added to O'Neill's *The Emperor Jones* clearly owes a debt to *Hallelujah. The Emperor Jones* operates intertextually as a critical reading of the earlier film, bringing to the fore *Hallelujah*'s implicit migration subtext. *Hallelujah*'s Zeke Johnson in many ways resembles Robeson's Jones, save for the fact that Zeke never takes the step that would seem to follow logically from his trajectory in the film. He does not move deliberately away from his family in search of economic opportunity and social advancement. Coupled with Jones's brief references in the dialogue to lynching and Jim Crow, migration references (in the narrative premise, in the mise-en-scène, and in these song lyrics) offer a critical glimpse of the sociohistorical upheaval, which breaks free of the film's overarching primitivist ideology.

From the angle of vision afforded by Johnson's lyrical arrangements, the film's transitions read as what Silverman would call "fault lines," opening up crucial gaps or holes in the diegetic enclosure and allowing us to recognize the sorts of social conflicts that typically fall beyond the horizon of the Mirror Screen. The construction of racial "interiority" as a state of confinement reinscribes a distinction between what is left outside and what is brought inside—what is excluded versus what is included—within the film fiction itself. This reinscription, following from the initial disavowal of propagandistic intent, founds white privilege (and the entire structure of racial difference) on a comparable "fault line" or legible contradiction. Therefore, the formal strategies of containment outlined above are legible in a second direction: they invite a dialectical reading practice. While, in the first place, these formal strategies signify stasis, fixity, and immobility, they signify, in a second, highly coded or distorted manner, sites of social struggle.

CHAPTER 1

"Black Became the Fad"

WHITE HIGHBROW CULTURE AND NEGRO FILMS

"Dorothy Mackail Is 'Blues' Enthusiast" reads the headline for an item in the First National studio's pressbook for *Safe in Hell*, a 1931 melodrama starring the white, English-born actress. One of several brief star profiles presented to exhibitors for use in advance promotional materials, this pressbook item reveals Mackail's musical tastes. She is "not only an admirer of the blues, but an expert at singin' 'em." The text goes on to point out that, while Mackail herself does not sing "blues" in *Safe in Hell*, the film contains "moments made melodious by the crooning of negro blues singers." The description is perhaps misleading. While the film uses what could be called blues melodies diegetically and nondiegetically, they are in fact instrumental performances. The only "crooning" in the film is Nina Mae McKinney's rendition of "When It's Sleepy Time Down South," a plantation song popularized by Louis Armstrong and not, strictly speaking, a blues. "Blues" in this context serves as a kind of umbrella term for African American popular musical styles, and one apparent purpose of the text's discussion of Mackail's enthusiasm for "blues" is to associate her with McKinney and the film's other featured African American actor, Clarence Muse. "Two celebrated negroes are in the cast," the text asserts, drawing a tenuous but important connection between McKinney, Muse, and the supposed African American "crooning" in the film, which, in turn, helps to define the white star's image.[1]

Safe in Hell's pressbook does not make any mention of blues music in its exploitation segment. For example, it does not offer any recommendations for product "tie-ups" involving phonograph records. The logic of the pressbook's references to blues, nonetheless, mirrors the logic of its suggested product tie-ups, such as those for gloves, handbags, Jantzen bathing suits, and Lucky Strike cigarettes.[2] These tie-ups use the female film star's association with and putative interest in the piece of clothing or accessory as a selling point.

At the same time that retailers could exploit this association and interest to make the commodity more desirable, the film would receive publicity outside of the cinema, elevating its own prestige by acting as a showcase for high-status commodities. The mention of Dorothy Mackail's "enthusiasm" highlights African American popular music's status as a fashionable object of consumer desire, while also serving to point out how prominently the film features it. In turn, the promotional materials suggest that this production feature might heighten the film's appeal for those viewers who would strive to emulate Mackail. Simultaneously, the text on blues and several items in the pressbook use McKinney's and Muse's roles in *Safe in Hell* to promote the film, characterizing them as African American quasi-stars ("screen favorites"). The pressbook repeatedly cites Muse's "creation" of "the title role in the Broadway production of 'Porgy,'" as well as his performance as Nappus in Fox's *Hearts in Dixie*. Without mentioning McKinney's performance as Chick in MGM's *Hallelujah*, the other all-African American–cast musical feature produced by a major studio in 1929, the pressbook bills McKinney as a "famous blues singer."[3]

Under what conditions does the white-controlled culture industry, the cinema in particular, become interested in producing and distributing African American musical and performance culture and fictional representations of African American life? What motivates the film studios to identify black popular music and appearances by familiar African American performers as potentially attractive production features? To which particular segments of the movie audience do the studios imagine these features to appeal? What internal resistances to the incorporation of black culture do the culture industry's own organizational structures and ideologies of race generate? How do these resistances shape and constrain what Geraldyn Dismond calls the "black film fad"?

During the Hollywood studios' conversion to synchronized-sound film production in 1929 and 1930, it became commonplace to speak of a "vogue" for "Negro films," which "echoed" the contemporary, New York–centered white "fad" for black musical theater, jazz music, and dance. Writers in both the white-controlled trade magazines and African American newspapers asserted a growing audience interest in films featuring African American characters and rooted in these entertainment contexts. For instance, the trade publication *Exhibitors Herald-World* framed *Hallelujah* in this way: "The negro and his religiosity form the theme of MGM's audien 'Hallelujah.' The negro, ever seeking an ultimate salvation and attaining an immediate pleasure in the seeking has had a vogue, both in flippant jazz and in serious sociology. 'Hallelujah' offers the materials from which this vogue has sprung."[4] Likewise, in 1928 *Variety* reported on how the "fad for all negro pictures on the coast is prompting a number of pictures and director and writers to become more familiar with the race," relating an anecdote about a party staged for a "troupe of colored stock players" at a white director's "palatial home."[5]

A writer in the African American weekly the *Pittsburgh Courier* assumed a larger public interest in "the Negro," which could attach itself to "Negro films," citing a white studio executive as an authority:

> Negro films will be the next type of picture to bask in the spotlight of public interest, Monte Brice, Paramount supervisor, prophesied Sunday in an interview.
>
> "The vogue for pictures dealing with the show business has passed its peak, in my opinion," Brice declared. "Public taste is a fickle thing and now I believe it is going to fasten its attention on Negro pictures."
>
> "It only remains for a few more clever colored boys and girls to find their place on the screen for a veritable deluge of Negro pictures to be made. Producers follow the demands of the public. Two years ago, none of them could have been persuaded to tie up money in such pictures."[6]

Brice here imagines "Negro films" as an emergent genre, reflecting a very recent shift in audience demand.

Although Hollywood's African American films during the transitional period indeed reflected or echoed the black-cultural "vogue" described in these publications, it would be misleading to say that this vogue simply extended into the cinema from other cultural venues, like jazz recordings, stage musicals, and cabarets. Rather, this preexisting vogue intersected with film production under a very specific set of industrial conditions wrought by the conversion to sound. In an effort to resolve the early talkies' problems with visual stasis, acoustics, and synchronization, some white industry personnel seized on African American performance (and vocal expression, specifically) as an ideal means for making the new medium technically and aesthetically viable. Hence, the kinds of African American musical performances featured on recordings, on stage, and in the cabaret found a new venue in the cinema. Of these different cultural venues, the interracial cabaret—the cabaret located in an African American urban district like Harlem or the South Side of Chicago, which featured black performers but catered to "slumming" whites—was the most important as a point of reference for "Negro talking pictures."

By depicting it as the practice of white aristocrats and celebrities, contemporary newspapers, magazines, literary texts, and theatrical productions associated slumming with cultural progressiveness and sophistication as well as (ironically, from an African American perspective) upward status mobility. Thus, the cabaret used as a slumming destination offers a theater of white "highbrow" culture, giving a particular symbolic value to cultural blackness and becoming the point of intersection for the dominant American cinema and the black-cultural "vogue" of the 1920s. By altering the landscape of film exhibition, the conversion to sound reshaped the studios' conception of their audiences. In the late 1920s and early 1930s, the studios began to focus their attention on metropolitan audiences patronizing first-run theaters wired for sound and owned by the studios, which charged the highest ticket prices and thus generated the most revenue. The studios understood this audience to be relatively more sophisticated or "highbrow" than its smaller-town or rural counterparts and thus more open to "artistic" cinematography, risqué subject matter, and novel forms of entertainment—such as the kinds of entertainment being featured on the contemporary Broadway stage.

In this context, black performance becomes a novel "production feature," which, the studios assume, will appeal to some "taste publics" (to use Richard Maltby's term) but not to others.[7] In an effort to appeal to the "class" audience, the studios begin to target the same people who might participate or at least be interested in cabaret slumming—given its high-status associations—with "Negro talking pictures." They make this appeal even at the risk of alienating the "mass" or "Main Street" audience, the film industry's own rhetoric about the undifferentiated national audience notwithstanding. Imagining an audience interested in the cinematic presentation of African American musical culture, the Hollywood film industry seizes upon the symbolic value of blackness for the white consumer. During this period, however, the studios remain ignorant of, if not hostile to, African American audiences in determining production schedules, thereby constraining their investment in "Negro films" and reinforcing a sense of white racial privilege and authority.

The Black Acoustic Object and the Future of the Talkies

In 1929, two years after the premier of Warner Bros.' *The Jazz Singer* (a "part-talkie" combining a recorded musical score with discrete passages of synchronized song and dialogue), the feature-length "all-talking" film was on the verge of becoming the industry standard, rendering silent films obsolete. Recognizing the popularity of all-talking films, major studios Warner Bros., Fox, Paramount, and MGM would complete their "conversion" to this mode of production during the 1929–1930 season, phasing out silent films, silent versions of sound films, and part-talkies. The wiring for sound of theaters around the country increased apace.[8] As film historian Donald Crafton highlights, 1929 was "a time of experimentation and concerted efforts by studio technicians, directors, and sound engineers to make the technology work."[9] Hence, the technical, aesthetic, and generic properties of the new medium remained in flux; films like *Hearts in Dixie* and *Hallelujah* were products of this transitional moment, when the industry had fully committed its resources to talking pictures, but before important aspects of the production process and ways of handling soundtrack-image relationships had been "standardized."

Dismond's "The Negro Actor and the American Movies" appears in the special "Negro in Film" issue of *Close Up* alongside an essay by Harry Alan Potamkin, a pioneering white film critic whose writings in the late 1920s and early 1930s address a wide range of aesthetic and ideological issues in international cinema.[10] In "The Aframerican Cinema," Potamkin makes a striking claim about the black film "fad," detailing a series of antecedent moments in literature and theater in which "Negro" culture becomes a source of fascination for (implicitly) white audiences:

> The present vogue for Negro films was inevitable. The film trails behind literature and stage for subject matter. There has been a Negro vogue since the spirituals were given their just place in popular attention. Many Negro mediocrities have ridden to glory on this fad. Many white dabblers have attained fame by its exploitation. The new Negro was suddenly born with it. Cullen and Hughes were crowned poets, but Jean Toomer, a great artist among the Negroes, has not yet been publicly acclaimed. He first appeared before the hullabaloo was begun. The theater took the Negro up. First Gilpin, and eventually came *Porgy*. Now the film. Sound has made the Negro the "big thing" of the film movement.[11]

Using a characteristically telegraphic style, Potamkin identifies "sound" itself as the agent that forces the American cinema's belated turn to "the Negro." "The Aframerican Cinema" does not directly address the question of why *sound* per se would cause this change. Potamkin highlights the possibilities for sound-film treatment of what he calls "the vocal experience of the Negro," but the essay devotes much more attention to the "plastic," sculptural qualities of moving "Negro" bodies as a vital "source" for film production.[12]

Potamkin's implicit claim, that "the Negro" voice possesses a unique acoustic quality, concurs, however, with a series of contemporary statements by filmmakers, industry personnel, journalists, and critics: that African American voices are especially well suited to the sound film's technologies of mechanical reproduction. Although Potamkin himself does not delve into this logic of racial-vocal difference, these statements serve to explain how and why sound "has made the Negro the 'big thing'" of film production in 1929. Film theorist Alice Maurice has delineated this rhetorical pattern, which constructs an affinity between "the black voice" and the "talking picture," and interpreted it as a response to prevalent anxieties within the American cinema about the aesthetic effects of the conversion to synchronized-sound recording.

As Maurice explains and as my own research into period debates about the "talkies" confirms, there were four major anxieties about recorded sound and its effects on the medium—and, by extension, four basic lines of attack open to critics of talking pictures. First, many observers worried that sound would make the movies static. The new emphasis on dialogue and the corresponding need for directors to capture the moving mouths of actors threatened to reduce the cinema to a kind of filmed theater, requiring longer shots and sacrificing the dynamic, poetic possibilities afforded by montage. Second, the recording apparatus itself enforced a set of technological limitations on camera movement, which, at least before 1929, made talkies seem visually uninteresting to many. The extremely sensitive early microphones required that the noisy film camera be housed inside a soundproof booth. The bulk of this booth made tracking shots extremely difficult, and the small window behind which the camera was situated permitted limited panning and tilting. Because of the newly static camera, filmmakers were thus eager to place new sources of motion and visual interest within the film frame.[13]

Third, moviegoers frequently complained that the human voices reproduced by the recording apparatus sounded artificial, lacking warmth, richness, and "personality." In what was a common criticism in the early American sound cinema, the addition of synchronized sound—which, hypothetically, should only enhance the abilities of the cinema to reproduce physical reality—diminished the illusionistic power of the film medium, making it seem ghostly and mechanical.[14] This discontentment with the sound of the recorded voice touched off an intense debate about what kinds of voices and ways of speaking were best suited to the apparatus. Finally, a range of problems with projection and speaker systems served, in some theaters, to diminish the illusion of image-soundtrack unity, disrupting the synchronicity of the two elements and making voices appear not to emanate from characters' mouths.[15]

Maurice argues that African American performers seemed, to some white observers, to offer remedies for these several ills of recorded-sound film–production. Responding enthusiastically to the landmark production *Hearts in Dixie*, some critics suggested that black musical performance—vernacular dance in particular—might be an ideal form of spectacle for filmic treatment, thus bringing dynamic energy back into the frame. As Maurice shows, critics like Kenneth MacPherson and *The New Yorker*'s Robert Benchley singled out the performance of Lincoln Perry (aka Stepin Fetchit) for particular praise, celebrating his kinesthetic skill.[16] Benchley's review, which appeared in the National Urban League's *Opportunity* magazine, also contains the most overt example of the argument that African Americans' voices were ideally suited to sound-film recording, registering on the soundtrack with more warmth and fidelity than the voices of other groups of people.

Writing as a skeptic who has doubts about the survival over the long term of sound films, Benchley waxes so enthusiastic in this review as to make the talking picture an inherently "Negro" medium. Not only is *Hearts in Dixie*, for Benchley, the first successful talking picture but, in the film's wake, it even becomes clear to him that "so long as there are enough Negroes to make pictures, and enough good stories for them to act in, the future of the talking picture is assured."[17] Beyond his description of Fetchit's vital, dynamic presence on the screen, Benchley bases this claim on the putative vocal "qualities" of black performers: "Voices *can* be found which will register perfectly. Personalities *can* be found which are ideal for this medium. . . . There is a quality in the Negro voice, an ease in its delivery and sense of timing in reading the lines which make it the ideal medium for the talking-picture."[18] In the most clear-cut instance that I have found of the discursive phenomenon that Maurice describes, Benchley sees/hears black vocal performance and synchronization as mutually enhancing one another. In a similar case, Frank Davis, a reviewer writing for *Sound Waves*, a semimonthly Hollywood-based newsletter devoted entirely to the new sound technology, lauded *Hearts in Dixie* for its perfect synchronization. Viewing a preview screening of the film, Davis begins to understand "color" as an audible phenomenon, which allows filmic elements to seem to cohere splendidly: "It is the colorful backgrounds, the inescapable melody and drama that is inborn in the Negro."[19]

Arguments like Benchley's and Davis's make a fetish of African American–produced sounds, creating what we might call a black acoustical (or, more specifically, vocal) object and using this object—its acoustic "quality" and "timing"—to facilitate the American cinema's transition to exclusive talkie production. As in Potamkin's succinct formulation, the black vocal object becomes the "big thing" during the conversion to sound, the "it" (Davis) that shores up the new medium's deficiencies—even rising, as Benchley suggests, to the level of a "medium" in its own right. Such pseudo-physiological arguments about the exceptional qualities of "the black voice" achieved currency in the early American sound cinema and were appropriated by African American cultural critics and cinephiles, who sought "to extend and to take advantage of growing opportunities for black performers in Hollywood."[20]

For instance, a writer using the penname "An Insider" in the black weekly *California Eagle* laid out an extensive physiological contrast between black and white voices: "It is a fact that nine out of ten Negroes who take the voice test for the talkies pass without having had previous training; while seven out of ten cultured and well-trained white actors fail to pass the voice test. The voice of the Negro actor registers smoothly and evenly because it is by nature well modulated and very mellow, while the voice of the white actor is high-pitched, sharp and rasping."[21] Writing in the *Pittsburgh Courier* in late 1929, Ruby Berkley Goodwin presented this understanding of "the black voice" as if it were an industry commonplace: "Directors will tell you that the Negro is a born actor and that his voice is more adaptable for the 'talkies' than that of any other race."[22]

Maurice astutely deconstructs the notion that the black vocal object offers a remedy to faulty synchronization and insufficient vocal "warmth," specifically, in early sound film. She claims that when commentators note some exceptional acoustic "quality" in "the black voice," what they really have in mind is a ready-made racial linkage between the voice and the body, which serves to supplement the tenuous "marriage of sight and sound in the early talkies." In other words, "the black voice" is a notion that conflates audible and visible properties, according to what Maurice calls a racial "synesthesia": the idea that racial "blackness," defined visually as skin "color," is something that can be heard as well. According to this analysis, when someone like Benchley claims to hear racial difference in "the black voice," he makes this synesthetic leap between sensory registers, grounding the voice in a racialized body. Thus, Maurice argues that African American performers seemed to offer a remedy to problems of sound-image connection on the basis of this habit of simultaneous seeing and hearing.[23] Racial ideology here furnishes the cinema with a surrogate form of synchronization, a means of making the talking picture whole.[24] In this fashion, the black vocal object acquires a particular cultural-symbolic value, which the cinema seeks to exploit; it becomes the next "big thing" in the cinema, the source of a new fad.

White Cultural Privilege and Cabaret Slumming

Using the phrase "Black became the fad" to frame the "Negro talking pictures" in production in 1929, Dismond identifies those productions as a second-degree fad that takes its cue from an earlier moment of white investment in black culture. She considers developments in the Hollywood cinema in the same terms as a writer in the 1931–1932 edition of the *Negro Yearbook*: "Negro films are becoming a field in themselves in Hollywood. The popularity of the Negro plays and dancers and musicians that originated in New York finds an echo in film production."[25] The instigators of Dismond's black fad, the people who confer this popularity, are white aesthetes with avant-garde pretensions ("dilettantes"), constantly seeking new forms of sensation and aesthetic pleasure. While Dismond does not describe these figures in detail, her historical referent is clear: the white bohemians who frequented African American cabarets and nightclubs in Harlem and Chicago during the 1920s.

Dismond was a firsthand observer of this particular phenomenon in New York. A member of the Harlem intellectual and cultural elite, she edited *the Inter-State Tattler*, an African American "National Pictorial Weekly" dedicated to society gossip. In her *Tattler* columns, Dismond often commented on the appearance of white celebrities at black Harlem premieres and parties.[26] Indeed, Dismond's rhetoric is echoed in a comment made by her friend and the most famous of these "white dilettantes," Carl Van Vechten. In a 1924 letter to H. L. Mencken, Van Vechten wrote: "Jazz, the blues, Negro spirituals, all stimulate me enormously at the moment. Doubtless, I shall discard them too in time."[27]

Van Vechten's investment in the culture of the Harlem Renaissance was, in the end, sustained and took on many forms. He assisted African American writers (Langston Hughes and Nella Larsen, most notably) in securing contracts with New York publishers; he promoted black artists and intellectuals through his photography and cultural criticism; he guided white literary and entertainment celebrities around a circuit of African American nightclubs catering to white trade and helped to stimulate a larger white "vogue" for "slumming" in certain Harlem districts; and he sought to disseminate on a larger scale his particular vision of black nightlife in his 1926 novel *Nigger Heaven*—to "exploit" this "exotic material."[28]

In accounts that circulated in literary texts, theatrical productions, and mass-market periodicals, slumming was represented as an emblem of elite cultural sophistication and an object of emulation for broader cultural publics. The existence of these earlier representations helps to explain why the trade-press reviewers and the distribution-sector personnel for whom they spoke would have treated contemporary African American musical culture as a desirable commodity for white white-collar audiences—even though most constituents of these audiences belonged to a very different class stratum than Van Vechten and his circle. The lack of precise demographic data in existing cultural histories makes it difficult to know to what degree less affluent white people participated in cabaret slumming. Nonetheless, contemporary coverage of the slumming "fad" illustrates that the practice was available at least as a site of vicarious indulgence in "highbrow," celebrity-driven culture.

In the mid-1920s, publications like *Harper's* and *Vanity Fair* featured stories on black Manhattan cabarets; even *Time* took note of Van Vechten's activities in Harlem. White New York papers helped to publicize the practice of white cultural tourism and "thrill-seeking" in the city, noting visits to cabarets like Happy Rhone's, the Cotton Club, Small's Paradise, and Connie's Inn by white celebrities from Broadway (Lenore Ulric, Marilyn Miller), vaudeville (Helen Morgan, Sophie Tucker), Hollywood (Jack Pickford, George Raft), and popular music (Jimmy Durante, Paul Whiteman). Further highlighting this association of celebrity and the Harlem cabaret, *Variety* magazine itself investigated Harlem clubs as part of its coverage of big-city nightlife.[29]

Historians like David Levering Lewis and period observers like Rudolph Fisher and Nella Larsen date the transformation of one Harlem district into a white nightlife destination between 1926 and 1927. In his satirical 1927 essay, "The Caucasian Storms Harlem," Fisher expresses a sense of estrangement upon visiting several Harlem nightclubs following a five-year absence from the city: "I found myself wondering if this was the right place—if, indeed, this was Harlem at all. I suddenly became aware of the fact that, except for the waiters and members of the orchestra, I was the only Negro in the place."[30] The shock of Fisher's discovery prompts "a moment's recollection" on the state of black cabarets "seven or eight years ago," before the white slumming fad had transformed their social atmosphere and entertainment offerings.[31] The protagonists of Larsen's *Passing,* Irene Redfield and Clare (Kendry) Bellew, discuss why Hugh Wentworth, a leisured white man and sometime ethnographer, would attend a black Harlem social function like the Negro Welfare League dance. Irene explains, "This was 1927 and hundreds of people of Hugh Wentworth's type came to affairs in Harlem, more all the time."[32]

As Irene's distinction of "type" makes clear, this form of cultural tourism was probably restricted to middle- and upper-class whites—as much because of cost as because of taste or racial attitudes. Citing a 1925 study of "the social atmospheres of New York dancehalls, restaurants, and cabarets," Nicholas Evans argues that cabaret-going in general was restricted to "wealthy (sub) urban sophisticates, business professionals of the middle and upper-middle class, and upwardly mobile youths."[33] Featuring African American entertainers in lavish revues and floor shows, the clubs that featured in popular accounts of white "slumming" were often owned and operated by whites, catered to white trade, and, in some cases, barred African American patrons from admission.[34] In an October 1929 cover story on the "Black Belt's Nite Life," *Variety* counted "11 class white trade night clubs," clubs patronized specifically by wealthy whites living downtown.[35]

Writing just after Dismond's piece was published and at the height of the putative "Negro film" fad, the *Variety* correspondent assures, "Never has [Harlem] been more popular," seeing the city as surpassing Broadway as a nightlife destination for those in the know.[36] He or she goes on to describe Harlem as a "high grade white locale," an amusement playground where white entertainers, politicians, and aristocrats ("celebrities in all walks of life") could be found indulging in various forms of black musical performance.[37] Deploying without noting this paradoxical racialization and class-marking of Harlem as a "locale," this report makes clear the established cultural association between cutting-edge African American culture and white "highbrow" taste that existed in the late 1920s.

"Classes" Not "Masses"

Much as film industry personnel promoted the movie palace in the late 1920s and early 1930s, portraying it as a temple of consumer democracy, the major motion picture studios sought to represent their audience as a homogeneous national mass, arguing that their products appealed to big-city, "de luxe" theater patrons and rural moviegoers alike. In his important essay "Sticks, Hicks, and Flaps: Classical Hollywood's Generic Conception of Its Audiences," Richard Maltby has demonstrated that this ideal image of an "undifferentiated and unified" audience was an ideological expedient, whereby "the industry [could] either claim a higher social status or else assert that it was performing a benign and unifying social function."[38] Adopted by the studios and the Motion Picture Producers and Distributors of America (MPPDA) alike, this "rhetorical pose" is belied, however, by the activities of distributors during the period and by controversies among exhibitors over the kinds of films available for purchase.[39] While Maltby concedes that filmmakers and studio executives involved in the production process did not have a clear sense of the composition and tastes of their audience, he demonstrates how the distribution sector attempted to predict what kinds of films would succeed in certain markets, thinking not in terms of one homogeneous audience but in terms of multiple "taste publics."[40]

The industry's division of labor made the distribution sector, represented by the studio sales departments, the keepers of practical knowledge about audience preferences. In order to "increase the efficiency with which the industry's output delivered the maximum number of viewers to exhibition sites," the sales departments attempted to compile information about these extremely diverse theaters.[41] Taking into account the physical location of these sites and available data about the surrounding community, the sales departments developed a categorical scheme for classifying theaters and, by extension, audiences. Making assumptions about the tastes of these audience types, distributors could make more informed, if still speculative recommendations to exhibitors about what films would be successful in their markets. In order to group theaters, then audiences, then films according to such categories, the distributors, Maltby shows, made general inferences about audience preferences based on their demographic profiles—where and how audience members lived plus their income levels. The distributors' assumptions about how localities determined tastes were informed at the same time by their dealings with exhibitors, who, claiming to speak on behalf of audiences, often demanded certain kinds of motion picture fare.[42]

Maltby assembles anecdotal evidence to show that the sales department helped to determine the "broad shape" of each studio's production schedule in a given year, with the personnel who staffed the regional film exchanges meeting in the spring to determine the proportion of films by genre that the studio would make.[43] Drawing on the sales departments' collective understanding of what would sell in each market, "the industry sought to provide a range of products that would appeal to different fractions of the audience" or, in a limited number of cases, "to include a set of ingredients that, between them, would appeal to the entire range of different audience fractions."[44] While a lack of documentation makes the histories of distribution and exhibition difficult to access, Maltby ingeniously uses trade-press film reviews to discern how the film industry understood its audiences.[45] Making predictions about what "fractions" of the audience will or will not find a particular film appealing (based on the "production features" it contains), reviews in trade magazines like *Variety* and *Motion Picture News* locate the film within an operative genre and taste category and thus can be read as a more or less reliable account of the film's intended addressees. Using a brassy tone and a heavy dose of slang, these reviews discursively divide the audience according to distinct but overlapping binaries.

Maltby's examination of trade-press rhetoric focuses on the same period with which the present study concerns itself—a period that sees the sharpening of these binaries in conjunction with changes in film production and exhibition venues. Between 1929 and 1933, the industry, Maltby argues, differentiated the audience first and foremost in terms of the "class" versus "mass" binary. The industry habitually linked this social-class binary to the taste binary of highbrow versus lowbrow or "sophisticated" versus "unsophisticated" and to a geographical binary, "Broadway" versus "Main Street."[46] Lining up terms along the respective sides of these binaries, the trade-press reviews illustrate how a dualistic vision of the audience conflated class or status with taste and locale. The trade magazines assume that the urban or metropolitan audience is wealthier and prefers more "sophisticated" forms of film entertainment and that the less-well-to-do rural or "hinterland" audience prefers simpler, more conventional fare. Within this discursive field, "sophistication" is an important, if quite flexible term. It can apply to artistic subtlety (fine "camerawork" or striking lighting) and narrative complexity, but also, in some cases, to what certain audiences might perceive as morally objectionable subject matter. Hence, these discursive audience divisions frequently concatenate issues of aesthetics, status, and public decency.

Upon this already complex framework of oppositions, the trade-press reviews overlay other binaries—principally of gender and age—in order to identify smaller segments of "trade" to whom films might appeal.[47] The way that the reviews deploy gender and age distinctions suggests that the patronage of certain trade groups was seen as more reliable than that of other groups. For example, the reviews address the "male audience" specifically less often than they do its female counterpart.[48] More specifically, the reviews disproportionately preoccupy themselves with whether a given film will interest the so-called flapper audience. In this context, "flapper" (sometimes abbreviated as "flap") is a term that conflates gender, generational, professional, regional, and status markers. "Flapper" designates a type-category comprised of young women working in salaried professions who attend movies frequently and whose moviegoing is part of a larger set of status-seeking consumption habits.[49]

Variety's treatment of "flaps" reflects the film industry's attempt to correlate production features with taste publics in a way that capitalizes on emergent patterns of aspirational, status-driven consumption. Making a series of bold assumptions, the reviews assert that this subset of the metropolitan, "Broadway" clientele enjoys scenic opulence and moral sophistication. Moreover, "flappers," to quote one contemporary review, desire "extra saucy lines and business"—the kinds of dialogue and screen action that trade-press reviewers often single out as unsuitable for nonurban, "Main Street" audiences.[50] Identifying specific production features as attractive and unacceptable for "class" and "mass," "Broadway" and "Main Street" audiences, respectively, these reviews highlight the degree to which the studios assumed that "very few pictures would play with equal success in all markets."[51] By the same token, the trade press's embrace of the "flapper" audience between 1929 and 1933—however patronizing its representation of that group—reveals how the industry favored the metropolitan, "class" public.

These invidious distinctions between "class" and "mass" represent, in part, an extension of efforts by the American film industry, which date back to the early 1920s, to augment its reliable, working-class patronage, with new, more affluent customers. That some industry figures and journalists observed in the late 1920s the rise of a "sophisticated" audience and the decline of the old "lowbrow" public was, in part, Maltby illustrates, an effect of new economic conditions accompanying the conversion of these same movie theaters to sound. Because first-run urban theaters were wired for sound more quickly than were smaller theaters in more rural markets, the American film audience was, at least until 1929–1930, effectively divided by locality.[52] Patrons of the former category of theaters had access to true "talking pictures," while patrons of the latter were treated to silent versions of the same films.[53]

While some commentators saw the closure of rural and small-town movie theaters as evidence that the first-run big-city theaters had drawn away their audiences, Maltby points out that the major studios' policies were responsible for the hardships faced by late-run exhibitors in such "marginal" sectors. The studios sought to exploit "the conversion to sound as a means of concentrating business in their theaters and profiteering from other theaters by greatly increasing film rentals." Hence, the disgruntled exhibitors working in these marginal areas correctly concluded that in this moment the studios were less interested in serving the rural, mass clientele; the studios' "production policies" increasingly were geared toward "material that would play with success in the theaters which they themselves owned: first- and second-run theaters in metropolitan areas, playing predominantly to employed urban working- and lower-middle-class audiences in their twenties and thirties."[54]

Observers in the trade press initially explained what they saw as a corresponding shift in film production toward artistic subtlety and experimentation, sophisticated and even risqué dialogue, lavish sets and costumes, and new kinds of musical spectacle as the film studios' spontaneous response to the demands of a "new," more sophisticated and discerning audience. In the articles that Maltby cites, the writers revel in the idea that this new audience, despite its "expensive tastes" (literary, musical, and theatrical), has embraced the "poor man's entertainment," painting fanciful pictures of "sophisticates" and "highbrows" filling theater seats. These self-serving images concealed and legitimated the studios' strategy of directing production budgets toward the most profitable market sectors. Notwithstanding the American film industry's desire to portray itself as a producer of universal culture, the studios actually began in this period to ignore certain sectors of the white audience and risked alienating "Main Street" exhibitors.[55]

As Maltby's precise demographic characterization of the patrons of "first- and second-run theaters in metropolitan areas" ("employed urban working- and lower-middle-class audiences in their twenties and thirties") suggests, the rhetoric of "expensive tastes" and elite sophistication contains an element of hyperbole. The actual social group that terms like "class," "highbrow," and "Broadway" generally targeted were white-collar workers, rather than wealthy elites or even people working in the traditional middle-class professions. In one of the reviews Maltby cites, the "flapper" audience is referred to as "the stenographer trade." As a "taste public," this group aligned itself with Broadway sophisticates, even as it belonged to an economic sector characterized by lower-paying clerical and service positions—the growing "armies of managers, supervisors, accountants, clerks, sales people, and other kinds of 'brain' workers" required by "corporations and service sector businesses."[56] The trade press's insistent linkage of these young workers in the rapidly expanding salaried professions with expensive tastes and high-status pursuits speaks to the aspirations of this group and the ways in which contemporary changes in the labor force had begun to alter existing concepts of class identity.

Representing what C. Wright Mills called the "new middle class," the white-collar sector encompassed such a wide range of occupations and salary levels that its growth troubled existing class categories. The attendant decline in the numbers of "old middle class" workers—independent farmers, entrepreneurs, and people in the traditional professions—meant that property ownership became less important as a determinant of class standing. Including highly compensated corporate managers and lower-paid subordinates, the white-collar sector tended to blur income-based distinctions. Some white-collar employees who considered themselves "middle class" and who identified with their managers as social peers actually earned less than skilled blue-collar workers.[57] As a result of this shift in class definitions and of the increasing importance of the consumer economy to social life, the white-collar sector promoted more fluid, status-based forms of class identification during this period. Consumer goods and services increasingly marked status distinctions, and an individual's ability to purchase and display these goods served to grant "middle-class" standing.[58]

As Steven Ross states, "Business leaders, advertisers, and politicians promoted a new discourse of class identity based on one's ability to consume rather than on one's occupation."[59] Hence, the flexibility of terms like "highbrow" and "classes" in trade-press discourse: the "ability to consume," and thus to style oneself according to one's own imagined or desired position, opened new pathways to elevated social standing for people holding a greater range of occupations. Yet for all of this revision of class concepts, the racial parameters of the expanding white-collar sector were extremely narrow. In 1940, the white-collar population was over 99 percent white.[60] Mills suggests that racial and ethnic homogeneity provided the new middle class with another claim to social prestige, making the whiteness of the white-collar sector a crucial feature of its social self-conception. Film trade-press reviews illustrate this racialization of class categories. While these reviews never identify white audiences as such, they mark African American audiences as a separate, usually stigmatized (and socially undifferentiated) group, illustrating the unspoken whiteness of terms like "class," "Broadway," and "highbrow."

Film Audience Typologies and "Negro Talking Pictures"

The reviews of "Negro talking pictures" published in *Variety, Motion Picture News, Exhibitors Herald-World*, and *Harrison's Reports* overwhelmingly predict that they will appeal to the "class," "highbrow," or "Broadway" sector of the American film audience.[61] The available reviews of African American–cast features (*Hearts in Dixie* and *Hallelujah*) and shorts (*Black and Tan, St. Louis Blues*, and *Yamekraw*) as well as *The Emperor Jones* evaluate the potential audience appeal of racial "themes" specifically, correlating black screen characters to (white) "highbrow" sensibilities—usually by comparing the films to Harlem Renaissance–era Broadway productions. Within this group of reviews, a handful point to a progressive racial "sentiment" or social agenda among white "highbrows," asserting an interest in "Negro films" that is intense if limited in scope.

At the same time, the reviews of these all or largely African American–cast films vary in how they treat the other pole of the audience binary. Some make no claims about the films' appeal (or lack of appeal) for "mass" or "Main Street" audiences; several assert that the very production features that will appeal to "highbrows" will alienate mass-audience members and/or will make the film unsuitable for southern exhibition; and a few, going somewhat against the grain, predict that the film will appeal to varied sectors of the audience. In describing how the films finesse matters of race relations to the point of becoming generally inoffensive, this last cluster of reviews resembles those of *Check and Double Check*—the one film in this group that, in the eyes of every reviewer, will have general audience appeal.

Films that feature African American performers in more limited capacities—*On With the Show* and *Thunderbolt*, specifically—draw notice for production features that, trade-press reviews typically hold, appeal to "highbrow" sophisticates: striking visual spectacles or groundbreaking uses of motion-picture technology, "symbolic" or "artistic" touches of lighting and cinematography, and "racy" or sexually charged "business." This cluster of production features also looms large in reviews of films like *Hearts in Dixie* and *Hallelujah*, where writers explicitly link scenes of black performance to the films' evocative, expressionist visual stylings. In the reviews of *On With the Show* and *Thunderbolt*, these connections tend to remain implicit. Read through the lens of Maltby's account of the explanatory value of trade-press discourse—as reflecting the audience-calibrated production decisions made by studios on a yearly basis—the reviews of "Negro talking pictures" demonstrate that the studios understood African American "themes" and musical spectacle to be production features that might appeal to white "class" audiences. While these reviews illustrate the studios' anxieties about "the southern box office"—and the ways in which such anxieties may have influenced the films' productions—they also indicate that the studios were sufficiently interested in "highbrow" trade to undertake a significant "experiment" in African American film production. The potential appeal of the films' production features for higher-paying (white) metropolitan audiences outweighed the likely disinterest of other less desirable (white) audiences.

Freddie Schader of *Motion Picture News* asserts that, while "highbrows" will love *Hearts in Dixie*, the "rank and file of fans" will not be interested in it; thus the film will do best in "little 'arty' theaters" in metropolitan areas.[62] Without using the term explicitly, *Variety*'s review of *Hearts in Dixie* points to the film's "class" appeal, highlighting its great "workmanship" and "pictorial" quality. While *Hearts in Dixie* is an original film scenario with no theatrical precursor, the reviewer employs a neologism popular in these reviews, calling the film "O'Neillish."[63] The reviewer not only compares the film to *The Emperor Jones* but also describes it as "a celluloid *Porgy*."[64] Contextualizing the film in terms of contemporary Broadway interest in African American subject matter and suggesting that it may appeal to a similar taste public, such comparisons are standard in the trade-press discussion of *Hearts in Dixie*. Both reviews published in *Exhibitors Herald-World* use Broadway shows to explain the film's appeal. Wilbur Morse Jr.'s account of the film's Hollywood premiere calls it "a worthy screen successor to the Heyward play," *Porgy*. T. O. Service's review compares the film favorably to Wallace Thurman's *Harlem*, which he claims to have seen the same night, and concludes that "the speaking screen is a better medium than the speaking stage" for African American performance.[65]

The combination of refined film aesthetics, theatrical interest, and African American subject matter makes *Hearts in Dixie*, the anonymous *Variety* reviewer concedes, "a novelty film" that will only appeal to certain niche publics: "That it is well made isn't going to particularly interest that clientele which wants its vital catch-as-catch-can stuff either in battle or on a couch."[66] In other words, the reviewer, assuming the "masses" to be oblivious to aesthetic refinement, determines that the film's lack of violent conflict or romantic situations will limit its appeal for that group. The film, this reviewer argues, is more "apt to appeal to the sympathies of the intelligentsia than the mob at large."[67] While the term "intelligentsia" clearly resonates with the conventional trade-press rhetoric of "highbrows" and "sophisticates," paired with the word "sympathies" it works implicitly to locate a spirit of racial "acceptance" within the "class" trade.

The term "novelty" works in an interesting way in trade-press discourse, seeming to mark something cutting edge (faddish?)—a production feature that will appeal to more daring or sophisticated viewers. Commenting on the Dudley Murphy–directed Duke Ellington vehicle, *Black and Tan*, *Variety* calls the film's setting, Harlem, "always a novelty."[68] While this statement is, on its face, illogical, it makes sense when considering the coding of Harlem as an ostensibly exotic, thrilling milieu in period popular culture. Although this reviewer concludes, without explicit justification, that this "slice of Harlem nite life should go anywhere" (that it should play successfully in any type of theater), his or her approach to the film implicitly opposes the "novelty" of the film's "all colored cast" and "real hot music" to the run-of-the-mill production features typically deemed to carry "mass" appeal.[69]

The reviews of *Hallelujah* echo the critical discourse on *Hearts in Dixie*. They stress the film's artistic and technical brilliance, suggesting that these production features, along with its all-black-cast format, identify it as a "class" or "highbrow" film. The anonymous reviewer for *Harrison's Reports* predicts "spotty" success for *Hallelujah*, which he or she also calls "a piece of art": "where 'Hearts in Dixie' drew good crowds, 'Hallelujah' should draw, too. Where it did not draw, it will be a suicide to show it."[70] In an extremely laudatory review, *Motion Picture News*'s Schader highlights *Hallelujah*'s "technical effects," pictorial "beauty," and "epic" qualities.[71] He further imagines Nina Mae McKinney, who plays "the role of the siren," acting the lead part of *Lulu Belle* on Broadway.[72] Indulging in the sort of casual racism visible in his other reviews (and common in trade publications more generally), Schader offers as proof of the film's quality the fact that "one can sit in [the] theater and be so absorbed in the story that one forgets that it is being enacted by negroes."[73] For Schader, the fact that this film transcends the limitations of its own casting is further testament to Vidor's directorial skill.

Variety, which published three separate reviews of *Hallelujah*, highlights the film's "highbrow" appeal but also considers whether the film might, in fact, appeal to "Main Street" audiences as well. Ambitiously, *Variety* seeks to use the film as a test case to gauge the degree to which "the colored race can appeal on the shadowy screen to all." The first of the reviews does assert that *Hallelujah* will have wider appeal, pointing to a series of mitigating factors in the film, which make it safe for "Main Street" audiences and inoffensive to white viewers with a range of racial-political sensibilities. Describing the film as "a big, gripping, all-colored (Negro) talker," the first reviewer predicts great success for *Hallelujah* "in the white man's theaters," broadly speaking, because white viewers "will accept it as a camera reproduction of the typical southland" and will discover in the film visual confirmation of their notions about how "the Negro" lives in that region's difficult conditions.[74]

Variety's first reviewer notes *Hallelujah*'s cinematographic brilliance, but, whereas this kind of language usually leads reviewers to conclude that a film has "class" appeal, this writer predicts that the film will "go into the hinterland houses and make money." The other reason for this atypical prediction is that, while the film "could have resorted to daring, risque, or vulgar bits," King Vidor has kept all of the instances of "lovemaking" morally "clean." The film contains erotically charged elements, but, according to this reviewer, the director's "deft, master hand" keeps them from devolving into the "extra saucy lines and business" deemed in trade-press discourse to appeal only to metropolitan audiences—and to "flappers" in particular. The reviewer calls the film "censorproof" and recommends its exhibition in "the sticks," offering no opinion about its chances in "Broadway" houses.[75]

Contrary to what *Variety*'s prefatory blurb asserts, the second reviewer of *Hallelujah* does not assert that the film will appeal to audiences in the "sticks"; instead, this reviewer goes to great lengths to contextualize the film in terms of the interracial cultural ferment of the Harlem Renaissance, which allows him to link the film with a white metropolitan "class" trade. The second review opens with a statement that anticipates Dismond's framing of "Negro films" within the larger "fad" or vogue for African American culture: "King Vidor's all-negro picture may be regarded as the climax and the popularization of that increasing body of sentiment which in recent years has found expression through such channels as the *American Mercury* and *The Nation*. It has tended to glorify the primitive negro life of the south and the emerging race consciousness and intellectual vigor of the colored people."[76] Strikingly, this particular invocation of the black fad suggests Alain Locke's discourse of "the New Negro" in its pairing of southern African American "folk" life and cosmopolitan, intellectual ferment.

Given this ideological background, the reviewer wonders, "Will 'Hallelujah' have any common denominator for the everyday white person detached from the liberal movement that centers in New York?" This fascinating question acknowledges a very specialized audience who will appreciate the film for its racial politics, making it "a worthy novelty for de luxe houses."[77] Moreover, the second reviewer sees *Hallelujah*'s religious worship scenes as potentially attractive production features for the first-run theater market. In other words, this "liberal" trade will go to the urban movie palaces to view the film. Leaving open the question of "the south" and of other "Main Street" markets, the reviewer sees *Hallelujah* as squarely rooted in the progressive, New York–based literary and theatrical culture of interracial "sympathy."[78]

Variety introduces the third *Hallelujah* reviewer, Ruth Morris, as specifically representing "the woman's angle" on the picture, and, more precisely still, the perspective of the "matinee" and "flapper" trades—terms Morris uses interchangeably.[79] While the reviewers of "Negro talking pictures" tend to link the films with a "highbrow" audience, they do not tend to make gender distinctions. Only the *Variety* reviewer of *Hearts in Dixie* mentions the typically emphasized "feminine audience," calling this group's interest in the film "doubtful."[80] Thus, *Variety's* devotion of a separate review to this audience in the case of *Hallelujah* highlights the complex intersection of race and gender ideologies in determining the film's intended audience.

Morris's review is a fascinating moment in the trade-press discourse of the "flapper" audience because it contradicts some of the conventional assumptions about this fraction of the audience's tastes as it seeks to imagine how young, working women might engage with an all-black-cast film. Morris opens her review by immediately declaring that the film is not "good matinee fare" and "not, in itself, a woman's picture": "There is nothing in it to attract the flappers or superficial lunchgoers who flock to a matinee after a morning's shopping in town. This element, wanting only a box of chocolates and a little light diversion, will be quickly bored by the picture, and take a rather indignant leave, as did several of its number at Monday's crowded matinee."[81] From here, Morris, asked to speak on behalf of these fractions of the female audience, goes on to defend the film against their supposed indifference to it; she even calls the film a "masterpiece." The resultant image that she constructs of the tastes of "flappers" and female matinee-goers is considerably more negative than the one that emerges from the reviews cited by Maltby.

Far from linking them with cinematic "highbrows," Morris describes these women as insensible to the film's well-wrought story, the "feeling for artistic composition [that] is in back of the photography," and its almost "musical" dialogue. These "femme dumb-bells" will, she asserts, be "bored with the fact that [*Hallelujah*] has no hey-hey nightclub scene, no handsome white hero and no sparkling gowns which usually set the pace for what should not be worn."[82] Morris links this audience's interest in movies to opulent commodified spectacle—the mise-en-scène of the fashion tie-up—and to vicarious romantic interest in white movie stars, production features absent from an all-black-cast film with a rural setting. Thus, while Morris's text implicitly supports the second reviewer's linkage between *Hallelujah* and the highbrow audience, it does so at the expense of the "flapper" contingent.

In the three paragraphs following the review's opening, however, Morris contradicts her own assertion that the film has "no hey-hey nightclub scene" and concedes that one part of the film might have significant appeal for "the matinee element." *Hallelujah* does feature an extended nightclub scene, a sequence in which the main characters sing and dance in an urban African American saloon. Further, according to Morris's own description, the scene features the kind of risqué appeal she has earlier asserted is missing from the film. It is as if, in order to review the film positively and to articulate her own enjoyment of it, Morris must first minimize the importance of the nightclub scene—she states that it is "relatively unimportant" and refers to it only in the final paragraphs of the review—and then displace any sign of interest in the scene onto the "flapper" audience, whose tastes she has already insulted. Evincing her own racial-sexual anxieties, Morris calls the film a masterpiece, but she seems to say that the sober, highly "serious" film she sees is not the same one that the superficially minded "femme dumb-bells" will see and enjoy.[83]

While Morris herself claims to find the idea of "a black and tan cabaret" to be "revolting," she concedes that the nightclub sequence will "draw in the matinee element" with its "naughty" aura, which according to Maltby's survey of the reviews, the "flapper" audience is said to prize above all else.[84] Morris even notes that the director has bathed the cabaret scene in "atmospheric colors with primitive, bold strokes"—rhetoric that recalls the other *Hallelujah* reviewer's interest in the film's primitivist aesthetic and its resultant appeal to white "highbrows."[85] Interestingly, Morris's description of *Hallelujah* mirrors a passage from a review of *Thunderbolt* that had appeared a few weeks earlier in *Variety*. Another film distinguished by the artistic "touches" of its prestigious director—"[Josef] Von Sternberg has gone symbolic with a vengeance"—*Thunderbolt* features a "black and tan cafe" scene.[86]

Evoking as it does the convention of white slumming in Harlem and Chicago South Side cabarets, the black and tan café was a significant production feature, which Paramount sought to market to interested audiences. One item in the studio pressbook trumpets: "Harlem—that strange black metropolis in the heart of the world's greatest city! The intriguing sounds and sights of its pulsing streets, its jazz-made night clubs, its hidden retreats."[87] Another item calls Los Angeles's "Central Avenue district" a "miniature Harlem" and claims that many of the black extras recruited from that neighborhood to work in the film also have lived in Harlem. This story even offers a sort of minihistory of slumming, suggesting either a perceived audience interest or a need to inform prospective viewers about an unfamiliar but glamorous practice: "Harlem, which extends from 125th to 140th streets, New York, brings heart-beats of southern plantations to metropolitan civilization. Sensation-seeking Broadwayites make these cafes possible, coming to dance shoulder-to-shoulder with habitués of this black metropolis to the beat of staccato jazz."[88]

A combination of racial hostilities and condescension toward the very "flapper"/matinee audiences whose perspective she has been asked to represent seems to keep Morris from endorsing *Hallelujah* on the basis of its "black and tan café"—and note that, strictly speaking, her description of *Hallelujah*'s intradiegetic cabaret's clientele as racially mixed is inaccurate. Morris appreciates the film as a piece of art and as a "serious" treatment of "the primitive" that does not "leer."[89] By the same token, she abhors the "'lowdown nigger' flavor" that the film acquires in those places where, she believes, it approximates the feel of the black and tan cabaret or, strikingly, the art of Miguel Covarrubias, the Mexican caricaturist and associate of Carl Van Vechten, whose stylized, primitivist drawings of African American figures were popular during the late 1920s.[90]

In the available trade-press reviews of African American–cast shorts centered around jazz music, two significant issues that remain more or less implicit and marginal in these feature reviews become explicit and central, specifically the use of striking, "artistic" cinematography and the representation of eroticism. In terms of the first issue, these reviews go further than the abovementioned pieces in highlighting how "Negro talking pictures" characteristically employ expressionist camerawork, suggesting that this "secondary" production feature strengthens their appeal for white "highbrows," the sector of the audience deemed to be attuned to it. For instance, *Exhibitors Herald-World*'s commentary on the Murphy short *Black and Tan* (whose very title is, in effect, a shorthand for a particular white "class" space) traces out a fascinating constellation of race, entertainment, and pictorial beauty.[91] Making the requisite comparison to *Porgy*, the *Exhibitors Herald-World* writer sees the short as "in a class by itself": "It's black men and it's music, the marvelous barbaric music of the Aframerican, plus superb direction, excellent recording and beautiful photography."[92] *Variety*'s reviewer also writes appreciatively of the film's seeming accumulation of "attractions." *Black and Tan* combines, he or she writes, a "first" production feature, "real hot music," with a "second" one, in the form of "fancy" and even "trick" photography, with "Harlem cafe life" as yet another attraction.

Although each of these features would seem to be most appealing to a select audience, according to the logic of trade-press discourse, the writer seems to conclude that their sheer quantity enhances *Black and Tan*'s chances of finding wide popularity. Looking at *Yamekraw*, another 1929 short built around a jazz score and using extensive expressionist cinematography, *Variety* reaches the opposite conclusion. The reviewer firmly states at the outset, "Too great an effort to be futuristic and overdo the Murnau art in photography and setting makes this one doubtful of mass appeal."[93] Here the reviewer clearly opposes "art" cinematography to "entertainment values"; *Yamekraw*'s emphasis on the former causes it to neglect the latter, making its presentation of "the moods and emotions of the Southern negro" alienating for the general audience.[94]

In terms of the second issue, the films' handling of sexually charged situations, the reviews of shorts rhetorically naturalize the links the films draw between African American jazz culture and "low-down" forms of erotic display. The reviews, however, reach different conclusions about how audiences—and film censors—might receive this putatively typical, "authentic" cultural linkage. *Motion Picture News* is concerned that the screen representation of sex and prostitution in *St. Louis Blues,* a Murphy short featuring blues singer Bessie Smith, may be too strong for "mass" tastes, lacking the "clean" treatment that could make the film widely appealing. Using racial terminology ("colored boys," "high yaller girl") in a way that indicates that he views screen representations of black sexuality through an exoticist lens, Schader wonders how "the story of this colored prostitute and her pander . . . ever got to the place where it was permitted to be filmed" and, moreover, how "the N.Y. Censor Board ever passed it" for exhibition. Unlike the *Variety* writer reviewing *Hallelujah* (whose cabaret scene is reminiscent of scenes in *St. Louis Blues*), Schader sees *St. Louis Blues* as fit only for "the blase Broadway mob"; even they, he suspects, might find the film "a little too rough."[95]

Interestingly, *Variety*'s review makes numerous equally overheated descriptions of the same production features—"hotsy-totsy trimmings," "sensuous Aframerican strutting so peculiar to the Harlem blacks," "low-down colored hot-cha-cha aura"—while averring that the film will "get by the censors on the ground of authenticity." Whereas *Motion Picture News*'s Schader sees the fact that African Americans act out this sort of "rough" material as making *St. Louis Blues* that much more shocking, the *Variety* reviewer sees it as lessening the film's violation of good taste. In this review, the expectation that "hotsy-totsy trimmings" like prostitution and suggestive dancing are simply a natural part of African American "low" life—"local color," as he or she repeatedly terms it—makes the film unobjectionable and, the review may want to suggest, more widely appealing to white audiences.[96]

While the reviews of the Warner Bros. musical spectacular *On With the Show* do not speak in terms of audience fractions, they highlight features of the film that, in trade-press discourse, typically carry "highbrow" associations and that normally would be linked to the flapper trade. Dealing with the travails of a stage musical headed for Broadway, the film uses sophisticated Technicolor cinematography and lavish spectacle to overawe the audience, incorporating scenes of African American song and dance performance. The *Motion Picture News* and *Exhibitors Herald-World* reviewers highlight the "sheer magnitude of screen entertainment" available in the film as well as its groundbreaking use of Technicolor; the very extravagance of the film's production values distinguishes it from other contemporary musicals.[97] Praising these same production values, the *Variety* reviewer notes the Warner Bros. studio's ongoing innovations in talking pictures and Alan Crosland's "class A directorial job."

With its technical sophistication and artistry, *On With the Show* will appeal, the reviewer implies, to the "class" trade—"anyone understanding pictures" in a sophisticated way.[98]

Somewhat more critically, the review points to an overabundance of material. Having included as many visually interesting music and dance spectacles as possible, the film becomes "overloaded" with production numbers. It is this strategy of organization that makes possible Ethel Waters's appearance in the film: "More than customary doses of girls, with several songs and a specialist without part in the plot, Ethel Waters, colored."[99] The reviewer makes positive, if somewhat bland, comments about a couple of these production numbers, including Ethel Waters's rendition of "Am I Blue?" which the reviewer predicts will be a "selling hit." The reviewer's weirdly legalistic presentation of Waters's name creates an interesting rhetorical tension: if this is "an all-colored musical," then what, the reader wonders, is the relationship between Waters's "coloring"—to use a term that appears throughout—and that of the film stock?[100] Waters's work in the film partakes of the aesthetics of abundance that allows *On With the Show* to combine musical spectacle with melodrama and romance, as well as lavish displays of what Morris's *Hallelujah* review calls "sparkling gowns."[101] These production features, which are generally linked to female or "flapper" audiences, surprisingly do not elicit such references here. The reviewers' unwillingness to identify specific audience fractions as privileged consumers of the film may suggest that they see it as widely appealing; all indeed predict that it will be a large box office draw. Nevertheless, the reviewers do not explicitly assert general or "mass" appeal for *On With the Show*.

Adapted from the wildly popular *Amos 'n' Andy* radio serial, *Check and Double Check* is the one film for which the trade-press reviewers unequivocally predict universal success. Speculating about the vast size of the duo's radio listenership, the *Variety* reviewer asserts that if even 70 percent of those fans turn out to see the film once, then they will fill "any theater anywhere" many times over.[102] *Motion Picture News* similarly asserts that the film "is geared for all kinds of [theatrical] runs . . . [but] should prove especially attractive in the smaller cities and neighborhood houses."[103] Moreover, the trade publications claim that the film will hold great appeal for children, as some of the most devoted radio listeners and *Amos 'n' Andy* fans. As a group whose tastes were most often held to be representative of the "Main Street" audience, children were a recently marginalized sector, whom some industry officials were eager to begin courting again.[104] An early report on *Check and Double Check* in *Exhibitors Herald-World* details RKO vice president Joseph Plunkett's "shaping of [the studio's] production program" in an effort to bring children "back into the theaters." At the annual sales convention, Plunkett hailed *Amos 'n' Andy* as an ideal vehicle for this turn to the child audience: "The point is," Plunkett stated, "that their stuff is always clean. On all sides I hear that, that the children idolize them as well as the grownups."[105]

Because of the radio program's reputation for clean, child-friendly entertainment and because of the characters' extensive, preexisting fan base, these reviewers are able effectively to bracket off questions of racial politics and thus do not explore the usual distinctions between "class" and "mass." The fact that *Amos 'n' Andy* relies principally on white blackface performance rather than on African American performance may also make the questions of white audience "sympathy" appear irrelevant to the reviewers. In fact, the reviewers seem so eager to emphasize what is familiar about the film (from the radio show) that they either neglect to mention the crucial production features in the film that are totally new or dismiss them as insignificant. These new features, which are significant indeed, include a veritable African American jazz performance (in a quasi-cabaret setting) and a plot involving upwardly mobile white characters (including women who wear "sparkling gowns"), making this film an important "Negro talking picture."[106]

The anonymous *Variety* reviewer insists that the "picture does not need its title of 'Check and Double Check.' It's just Amos and Andy." This reviewer calls the other "story" (the white romance and inheritance plot) "drivel," which serves the expedient of "allowing [Amos and Andy] to pace their bits and laughs, without being continuously on the screen." Given the ways in which the white characters' plot threatens to subsume that of Amos and Andy, the reviewer's assertion that "nothing [else in the film] means anything . . . it's just Amos and Andy" is patently untrue.[107] Indeed, Amos and Andy's social "meaning" in the film is largely determined by the ways in which *Check and Double Check* stages their interactions with the other characters and even links their destinies through an antecedent connection, the fact that the duo worked for the white protagonist Richard's father in Georgia.[108]

The film uses a sort of "black and tan" cabaret sequence to establish the initial connection between Amos and Andy and Richard, the characters existing in the film's parallel story lines. Amos and Andy, who run a taxi business, are charged with driving Duke Ellington and his orchestra to the suburban manor where Richard is staying. In the film's one scene of veritable African American performance, the band plays before a white audience, while Richard and his love interest, Jean, steal a romantic moment. Although this sequence lacks any of the "naughty" elements that Ruth Morris found in *Hallelujah*'s nightclub scene, it presents a fascinating attempt by the filmmakers to situate African American jazz in an atmosphere of cultural sophistication.

The reviewers' attempts to erase this aspect of the film notwithstanding, the Ellington sequence—and perhaps the entire Richard-Jean plot—seems like a "production feature" tacked onto the *Amos 'n' Andy* milieu for the express purpose of appealing to the sought-after "Broadway" trade—and even Morris's "matinee element." It is as if the studio thought that the humble world of Amos and Andy's taxi stand would not offer enough commodity-rich, visual pleasure for these desirable fractions of the audience. Thus, the filmmakers at once draw from *Amos 'n' Andy*'s "Harlem" setting a cultural commodity (in the Ellington band) deemed desirable for white sophisticates, while at the same time providing the white audience of the aspirationally highbrow status a point of identification in Richard, Jean, and the film's other intradiegetic listeners and dancers.

Motion Picture News's review of *Check and Double Check* also illustrates the attention given by the trade press to the southern box office, conceptualized as a homogeneous white audience extremely hostile toward any perceived violation of strict racial hierarchies on screen. By way of explaining the RKO film's universal appeal, the reviewer stresses, "Southern cities, where racial feeling may be pronounced, will find nothing in the picture to cause objection."[109] The rhetoric here echoes the terms used in the discussion of *Hearts in Dixie* and *Hallelujah*, signaling that the film will not offend white sensibilities because it does not seek to advance a social critique or to show African Americans and whites in "familiar" relationships. There is no consensus, of course, that the all-black-cast films will pass muster with white southern audiences, and the *Harrison's Reports* writer wonders "how such a picture [as *Hallelujah*] will be received, particularly in the South."[110] Likewise, the second *Variety* reviewer of *Hallelujah* predicts that "the film will not be universal in appeal," precisely because the film is so progressive (in the writer's view) in its representation of African American culture.[111]

In a groundbreaking article published in 1970, Thomas Cripps noted the trade press's abiding preoccupation with the tastes of white southern audiences in the period spanning 1920 to 1940. In what was the first (and appears still to be the only) film-historical study of racial rhetoric in trade magazines, Cripps argued that the studios' preoccupation with a "monolithic," racially intolerant southern box office limited the number of films that they produced featuring substantial black characters and encouraged them to maintain long-standing patterns of stereotype.[112] Cripps's study identifies a rhetorical pattern in the reviews, whereby the writers "predicted failure" for films with what he calls "Negro themes" in southern markets. My research illustrates that, where early sound-period "Negro talking pictures are concerned," such predictions were often countered by predictions of success for "Negro-themed" movies.

Cripps is no doubt correct that the studios' (perhaps exaggerated) concern with the southern box office shaped their production schedules and their ways of handling black "themes" and characters. The handling of cross-racial relations in *Check and Double Check* clearly bears out this point, as does King Vidor's initial struggle with MGM studio executives to get approval for *Hallelujah*.[113] Yet Cripps's need to support his main thesis—that the studios' South-fixation kept them from making greater numbers of "Negro-themed" films—encourages him to overstate the importance the industry placed on this box office. Writing before Maltby's important intervention, Cripps likewise fails to place these references to the southern box office into the larger context of trade-press discourse, which routinely pits specific segments of the audience against one another. In short, Cripps fails to recognize the degree to which the studios' interest in "class" or "Broadway" audiences during the early sound period would have encouraged them to make more African American–cast films and film sequences, in spite of the threat of a loss of southern business for these productions.

Unlike Maltby, Cripps does not attend to the division of intellectual labor within the film industry, in which the task of audience research falls to the distribution sector—to the studio sales departments that market groups of films to exhibitors on a regional basis. Moreover, Cripps unwittingly subscribes to the myth that, during the classical era, the Hollywood studios thought of their audience as homogeneous and undifferentiated. Thus, Cripps approaches the trade-press rhetoric not as a reflection of the distributors' habitual division of the larger audience into specific taste publics, but as evidence that producers used the assumption that films with "Negro themes" could not be exhibited successfully in the South to justify not making such films at all.

As a result of the contradictory maneuver that Cripps makes, using the trade-press discussion of extant "Negro-themed" films to explain the studios' refusal to make such films, it becomes impossible to offer a positive account of why "Negro talking pictures" would have been made at all. If we take into account the process described by Maltby, whereby the studios sales departments helped to set the next year's production schedule, then it becomes clear how (as Cripps himself argues) the assertion of the intransigent southern box office could limit, over the long term, the number of productions released by the major studios featuring African American characters. Indeed, the "deluge of Negro pictures" that Paramount's Monte Brice proclaimed in the 1929 statement quoted earlier in this chapter never materialized. Due to his less nuanced approach to the relationship between trade-press rhetoric and production decisions, Cripps, however, forecloses the possibility that such films might actually have been made for the express purpose of meeting a perceived audience demand during a given period.

Within the larger discursive context of audience classification that Maltby lays out, a slightly different reading of the rhetorical pattern that Cripps analyzes becomes possible. Rather than being a unique formation, the so-called southern box office represents a subset of the "Main Street" market. With the exception of a few major cities like Atlanta and Memphis, the southern market was mainly rural and featured fewer, smaller, and cheaper theaters. Indeed, Cripps's work astutely illustrates how, due to a combination of legal, cultural, and economic conditions, the southern market was relatively insignificant to the studios' business.[114] Cripps assumes, however, that the industry refused to recognize this economic reality and reads the trade-press reviews' predictions of southern box office failure as evidence of that refusal. Following Maltby, it becomes clear that such rhetoric reflects the distributors' conventional strategy for directing films to specific markets based on their assumptions of how different production features would appeal to different taste publics. Thus, as the reviews of the films examined here illustrate, negative references to the southern box office accompany—and are often secondary to—positive statements about the appeal of "Negro talking pictures" to the metropolitan, "class" audiences.

The film in this study that is most decisively declared to be unsuitable for white southern exhibition is *The Emperor Jones*. The response is not surprising, given that the film features perhaps the most socially assertive African American character—*Motion Picture Herald* calls Brutus Jones an "ambition-crazed Negro"—and the most extensive scenes of interracial dialogue in this corpus.[115] *Variety*'s highly positive review of *The Emperor Jones* laments the "doubtful" nature of the film's success "as a commercial property," predicting low "exhibitor acceptance." In light of the film's subject matter and treatment, "the south is entirely lost to it for consumption by whites." In a surprising twist, the reviewer notes that, at the same time, "colored [theater] operators below the Mason-Dixon line are objecting to the use of the term 'nigger,' which may have to be cut where occurring if exhibition is wanted for the Ethiopian trade."[116] The anonymous reviewer's own linguistic condescension notwithstanding, he or she strikingly acknowledges a regional African American audience, whose exhibitors have sufficient clout to affect the film's commercial success.[117] This anomalous moment is so striking because the trade magazines tend to treat African American audiences with undisguised contempt, implying that exhibitors will (and ought to) discourage black patronage of their theaters—as if the potential African American–audience appeal of "Negro talking pictures" is a liability for the same northern, metropolitan theater owners catering to the white "class" public interested in these films.

The *Variety* writer discussing *Hearts in Dixie* alludes to the "worry of whether any house playing it will thereby work up a strong Negro patronage," suggesting that exhibitors might shy away from the film because it is liable to attract African American viewers. For reasons that are left unclear, the reviewer dismisses this possibility and asserts that "members of the race" are only likely to attend initial screenings and not in sufficient numbers to deter whites.[118] In its review of the same film, *Motion Picture News* explicitly warns the potential exhibitor to "guard against" black trade: "[*Hearts in Dixie*] will undoubtedly draw the entire negro element in the vicinity of any house where it is played. That is one angle that the exhibitor must guard against." The reviewer notes immediately that this "angle" creates a paradox. The fact that the film has a "wholly negro cast . . . [and] is the first one of the feature length sound pictures with negro players" is also the only "angle" the exhibitor has to lure white trade into the theater.[119] The very novelty liable to attract the "negro element" also distinguishes this film among its competitors for "highbrow" white trade. This conclusion neatly points out the difficult position occupied by "Negro talking pictures," between a claim to novelty and niche interest for white viewers and an incipient African American interest that neither the exhibitors nor the studios seem to want or to be prepared to handle.

Notwithstanding the attitudes of the white "intelligentsia" toward African American filmic subject matter asserted in these reviews, the presence of African Americans in the theater audience would represent, these reviewers suggest, a nuisance for these spectators. This suggestion illustrates the assumed limitations of these patrons' "sympathies," as well as the marginal position accorded to African American patrons in first-run movie exhibitions, even in major, northern metropolitan areas.

The next chapter examines the precise ways in which films like *Hearts in Dixie* dramatize what one *Variety* writer called "the body of sentiment which in recent years has . . . tended to glorify the primitive negro life of the south and the emerging race consciousness and intellectual vigor of the colored people."[120] It focuses, specifically, on what it means that such white "highbrow" interest in "primitive negro life" coincides with the Hollywood film industry's resistance to African American audiences, which typifies American mass culture in the period. Does what this reviewer calls "emerging race consciousness and intellectual vigor" manifest itself in "Negro talking pictures"? Or is the other trope, "primitive negro life" with which the reviewer lumps these ideas, dominant? At what points do the film texts themselves demonstrate resistance to this Harlem Renaissance–era "race consciousness"?

The *Variety* review of *The Emperor Jones* nicely throws these questions into relief. The anonymous writer squarely locates the film in terms of the "Broadway" audience's tastes. Praising *The Emperor Jones*'s "cinematic achievement" and Paul Robeson's performance in the lead role, the writer asserts that the film has "class rather than mass appeal and thus its best grossing possibilities are limited to the larger urban centers of the U.S."[121] Setting aside the white South, where the film "is entirely lost," the reviewer asserts strong Broadway interest, which necessarily correlates to strong aversion on Main Street. He or she calls the film "too highbrow and O'Neillish" for "smaller localities."[122]

Although this reviewer does not assume that "the classes" will necessarily be more "sympathetic" to the film's racial politics, he or she does acknowledge the presence of differing "viewpoint(s)" within the northern, urban audience that should have access to the film: "the picture is still a character study of a Negro whose audience acceptance will either be sympathetic or unsympathetic according to its viewpoint."[123] By conjoining this binary—"sympathetic" versus "unsympathetic" to an individuated, dramatically compelling "Negro" protagonist—with other more familiar ones—"class" versus "mass," "larger urban centers" versus "the south"/"smaller localities"—the reviewer suggests a potential linkage between at least one fraction of the class trade's tastes and its racial attitudes. If "mass" aversion to the "highbrow and O'Neillish" lines up with racial hostility, then, by the binary logic of the trade-press review, the "class" desire for these same elements might also—but not necessarily—entail "acceptance" of complex African American "character stud[ies]."[124] But "acceptance" in what sense precisely? How do "Negro talking pictures" construct black characters in social terms? Do African American characters possess the kind of upward mobility enjoyed or sought by the white people belonging to the "highbrow" audience? Or might this audience be unwilling to extend its "sympathies" this far, thus making stories of African American social movement like that of Brutus Jones unacceptable?

CHAPTER 2

"The Negro Invades Hollywood"

THE GREAT MIGRATION, THE STUDIOS, AND THE PERFORMANCE OF AFRICAN AMERICAN SOCIAL MOBILITY

Generally regarded as the first of Hollywood's "all-black-cast musicals," *Hearts in Dixie* (Fox, 1929), in fact, features a white actor in a crucial role.[1] When Chloe (Bernice Pilot) and her baby, Truelove (Richard Brooks), fall seriously ill, her father, the kindly widower Nappus (Clarence Muse), expresses a desire to call in the local white physician, Doc Shelby (Richard Carlyle). Respected figures in the community, the Deacon (Zack Williams) and his wife, Emmy (Gertrude Howard), however, oppose Nappus's plan, trusting only the healing arts practiced by the Hoodoo Woman (A.C.H. Billibrew). Despite the Hoodoo Woman's attempts to drive out the "swamp fever," Chloe's and Truelove's conditions deteriorate. An agitated Nappus summons Doc Shelby, against the objections of the Deacon and Emmy, who, like Chloe herself, believe that his medicine is "only good for white folks" and that his presence will stifle the Hoodoo Woman's powers. The doctor arrives only to discover that mother and child have been dead for some time, even as the Hoodoo Woman continues her elaborate ritual, interpreting "signs" from the natural world and promising that the "hot"—the normal temperature and vitality—is about to "return to the body."

As the climactic moment of the first half of *Hearts in Dixie*, the loss of Nappus's child and grandchild motivates the narrative thread of the second half: Nappus's plan to send his much younger son, Chincapin (Eugene Jackson), "up North," so that he may receive an education. In the dialogue, the film establishes only a loose connection between Chloe's death and Nappus's plan for Chincapin; yet the sequence of events in the plot, coupled with Chincapin's own final speech, makes these deeper motivations evident. Nappus wants his son to gain access to Doc Shelby's scientific rationalism, so that Chincapin, as he himself suggests, might one day may become "a big doctor" and return to aid the community.[2] Once again meeting with resistance from the Deacon and Emmy, Nappus secretly sells his farm and his mule to finance Chincapin's trip. Only Doc Shelby supports Nappus's plan, acknowledging to him the need of "your people" for such opportunities and providing him with information about an unnamed "place" where Chincapin might learn. Against the backdrop of this antagonism between individual and community—an antagonism that, I will show, is patently false—Chincapin's eventual departure reads like a moment of social rupture. The concluding shots of the film visually emphasize the sorrow expressed by Nappus and the rest of the community, suggesting their potentially irreparable alienation from Chincapin.

The social antagonism that *Hearts in Dixie* establishes is, first and foremost, an allegory of the film's attempt to negotiate a crisis in African American screen representation. The film's focus is divided between a stable, insular community that exists, as it were, out of time (and that serves as the basis for the film's many musical sequences) and an individuated character who, according to the classical narrative paradigm, is able to change social positions and to motivate narrative action. Nappus and Chincapin jointly occupy this latter position in the film, the father plotting a course for the son that he himself cannot carry out. This course links the film historically to the Great Migration of African Americans from the rural South to the urban North, the first phase of which tapered off during the year that *Hearts in Dixie* was released. By associating migration with a shift in African American screen character, the film represents a symbolic change or "metamorphosis" not unlike that described by Alain Locke during the mid-1920s in his discussion of the emergence of a "New Negro." Thus, *Hearts in Dixie* uses the motif of migration to project or imagine an individuated black screen protagonist. It does so, however, in a way that is at best ambivalent, and at worst misconstrues the relationship between what Locke would call rural "folk" culture and the black-metropolitan culture of the "New Negro" as one of strict antagonism rather than of productive dialectic.

In order to contain the transformative potential that accompanies Nappus's plans and Chincapin's actual departure, the film goes to great lengths to ground its characters diegetically. The African American–cast format helps to create the image of a stable community, in which individual members do not differ substantially from one another, and the film underscores this notion through a quasi-anthropological prologue, in which a white actor steps out from behind a curtain and speaks into the camera. As Arthur Knight explains, the narrator both asserts the presumptively white audience's common ground with "the race" depicted on screen and exoticizes the film's characters. Claiming "we all laugh when we are happy; we cry when we are sad," the narrator casts African Americans in a condescending, "primitive" light (as if their emotional expressions were somehow more elementary than those of white people) and apologizes for the film's departure from the white norm (as if the bare humanity of the film's subjects needed to be vouched for). The film's characters are "other people" whose screen representation will enable the white theatrical audience to set aside "for an hour the cares and trouble of everyday life . . . to relax and enjoy" itself.[3] Following this prologue, the film moves episodically, relying heavily on extended musical sequences that further ground the characters in what Kaja Silverman would call a "recessed" diegetic space.[4] These musical sequences seem to embody the film's notion of a dehistoricized "folk" culture. Only in its final sequence does the film seem to breach this carefully constructed diegetic envelope.

By leaving his place of birth, Chincapin allegorically steps beyond the horizon of what the film can imagine as "Negro" social and cultural space. He becomes illegible with respect to the available frameworks for constructing an African American character. In this regard, the opposition the film establishes between Chloe's husband, Gummy (Lincoln Perry, aka Stepin Fetchit), and Chincapin is instructive. Gummy's defining trait is his laziness: he is constitutionally incapable of work, yet music can dramatically animate him. Indeed, early critics of the film fixated on Perry's physical grace and skillful dancing in this role.[5] For all of his movement within *Hearts in Dixie*'s musical spectacles, Gummy is another icon of social immobility; he even holds himself up to Nappus as an (ironic) example of what Chincapin could become should he stay in his current place. Chincapin, for his part, does not appear in the singing and dancing scenes.

Given that *Hearts in Dixie* attributes Chincapin's alienness to his changed relationship to the diegetic black community, it is not surprising that the film must end with his leaving, even though this feels more like a point of narrative departure than conclusion. By ending at this unsettled moment, the film briefly identifies an African American character as a subject, rather than object of what Kaja Silverman would call "enunciation."[6] Chincapin (through Nappus's dogged efforts) becomes capable of making narrative action happen. Thus, the film undermines the rigid racial divide it establishes at the outset between the cinematic interior (the diegesis of the all-black-cast film) and exterior (where the white narrator seems to verbally conjure the characters into being)—but only for a brief instant. Chincapin's metamorphosis is finally more an unrealized potential than anything tangible. With this conclusion, *Hearts in Dixie* exemplifies the muted but decisive ways in which almost all of the films examined in this study represent the Great Migration. While Hollywood's African American films from the transition to sound do not explicitly depict a mass movement of people, they refer to the Great Migration through striking allusions in song and dialogue, bits of narrative exposition, and images of individual relocation.

For early sound-era "Negro films," African American migration represents both a physical change of location and a symbolic movement or change in social position or role. With this symbolism, the films partake of preexisting discourses of migration: the dominant white culture's alarm over a perceived African American "invasion" of northern urban centers and, more important, Alain Locke's interpretation of migration as an effect of collective metamorphosis. The films' references to migration become more complicated in light of the fact that Locke himself, along with other late Harlem Renaissance–era observers, applied both of these tropes (invasion and metamorphosis) to African American performers' changing position in the Hollywood studio system during the "experiment" in "Negro films" of 1929 and 1930.

Describing such film-industrial shifts, these writers discursively link African American actors' new positions within the economic hierarchy of the movie studios with the loosening of typologies of black screen character and with the symbolically charged figure of the "New Negro." Locke, Sterling Brown, and Floyd Covington forecast that, just as the "New Negro" has exploded the dominant racial myths of the early twentieth century, African American film stars will move from periphery to center, from confinement within the logic of racial "type" to the freedom of singular self-expression.

This chapter turns the discourse of the cinematic "New Negro" back onto a series of feature and short films from the transitional period in order to analyze their own multifaceted treatments of migration. *Hearts in Dixie* presents an internal crisis in African American representation, whereby one character's decision to migrate decisively individuates him, giving him the potential for self-expression and self-determination, but placing him, at the same time, in opposition to the film's static, undifferentiated community. While *Hearts in Dixie* hesitantly opens a space for this figural metamorphosis, *Rufus Jones for President* (Warner Bros., 1933) pushes the logic of migration as self-expressive decision much further: the film stages the emergence of a black film star, Ethel Waters, who performs a pair of songs celebrating migration as an irrevocable shift in African Americans' social position or standing. By contrast, *Yamekraw* (Warner Bros., 1930) returns its migrant protagonist to the rural southern (plantation) setting, representing Harlem as a space in which he cannot survive and which, allegorically, defies the Hollywood cinematic imperative to locate African American characters in a familiar visual and narrative context.[7]

These last two films, which are shorts, rely heavily on strategies of visual and narrative containment; they are African American–cast films and use circular narrative structures. After brief journeys and changes in social status, their protagonists return to the settings in which they began. The very strategies the films use to envelop African American social experience, however, yield film-textual fault lines that indicate their simultaneous recognition and disavowal of black mobility. *Rufus Jones for President* comes the closest of all of these films (*Hearts in Dixie* included) to representing movement and metamorphosis sympathetically. Ironically, the film's musical numbers become the staging ground for this alternative discourse of migration. While emanating from what is the most intensively grounded or recessed space in the diegesis, these lyrics convey a more liberal racial-political sensibility, making it possible for the film's star vocalist to associate migration with liberation, rather than with alienation, and thus to evoke the "New Negro." As in *The Emperor Jones* (United Artists, 1933), vocal performance in *Rufus Jones for President* helps to draw attention to the fault lines that form around the film's attempt to contain diegetically its mobile black protagonist.

None of these films, however, offers a strong, emancipatory vision of migration; nor do they present a narrative in which a character realizes migration's potential to bring about metamorphosis. Such a representation is only conceivable in a film-production context in which African American artists—screenwriters and directors in particular—are employed in addition to African American actors. While early observers like Locke, Brown, and Covington believed that these production-sector jobs would follow from the initial wave of enthusiasm accompanying "Negro talking pictures," their ultimate lack decisively checked the putative black "invasion" of Hollywood. To exploit the imagined white audience demand for black performance, the studios participated, willingly or unwillingly, in a kind of "migration" at the level of industry demographics and labor relations. Yet the industry radically limited the scope of this shift, employing more African American performers while refusing to hire their behind-camera counterparts. This move assured that the range of African American characters and story material in Hollywood films would not significantly or permanently change. In making "Negro talking pictures," the industry remained focused on the appeal of black culture for white audiences, involving itself somewhat ambivalently in fictional treatments of black desire and social agency; it made opportunities available for black performers but continued to disregard the concerns and interests of black audiences.

The Cinematic "New Negro"

Alain Locke begins his 1925 manifesto "The New Negro" by critiquing entrenched forms of public opinion, which claim to "account for" the "American Negro" as a homogenous, collective subject. Locke posits that a psychological and spiritual transformation has taken place among the African American "masses," making existing racialist discourses "obsolete."[8] While conventional authorities on "the Negro problem" (white social scientists, philanthropists, and politicians) have used "formulae" to generalize about African Americans, these collective abstractions no longer hold any explanatory value—if they ever did.[9] Locke identifies as the major cause of this sudden and surprising group transformation "that shifting of the Negro population which has made the Negro problem no longer exclusively or even predominantly Southern."[10] Locke's argument thus depends on a particular interpretation of the Great Migration, the movement of an estimated one and a half million southern African Americans to northern cites like Chicago, New York, and Detroit between 1916 and 1930.[11]

African American mass migration carries immense symbolic significance for Locke, who reads it as a performance of historical agency, a "deliberate" embrace of "a new vision of opportunity, of social and economic freedom."[12] Locke is one of the "socially oriented observers" who, according to the historian James Grossman, emphasizes the "push of racial discrimination in the South and the pull of less oppressive race relations in the North" above economic motivations.[13] Indeed, Locke is so determined to combat arguments that impersonal economic forces have spurred a "blind flood" of humanity into the North that he attributes migration almost exclusively to African Americans' coming to historical self-consciousness—to a shift in collective "spirit."[14] Thus, Locke minimizes what Grossman would call "macro-historical" causes of migration, such as the opening of higher-wage jobs in northern factories due to the World War I–era economic boom and the wrecking of the cotton-farming economy by infestation and flooding. Likewise, Locke gives the new "vision" at work in the African American masses credit for enabling them to see "micro-historical" factors—"pushes" like lynching, white terrorism, and Jim Crow, and "pulls" like access to the ballot, better schools, and personal freedom—as "chance[s] for the improvement of conditions."[15] For Locke, the Great Migration exemplifies "metamorphosis" and "self-determination" and thus provides the historical backdrop for the appearance of the "New Negro."[16]

Indicating how "stock figures" from American popular culture have shaped racial ideology, Locke makes clear that he sees the "New Negro" as a dramatic figure, both literally and figuratively. "The day of 'aunties,' 'uncles' and 'mammies' is . . . gone," Locke argues: "Uncle Tom and Sambo have passed on. . . . The popular melodrama has about played itself out, and it is time to scrap the fictions, garret the bogeys and settle down to a realistic facing of facts."[17] Casting African Americans as subservient and dependent, such theatrical and literary stereotypes have conditioned the dominant understanding of "the Negro." Locke therefore stresses how, by defying this understanding, the "northward and city-ward" movement of large numbers of African Americans actually amounts to a dramatic performance of as yet uncodified "roles."[18] In an interpretation of the motives of "mass migrants" that is heavily indebted to Locke's, Amiri Baraka later would use similarly theatrical terms to depict a "change within the Negro as far as his relationship with America was concerned." Baraka asserts that the event of mass migration "must have been preceded by some kind of psychological shift; a reinterpretation by the Negro of his role in this country."[19]

Not only does the Great Migration dramatize collective self-determination, but it also reveals "the Negro" to be "rapidly in process of class differentiation": "If it was ever warrantable to treat the Negro *en masse*," Locke states, "it is becoming with every day less possible, more unjust and more ridiculous."[20] Thus, Locke sees in a postmigration center like Harlem a melding of groups with their "own separate motives . . . [and] special ends," a diversity that further challenges reductive "formulae."[21] As a combined effect of psychological metamorphosis, geographic movement, and intraracial differentiation, the very rhetorical form of "the Negro problem" becomes outmoded, making self-expression alone an adequate representation of the shifting "inner and outer life of the Negro in America." The very assumption that outside authorities might be able decisively to explain the difficulties and aspirations of an entire social group no longer holds.

Privileging a "literature" that is "of" rather than "*about* the Negro," Locke makes "self-expression," along with "self-determination," the key trope in his discourse of the "New Negro." The time for "external view and commentary" has passed, he asserts, and the "truest social portraiture" must come from African American arts and letters themselves. Locke explains the purpose of the cultural anthology to which his essay gives its name as one of cultural group self-portraiture: "So far as he is culturally articulate, we shall let the Negro speak for himself."[22]

In an article that draws heavily on Locke's discourse of the "New Negro," Floyd Covington, executive secretary of the National Urban League's Los Angeles chapter, identifies the sound film as a crucial venue for aesthetic and social self-articulation. Published in the April 1929 issue of *Opportunity*, Covington's "The Negro Invades Hollywood" sets out to examine the position of African Americans within the Hollywood studio system. Addressing "the casual observers who live outside the environs of 'Filmland,'" Covington promises at the outset to address these questions: "What part, if any, does the Negro play in the motion picture industry of California? Behind the walls of the legion of studios which festoon the Hollywood district, what place has the Negro taken in the cinematographic world?"[23] As Covington's title indicates, the African American "part" and "place" within the studios and on screen have begun to change as a result of the transition to sound film production and the industry's concomitant enthusiasm for "Negro films."

Covington's title is more a (humorous) projection of a desired movement into the studios than an accurate description of actual trends. Strikingly, this title draws on a preexisting rhetoric of migration. As Gilbert Osofsky has demonstrated, "invasion" was just one keyword in "the language of war" used by frightened white property owners to represent their struggle to maintain hold of "their" neighborhoods in important migration zones. Beginning in the second decade of the twentieth century, the rhetoric of black "hordes" or "enemies" advancing on white enclaves typified the reaction to migration in Harlem and elsewhere.[24] While Covington writes about established and aspiring African American actors who, for the most part, already reside in Los Angeles, his title ironically suggests a comparable siege on the film studios—"Filmland," the insular "cinematographic world." Covington further echoes Locke's interpretive account of African American mass movement by making the consequences of this "migration" both material and symbolic or expressive.[25]

Covington sets out not only to document the number of African American actors working in Hollywood, the types of work and contracts they receive, and their salaries, but also to reflect more broadly on the cultural implications of these facts and figures. Just as Locke speculatively interprets the social and cultural significance of African American migration, so does Covington reflect on how the incipient black "invasion" of Hollywood will affect African American screen representation. Because Covington's article deals with African American film actors and the screen roles they play, his Lockean rhetoric of "parts" creates productive ambiguities.[26] While at times Covington refers to actual movie "parts"—the casting of characters in specific films—he treats the film industry itself as a social theater in which new screen roles for African Americans necessarily bring about a more general shift of African Americans' collective position within the industry's hierarchy. In this respect, Covington's use of terms like "part" and "role" resonates with Locke, who, on the one hand, blames "popular melodrama" for the misrepresentation of African Americans in the national consciousness and, on the other hand, sees "theatre and performance [as] an outlet for expression and social change."[27]

At the start of his article, Covington establishes that "Negroes have been employed in the motion picture industry in various capacities for a period of years," identifying three general categories of employment. For African American actors, the largest and most significant category traditionally has been that of "extras": actors "employed . . . to create atmosphere in jungle, South Sea Islands, and African scenes as natives, warriors, and the like."[28] Covington details the "place" of African American "extras" in the studios at some length. He offers a range of anecdotes and supporting data about the Central Casting Corporation, "a clearing house for 'extras' of all types" founded jointly by the major studios in 1926, and notes that the agency employs a "Negro casting director," Charles Butler, who takes calls from studios seeking black extras and sends registered actors to their assignments.[29]

Covington's reference to Charles Butler points to a new development also drawing notice in white-run industry publications. *Sound Waves*, a short-lived Hollywood newsletter covering the transition to sound, cited Butler's work in an odd editorial cartoon carrying the caption "Negro Finds Talker Voice."

Representing African Americans through grotesque, minstrel caricature, the cartoon uses the image of a lifeboat filled with scared whites to represent "the Negro" securing his "place" in Hollywood.[30] (It is unclear what significance the alligator carries other than being a cliché from the cartoon's "primitivist" milieu.) Passing on no opportunity for racial insult, the text below the image plays on the idea of "place." "Dis-location" is a dialect coinage that seems to refer both to the "Negro" move into ("invasion" of) Hollywood and to Central Casting as a "location" itself—one that now includes African Americans though under "separate" auspices.

Covington uses statistics supplied by Central Casting to point out the significant increase in the number and aggregate wages of African American extras employed in 1928. Whereas "the total number of placements for 1927 was 3,754"—a typical figure for the years for which Covington supplies data—and "the total amount paid in wages for that year was $30,036," 1928

Figure 4. Editorial cartoon from *Sound Waves*, March, 1, 1929. Courtesy of the Academy of Motion Picture Arts and Sciences.

saw "an approximate increase in placement of 345 per cent"—to 10,916 total placements—"and an increase of 335 per cent in wages received"—to $89,703. Covington also quotes Butler as saying that African American extras are the highest paid in the industry, save for "Chinese" extras, with an estimated average daily salary of $7.50.[31]

In addition to "extras," Covington defines two other employment categories for African American actors: "bits" and "parts." "In scenes requiring domestics of color," Covington explains, "the Negro is employed to do these 'bits.' Others are employed to do individual roles or 'parts' such as mammy types and other character sketches that receive camera close-ups and remain prominent throughout the film."[32] While the "parts" that Covington describes might also be "domestic" roles (maids, butlers), the distinction between "parts" and "bits" lies in the amount of screen time as well as the individual credit that the actors receive. "Bit" players are distinguished from extras because the former appear individually rather than as part of a crowd—and may, therefore, have a more specific action to perform. "Bit" players, however, remain "atmospheric" or background figures, rather than defined characters with a significant presence in the narrative, and might appear only in one scene. By contrast, "part" players do portray characters (albeit minor ones) that appear "throughout the picture" and receive significant screen time. Moreover, "their names are included with the other principals" in a given film's credits, and they work under long-term contracts with individual studios.[33]

While Covington shows greatest interest in this last, most prestigious group of performers, he is unable to supply as much information concerning their contracts and salaries as he is regarding "extras" registered with Central Casting. As Covington explains, the individual studio "offices are reluctant to give any information concerning salaries or length of contracts."[34] Despite this lack of information, Covington does go on to suggest how conflicting forces shape the position of African American "part" players within the studios. The all-black-cast productions that are responsible for the great surge in African American "extra" placements in 1928 have also drawn attention to talented African American "part" players. Some of these actors, like Clarence Muse (*Hearts in Dixie*) and Daniel Haynes and Nina Mae McKinney (both *Hallelujah* [MGM, 1929]), therefore have the potential to become "stars." But insofar as the actual screen "parts" available to actors of this stature remain constrained by the logic of "type," no viable African American star will emerge; this logic will continue to make African American actors seem "interchangeable," thus constraining even the most "distinctive" screen personalities.[35]

Because studio films continue to employ black actors "principally for *atmosphere* in large numbers and [to] dispos[e] of them chiefly *en masse*," Covington must conclude that there "has been no Negro star to date."[36] At the same time, he holds out hope that the studios' trial run of African American–cast films will yield or even has begun to yield a few black stars. Covington's use of the term "*en masse*" recalls Locke's critique of the American racialism that insists on "treat[ing] the Negro *en masse*," despite significant intragroup diversity. Alluding to Locke's earlier essay, Covington subtly compares "the Negro's" shifting position in the Hollywood studios and "the Negro's" shifting stature relative to sociological "formulae" and "stock" figures from popular culture. According to Covington's analogy, the black film star would be a *figural* equivalent of Locke's "New Negro."

Pushing this analogy further, Covington predicts that African Americans will move from the periphery to the center of the film industry. While Covington laments how the industry's "Negro as atmosphere" logic limits African American actors' roles, he is hopeful that "with the introduction and improvement of talking pictures, comes, perhaps the Negro's real opportunity to produce stars in his own right."[37] At this point, Covington refers to the work of Muse, Haynes, and McKinney in the first two all-black-cast features as a kind of first test of this opportunity. The relative success of productions like these will determine whether African Americans' place within the studio system will change significantly.[38]

While admitting a degree of uncertainty about the outcome of the "Negro film" experiment, Covington remains sufficiently optimistic to assert that the position of African American actors in the industry has already begun to change: "Apparently, then, with the current venture of all-Negro talking pictures, the Negro emerges from a somewhat obscure place in the industry to take a place in the center of the stage."[39] In "all-Negro talking pictures," African American characters are primary, at the center of the frame, if not the "stage" *per se*. These same films point toward black stardom and, "it is hoped," toward a day when there may be African American "directors," "technicians," and "scenarists" working in the studios. Further, Covington describes a film-industrial movement to center stage that, like Locke's account of the "new figure on the national canvas," enables African American self-expression.[40] In what is effectively an unmarked quotation of Locke, Covington concludes, "In the wake of this new experiment in all-Negro pictures comes the Negro's chance to be articulate on his own behalf."[41]

At the same time, Covington acknowledges that by focusing on African American actors, he has addressed only one determinant of "the Negro's . . . place in the cinematographic industry": for African Americans to establish a more central and "permanent" place would seem to require the opening of other production-sector jobs to them. The cinema's complex industrial and collaborative structure, however, makes racial self-expression an even more elusive goal than does literary fiction, poetry, or stage drama. Covington looks forward to but stops short of the sort of critique of media power that Harold Cruse would make almost forty years later. In *The Crisis of the Negro*

Intellectual (1967), Cruse argues that Harlem Renaissance artists and intellectuals were misguided to pursue their aesthetic and social aims within mass-cultural media owned and managed by whites. Lacking a coherent philosophy of black economic nationalism, Cruse argues, black intellectuals and artists in the 1920s had to rely on white patronage and (in the case of the theater) on the interest of white playwrights to achieve a measure of visibility, a visibility that, further, came at the expense of profits and capital accumulation.[42] Although Cruse does not discuss the film industry, his critique of the relations of production in the "legitimate" theater translates easily to this context: media ownership, for Cruse, is a prerequisite of cultural power.[43] From Cruse's black-nationalist perspective, the "Negro film" movement's failure to found a significant, lasting African American studio presence seems inevitable. But however shortsighted Covington may seem in retrospect, in 1930 he was not the only African American critic to observe an incipient change in the black industry position and screen image.

The Individual and the Mass: Beyond Type

Covington pays tribute to James B. Lowe, an African American "part" player who had the title role in the 1927 Universal (silent) adaptation of Harriet Beecher Stowe's *Uncle Tom's Cabin* and "who by sheer force of ability or because of the value of their distinctive type [has] outstripped [his] fellows."[44] Characterizing Lowe's Uncle Tom paradoxically as a "distinctive type," Covington echoes a contemporary discussion of African American representation in Hollywood coauthored by Alain Locke himself. In conjunction with poet, cultural critic, and fellow Howard University professor Sterling Brown, Locke assessed the state of African American Hollywood in an extended review of the first two all-black-cast features, *Hearts in Dixie* and *Hallelujah*, titled "Folk Values in a New Medium."[45] Like Covington, Locke and Brown express their appreciation of Lowe's performance in apparently contradictory terms: "a fairly genuine type portrayal."

For Covington, "type" roles are standardized and interchangeable, allowing the studios to cast African American actors "*en masse*" and without regard to individual attributes and skills. For Locke and Brown, "type" is a product of the "traditional sentimentalities" of blackface minstrelsy and the "plantation" tradition of American theater and film; "type," therefore, signifies inauthentic or "formulaic" in their essay. However peculiar the use of the adjectives "distinctive" and "genuine" to modify "type," both Covington's and Locke and Brown's labels accurately capture the ambiguity of Lowe's performance. Although Lowe first appears in *Uncle Tom's Cabin* wearing the same fixed grin and wide-eyed stare common to all of the African American extras who play slave characters in the film, he later abandons this grin, using his face to express emotions that seem inconsistent with the "traditional sentimentalities" of minstrelsy and plantation melodrama. Lowe uses pensive expressions to point inward, toward an affective "depth" or complexity that exceeds the limitations imposed on his character by type. In turn, Lowe distinguishes Uncle Tom from the "interchangeable" African American extras, who serve to create plantation "atmosphere" in the film.

For Locke and Brown, Lowe's performance is only a prelude, however, to the much more drastic shift in the filmic construction of "the Negro" by all-black-cast sound films like *Hearts in Dixie*. Despite the strength of Lowe's work in the film, the setting and plot of Stowe's novel, as well as its focus on white characters, dictate a limited and largely static African American protagonist. By contrast, films with contemporary settings and newly invented plots necessarily provide African American characters with greater autonomy, agency, potential for change, and mobility, not to mention that synchronized sound itself literally gives, as Covington points out, "the Negro" an opportunity to speak "on his own behalf." Even *Hearts in Dixie*, which relies on a highly stereotyped screenplay and seeks, like other films from this period, to package black musical spectacle for white "highbrow" consumption, must construct an extended narrative framework around autonomous African American characters, inserting these characters into the classical Hollywood narrative paradigm in an unprecedented way.

According to David Bordwell and Kristin Thompson's canonical account, classical Hollywood narrative is driven by "*individual characters as causal agents*."[46] Individual desire oriented toward a more or less concrete goal motivates film narrative, requiring autonomous characters capable of inducing and experiencing change.[47] As one consequence of the studios' experiment, African American protagonists who express desire emerge on the screen. Situating these protagonists in contemporary, often urban settings, some of the films examined in this book associate them with the historical forms of desire that were the industry's lingua franca in the late 1920s and early 1930s: consumer desire and the desire for upward mobility in social status.[48] Marking a significant shift in the racial politics of the Hollywood cinema, the individuated, desiring black protagonist's emergence is accompanied by obvious anxieties.

Locke and Brown keenly highlight what is "new" in *Hearts in Dixie*'s rendering of "Negro life" on screen. They chart how the film, while still reliant on "type" to create "atmosphere" in group scenes, presents three individuated, complex main characters:

> The usual types are there—the Daddy, Uncle, the Mammy, and the inevitable pickaninnies, but in this group they are real flesh and blood Negroes evoking a spontaneous and genuine human interest. In fact, they have real

> individuality. Lazy Gummy is new because he is crafty as well as lazy; the grandfather too because he is ambitious as well as pious, loyal, and humble, and little Chinquapin because, though the most lovable of pickaninnies, as we see him leave on the river steamboat to go "up Nawth to school," we feel that he might just as reasonably turn out a Booker T. Washington as a roustabout or longshoreman.[49]

While listing those character traits that fit the "type" to which each character belongs, Locke and Brown note the presence of complicating traits: "craft," "ambition," and the will to leave home. Tellingly, all of these traits relate to character desires capable of motivating narrative.

Locke and Brown's account of *Hearts in Dixie*'s main characters only begins to illuminate the complex ways in which the film links narrative drive with individual, subjective agency. In narrative terms, *Hearts in Dixie* is a static film, devoting most of its eighty minutes of screen time to extended singing and dancing performances by large groups and to comedic dialogues featuring Gummy. This emphasis reflects the film's ostensible purpose as highlighted in the spoken prologue, to depict what we might call an "organic" community, whose members exist in harmony with one another and with their surroundings. While the characters clearly live under meager economic conditions, harvesting cotton on what appears to be a large plantation near the Mississippi River, the film, like *Hallelujah*, completely mystifies issues of land ownership and tenancy. Moreover, *Hearts in Dixie* offers no markers that decisively place the film's setting in historical time.[50]

While Walter Weems's original story for the film and Paul Sloane and A. H. Van Buren's adaptation set the action in the immediate postbellum period, the film finally released by Fox neither affirms nor contradicts this premise. Adhering to what Paula Massood calls the "idyllic chronotope," the film "referenc[es] forms of preindustrial, and antebellum, labor, thereby erasing the distinctions between historical moments." The film's costumes, dwellings, and props (like mule-drawn wagons and the steamboat) suggest a "southern agricultural economy" existing, as Massood suggests, in a mid-nineteenth- or an early-twentieth-century setting—or, indeed, any time in between.[51] Certainly, Nappus's vision of the North as a land of educational opportunity links the film with the contemporary events of the Great Migration. And the fact that, through several drafts of the screenplay, the writers purged any references in the dialogue to slavery, emancipation, or Nappus's former masters means that *Hearts in Dixie* does nothing to dissuade the viewer from assuming a contemporary setting. Yet the film's idyllic chronotope, conjuring a temporality of "stasis and circularity," a "self-contained" realm with "the distinct characteristic of 'not being related to the rest of the world,'" may have encouraged some audiences to view the film as a period piece.[52]

It is conceivable that the story and early screenplay draft's references to slavery were eliminated as too threatening to dominant racial ideology. In these early drafts, Nappus links his desire to educate Chincapin to his own frustrated desires as an enslaved young man to "read, an' write, an' talk lak de white folks." In a pointed speech to the Deacon and Emmy, Nappus equates slavery with a total lack of opportunities for uplift. Although the Deacon points out that "Massa Taylor" might have given Nappus his farm when he "wuz freed," Nappus himself alludes to having had a "hard master." As a chattel slave, he had no control over his education; once emancipated, he can choose not to let his child remain a "slave to ignorance."[53]

In a clear sign of the original story's ideological double vision, Nappus's eloquent comments on physical and mental enslavement meet with the Deacon's and Emmy's extreme racialist counterarguments. Although the film in its finished state filters these characters' racialism through the controversy surrounding Chloe's and Truelove's medical care, in the original story they overtly reject Nappus's argument in favor of African American education, suggesting that a trip up north will fill Chincapin's head "wid high notions that his color won't 'low him to live up to." Emmy goes so far as to essentialize human capacity on the basis of physiology. She "kain't understan' why folks ain' satisfied to stay where de Lawd put 'em."[54] While jettisoning this frank discussion about race and social opportunity, the finished film maintains the Deacon and Emmy in the position of spokespersons for a fixed, essential racial order. In the film, they worry only that Chincapin's departure will break Nappus's heart, not that he will acquire social ambitions above his station or ability.[55] Echoing the original story's dynamics, however, the characters' opposition to Nappus's calling Doc Shelby tends to reinforce racialist logic.

By itself, the Deacon's and Emmy's opposition need not necessarily be read in this way. The Hoodoo Woman evokes, in however distorted or simplified a fashion, the figure of the traditional healer, herbal doctor, or rootworker—a figure from what Valerie Lee calls the "cultural system" of conjure or "African based" folk medicine.[56] Thus, in a different context, the Deacon's and Emmy's rejection of Doc Shelby's "Western," "scientific" medicine and trust in the Hoodoo Woman's herbal and "magic" healing practices might reflect a legitimate, reasoned way of negotiating between competing cultural systems. As Lee has demonstrated, "Western science" is no less "rooted in [a] larger cosmology of [a group's] views on life and death" than is conjure or traditional medicine, and so the efficacy of each set of methods must be judged in the context of this larger cosmology. The scientific and professional medicine historically practiced by white men has claimed legitimacy and prestige for itself precisely by denying its own cultural mediation and at the same time reducing the medicine practiced by black women healers (midwives, rootworkers, herbalists) to a mere product of ignorance and superstition.[57]

Against this background, it is tempting to see the Deacon and Emmy as expressing deep communal respect for the Hoodoo Woman, much as the healers that Lee discusses have been revered by the generations of people to whom they have ministered. Georgia Douglas Johnson's 1927 drama *Plumes* is an interesting point of comparison for *Hearts in Dixie* in this respect. Like the film, Johnson's one-act play presents an African American parent who, facing the loss of a child, struggles to choose between the methods of a white male doctor and the traditional remedies in which she herself is versed. At the beginning of the play, Charity Brown and her friend Tildy prepare a poultice for the sick child, Emmerline, expressing skepticism about Dr. Scott's ability to heal her through surgery. Charity and Tildy have seen too many cases in which white doctors' attempts to heal members of their community have been unsuccessful, leaving the family broke, unable to pay for a suitable funeral for their deceased relative.[58] For the two women, a suitably "grand" funeral is a crucial part of the larger cultural system in which they understand a person's life and death, and thus this expenditure must be weighed in making decisions about the sick child's care.[59] Johnson's drama implicitly validates Charity and Tildy's trust in traditional methods: the coffee grounds that they read, indeed, "don't lie," accurately predicting that Emmerline is too sick to be saved and casting doubt on Dr. Scott's conclusion that he should still operate.[60]

As Lee argues, *Plumes* exemplifies African American women writers' persistent questioning of "Western" medicine's claim to total scientific objectivity and their interest in the cultural value of conjure and traditional healing. From the vantage point afforded by Johnson's play, it is clear that *Hearts in Dixie* invidiously distinguishes these two types of medicine.[61] By portraying the Hoodoo Woman as unable to discern that her patients have died, the film makes the community's trust in her herbal and magic remedies seem like a kind of self-degradation. Yet for all its mockery of conjure methods, the film fetishizes a harmonious, organic black community radically other in its sensibilities to white (modern, urban) society. Even as *Hearts in Dixie* proves Doc Shelby correct, it raises the possibility that his intrusion into the community's affairs—through his advice to Nappus and behind-the-scenes guidance of Chincapin's education—might be disruptive to the racial order itself, stripping the African American community of the "timeless" quality that makes it ostensibly appealing to the (white) spectator.

Hearts in Dixie opposes the static, rural collective and the mobile, urban-directed individual in a way that is patently false. In contrast, Locke's discourse of the "New Negro" posits a reciprocal relationship between urban "capitals" like Harlem and the rural areas from which its new migrants come, between the avant-garde artists of the Harlem Renaissance and the "folk" whose culture they have begun to transform. In some cases, Locke stresses, community leaders (like clergymen and lawyers) have become the followers of the masses, whose northward movements are the driving force in shaping a common "race consciousness" that crosses class and regional barriers.[62] By ignoring this dialectic and positing an insular, vulnerable black "community," *Hearts in Dixie* demonstrates a strategy of containment that is characteristic of "Negro talking pictures." First, the film tries to deny migration's grounding in and effects on black rural-communal life. Second, it naturalizes the "folk" community's seeming isolation and insularity: these, the film seems to say, are not oppressed, landless workers but people "outside of time" who enjoy laboring in other people's fields.

By having the activity of picking cotton seem spontaneously to produce song and comedic banter, the filmmakers attempt to make labor indistinguishable from the leisure activities represented in the film. *Hearts in Dixie* presents musical performance as something that emanates "naturally" from the film's African American characters. Using innovative cinematographic and sound-editing techniques, the filmmakers also seem to explore the possibility that such performance, as "pure" cinematic spectacle, can sustain an entire film.[63] At the same time, *Hearts in Dixie* concedes that some form of narrative development is required to provide continuity and maintain spectator interest. By weaving a pair of narrative threads (the deaths of Nappus's daughter and grandson and Chincapin's migration) into the larger representation of an unchanging, uniform collective, the film necessarily distinguishes "characters as casual agents," creating thematically significant tensions between narrative and spectacle, individual and group.

Hearts in Dixie is thus pulled between two opposing impulses: pure musical spectacle, on the one hand, and narrative progression, on the other. As a result of these competing impulses, the film sets up a conflict between the undifferentiated, performing collective, which seems to exist outside of space and time, and the complex, individuated, and changing African American characters like Nappus and Chincapin. Implying that such characters threaten the stability of the community, *Hearts in Dixie* suggests that by differentiating himself through movement into the wider world, Chincapin will transgress a racial barrier held to be absolute. If Chincapin returns with the sort of medical and scientific knowledge that the film equates with white culture, then what will happen to the African American community? Will the racialist difference that the film insists is organic or natural be somehow undermined? Thus, while the film (however patronizingly) shows some sympathy toward Nappus's desire to educate his son, it stages Chincapin's departure from the community in an almost allegorical way as a crisis of African American figuration.

The crisis here is, perforce, in the eye of the spectator—the white ideal addressee that *Hearts in Dixie* constructs from the outset—yet the film projects this crisis onto the diegetic community itself. Once he decides to leave, Chincapin becomes illegible in terms of the film's semiotic system for representing

African American characters; he becomes alien to the dominant "atmosphere" of the cotton field and the cabin—to their "traditional sentimentalities." His decision physically removes him from the community and, more symbolically, halts the production of musical spectacle in the film. Strikingly, the film ends at the moment of Chincapin's departure, as if the filmmakers lack the scenic and dramatic resources necessary to represent, or "account for" (Locke), an African American character seeking his education in the North. The film underscores the impact of Chincapin's decision to leave through a striking visual device.

Having otherwise used no subjective cinematography, *Hearts in Dixie* concludes with the camera mounted on the moving steamboat, representing Chincapin's physical perspective. This shot takes in the mournful community, whose members are lined up along the riverbank. At the moment at which Chincapin stands opposed to the rest of the community, he becomes a full-fledged character, possessing a distinct subjectivity or interiority and becoming the controlling narrative agent in the film. This particular shot exemplifies the moments of rupture that mark "Negro talking pictures." It is what Thomas Cripps might call a "small gesture": if, when weighed against the dominant visual patterns of the film, the shot appears inconsequential, then its force lies in it exceptional status—in how it unsettles the film's dominant racial constructs.[64]

Locke and Brown do not explicitly gloss it as such, but Chincapin's decision "to go 'up Nawth to school'" aligns him with the Harlem Renaissance poetics of migration—the film's historical ambiguity notwithstanding. For Locke and Brown, the film's refusal to reveal the outcome of Chincapin's migration—his "destiny" remains an open question at the end of the film—makes the narrative all the more powerful. Like the figure of the "New Negro" in Locke's original essay, by deciding to seek an open-ended future in the North, Chincapin becomes capable of metamorphosis, and this capability renders him unrecognizable in terms of "stock images" or racial "formulae." Eluding the film's logic of type and its pastoral setting, Chincapin moves to the "center of the stage" and gains the potential for self-expression, but only for a brief moment.

Nominating Herself: Ethel Waters as Star and Migrant Character

While previously obscure, *Rufus Jones for President*, an all–African American–cast musical short film made by Warner Bros. during the early sound period, has been brought into view with recent commentaries on cinematic "black presidents." Several of these commentaries cite *Rufus Jones for President* as the earliest of the "black president" films that have "paved the way" for Barack Obama's election.[65] Running approximately twenty minutes, the film embeds a series of musical performances in a two-stage narrative, consisting of a framing plot and an inset fantasy or dream sequence.

Rufus Jones for President opens with a long shot of Ethel Waters's character hanging laundry on the front porch of a wood and brick house. She calls for her son, Rufus (Sammy Davis Jr.), and scolds a boy with whom he has been fighting offscreen.[66] Rufus enters the shot with his face covered in white frosting, from a cake with which his adversary has struck him. In order to comfort Rufus, Waters tells him that he will become a "great man" some day: "the book says that anybody born here can be president." Singing a soothing melody and then reiterating her prediction, Waters says that she can "see [him] now." At this point, both characters appear to doze off, the film dissolving into a fantasy scene of a nighttime rally and parade, where raucous supporters campaign for Rufus. After the victorious Rufus performs "You Rascal You (I'll Be Glad When Your Dead)" for the crowd, the setting shifts to a neoclassical set of stairs and pillars, marked by a sign reading "Senate," and the young boy is inaugurated as president of the United States. At this point, Rufus's mother takes over, nominating *herself* "Presidentess" and beginning to "debate" the male senators seated before her in an exchange of jokes modeled after a blackface minstrel show. Following a series of musical numbers that I discuss in detail below, mother and son pose for a picture. As the smoke from the camera flash clears, the film returns to the front porch setting. The narrative frame closes with Waters finishing the melody she had begun before the shift to the campaign scene.

Everything in *Rufus Jones for President* is double, and by pairing characters, plot devices, and discourses, the film establishes a pattern whereby the first element in the pair appears to mask or even restrict the importance of the second. To carefully trace these dual structures, however, is to see how the first element fails to negate the second and even serves to make the second, dialectically, meaningful. *Rufus Jones for President* has two main characters, two plot devices, two settings, two geographical points of reference (North and South), and two conflicting discourses of social relations across the color line. While the eight-year-old Davis's character receives titular billing, the film's true protagonist is Waters, whose predictions about Rufus's future become the basis for the inset fantasy plot and who assumes the responsibilities of running the film's peculiar legislative space. Moreover, the lyrics of her songs comment extensively on African Americans' movement from the rural South to the urban North. In her sung references to migration and to social mobility more broadly speaking, Waters contradicts herself. At times, she counsels submissiveness and strict observance of existing boundaries, while at other times she defiantly proclaims geographical and social mobility as an African American prerogative.

The lyrics of Waters's consoling tune, coupled with an odd visual detail in the opening sequence, announce cross-racial social tension as *Rufus Jones for President*'s central theme, the underlying idea that serves to link together, if not to reconcile, the multiple facets of this surreal film. The "boy" with whom Rufus scuffles is represented only by an offscreen voice. Waters scolds this child, referring to him as "Sinbad Johnson" and calling him "common trash," before the dejected Rufus comes into the frame for the first time. Marking Rufus's foray into an otherwise unseen social space, Rufus's frosting-covered visage is a bizarre, gratuitous image that puts him in virtual whiteface. The frosting mask is a displaced reference to the unseen Sinbad Johnson's racial identity, which evokes the child's traumatic proximity to hostile white neighbors.[67]

The refrain that Waters sings to her son lends support to this speculative reading by suggesting that Rufus's scuffle resulted from his crossing a dividing "line" between black and white sections of a neighborhood or town. More than simply consoling Rufus, she instructs him in how to negotiate such invisible barriers and in how to protect himself by observing a certain racial etiquette. Holding Rufus in her arms, Waters sings, "Stay on your side of the fence. Don't try to cross the line." The long and medium establishing shots of the front of Waters's house do not offer enough background details to situate it in a particular milieu, nor do the dialogue and mise-en-scène in the rest of the film serve to locate the film's setting geographically. To invoke the North-South axis introduced later in the film, the characters could live in an urban or semi-urban southern locale—in which case Waters's lyrics would refer to what Richard Wright called "the ethics of living Jim Crow."[68] Or they could live in a similar northern locale undergoing a demographic shift as a result of African American migration—in which case Waters's lyrics would speak to postmigration backlash by hostile whites.[69]

These lyrics represent Waters's character as a figure of accommodation. Appearing in the kind of matronly costume and domestic setting that would characterize her later Hollywood roles—but that is less typical of her roles in this period—she counsels caution and patience. Yet this counsel seems to go against the advice she gives initially. Remarking that Rufus will become a great man, even president, Waters initially favors an egalitarian spirit of individual achievement, only to retreat into an acceptance of racial segregation and hierarchy ("Don't try to cross the line"). When Rufus does indeed become president, Waters shifts her stance once again, this time endorsing black social mobility. And yet within the fantasy plot itself, the film packs the dialogue with a litany of racist, minstrel-show clichés, as if to mask—or perhaps make possible the inclusion of—Waters's critical, emancipatory discourse.

For recent commentators on this film like Jabari Asim, *Rufus Jones for President* presents a conundrum: while it would seem to be the "first cinematic treatment of a black chief executive," the film's vague setting, racially exclusive cast, and lack of explicit references to the nation make the viewer doubt that Rufus is "supposed to be president of *the United States*."[70] As Asim aptly notes, Rufus presides over a group of African American men whose dialogue reflects

Figure 5. Ethel Waters sings to Rufus (Sammy Davis Jr.) about not crossing lines in *Rufus Jones for President* (Warner. Bros, 1933).

every cinematic cliché of African American appetite and irresponsibility, referring multiple times to dice, razors, chickens, pork chops, and watermelons.[71] Rufus and his mother seem to be participating in a minstrel show, whose object is to parody the idea of African Americans crafting and debating legislation, and the opening shots of the Senate sequence conjure *The Birth of a Nation*'s "historical facsimile" of the South Carolina legislature during Reconstruction.[72]

In light of the film's overarching theme (interracial social tension) and of Waters's complex performance of self-determination, the ensuing scenes inside the Senate tend, in fact, to undermine these stereotypes and even to reframe them critically. Excessive and grotesque, these stereotypes undeniably bring a strong element of racial insult into the film's diegesis. It is crucial, nonetheless, to consider how they participate in the film's larger network of tropes of racial obstacles and barriers. Waters's declaration, "I've nominated myself to the office of Presidentess," takes place against a backdrop of ridiculous images such as Rufus's being sworn in on a telephone book, putting into relief the social depths from which Waters establishes an authoritative voice.

After bantering with the senators, Waters sings two songs. The first, "Am I Blue?" is a blues-inspired ballad that became Waters's signature tune after she performed it in her film debut, *On With the Show* (Warner Bros., 1929).

In *On With the Show*, Waters sings "Am I Blue?" in the guise of Bertha, her character in this backstage musical's intradiegetic show, *The Phantom Sweetheart*. Standing in front of a stylized stage backdrop that depicts a cotton field, Bertha sings about the man who has left for Chicago, while she remains "down here in Birmingham, trying to get the money to go and find [her] honey." In a later number in *On With the Show* that recapitulates the song's melody, Bertha has arrived in Chicago (represented by a painted backdrop of skyscrapers) and found her "lovin' Sam." This later number represents Bertha's journey north as a mixture of romantic consummation, revenge (Sam has stolen her "diamonds" and "dough"), and even collective self-assertion. Bertha's insistence that "we's in Chicago" resonates with the history of black mass migration and suggests motives for her leaving the South that go beyond the song's main tropes. While directed overtly at Sam, Bertha's repeated injunction, "treat me fair," points to a broader historical context.

By having Waters reprise a portion of her *On With the Show* performance, *Rufus Jones for President* makes the subject of migration explicit and, in turn, significantly complicates the film's developing discourse of interracial tension. Rufus and his mother's entrance onto the political stage becomes an opportunity for her to comment musically on migration, with the election fantasy plot thus symbolically representing migration as historical self-translation. Depending on how we interpret the film's initial setting, Waters's songs either speak to her and her son's status as recent migrants or imagine the consequences of their hypothetical migration.

Fittingly, in *Rufus Jones for President*, Waters follows "Am I Blue?" with a slightly more up-tempo number, "Underneath the Harlem Moon," which explicitly celebrates African American migration and urban life, this time as collective phenomena; the "I" of "Am I Blue?" decisively becomes a "we" in the second song. "Underneath the Harlem Moon" offers a mocking but finally sympathetic Hollywood version of Alain Locke's discourse of the "New Negro." Written in 1932 by a pair of Jewish Tin Pan Alley songwriters, Mack Gordon and Harry Revel, the tune had already been a hit on records and in nightclub performances by several African American jazz bands, including Fletcher Henderson's and Don Redman's.[73] "Underneath the Harlem Moon," then, emerges from the same formation of "black-Jewish relations" in American mass culture as "Am I Blue?" which was written by the duo of Harry Akst and Grant Clarke.

Jeffrey Melnick has persuasively demonstrated how Tin Pan Alley songwriters working in this formation, many of whom had experienced a racially mixed "streetlife" as their means of American "acculturation," constructed a pluralistic style of "racialness."[74] According to this style, Jewish songwriters understood "Jewishness" as granting them a sympathy for or privileged access to African American experience (through shared histories of forced movement and persecution) and culture (music especially).[75] Melnick does not discuss specifically the songwriting duos whose work is featured in *Rufus Jones for President*, but the lyrics of "Am I Blue?" and "Underneath the Harlem Moon" are notably attentive to contemporary African American urban experience, suggesting the style of interracial sympathy that he describes. Thus, we can point to a clear cause for these songs' relatively progressive content, for their departure from the usual minstrel or pastoral clichés about African American life. It is certain, in the case of Akst and Clarke's work, and plausible, in the case of Gordon and Revel's work, that this lyrical content reflects a process of collaboration across the color line akin to the one employed by Harold Arlen, the white Jewish composer of tunes like "Stormy Weather." Melnick explains that Arlen was influenced by and wrote for the African American singers and jazz bands whose music he encountered in cabarets and on race records.[76] As I discuss further in the next chapter, the duo of Akst and Clarke worked collaboratively with Ethel Waters on more than one occasion and even incorporated her suggested changes into "Am I Blue?"

In a simplified but humorous way, "Underneath the Harlem Moon" challenges white viewers' stereotyped associations with African American life. The lyrics juxtapose images of city life in Harlem with these stereotypes, undermining cultural "stock figures" and contradicting the idea that African Americans constitute a homogeneous group. "Underneath the Harlem Moon" sets up tidy binaries like North/South, urban/rural, luxury/poverty, and younger generation/older generation, privileging the first term in each case. For instance, the lyrics declare, "There's no fields of cotton. Pickin' cotton is taboo." Harlem residents, Waters sings, have traded "cabins" for "penthouses" on St. Nicholas Avenue, a street running through the then affluent Sugar Hill section of Harlem.

Through these contrasts, the lyrics imply that the second term in each binary represents an outmoded way of life, acceptable to earlier generations—what "our old folks used to" do—but not to Waters's own generation. The "old" versus "new" distinction in play here evokes Locke's rhetoric in "The New Negro," especially given that the lyrics challenge "stock figures" of African American life long etched into the (white) public mind but increasingly removed from any social reality. The song lyrics make a Lockean point: rendering conventional frames of reference used to generalize about African Americans "obsolete," the metamorphosis of "the Negro" has yielded a "new figure on the national canvas and a new force in the foreground of affairs," whose social significance is hard to fathom.[77] From nominating herself "Presidentess" to physically occupying the center of an explicitly national "stage," Waters literally performs certain facets of Locke's discourse. At the same time, by linking Waters's self-nomination to migration, *Rufus Jones for President* establishes a Lockean context.

Waters's central position in the Senate sequence enables her to comment critically on racial stereotype. She alludes to a historical African American "metamorphosis" and questions the relevance of "stock figures" from popular culture to contemporary black life, reiterating the sort of critique that, according to Locke, the emergence of the "New Negro" necessitates. In a way that highlights the film's ambivalence and confusion, she utters her critique of "stock images" in a diegetic setting where such images abound. Just as the lyrics assert that "Parisian hats" replace "bandanas" and that "shoes and spats" replace bare feet, so does Waters's own attire dramatically change from the opening scene to the Senate scene—a house dress and hair covering give way to an evening gown. This overlap between song lyrics and shifts in mise-en-scène works simultaneously on two registers. First, Waters shows how tropes held to be objective features of African American character—like the film's own tropes of black appetite and irresponsibility—might be reframed as products of white misperceptions. While the particular (cinematic) clichés of African American life that she refers to in "Underneath the Harlem Moon"—cotton picking, living in cabins, wearing bandanas—do not figure in this film's mise-en-scène, Waters's aggressive challenge to white viewers undercuts the explanatory value of such images and may even invite audience members to reconsider the film's earlier minstrel-show banter. Second, Waters's transformation works metacinematically to signal her emergence as an African American would-be film star.

In this respect, *Rufus Jones for President*'s homage to *On With the Show* is crucial. When Waters's Bertha character reappears in *On With the Show*'s intradiegetic stage musical, she has changed costumes, from a polka-dotted dress and matching bandana to a tailored jacket, flowered sash, crepe skirt, and turban-style hat adorned with ostrich feathers. Given that *On With the Show*'s backstage sequences play up Waters's status as a performer of note—another white female character expresses her interest in hearing "Ethel Waters" sing—the change to glamorous, opulent attire plays into the film's attempt to introduce her as a star.[78] By self-consciously replaying her costume change from the earlier film, *Rufus Jones for President* again works metacinematically as a vehicle for Warner Bros. to craft a glamorous star image for Waters.

In the final verse of "Underneath the Harlem Moon," Waters repeats the line about the "taboo" on cotton picking but follows it with a crucial twist. "All we pick is numbers," she sings, "and that includes you white folks too. Because if we hit [that is, pick the right number], then we pay our rent on any avenue, if we hit." Waters's interpolation—"and that includes you white folks too"—is logically tricky, shifting as it does away from the immediate context of playing the numbers (participating in an illegal lottery). Waters seems to have in mind the idea of "having a person's number"—of grasping someone's true motivations. Her point is that, with the necessary money to afford rent, African Americans—specifically those living in northern, urban settings—will live in any apartment they might choose, regardless of white people's objections. And even if the sorts of affluence about which the song fantasizes are not in reach

Figure 6. Ethel Waters sings "Underneath the Harlem Moon" in *Rufus Jones for President* (Warner Bros., 1933).

of all of the African American people to whom it refers, the force of the assertion is the same.[79]

With these lyrics, Waters shows that she has got the "number" of those white audience members who would participate in or sanction residential segregation. Waters's tone here is assertive and authoritative, quite at odds with her accommodating tone in the opening scene. Further, her statement here—that African Americans will live where they please—directly contradicts her advice to Rufus to "stay on [his] side of the fence." "Underneath the Harlem Moon" is about defying the very "line" she has earlier counseled Rufus to observe. And *Rufus Jones for President* follows this song with yet another song (and production number featuring the Will Vodery Girls, a Cotton Club–style ensemble of light-skinned African American chorines) whose lyrics uses Harlem high society and cabaret culture as shorthand for cultural trends that defy existing racial optics: "You can't see [African American elite] society from down in Alabam."

In light of the film's extended fantasy sequence, the closing portion of the framing plot of *Rufus Jones for President* appears quite incongruous. As if to cancel out or contain the discourse of migration and black self-determination, Waters reprises part of the "Stay on your side of the fence" advice back on the front porch. Given the length and aesthetic power of the fantasy sequence, this is a decidedly weak containment strategy. The film's brief return to its original setting and discourse does little to offset its extensive endorsement of African American migration and self-assertion. And while the "version" of Waters who sings "Underneath the Harlem Moon" is restricted to the fantasy "Senate" space, this version registers much more powerfully in the film—particularly insofar as this is the glamorous, self-assertive film star of the earlier Warner Bros. vehicle.

The Distorting Mirror of the City: *Yamekraw*

Although *Yamekraw* never shifts into the realm of overt fantasy, it employs a frame narrative that also requires the main character to begin and end his journey in the same place, canceling out his intervening change in status. In this case, the migration event is itself the negated change, pointing to how *Yamekraw* more decisively denies African American migration and the concomitant figural metamorphosis of "the Negro" than does *Rufus Jones for President*. By nostalgically refiguring the initial setting (a cabin in the vicinity of cotton fields somewhere in the South) and by making the postmigration urban space threatening, the film recasts the protagonist's migration as a bad dream that can be wished away in the dissolve that instantly transfers him back home. Following a brief montage of northerly train travel, *Yamekraw*'s protagonist arrives in an urban place, the décor and cultural trappings of which rely on the idea of "Harlem as sign."[80] Precipitously returning the protagonist to the original setting and to his family, *Yamekraw* uses an envelope plot to cancel out the migratory move.

Yamekraw is a stylistically unconventional work that uses sound and expressionist mise-en-scène in a way that makes it unique among these films. *Yamekraw* is not a synchronized-sound film in the usual sense: it has no dialogue, and the images primarily act as accompaniment to a ten-minute orchestral piece.[81] As a result of the composition of the soundtrack, the action of *Yamekraw* unfolds primarily through pantomime and dance, with changes of scene serving to advance the narrative. Hence, the visual register of the film illustrates the music, using expressionist sets, lighting, and gesture to create an apposite mood or atmosphere. The film is based ostensibly on the great African American stride piano player James P. Johnson's long-form symphonic work, *Yamekraw: A Negro Rhapsody*. A composition "for piano and orchestra," *Yamekraw: A Negro Rhapsody* debuted on 27 April 1928 at Carnegie Hall, "with W. C. Handy conducting and Fats Waller as a [piano] soloist."[82] Jazz historians' accounts of the concert suggest that the work was strictly instrumental, and the one extant recording of the piece also contains no vocals.[83] The film, however, interpolates extensive Stephen Foster–like lyrics into Johnson's music.[84]

One of the film's opening titles embellishes the subtitle of Johnson's original composition: "A negro rhapsody which expresses the moods and the emotional side of negro life. YAMEKRAW is a settlement on the outskirts of Savannah, Georgia."[85] Identifying the film as a "mood" piece, the purpose of which is to evoke the "emotional" rather than to represent a particular subject or theme, the filmmakers align their project with that of Dudley Murphy's cinematic "Negro things." The film shares Murphy's ethos both in its expressionism—it seeks the graphic or plastic rendering of interior states—and in its romantic racialism—it conceives of "negro life" in essentialized terms, as a subjective disposition toward the "emotional." While *Yamekraw*'s expressionist "mood" emphasis and romantic racialism are consistent with Murphy films like *Black and Tan* (RKO, 1929), the film obviously differs from Murphy's *The Emperor Jones* (United Artists, 1933) in its construction of the "primitive."

Following the terms laid out in O'Neill's play, Murphy's *The Emperor Jones* clearly associates blackness with chaos and "primal" fear in a quasi-metaphysical sense; *Yamekraw*, by contrast, offers a more picturesque and comedic vision of American "negro life." *Yamekraw* evokes a narrower range of "moods," altogether avoiding the haunted or phantasmagoric register of *The Emperor Jones*'s expressionist jungle scenes. The carefree, whimsical tone of the film dissipates only in the Harlem scene, during which the film uses a second set of expressionist techniques to evoke alienation and disorientation.

All of the action in *Yamekraw* unfolds within highly stylized sets, the construction of which evokes the famous distorted style of *The Cabinet of Dr. Caligari* (dir. Robert Wiene, 1920). Rendering familiar objects in simplified, abstract ways, these sets flatten space into two-dimensional surfaces and use the vertical axis to simulate depth (objects farther back in three-dimensional space are placed higher in the frame and vice versa). Pairing sinuous and broken lines with asymmetrical, angular forms, these sets dispense with naturalistic illusion in order to graphically render otherwise invisible subjective states.[86] But whereas *The Cabinet of Dr. Caligari* uses graphic distortion in sets to "exteriorize" the madness of the characters introduced in the frame narrative and thus ideally to "create states of anxiety and terror" for the viewer, *Yamekraw* initially uses this design technique to render a tableau of domestic harmony. Rather than signifying madness, *Yamekraw*'s broken, unusually curved, and angular forms convey what I would call a gentle "rhythmic torsion" of physical reality, in which the characters' surroundings offer a visual compliment to the soundtrack.

Yamekraw's primary set is a cabin, rendered as a flat surface with bold, abstract details that recall a child's drawing. The cabin sits at an oblique angle to the horizontal axis, and the two sides of the roof meet at a point significantly off center. The windows and the door are asymmetrical and set at clashing angles, while the chimney looks as if it is about to fall over. Because of the set's flatness, the cabin itself seems to sit on top of a hill, with characters positioned in various places from the porch (at the top of the frame) to grassy patches along the path that leads away from the cabin (at the bottom of the frame). To further emphasize abstraction and flattening of space, the cabin is heavily backlit, seemingly surrounded by a penumbra of light, with objects at the edges of the frame (like the branches of a weeping willow tree) rendered in silhouette.

In this opening tableau and in the series of medium shots and close-ups to which *Yamekraw* cuts away, characters engage in a variety of stereotyped activities: a "mammy" figure in a rocking chair holds a baby, a young boy eats a huge slice of watermelon, and an older man sits smoking a pipe. Strikingly, all of these figures rock or sway in time with the slow music, engaging in repetitive, nonnaturalistic movements that help aesthetically blend them into their rhythmically contorted surroundings—again in expressionist fashion.[87] Rather than creating a sense of overt "distortion"—in a disturbing sense—the film's rural sets help highlight the characters' leisure and lack of worldly concern (as conveyed through their marking time with purposeless swaying). Moreover, the cutaways underscore the iconicity of the film's vision of "negro life." In almost all of these shots, the filmmakers employ Dutch angles or extreme low angles as well as chiaroscuro lighting to add stature and substantiality to the figures in the frame. Whereas *The Emperor Jones* uses expressionist chiaroscuro in the jungle sequence to create a diegetic enclosure that underscores the protagonist's sense of entrapment and mounting anxiety, *Yamekraw*, eschewing perspectival depth altogether, uses this lighting technique to give a sense of dimension to bodies. Creating stark light-dark contrasts, *Yamekraw*'s harsh, oblique lighting models the characters' bodies, bringing them into relief in the frame. Unusual camera angles like the Dutch angle give these bodies a further "tangible" quality, the effect Lottie Eisner calls "depth without depth."[88]

The film's preference for the iconic and the preservation of mood over diegetic continuity and narrative development adds to the monumental quality of these shots. For instance, the shot that introduces the protagonist (Jimmy Mordecai) and his girlfriend is a medium, extreme-low- and Dutch-angle shot, in which the actors pose in front of an abstract, geometric background (horizontal stripes that appear to be the silhouette made by bars positioned out of frame).[89] A harsh key light illuminates portions of the characters' faces as they embrace, smile, and sway toward and away from the camera, even seeming to acknowledge the camera's presence. The result here is a more or less discrete tableau that (again in conjunction with the soundtrack) underscores the "mood" of romantic love between the two characters and gives them a corporeal "depth without depth."

At the end of this sequence, Mordecai playfully chases his girlfriend, catches her, and puts a ring on her finger. In an extreme high-angle shot, we see them both kiss the ring, at which point the action returns to the cabin backdrop.

Then, for reasons that neither the soundtrack nor the progression of images makes clear, the father character descends the path from the cabin and hands a suitcase to Mordecai. A poetic montage of charging steam engines and trains speeding along the tracks indicates the character's journey north. The tempo of the music increases here, the rhythm picking up the train's insistent pulse, while multiple exposures of rails create abstract grids in the frame. As the pace of the editing increases in kind, brief recurring shots of a train headlight rushing toward the camera intensify the montage. In the ensuing sequence, the film maintains this frantic energy, using expressionist aesthetics for the first time to convey true distortion and fragmentation.

Yamekraw uses an expressionist barbershop facade, complete with a zigzagging rendition of the conventional striped barber's pole, to convey a northern-urban setting, Harlem perhaps. As up-tempo jazz carries the soundtrack, shots of street life give way to a scene in an apartment, in which Mordecai straightens his tie in front of a warped, funhouse mirror that reflects only a distorted blur. A medium close-up of the amorphous reflection itself accentuates this point. Highlighting the mood of musical frenzy and tropes of distorted reflection established here, the following scene unfolds in a cabaret. The scene opens with a close-up of a spinning, mirror-encrusted bowl on the ceiling; the mirrors project dots of light around the dark room, making the space seem to spin or even fragment. A Dutch-angle adds to the unbalanced feel. As Mordecai enters, he takes a seat at one of the tables and fixates on a woman dancing an energetic Charleston. Emphasizing their gazes, alternating medium close-ups establish their mutual interest, and Mordecai eventually approaches her.

Once the couple begins to dance, the cinematography mimics the intensity of their movements, drawing out the connotations of this desirous encounter for the main character. It is as if the speed and sensuality of the city have now begun to transform Mordecai—he has forgotten about his fiancée back home and begun to contemplate infidelity with a sophisticated, urban woman. The camerawork registers this metamorphosis: when the couple, isolated at the center of the frame in a high-angle shot, begins to dance, the filmmakers use a faceted lens to make the room appear to dissolve into multiple images. In an oscillating motion, the components of the image repeatedly separate into multiple exposures and come back together. Then, as the dancers begin to execute rapid turns around the dance floor, the camera itself begins to spin, making a number of complete circles that turn the contents of the frame upside-down until they become a round blur in the frame.

Following this spinning blur, the film cuts to a shot of Mordecai entering the cabaret, much like the one used earlier; the viewer deduces that he has returned on a subsequent night, looking for his dance partner. He sees her at the other side of the cabaret, sitting on a sofa with another well-dressed man. Dejected, Mordecai leaves the cabaret and walks glumly along the sidewalk in front of the barbershop. Then, all of the sudden, *Yamekraw*'s setting flips back to the rural South. The cabin appears again, and, in a brief concluding scene, Mordecai returns toting his suitcase. His fiancée runs out and throws her arms around him. As recurring shots of the cabin throughout the film have emphasized, this is a place where nothing changes. Characters remain in a state of picturesque repose, mirroring the rhythmic torsion of their surroundings with their gestures. Thus, Mordecai's physical homecoming also indicates his return to a representational context of familiarity or legibility. It is in these terms that we must read the film's use of two contrasting expressionist registers: gentle rhythmic torsion versus outright distortion and fragmentation.

In the film's urban or Harlem setting, the second of these registers coincides with the protagonist's move into an unfamiliar "African American modernity" (to use Paula Massood's term), the pace and libidinal energy of which prove initially enticing but finally upsetting. Whereas the rural-southern scenes have a harmonious atmosphere, indicating a certain kind of "emotional" tranquility on the part of the characters, the Harlem scenes convey extreme tension—not only conflict between Mordecai and his rival for the Charleston dancer's attention but even a disturbance in his own self-image. Within northern, urban space, the "emotional side of Negro life" becomes distorted, to the point that the African American subject seems no longer to recognize himself.[90]

Yet as the films examined throughout this chapter highlight, the subjectivity in question here is, first and foremost, a white projection. Indicating the thrill and threat of city life, the fragmented, spinning images in the cabaret objectify the supposedly subjective impression of Mordecai's blurred image in the mirror. In the cabaret scenes, the camera itself becomes a fun-house mirror for the viewer, exteriorizing a putative crisis of "the Negro." While *Yamekraw*, like most "Negro talking pictures," certainly is interested in presenting the assumed white spectator with a glimpse of black cabaret life, it cannot imagine a larger social and psychological context for this activity. For instance, where would someone like Mordecai work? Hence, *Yamekraw* must restore the protagonist to the familiar setting of rural southern life, rendered through a few simple visual clichés—characters in repose surrounded by baskets of cotton. This setting, in turn, becomes self-consciously iconic, making it appear as if the figures situated therein are in their proper place, at home.

We know that *Yamekraw*'s sense of figural crisis is a white projection because even the most basic attempt to make sense of the progression of the narrative begs the question of why Mordecai would want or need to leave home in the first place. If the brief stint away from home makes him appreciate this place and the company of his fiancée all the more, then what motivates him to depart? *Yamekraw* makes this an impossible question to answer, thereby opening a certain "fault line" within the narrative structure. *Hearts in Dixie* is the one film of the three to actually posit conscious motivations for African

American migration; however, it ends before fully exploring the attendant "metamorphosis" that this migration causes. As a film that either commences postmigration or reimagines migration as political election, *Rufus Jones for President* lyrically and visually explores this metamorphosis, eventually canceling it out, but not before giving its protagonist the opportunity to affirm black self-determination as a force of psychological and social change. In the end, however, even Ethel Waters and Sammy Davis Jr. end up rocking on the porch at the close of this film. In the two short films, the closing of the diegetic envelope works to replace the physical movement of migration with stasis or motion in place—musical performance occurring on the porch or in the front yard of a home to which the characters have returned. It is as if these films trade Chincapin's movement "up North" for the repose and occasional motion-in-place of Gummy, thereby identifying the closing of their respective diegetic envelopes as anxious responses to African American mass migration and the emergence of the "new Negro."

CHAPTER 3

On (With the) Show

RACE AND FEMALE BODILY SPECTACLE IN EARLY HOLLYWOOD SOUND FILM

In "Entertainment and Utopia," Richard Dyer argues that the Busby Berkeley–choreographed spectacles of *Gold Diggers of 1933* (Warner Bros., 1933) expound the same bleak "lessons of the narrative—above all, that women's only capital is their bodies as objects," although in a very different way.[1] On the one hand, the narrative is sympathetic to the struggles of its "showgirl" protagonists. Lacking financial resources, the film's four single, straight, white women seek steady work in a theatrical industry where men control capital and the means of production. With the Depression crippling this industry, two of the women, Carol (Joan Blondell) and Trixie (Aline MacMahon) pose as "gold diggers" in order to keep their show going. While their complex motivations for this performance absolve them from the stigma of prostitution that attends to the figure of the gold digger, Carol and Trixie ultimately succeed in exchanging the prospect of access to "their bodies as [sexual] objects" for the financial support of wealthy white men.[2] On the other hand, *Gold Diggers of 1933*'s spectacles celebrate the transformation of women's bodies into images: the realization of the latent capital of the eroticized female body through its mechanical reproduction as an object of visual pleasure.

As is the case in *42nd Street* and *Footlight Parade*, the other two Warner Bros. backstage musicals for which Berkeley choreographed and photographed "dance" sequences during the same year, *Gold Diggers of 1933* molds large groups of white women of similar physiques and appearances into intricate formations, representing abstract patterns or discernable shapes. In some sequences, the mise-en-scène, cinematography, and editing isolate the women's limbs; other sequences literalize the commodification of women's bodies through props and costumes, such as the large coins that the performers wear and carry in the opening number of *Gold Diggers of 1933* ("We're in the Money"). Lucy Fischer has theorized that Berkeley's films equate women with spectacle itself. The films revel in the women's reduction by men (the producers in the backstage musicals, the characters in the stage shows whose fantasies some of the sequences seem to manifest, and, finally, Berkeley himself) to the status of image: passive, two-dimensional, manipulatable, reproducible, hypervisible, to-be-exhibited, and to-be-looked-at.[3] As Fischer brilliantly explains, the Berkeley–Warner Bros. musicals go so far as to acknowledge the fetishistic nature of "woman as image." The female image acts "as a virtual *substitute* for woman herself."[4] Possessed of all of the qualities listed above, "beautiful [white] girls," are, Berkeley believes, "what people want to see," why they come to the cinema at all.[5]

This chapter examines the positions or roles that African American women occupy within the spectacular economy of early Hollywood sound films, particularly the first backstage musicals. If, as is the case in the most canonical films in this subgenre, women become "image" by capitalizing upon their bodies as objects in order to enter "show business," then under what terms do black female performers undertake this process of exchange? In the aesthetic context of superabundance, what "values" do African American women's bodies possess? Do African American performers ever occupy the position of "showgirl," the category that names the female body's commodification and resolute framing as scopophilic object in show business? At what points do "Negro talking pictures" overlap with the backstage musical subgenre?

This chapter focuses on Ethel Waters's complex role in the groundbreaking but critically neglected *On With the Show* (Warner Bros., 1929), a backstage musical that works in the same post-Ziegfeld tradition of "glorifying" the white showgirl as do the Berkeley–Warner Bros. films, while anticipating some of the later films' signature visual strategies. In her role as a "specialist" in the film—a performer who appears "as herself" and has virtually no role in the backstage action—Waters occupies a unique position. Prominently featured in the film, her two numbers are important "attractions"; yet she has no real character in the film apart from the one she dramatizes in these numbers. At the same time, Waters's exceptional status in *On With the Show* has ironic consequences. She is a singularly individual figure who is not subsumed into any larger mass of interchangeable members—the plight of all of the other female performers in the film.[6] The film thematizes the white women's abstract equivalence as members of a "beauty chorus"—as bodies turned into images in Fischer's sense. Likewise, the other African American women are interchangeable, having nonspeaking, stock roles meant to add "atmosphere" to the stage show (the plantation "mammies") or to provide foils for the white performers (the star actress's maid) backstage.[7]

On With the Show also adheres to racially exclusive criteria, derived from the Ziegfeld Follies tradition, for judging particular "types" of female bodies suitable for "show." Again, racial exclusionism has an ironic effect, exempting

Waters from having to be, first and foremost, an object of erotic display on stage. By the same logic, she is never subjected to the invasive, voyeuristic camera that the film trains on performers' undressed bodies backstage. In this respect, Waters's role in *On With the Show* provides an important counterpoint to Fredi Washington's in Dudley Murphy's *Black and Tan* (RKO, 1929), an African American–cast musical short with "backstage" elements. *Black and Tan* is a rare early sound film that, drawing on the cabaret and stage tradition of the putatively exotic-primitive, light-skinned African American showgirl and ignoring the Hollywood studios' growing anxieties about representations of interracial desire, frames black female bodies as objects of erotic spectacle.

If Waters's character lacks the "to-be-looked-at-ness" that defines female representation in general in *On With the Show* and *Black and Tan*, then this lack translates into her possession of what I call "fictive capital," a cultural value located outside of her "body as object." This fictive capital can be read, from one angle, as a sign or manifestation of Waters's singular, autonomous standing in the film and, from another, as the cause of that singularity and autonomy. Waters's character in the show-within-the-show both demonstrates an exceptional economic self-sufficiency and geographical mobility and makes exemplary claims to women's control of capital. By a similar logic, Waters herself enters the film as a recognizable "star" performer, whose popularity in other venues (in Harlem nightclubs, in vaudeville, and on phonograph records) acts as a kind of noncorporeal cultural capital that enables her to retain significant creative control over the material she performs. To make this claim is not to validate these screen representations as alternative, "positive images" of black female character; to minimize the effects of racial exclusion and marginalization on these representations; or to claim that the films manage to adequately "reflect" historical challenges facing African American women during this period. The capital that the films attribute to these characters is decidedly abstract or fantastical. To use a crucial trope from *On With the Show*'s intradiegetic musical comedy, Waters remains a "phantom" being within the film narrative.

On With the Show: Backstage and Onstage

On With the Show features Ethel Waters in a starring role, connecting it with the early sound-era "Negro film" movement, even as it works in the backstage musical tradition of aesthetic "superabundance."[8] Alternating between backstage and onstage perspectives, *On With the Show* follows one evening's performance of a musical comedy, *The Phantom Sweetheart*. At the beginning of the film, the production's goal of making it to Broadway is in doubt. The show's funds have run dry, and the cast and crew have not yet been paid. The house is full, but the actors bicker with the producer and threaten not to perform until they receive their wages. Thus, *On With the Show*'s backstage action develops the tensions between numerous characters involved in the production. Most of these tensions relate, at least indirectly, to the financial difficulties facing *The Phantom Sweetheart.* While a crude plotline for *The Phantom Sweetheart* emerges over the course of the numerous, relatively lengthy onstage production numbers that the film features, *On With the Show* leaves viewers with fairly substantial gaps in their understanding of this fictitious musical comedy. The exact setting that the stage show is supposed to depict remains uncertain, and the featured scenes fail to explain important relationships between major characters.

As is typical of films in this subgenre, *On With the Show*'s backstage action gives the film narrative coherence, with the stage numbers offering diverting bits of musical spectacle that need not be "integrated" into the rest of the diegetic action. Yet *On With the Show* stands out from other early backstage musicals like *The Broadway Melody* (MGM, 1929) in the effort it makes to at least evoke a coherently plotted stage show. Further, the film establishes subtle but important analogies between events, motifs, and themes occurring onstage and backstage.

On With the Show's large cast of white characters divides into three groups based on their roles in the production of *The Phantom Sweetheart*: crew, cast, and producers/financial backers. The first group centers around Kitty (Sally O'Neill), a young, aspiring Broadway actress, who runs the theater's coat-check room. Kitty works alongside her boyfriend, Jimmy (William Blakewell), the head usher, and her father, the doorman, whom everyone calls Dad (Thomas Jefferson). The stage manager, Pete (Lee Moran), rounds out the members of the crew who figure as significant characters.

The chief actress character in the film is Nita French (Betty Compson), who plays the title role in the stage musical. Harold Astor (Arthur Lake) is the actor playing the lead role in the stage show, the young man who becomes smitten with the Phantom Sweetheart, even though he is engaged to be married to someone else. Nita's rival in the backstage action, Sarah Fogarty (Louise Fazenda), has no evident role on stage, despite her jealousy over the adulation that Nita receives.[9] The actress-character who plays the fiancée of Harold's character in *The Phantom Sweetheart* (Josephine Hutton) is unnamed and barely features in the backstage action. Joe Beaton (Joe E. Brown) is a stage comedian whose solo scenes feature prominently in the onstage action, while Bert (Otto Hoffman) plays a buffoonish butler in *The Phantom Sweetheart.*

At the outset, Beaton and Nita have the most significant connections with the third group of characters. They confront the show's producer and manager, Jerry (Sam Hardy), with their demands for the wages owed them. The owner of the props and scenery, Sam Bloom (Purnell Pratt), has also come to the theater to demand the money due him, threatening to carry away all of the pieces on which Jerry owes rent. The show's "angel," or major financial backer, Bobby Wallace (Wheeler Oakman), is also present from the outset. Wallace is romantically involved with Nita but reveals early on that he has romantic designs on Kitty.

The major action of *On With the Show*'s backstage plot concerns the squabbling between members of the three groups of white characters. Kitty, Jimmy, and Dad try to stall Bloom in order to keep the show going, making a pair of proposals to the producer, Jerry, which he in turn rejects. First, Kitty proposes to entice Wallace to give more money to the show, by effectively offering herself sexually to him. Then, Jimmy suggests that they rob the box office to pay the actors' salaries. When someone later does hold up the box office, the suspicions of the house detective (Harry Gribbon) predictably turn to Jimmy. Dad is later revealed, however, to be the thief. In a characteristically knotty and improbable bit of logic, the film explains that, having poured his savings into the show, Dad could not afford to see it fold. Likewise, a scenario very much like what Kitty earlier has proposed unexpectedly comes to pass. She finds herself alone with Wallace, who plies her with alcohol, propositions her, and tries to assault her. While Kitty attempts to fend him off with a broomstick, Wallace manages to kiss her, at which point Jimmy enters. He punches Wallace but, smelling alcohol on Kitty's breath, turns his wrath on her, assuming that she has willingly acquiesced to Wallace's desires.

In the meantime, Nita has refused to take the stage until she receives the $1,500 salary owed her. Still somewhat shaken but exhorted by Dad and Jerry, Kitty, who knows the lines and songs by heart, takes the stage in Nita's place. (The Phantom Sweetheart wears a veil until the final scene of the show.) Kitty is a huge hit, and Nita, of course, is furious, until a despairing Jimmy informs her of Wallace's actions. Nita apologetically explains Wallace's philandering tendencies to Jimmy and convinces him to forgive Kitty. Then, Nita attacks Wallace, whipping him (perhaps with a stage prop from the hunting scene; the action occurs offscreen), until he must be dragged out of the theater by two other men. In order to pacify Nita, Wallace agrees to renounce his claim on the $10,000 he has put into the show and to give Jerry further backing. Wallace also refuses to press charges against Dad for having stolen what was rightfully his money. Having exacted her retribution in this way, Nita makes a surprising disclosure. She and Wallace recently have been married, and he has agreed to relocate to California with her, in order precisely to get himself away from the temptations of the theater, with its ubiquitous showgirls. These major tensions and rivalries having been resolved, the show goes on to a triumphant finale, with Kitty, now the star, receiving the crowd's adulation.

The African American characters in the film hold markedly different positions in both the backstage and onstage lines of action. With the exception of Ethel Waters, the black dancers and vocal performers appearing in the film are not named either as characters onstage or as actors backstage. In fact, these doubly nameless performers do not appear backstage at all, as if they change and rest in some other space altogether. Like her counterpart in *42nd Street*, Dorothy Brock (Bebe Daniels), Nita has an African American maid (unnamed in the script and uncredited in the film), who appears briefly in two backstage scenes.

For all of the attention her musical numbers receive, Ethel Waters holds a highly ambiguous position in *On With the Show*. In a sense, the film presents her as the star attraction for the diegetic audience of *The Phantom Sweetheart*. The opening shots follow a couple into the theater who express their eagerness to hear "Am I Blue?" a song composed especially for Waters by the film's songwriters, Harry Akst and Grant Clarke. Nita echoes this sentiment later, when, waiting in the wings, she announces to Sam Bloom, "Ethel Waters is going to sing 'Am I Blue?'" In this didactic moment, Nita seems to speak as much to the film's viewer as to the other character. Not surprisingly, then, "Am I Blue?" acts as the *de facto* theme for both *The Phantom Sweetheart* and the film as a whole. An instrumental version of the tune plays during the film's opening titles; an actor in the show hums the melody backstage; and the melody features as a motif in the extradiegetic soundtrack music several times. Nevertheless, Waters herself scarcely figures in the backstage action, appearing in a backstage sequence only once. Right before Waters takes the stage to sing the much-anticipated tune, she playfully nudges Nita out of her way with her prop, a large basket of cotton.

Apart from this moment and the duration of her two onstage numbers, Waters exists in the same fictional void as the other African American characters. Waters's second number gives her character a name within the stage show, Bertha from Birmingham. Yet the Bertha scenes appear to take place in an entirely different setting from the other scenes of *The Phantom Sweetheart*, such that the film viewer wonders whether, indeed, she is acting in the same show. Waters's "specialties" are the only numbers that have no evident connection to the crude plotline of *The Phantom Sweetheart* or any of its settings, beyond shared vague references to "the South." While the film makes a point of situating the play's main "plantation" setting near a river, presumably the Mississippi, Waters's character locates herself first in Birmingham, Alabama, a city nowhere near the Mississippi, nor, for that matter, in direct proximity to any major river. In the second number, Bertha has traveled to Chicago, the show's only northern point of reference.

At first glance, Bertha seems like less of a full-fledged character than the other major figures in the stage show and more of a lyrical persona used to link Waters's two songs together. More significant, Waters herself is not a character in the film in the same way that the white characters are. Whereas the film actress Betty Compson plays the stage actress Nita French, who plays "the Phantom Sweetheart" in the show-within-the-show, Waters remains "herself."

Witness the opening titles, which identify her character's name as "Ethel" and Nita's crucial reference in the dialogue to Waters's full name.

Excluding a pair of brief cutaways to onstage action, *On With the Show* depicts a total of eleven individual scenes that are supposed to comprise the stage musical, *The Phantom Sweetheart*. As mentioned earlier, there is enough continuity between the action, dialogue, and song lyrics in these scenes to suggest a crude plot; at the same time, several key scenes devolve into musical or comedic spectacles that have almost no narrative or thematic connection to this plot, suggesting a revue-style production. The first scene depicts the return of an older man's young relative (Harold), perhaps a grandson, to his southern home, somewhere along the Mississippi. Harold arrives on a steamboat to the eager welcome of a large crowd, which includes his "schoolgirl sweetheart," who is "all smiles to greet him."

The setting of *The Phantom Sweetheart* appears to be contemporaneous with that of the film. As in several subsequent scenes, the white characters in the riverside homecoming scene sport up-to-date fashions. The members of the white women's chorus wear short, pleated skirts consistent with the 1920s "flapper" aesthetic. At the same time, *The Phantom Sweetheart* occasionally features anachronistic or period markers in its costuming and decor, which specifically evoke the antebellum period. For example, some of the same female chorus members wear floor-length hoop skirts during the fifth scene, while the Spanish moss–draped piazza of the southern manor constructed on stage further evokes a romanticized, pre–Civil War plantation setting. Indeed, a character in the stage show refers to this setting as "the old plantation." The uncertain logic that marks the narrative organization of the show-within-a-show thus extends to its setting; the filmmakers have sought to present an overtly contemporary milieu while also capitalizing on the signifiers of antebellum luxury. It is as if the filmmakers believed that these signifiers should necessarily be included in any cinematic representation of the South, or, at least, that they could add value to the commodified opulence of the film, without causing any cognitive dissonance for the viewer. The manner in which the show incorporates African American performers, costumed in historically ambiguous dress and cast in domestic service and manual labor roles, works off of a similar logic, which I address in more detail below.

Just as soon as the scene of Harold's arrival on the steamboat concludes, the young man remains on stage alone, and a mysterious, veiled woman (Nita) appears in a tree and begins singing to him. The lyrics of her song, "Let Me Have My Dreams," state that she has been dreaming of and waiting for him for a long time, even though he has "torn" himself away from her out of "angry pride"; she pleads with him to return to her, even though "there's someone else it seems." While this veiled woman becomes the play's Phantom Sweetheart, the subsequent scenes offer no further explanation of her relationship with Harold.[10]

The fourth scene from the stage show depicts a lavish engagement party for the protagonist and his "schoolgirl sweetheart," set in the front yard of a plantation manor. The revelers sing "Lift the Juleps to Your Two Lips," calling for a toast to the health of the bride and groom to be. In the following scene, the Phantom Sweetheart appears again and interacts with the protagonist. Contradicting the suggestions she makes in "Let Me Have My Dreams," the young man seems not to recognize her as someone with whom he has a prior relationship and wonders if she is just a "phantom" of his imagination. The two characters also interact in the following scene, which begins as a fox hunt featuring real horses and dogs. The young man falls off of his horse, at which point the Phantom Sweetheart arrives to comfort him. She instructs him to dream, and the scene shifts into a fantasy tableau in which she appears as a queen and he as her suitor. The song that concludes the scene identifies this realm, self-reflexively, as "The Land of Let's Pretend." Having no relation to the rest of *The Phantom Sweetheart*, "The Land of Let's Pretend" centers around a lavish fashion show in which Nita and members of the chorus parade down a large staircase situated at the rear of the set, wearing elaborate gowns and headpieces.

In the seventh scene, the young man and his fiancée perform a romantic duet in which she expresses doubt about the strength of his affections. The eighth and ninth scenes are set immediately before the wedding with the guests engaging in comedic banter in the former and the groom once again encountering the Phantom Sweetheart when he is alone in the latter; this scene marks Kitty's first appearance in the stage show as the Phantom Sweetheart. The eleventh and final scene of the stage show begins with a wedding march, during which the young man shocks the gathering by introducing the Phantom Sweetheart, whom nobody else has yet seen, as the woman he intends to marry. To the viewer's surprise, his fiancée appears only mildly upset by this revelation, and the comedic drunk (played by Beaton) has no difficulty consoling her. The bridal couple ascends a staircase at the back of the set, and the rest of the cast joyfully runs through a medley of the show's songs.

In both this final scene and the curtain call during which the cast members take their bows before the diegetic audience, none of the African American performers who appear in the earlier song and dance numbers reappear, further underscoring their uncertain place within *The Phantom Sweetheart*. African American characters appear onstage at the very beginning of the first scene in a background, or atmospheric, capacity, some dressed as stereotypical "mammies," others playing banjoes. Several African American men, wearing brightly striped overalls, shirts with flowing sleeves, and straw hats—the stock Hollywood costume of black stevedores—appear on the steamboat that brings the young white protagonist onto the scene. A mixed, male and female African American quartet, The Four Covans, performs a fast-paced synchronized tap routine during the ensuing production number; all four members wear the same stevedore's costume. During the engagement scene, The Four Covans dance wearing bellhop's or waiter's livery, carrying trays with (attached) wine bottles and goblets and entertaining the white guests in front of the plantation manor.[11]

By costuming and positioning African American figures as laborers and servants who are literally timeless—located in no particular historical moment or social configuration but always laboring happily for white southerners—*On With the Show* certainly indulges in what Paula Massood calls the "idyllic chronotope," a mystifying representational strategy typical of early sound-era African American films.[12] At the same time, Waters's scenes in *The Phantom Sweetheart* keep the themes of exploitation and slavery in view in a way that becomes highly ironic, in light of the film's preoccupation with these themes in the dialogue of the backstage sections. Moreover, Waters's Birmingham and Chicago stops further cloud the stage show's sense of space and time.

All-Color versus All-Colored

Given the challenges that *On With the Show* presents to the viewer's comprehension, with its many backstage conflicts and its incoherent southern fantasia onstage, the film may best be understood in terms of the technical and generic considerations that have shaped it. *On With the Show* is, first and foremost, a prestige production that seeks to exploit the full capacities of the cinematographic and sound-recording apparatuses that the Warner Bros. studio had at its disposal in 1929: not only the Vitaphone sound-on-disc system but also the new Technicolor Process Number Three, which had become available the previous year.

Process Three was a refinement of the existing "two-color" process, in which the Technicolor camera exposed two sets of adjacent frames simultaneously, one behind a cyan (often called green) filter, another behind a magenta (often called red) filter. In Process Two, each set of frames had been printed on a strip of very thin positive film stock, and the two film strips were cemented together to form a release print. While this "subtractive" process made possible the wide distribution of Technicolor films, which subsequently could be run through standard projectors, it resulted in fragile prints that cracked, buckled, and lost focus easily.[13] By using a "dye transfer" printing technique, Process Three generated a single-thickness release print from the two color-filtered (or "toned") negatives. Process Three remained the state of the art for only a few years, however.[14] In 1932, the Technicolor Corporation debuted a "three-color" process that added a yellow-filtered negative strip and made it possible to register a wider spectrum of colors on film.[15] In exploiting the new Technicolor Process Three, *On With the Show* aims to solidify the Warner Bros. brand's claim to being the most innovative and technologically sophisticated film studio in the early sound era.

On With the Show seeks to make an attraction of the cinematic apparatus, much as the studio had made the Vitaphone itself a focal point in marketing earlier synchronized-sound productions.[16] Technicolor here acts to extend further the range of the film's claims to naturalness and spectacular power, and *On With the Show* lays legitimate claim to being the first "all-color, all-talking" feature film.[17] The logic of these claims, which emphasize multiplicity and novelty of sight and sound, on the viewer's attention also informs the film's choice of subject matter, setting, and performance styles. In every respect, *On With the Show* assumes that more is better. Everything included in the film serves to add another measure of visual spectacle, to increase the film's novelty, and to distinguish it from comparable products in the cinematic marketplace.

In his work on Busby Berkeley, Martin Rubin has called such an aesthetic principle of inclusion "superabundance." For Rubin, superabundant entertainment confronts audiences with heterogeneous, "aggregate" spectacles, containing "more than could possibly be absorbed at a single sitting by any single spectator."[18] In such entertainments, narrative material (like *On With the Show*'s backstage and onstage plots) serves a secondary function, overlaying a semblance of continuity on the dizzying variety and intensity of spectacle. The materials included in *On With the Show*'s pressbook and its trade-press reviews clearly demonstrate how considerations of superabundance determined the film's contours.

The majority of the stories in the Warner Bros. pressbook for *On With the Show* trumpet the film's novelty and multiple forms of spectacle as not just "all-color" and "all-talking" but also all-singing and all-dancing. The pressbook's stories and the accompanying posters and lobby display cards that were sold by the studio frequently substitute "100%" for "all," a turn of phrase that suggests breakfast cereal advertising, especially when used in a motto like "First 100% Natural Color, Talking, Singing, Dancing, Picture."[19] The promotional materials use the phrase "Natural Color" to characterize the representational capabilities of the new Technicolor process: "'On With the Show' marks a distinct innovation in the picture industry, being made by a new process, which reproduces colors in their true values, and is no more to be compared to previous color films than the gaudy cover of a cheap magazine to the fine color-plate reproduction of the National Geographic Magazine."[20] The pressbook pieces locate a very specific marketing value in the Technicolor film stock and dye transfer process that precisely and truly register color "values"—their subtle differences of hue relative to one another. The new Technicolor process realizes the full potential of costume and set design by giving the most lifelike reproduction possible of the opulent material realm in which the film seeks to immerse the viewer: "Gorgeous costumes and settings are seen in their own brilliant coloring; and the tintings make the players all but living."[21] Thus, the objects and bodies that comprise the film's mise-en-scène become fully accessible to the viewer, who may realize their exhibition value as commodities.

In order further to illustrate the film's value as a cinematic "extravaganza," *On With the Show*'s pressbook points to the quantity of money, materials, technologies, and human labor expended in the production. One advance story to be distributed by theater owners informs the reader, "All costumes were especially designed for this picture, as stock costumes even for minor characters, which would have been suitable were the picture being filmed in black and white, could not pass muster because color film is used." As evidence of the special nature of the film's costumes, the same story notes that in the "Land of Let's Pretend Scene," Betty Compson wears "a gorgeous headdress which she insists weighs more than twenty-five pounds."[22] Other pieces highlight both the large cast of name actors and the huge white female chorus—"a dazzling beauty chorus of 100"—or attempt to quantify the number of actors, extras, and technicians working on the set at any given time: "in [its] making [the fictional musical comedy, *The Phantom Sweetheart*,] was enjoyed daily by several hundred players, extras, and technicians at the Warner Bros. Vitagraph studio in Hollywood"; "from two hundred to two thousand people were before the cameras constantly from the start to the finish of this production."[23] The pressbook even devotes one advance story to the array of "thirty-eight microphones" used to facilitate shooting in the "theater" specially built on the movie lot to film both backstage and onstage action.[24]

On With the Show's reviewers in the trade publications *Motion Picture News* and *Variety* forecast the film's success at the box office, hailing it as a milestone in sound and color film production and noting the sheer "magnitude of screen entertainment" that it provides.[25] The *Motion Picture News* reviewer offers unqualified praise: "It has music, dancing, singing, comedy, drama—in fact everything for eye and ear entertainment." While the *Variety* reviewer also highlights the film's sheer "plenty of entertainment," he or she worries that "the talker [is] as a whole overloaded" with action and spectacle and, at more than two hours of running time, overly long. Nonetheless, this reviewer assumes the film to be "a cinch for any picture house" and a particularly strong draw at first-run, urban movie palaces charging top ticket prices. Indeed, the *Variety* reviewer treats *On With the Show* as a "class A" production that has both aesthetic—the film "will give anyone understanding pictures lots to think over"—and broad box-office appeal. The film, he or she asserts, will solidify Warner Bros.' reputation as the cutting-edge sound-film studio: "Warners are the first of the talkers. Other credits due are a first also for operetta as with 'The Desert Song' and now again another first for its initial all-colored musical 'On With the Show.' So the Warners continue leading with talking innovations."[26]

If the film merits notice for its vivid "coloring," then it is also distinguished by its "more than customary doses of girls" in the chorus and main cast alike. By addressing "girls" as one production feature among many to be quantified and registered in its unusual abundance, the *Variety* reviewer mimics a strategy used frequently in the pressbook.[27] Yet the *Variety* writer's language complicates the pressbook's logic of uniformity and all-inclusiveness. Rather than using the more conventional word "all-color" to describe the film's pioneering Technicolor cinematography, he or she calls it an "all-colored" musical. By using this participle, the reviewer, perhaps unwittingly, risks confusing *On With the Show* with another classification of films being advertised on the basis of another "all." As Alice Maurice has shown, film studios promoting both feature-length musicals (*Hearts in Dixie* [Fox, 1929], *Hallelujah* [MGM, 1929]) and comedy shorts (the Christie-Cohen series) with all–African American casts employed phrases like "all-colored" or "all-Negro," playing on the promotional discourse of the early sound cinema.[28]

Just as industry personnel coined phrases like "all-talkie" and "all-talking" to promote the sound-film medium—to distinguish films with synchronized dialogue throughout from those with isolated talking sections ("part-talkies")—so did the studios seek to highlight the novelty of films that featured African American performers throughout and in large numbers.[29] But whereas the other "all-" labels that circulate in early sound cinema promotional discourses work on a logic of uniformity and inclusivity, "all-colored" and "all-Negro" are coded signs of racial exclusivity. The all-black-cast film effectively segregates film production and narrative space, making it possible to feature a wider range of African American characters—including characters who elude the constraints of existing stereotypes—and social situations in which these characters might appear. This subgenre achieves this range, however, by locating these characters and situations in a fantasy space where evidence of white discrimination and threats to white privilege are missing—in what James Baldwin called a cinematic "vacuum."[30] By using the ambiguous term "all-colored" to characterize *On With the Show*, the *Variety* reviewer ironically highlights this film's complex racial dynamics: it is a musical film that prominently features an African American star performer—marking her as such both diegetically and extradiegetically—but that situates her within a predominantly white cast, thus foregoing some of the insulating properties of the "all-Negro" casting strategy.

Thus, the *Variety* writer's language serves to point out the structures of racial division and exclusion that underlie *On With the Show*'s numerous claims to work by addition and full inclusion. In specifying the various numbers in which the "more than customary" number of "girls" appear, the writer first mentions "a specialist without part in the plot, Ethel Waters, colored." If Waters is one of the more important "girls" that appear in such abundance in this film, then, the writer also notes, she is "colored," albeit not in the same sense as the film stock itself. Assuming whiteness as the normative racial category, which in its claim to represent universal humanity does not need to be marked as a category, the reviewer feels compelled to identify Waters in racial terms.[31] In the context of the early sound cinema, the racial designation serves to highlight Waters's ambiguous status as "specialist."

On the one hand, the reviewer assumes that the appearance in the film of a popular African American recording artist is an attractive production feature, especially for the "class" or "Broadway" sector of the overall film audience. On the other hand, the reviewer recognizes that Waters's appearance could be seen as a possible violation of racial etiquette onscreen by those exhibitors and segments of the audience who will not tolerate any representation of racial "mixing" or social "equality." The writer's note explaining that Waters has "no part in the plot" likely serves to allay these concerns, in keeping with his or her larger belief that the film is "a cinch for any picture house."[32] In a similar vein, the studio's own promotional materials register the ambiguous status of the African American cast members, while also serving to characterize their role in the production in restricted terms.

In an advance piece celebrating the work in *On With the Show* of the African American dancer John William Sublett, who plays Bertha's boyfriend, Sam, the pressbook obsessively repeats the terms "color" and "colored."[33] Repeating these terms, the piece melds their visual-cinematic and racial-social connotations, illustrating how, by including African American performers, *On With the Show* adds yet another measure of novelty to the production's spectacular balance sheet, increasing its superabundance. Sublett's appearance in the film "augments the rainbow glories of 'On With the Show.'"[34] At the same time, the pressbook materials contend with the potential liability posed by Sublett, Waters, and the other African American cast members for white exhibitors and viewers who are unwilling to tolerate any disruptions of the social order, even fictional ones.

An adjacent piece profiling the Harmony Emperors Quartet, who provide backup vocals for Waters on "Am I Blue?" highlights the singers' constrained position both within the film's complicated narrative space and on the set (during the actual production). This piece makes clear that the Harmony Emperors appear only in the film's stage show portions and not in the backstage portions, where "most of the dramatic action takes place." Further, the "darktown jazz stuff" in the film "is set in the cotton fields down South." In other words, the piece highlights how the film uses a stock setting to contain African American performance within a familiar and reassuring space and time set apart from the rest of the film. (Strictly speaking, the claim is even inaccurate, Sublett's own scene being set in Chicago.) Indeed, the pressbook article goes so far as to make reference to the vocal quartet's impromptu performances on the set to entertain the (white) cast and crew during lulls in shooting.[35] These African

American performers, the article suggests, serve the same role for the other actors on the set as they do for the film's own viewers; they are there always and only to entertain.

The Girl-Glorifying Ziegfeld

Celebrating *On With the Show*'s "more than customary doses of girls" and "dazzling beauty chorus of 100," the reviews and pressbook begin to reveal the filmmakers' basic assumptions about the place and purpose of female embodied spectacle on screen. The film exhibits "girls" as objects of visual pleasure and erotic contemplation; the very exhibition of their bodies adds a certain scenic "value" to the film (just as adding Technicolor cinematography enhances the film's color "values"), while, in turn, these performers act as mannequins for valuable commodities (the opulent costumes). At the same time, the film has been shaped by crucial decisions about what "types" of female bodies—judged according to norms of race, class, and sexuality—are suitable for exhibition and, more significantly, will bring the maximum glamour or scenic value to the film. *On With the Show*'s handling of these questions is evident in Ethel Waters's complicated position. The *Variety* reviewer's synopsis includes her in the film's large cast of "girls," while marking her separation from this cast in multiple ways, as a "specialist," as someone with "no part in the plot," and as the only performer identified by race ("colored").

In the ways that *On With the Show* scripts and casts scenes of female embodied spectacle, deciding what "types" of bodies may or may not appear in particular settings, the film clearly taps into the theatrical legacy of the preeminent Broadway producer in the years between 1910 and 1930, Florenz Ziegfeld Jr., and on the image of the showgirl that he sought to fashion. Indeed, the film explicitly seeks to link itself to the man whom one pressbook article calls "the girl-glorifying Ziegfeld." The piece describes the film as "equaling" Ziegfeld's productions in its scenic sumptuousness and in its abundance of beautiful "girls."[36]

As Linda Mizejewski has illustrated in her definitive study, *Ziegfeld Girl: Image and Icon in Culture and Cinema*, Ziegfeld styled himself and was accepted by the popular media as the ultimate arbiter of American female beauty during the first three decades of the twentieth century. For Ziegfeld to identify a young woman as suitable material for exhibition in his Follies was for him to see in her a potential value as an object of display and visual consumption, what was called "glamour" in period discourse. Mizejewksi defines "glamour" as the "public visibility of a desirable object, its management or control, and its resulting value as a class marker or commodity."[37] Mizejewski's definition suggests a more specific, classed, and gendered version of what Walter Benjamin calls "exhibition value" in his famous "Artwork" essay.

Playing on the classical Marxian concepts of "use value" and "exchange value," Benjamin coins the term "exhibition value" to illustrate how, under conditions of late capitalism and technological reproduction, works of art are valued for their ability to display representational objects in public in many different places and at the same time. In mass-cultural media like film and photography, Benjamin argues, ritual and even conventional aesthetic functions wither away, opening the "work of art" to a new purpose, that of sheer public exhibition.[38] Hence, Benjamin's term is useful for understanding emergent mass-cultural phenomena like Ziegfeld stage revues and the backstage musical films influenced by these revues. As "girl" shows, such stage revues and films appeal to their audiences on the basis of their selection and public display of female bodies. Zeigfeld's obsession with "glamour" thus represents his attempt to realize the "exhibition value" of the female body: to "glorify" it by making it publicly visible as a desirable object and imbuing it with more specific class, racial, and national meanings.

As Mizejewski argues, for Ziegfeld to brand or "trademark" female beauty was to evaluate bodies with an eye to achieving standardization or uniformity, on the model of the products marketed by other national brands. In this model, the familiar brand name or trademark acted as a guarantee, enabling the prospective consumer to make a purchase with a set expectation of the commodity's quality.[39] Over the course of Ziegfeld's career, this project of "branding" female beauty followed very specific assumptions about what sorts of bodies and subjects were suitable for public display. Ziegfeld sought to associate the "Ziegfeld Girl" brand with class prestige and social "respectability," thus creating a new kind of showgirl, one stripped of the negative associations with promiscuity and even prostitution that clung to the figure of the "chorus girl."[40]

In its portrayal of Kitty's and Nita's relationships to Wallace (*The Phantom Sweetheart*'s patron), *On With the Show* picks up on the same anxieties about the chorus girl to which Ziegfeld responded, portraying backstage as a space of flirting and deal making (exchanges of bodily display onstage and companionship offstage for money or goods). The narrative ultimately allays these anxieties by highlighting Kitty's relationship to Jimmy (and to Dad), on the one hand, and Nita's inherent goodness and skillful management of Wallace, on the other. Nita spares Kitty from having to accept Wallace's proposition of "practical love" ("the kind of love that comes wrapped up with jewelry") and vows physically to remove Wallace from the temptations of backstage encounters with showgirls. She will, the end of the film suggests, settle down with Wallace in conventional married life, away from the promiscuous world of the theater. These comforting representations notwithstanding, the film serves to point out, as I argue below, the vulnerability and economic dependence of the female theatrical performer, chorus member and leading lady alike, even as it participates in her exploitation.

On With the Show borrows another strategy from Ziegfeld for "glorifying" the showgirl and guaranteeing her quality as a walking commodity, linking theatrical performance with fashion modeling. Because fashion was associated with elevated class status, with the ability to dress tastefully, the fashion model seemed to project "good breeding." Moreover, the model could be presented more as a depersonalized mannequin than as a vital, sensual body. Just as *On With the Show*'s pressbook trumpets the many fine, expensive costumes produced specially for the film, so did Ziegfeld disseminate detailed information to the press about the actual cost of the costumes worn onstage by his "Girls."[41] The film's highly touted fashion sense, "The Land of Let's Pretend"—itself a direct imitation of the *Follies*' famous "Ziegfeld Walk"—also makes *On With Show* an obvious film to promote through fashion "tie-ups."[42] One item in the pressbook recommends that theater owners exhibiting the film consult with local department stores and "women's wear shops" to "display their dresses of newest shade and designs, with posters and cards for the show [the film]."[43] The film's combination of "natural color" and "many beautiful, new, and unusual creations" makes it a kind of cinematic shop window; it gains prestige from its dabbling in high fashion, even as the fashion tie-up serves to draw actual female department store shoppers from show windows and floor displays to the theater.[44]

As a national brand name, "Ziegfeld" functioned not only as a guarantee of the uniform "quality" of the "girls" who bore it but also as an acceptable symbol of Americanness, becoming enmeshed in the dominant culture's attempts to delineate and police the racial and ethnic boundaries of this concept. Ziegfeld's choruses favored white women possessing physiques and physical features deemed indicative of good "breeding" and adhered to the racial and ethnic hierarchies of early-twentieth-century eugenics, altogether excluding African Americans, Native Americans, Latinas, and Asian Americans.[45] Yet Ziegfeld revues frequently defined (white) American beauty and glamour in relation and/or in opposition to images of "exotic" femininity. Within the fashion-show format, Ziegfeld showgirls participated in spectacles of touristic masquerade, appearing in Turkish, Egyptian, Japanese, and Hawaiian settings; such spectacles reinforced white female privilege by appropriating the allure of simulated exoticism.[46] Ziegfeld Girls even donned "café au lait" makeup for certain performances; this variation on blackface performance represents what Mizejewski calls the Ziegfeld shows' "specific appropriations of the representation of the dusky belle."[47]

The "dusky belle" was the black Broadway show's equivalent to the Ziegfeld showgirl: the "high yellow," or light-skinned, African American chorines who were featured in shows like *Chocolate Dandies* (1924), *The Plantation Revue* (1922), and *Dixie to Broadway* (1924). The latter two shows were overseen by the white producer Lew Leslie, who later opened the Plantation Club restaurant and cabaret in Harlem.[48] As Jacqui Malone explains, *The Plantation Revue* brought performers from the floor show of Leslie's club to the Broadway stage, initiating a series of productions that popularized vocal, jazz, and dance styles being developed in Harlem cabarets among white audiences. Leslie's productions also introduced major stars of the African American vaudeville circuit to these audiences and helped to launch some of their careers in film.[49]

Mizejewski argues that the light-skinned African American chorines in shows like *Dixie to Broadway* carried an aura of "forbidden desirability."[50] By a similar logic, Ziegfeld revues, mimicking these Broadway shows' representations of the "dusky belle" chorine, both appropriated the value of the exotic and reinforced white glamour and privilege. *On With the Show*'s "beauty chorus" is an all-white ensemble that engages in no ethnic masquerade or minstrelsy, and the film does not present any African American women in the role of "dusky belle" as represented by black Broadway shows. While it would be absurd to see these absences as deliberate "omissions" by the film—neither of these representations of the "exotic" showgirl being by any means typical in contemporary American theater—it is possible to read them as symptomatic of *On With the Show*'s observance of a taboo on interracial desire, an observance even more rigid than the one that characterized the Ziegfeld Follies.

On With the Show must be understood, in the first place, as a film shaped by the dominant conservative racial politics of the Hollywood studio system, which enforced a taboo on interracial desire in contemporary film productions. The industry's governing body, the Motion Picture Producers and Distributors of America (MPPDA), had issued a list of "Don'ts and Be Carefuls" encouraging the studios to censor their own productions with respect to certain "objectionable" or taboo topics. The sixth "Don't" on this list identified "Miscegenation (sex relationships between the white and black races)" as a topic that was utterly off-limits.[51] The 1930 Production Code that supplanted the earlier list repeated this prohibition. While the 1930 code was more extensive and stringent, it was not observed seriously until 1934, when the MPPDA formed a censoring body to enforce it, the Production Code Administration (PCA).[52]

As Susan Courtney has argued, the PCA's enforcement of the "miscegenation clause" was uneven or contradictory, beset by the ambiguities inherent in the notion of "miscegenation" and by the blurry nature of racial categories. Nevertheless, the PCA tended to take a broad view of "miscegenation." The organization used the clause to justify censoring characters and situations that suggested a prior "sex relationship between white and black" individuals, and it bowed to pressures exerted by southern exhibitors and audiences to construe the clause as barring racial "mixing" in a general (nonsexual) sense.[53] Therefore, mixed-race characters posed problems for censors not only as subjects or objects of sexual desire for/by white characters but also as embodied representatives of historical "miscegenation."[54] At the same time, the PCA used the "miscegenation clause" to police the "color line," steering studios away from any depictions of "social equality" in the form of "mixed" contacts not built around clearly marked, hierarchical distinctions.[55]

While *On With the Show* predates the Production Code, it abides by the spirit of the "miscegenation clause" as instantiated in the list of "Don'ts and Be Carefuls" and constructed by the PCA after 1934. The film contains no representations of African American women as objects of erotic desire (whether through actual black performance or white masquerade) and is scrupulous in how it manages onstage and backstage interactions between white and black characters, avoiding any suggestion of illicit "contact" or "social equality." In this last feature of the film, the filmmakers' goals for *On With the Show* become clear. It is a "class A" feature by a major studio seeking to capitalize on all of its technical resources and to pull off the difficult feat of appealing simultaneously to "Broadway" and "Main Street" audiences (including the notoriously intransigent "southern box office").

For all of its insistence that *The Phantom Sweetheart* is a viable piece of Broadway entertainment—the film's original title was *Broadway or Bust—On With the Show* is unwilling to cater strictly to "Broadway" standards of taste (as held by actual Broadway theater patrons and the "highbrow" segment of the film audience labeled in this way). This reluctance extends to Broadway's notions about what sorts of raced images were acceptable for stage exhibition, which were more liberal than the Hollywood cinema's own. In this respect, the comparison between *On With the Show* and *Black and Tan*, an exceptional early sound film set in the putatively risqué world of the interracial cabaret and trading in the types of entertainment available in African American Broadway shows, proves instructive. As is the case in *On With the Show*, *Black and Tan*'s own construction of the taboo on racial mixing and on the sorts of desire that may or may not be forbidden for white viewers correlates directly with its goals and sensibilities as a film.[56]

A short film produced by a nascent "production-exhibition conglomerate," RKO, *Black and Tan* has a decidedly experimental feel.[57] The film bears the stamp of its writer and director's cosmopolitan sensibilities and unusual career trajectory within the Hollywood cinema. An associate of Carl Van Vechten, Murphy accompanied him on numerous "slumming" expeditions in Harlem. Murphy conceived of African American culture in thoroughly symbolic ways: as simultaneously primitive and modern but always exotic and spectacular. This conception clearly shaped *Black and Tan*, as did Murphy's background in the avant-garde cinema and abiding interest in creating a specialized art cinema within the Hollywood studio system.[58] Most significant here is the way that Murphy uses visual techniques honed in avant-garde film practice to hypereroticize light-skinned African American female bodies and to make them available to extreme visual consumption by (implicitly) white spectators. Through these techniques, Murphy combines his racialist and cinematic preoccupations.

Compared to *On With the Show*, *Black and Tan* does not represent simply a road not taken for the mainstream American cinema with respect to exoticist, primitivist racial and erotic spectacle. Instead, it highlights the ways in which the Warner Bros. backstage musical extravaganza trains comparable, if less extreme visual strategies on white female bodies, indulging this sort of intensely erotic gaze, while restricting it to an intraracial context. The same fantasies of scopic access that are encoded in Murphy's representations of "dusky belle" chorines feature in *On With the Show*'s invasive backstage depictions of white showgirls.

The Body of the Woman Owning the Legs

Black and Tan portrays an aspiring dancer, played by Fredi Washington, and her boyfriend, an ambitious jazz composer, played by Duke Ellington. At the beginning of the film, Fredi (all of the characters have the same names as the actors) arrives at Duke's apartment to inform him that she has secured them a job for that evening. He protests, reminding her of "what the doctor said about [her] heart": that "[she] cannot dance." While *Black and Tan* offers no further explanation of this mysterious heart ailment, it ultimately kills Fredi after she insists on performing.

Following the opening scene in Duke's apartment, the bulk of the film consists of a series of musical performances in a "black and tan" cabaret meant to evoke Harlem's Cotton Club, where Ellington and his orchestra were appearing at the time of the film's production. *Black and Tan* organizes these performances around Fredi's declining health. She begins by watching in the wings, swooning and looking faint, starts her dance, and then collapses on stage. The concluding scene takes place back in Duke's apartment, where Fredi lies on her deathbed surrounded by Duke at the piano, his orchestra sidemen, and members of the Hall Johnson Choir, who perform a vocal version of Ellington's "Black and Tan Fantasy." In this scene, the film uses directed, high-key lighting and high-angle shots to create expressionist chiaroscuro.[59] Long shadows play on the wall, and, as Fredi loses consciousness, the film cuts back and forth between medium close-ups of Fredi and of Duke at the piano as seen from her point of view. As the orchestra plays the song's final bars, a quotation from Chopin's "Funeral March," the medium close-up of Duke's face goes out of focus, indicating Fredi's passing.

Although *Black and Tan*'s simple narrative attributes Fredi's death to her heart, the film's visual rendering of her illness and collapse suggests an alternative, more esoteric explanation that thematizes the traumatic subjection of African American bodies to (white) erotic gazes. Giving the soundtrack over entirely to the orchestra's music, the cabaret sequence evokes Fredi's illness strictly through her disoriented vision, suggesting that her awareness of the gaze to which she is about to be subject is itself what makes her disoriented and finally unable to continue performing. The cabaret section begins with performances by the members of a male tap quintet, costumed in white ties and tailcoats, who perform synchronized precision routines to segments of "The Duke Steps Out" and "Black Beauty." In these first dances, the camera frames the dancers and the musicians on the elevated stage behind them with extreme long shots, suggesting the perspective of the cabaret patrons seated at floor-level tables a short distance from the stage. (Although the patrons' applause is audible between songs, they never appear on screen.) This default perspective provides a full view of the stage, including the proscenium framing the stage and the wings through which the dancers enter and exit. From this view, the film cuts to brief long shots at a slight low angle of the dance quintet, isolating their legs and feet in the frame as well as the reflection of their bodies visible on a mirrored section of the dance floor.

When these dances conclude, the film cuts to a shot of Fredi just offstage, perched on a high stool and slumped forward. Her stage costume consists of a white sequined bikini, the two pieces of which are connected by a web of beaded strings. She wears a similar lattice over her hair, which joins in a chin strap to resemble a harness, and a kind of skirt made up of numerous beaded strings. As the band begins playing again, Fredi stands to get a better view, staggering and holding her hand to her forehead. In a piece of editing that initially disorients the viewer, the film at this moment reprises the two prior dances by the male quintet. Thus, the film effectively moves backward in time, disrupting temporal continuity in order to emphasize the character's unique perspective. The viewer thus observes what he or she has just seen from the perspective of the intradiegetic audience a second time, from the subjective point of view of the character.[60]

In this second version of the sequence, *Black and Tan* uses a myriad of unusual shots to illustrate Fredi's distress and disorientation. The camera pans across the band members' faces in medium close-up, going in and out of focus. Then the film begins to cut between shots of the band and dancers photographed with a special, faceted lens that creates nine roughly circular segments in the frame, in which the same image appears. Murphy rotates and stretches this grid of repeated images to create the effect of looking into a kaleidoscope.[61] Cutting away to medium close-ups of Fredi leaning against the wall and swooning, the film repeatedly reestablishes her point of view. Focusing on the dancers' bodies, the faceted shots have the effect of isolating and multiplying their body parts, thus compounding the effect of their choreography and positioning. (At one moment, they execute a graceful march passage in single file, with almost no space separating the dancers.)

Figure 7. Fredi Washington's kaleidoscopic view of the male tap quintet in *Black and Tan* (RKO, 1929).

Following this sequence, Fredi takes the stage and begins to perform a solo dance to Ellington's "Cotton Club Stomp." The film frames her more closely than it has framed the male dance group, and the camera moves with her, highlighting her bare arms and legs as she shimmies and executes high kicks and spins. In the middle of this performance, Fredi steps onto the mirrored floor, and the film cuts to a shot photographed from directly underneath her. The floor is not, in fact, a conventional mirror, but tinted and polished glass, through which the action above is visible. At this moment, *Black and Tan* leaves behind any perspective that could be occupied by a character or a diegetic audience member and enters the realm of pure cinematic fantasy and scopophilia. As Fredi turns, the strands of her skirt swirl in mesmerizing patterns, and the viewer has a kind of impossible visual access to the lower half of her body. Manipulating space to achieve near-abstract visual effects, while emphasizing the female genital area, Murphy's film provides a striking instance of the stock "crotch shot," while also anticipating Busby Berkeley's cinematographic techniques.[62]

Moments after *Black and Tan* returns to the more conventional view of the action, Fredi collapses on the floor and is carried offstage by the other dancers. At the behest of the cabaret's proprietor, the orchestra continues playing,

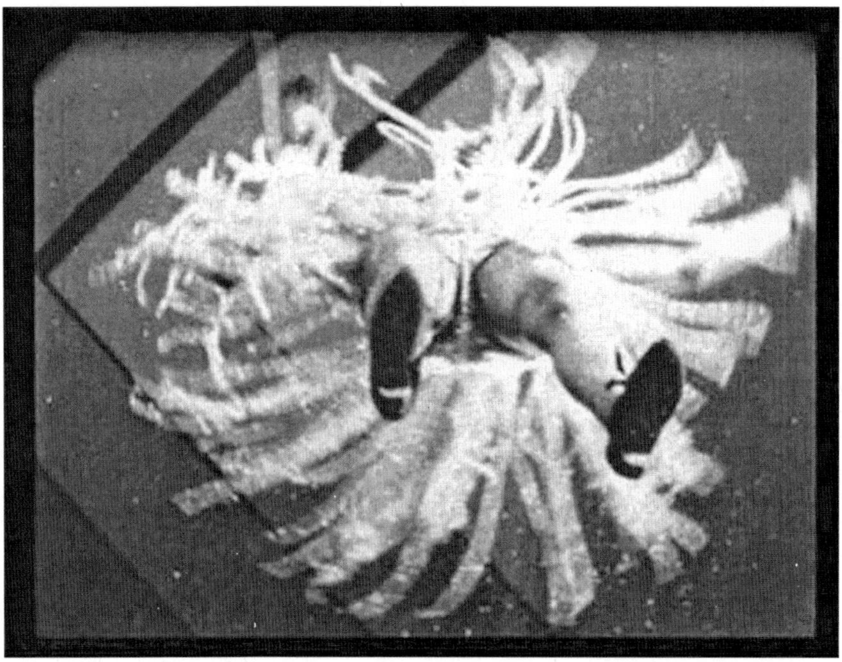

Figure 8. Fredi Washington dances on a transparent floor in *Black and Tan* (RKO, 1929).

breaking into "Hot Foot" as a group of five female dancers take to the floor. This quintet represents a smaller version of the choruses of light-skinned African American women that were a fixture in black Broadway shows and a featured attraction at Harlem cabarets during the late 1920s and early 1930s.[63] Their costumes are a variation on Fredi's, or, perhaps more to the point, her costume is a variation on theirs. Accentuating the women's bare skin, while attaching to them the signifiers of the exotic-primitive, the chorines wear very minimal two-piece costumes, with clusters of long feathers on their heads, hips, and ankles. These chorines dance briefly before Duke and his bandmates quit playing and leave the stage, out of concern for Fredi.

Without returning to the special lenses and extreme camera positions that it reserves for Fredi's view of the action and her dance, in this scene *Black and Tan* uses a cinematographic style like the one established during her number. The framing tends to emphasize the dancers' legs and their reflections in the floor. One particularly lengthy close-up isolates two dancers' legs as they shimmy from side to side and kick. Enclosing the women's legs from the upper thigh to the foot, this tight framing allows the viewer to study the movement of flesh as their leg muscles strain and relax.

Black and Tan establishes such a direct link between the mechanics of the erotic gazing and Fredi's trauma on the dance floor that it is tempting to posit a relationship of cause and effect between the two. When the film replays the male tap quintet's numbers from Fredi's point of view, it seems to illustrate her knowledge of the types of gazes to which she will be subject as a dancer performing in the space of the interracial cabaret.[64] It is as if she imagines an exaggerated version of the cabaret audience members' way of seeing the dancers, as identical to one another, interchangeable, and an assemblage of moving limbs. But not these particular dancers. Allowing for the complex range of desiring gazes that viewers of different sexualities, genders, and races might bring to these numbers, the male quintet's performance does not appear to have erotic exhibition as its primary purpose in the film. Whereas all of the female dancers that follow are positioned, through their costuming and choreography, primarily, though perhaps not exclusively, for erotic exhibition, the male dancers are fully clothed in conventional evening wear and dance in a style that emphasizes precise footwork over dramatic movement (especially of the torso or pelvis).

In a way that is fully consistent with the "gendered division of labor" of erotic spectacle in American narrative film documented by feminist film theorists, *Black and Tan* gives a particular erotic charge to women's dance, coding female bodies with "to-be-looked-at-ness."[65] Crucially, the film does not begin to use cinematographic techniques that isolate the parts of the body into the nonsubjective point of view until Fredi and then the five chorines take to the stage. At this point, the extreme-long and long shots *Black and Tan* has previously used to render the neutral/objective point of view—to give the film spectator a reasonable simulation of the diegetic audience's perspective—become somehow insufficient to the task of giving the viewer access to the spectacle of bodies in motion. Only then does the exhibition of the dancers' bodies need to be supplemented by shots that give viewers privileged, and even impossible, voyeuristic access to the women's legs and crotches. And only then does the imagery of fragmented and multiplied body parts achieve its particular erotic and fetishistic effect.

By incorporating these shots into the female dancing montages, the film explains why the prospect of performing in this setting might have produced such anxiety in Fredi. The very dramatic fragmentation and probing by the camera to which she is subjected thus seem almost to affect the character's action within the fictional realm of *Black and Tan*, bringing her dance to a dramatic stop. Although Fredi is a star performer who dances alone and is introduced by name, the camera relates to her in an even more invasive and voyeuristic way than it does to the five chorines who, tellingly, take over for her when she collapses. Just as the chorus is interchangeable for her in the cabaret's floor show, so could Fredi be another of its anonymous members.[66]

On With the Show spares its African American female performers the sorts of scopophilic exploitation and even violence imposed by *Black and Tan*. Interestingly, *On With the Show* does train voyeuristic camera gazes on white female chorines in various states of undress and makes these chorines into figures of abstract equivalence, even as it neglects or refuses to feature African American women in this vulnerable role. In creating a huge assembly of white "girls," the "dazzling beauty chorus of 100," *On With the Show* requires that each woman minimize her individual particularity and become submerged in a uniform body. While the chorus role certainly tolerates individual differences of appearance, movement, and expression, it does make each member equivalent in an abstract sense, through the guarantee of uniform quality. Each member possesses the same "exhibition value." In trading individual distinction for abstract and equivalent valuation, the white chorus girls become "phantom sweethearts," to pick up on the film's suggestive trope: living commodities and objects of erotic contemplation.

Although *On With the Show* differentiates the white female leading actresses from the chorus girls both in the defined parts they play in the stage show and in their individuated roles in the backstage action, the film also suggests that these actresses are interchangeable and exist, first and foremost, as objects of erotic contemplation for their male patrons. Recall that the role of the Phantom Sweetheart in the stage show acts as the site of multiple substitutions in the film. In the first place, the Phantom Sweetheart character is the woman for whom the protagonist of the stage show substitutes his fiancée. Without belaboring or explaining this substitution, the show allows him to cast off the other woman in favor of this mysterious, unnamed apparition. By the same token, the role permits Kitty to substitute for Nita on stage; Kitty simply takes over the part midway through the performance, allowing the show to continue uninterrupted. Nita actually faces this danger of replacement from the start, as part of her role—the laugh—has been contracted out to Sarah.[67]

Moreover, Kitty tries to enable the cast to go "on with the show" by putting herself in Nita's place backstage. She volunteers to entertain the advances of the show's wealthy "angel" in order to secure the money needed to pay for the props and to cover back salaries. Preparing to face Wallace, Kitty acknowledges what is at stake in this transaction. In exchange for the money needed to fund the production, she must trade her physical body—or at least the prospect of access to it—to Wallace. Kitty fantasizes that she will be able to make Wallace her "slave without even allowing him to touch" her. When Wallace attempts physically to assault Kitty, the film reveals the true dynamics of exploitation at work in their relationship and, by extension, in the relationships of all of the female theatrical performers (chorus girls, stars, and aspiring stars alike) to the men who support them. As women who exchange their physical appeal or their bodies for money, however indirectly, these figures are, the film wants to suggest, dependent and vulnerable to all kinds of exploitation.

Although she is the show's star, Nita speaks throughout the film as the experienced ex-chorine who is always in danger of losing her privileged status to another aspirant from the chorus and who must compete with these women for her husband's attention. The film actually tones down this dimension of her character as drawn in the final draft of the screenplay, leaving out a tart speech that Nita makes to Jimmy. Nita tries to explain to Jimmy that Kitty's plan to work in the theater will require her to do things that he will not like: Kitty will likely land a part that "calls for B.V.D.'s." At this time, BVD was a brand of men's and women's undergarments; the implication here is that she will appear onstage in little more than underwear. Further, Nita explains that Kitty will face "yaps from Oshkosh staring their eyes out across the foot-lights."[68] The film is hesitant to admit this sort of relationship between male members of the theatrical audience and female stage performers and even tries to avoid the impression that it is making any appeals to such "yaps."

On With the Show's promotional materials attempt to dignify the production by emphasizing the "intriguing concealment" of its showgirls under longer and more modest skirts. One advance story claims that the filmmakers have made a point of excluding "baldheads" from the diegetic audience of *The Phantom Sweetheart*. "Baldheads" are the pressbook's equivalent of Nita's "yaps from Oshkosh": middle-aged, professional (and probably married) men who come to leer at these "girls." "Baldhead" comes from the slang term "bald-head row" used by burlesque performers to characterize the stereotypically older, balding businessmen who could afford to pay for front-row seats and were, thus, unusually visible to the female performers moving along the stage and runways.[69] The pressbook piece argues that by harkening back to the theatrical styles of the 1870s, including longer skirts, shows featuring chorus girls may frustrate the efforts of the "baldheads" to gain privileged visual access from the front row. The film's choreographer, Larry Ceballos, presents his costume choices as a model of such a change in fashion, which, supposedly, discourages leering and invasive male gazes.[70]

These disclaimers notwithstanding, *On With the Show* makes obvious and gratuitous gestures toward satisfying the prurient desires of the "baldheads" in the *cinematic* audience, presenting the chorus girls' unclothed limbs and bodies as objects of a voyeuristic gaze. One of the early backstage sequences evokes voyeuristic scopophilia by using a suggestive match cut as well as angles and placements that are atypical for the film. The departure from the film's dominant cinematographic style of long shots and "objective" point of view that takes place in this sequence makes it all the more noticeable and seemingly gratuitous. Just as the stage show is about to begin, *On With the Show* cuts from a shot of the curtain going up on stage to a shot of a rack of costumes,

Figure 9. Costumes coming off the rack in *On With the Show* (Warner Bros., 1929).

which, being set directly in front of the lens, occupies the entire frame. As these costumes are taken off of the rack, the shot reveals the inside of the backstage dressing room, and the viewer realizes that he or she is observing the scene from a concealed position inside a closet.[71]

The removal of costumes mimics the opening of the stage curtain revealing the scene, but, whereas the action on stage is a deliberate exhibition, the action in the dressing room is observed furtively. The more clothes that come off of the rack, the more of the partially undressed women's bodies we see. To sustain the voyeuristic fantasy further, the film cuts from a long shot of the balcony outside of this dressing room to an extreme low-angle shot looking up the iron spiral staircase leading from this balcony to the stage level—a shot not unlike the under-the-floor shot in *Black and Tan*. As the chorus girls descend the staircase, the viewer is treated to an extreme version of the "baldhead" vantage point from the front row of the theater.[72]

In light of the totally liberated camera of the early 1930s Berkeley performance numbers, capable of tracking "through the legs," these voyeuristic shots of women's bodies "behind the scenes" seem almost quaint. Yet by preserving the voyeuristic glimpses of backstage flesh, and thus supplementing the pervasive erotic exhibition that happens onstage, the backstage musical offers the fantasy of a kind of total access to the showgirl's body. There is no space outside or refuge from the spectacle that would reveal the labor that gives rise to it. Even in the space where the production of the spectacle begins, the female body in show business is already available as an object of erotic gazing, its public visibility as image always assumed.

As earlier drafts of the story materials for the film illustrate, the thematizing of female bodily display was integral to *On With the Show*'s conception from the start. In the short play "Shoestring," from which the eventual screenplay was adapted, Jimmy sarcastically describes Nita as playing to the "husbands"—"baldheads"?—in the crowd by letting "her draperies fall apart."[73] The play's stage directions also make a point of having Nita walk around backstage in a thin negligee. The final draft of the screenplay sketches out a scene, not unlike the film's dressing room scene, which even more explicitly insists on the metonymy between the female body and "scenery." It calls for a "MOVING SHOT," showing "A pair of exquisite feminine legs moving along behind a piece of scenery carried by two stage hands": "The scenery veils the body of the woman owning the legs. The stage hands turn diagonally so that we can see the woman—Nita French, wearing as little as possible and looking gorgeous." The film's dressing room scene plays out, on a larger scale, this same backstage game of concealing and revealing the bodies of the female performers, stars and chorines alike.[74]

A color promotional poster produced for *On With the Show* offers a final, peculiar variation on this theme of voyeurism. Above a text touting "A Chorus of 100 Dazzling Beauties," a drawn image of a "chorus girl" appears: she faces away from the viewer, looking through what appears to be a small peephole. We can assume that this is a hole in the curtain and that she furtively watches the action on stage through it. But her pose while engaging in such spying serves as an occasion for the viewer of the poster to gaze voyeuristically. In cinematographic terms, the perspective in the drawing suggests what would be a slight high-angle shot, emphasizing the length of her legs, which are visible up to the tops of her thighs. Perched on high heels and bending slightly at the waist toward the peephole, she wears a stiff, ruffled skirt (like a ballerina's tutu), which, in this pose, reveals her contrastingly colored undergarments. The image of the showgirl having her voyeuristic pose consumed voyeuristically by another spectator suggests that she finds herself in a closed circle, with no escape from the scopophilic regime that demands that her body be available in every instance to the camera's erotic gaze. The showgirl is available in this way because she "owns" nothing but her body as an object, including crucial parts like legs, which, having already been expropriated by the film, are always subject to its designs.

Ain't No Foolin' Birmingham Bertha

If the constellation of issues addressed above—the framing of female bodies in the film as interchangeable, fragmented, and perpetually subject to erotic gazes—defines female performance generally in *On With the Show*, Waters has no part in it. Waters's Bertha character appears in a romantic fictional setting, lamenting the departure and infidelity of her boyfriend, Sam, but is never overtly framed as an object of erotic gazing. Moreover, Waters is not involved in the forms of collective representation (explicit and implicit) that the film reserves for African American women: the "mammy chorus" that appears in early scenes from *The Phantom Sweetheart* or the backstage maid "type" figure.[75] The other two African American women who dance in the film, the two female members of The Four Covans, appear in identical costumes to those of the men in the group—masculine-gendered workers' uniforms—and perform within the same male dance vocabulary; by tacitly gendering these dancers as male, this group's aesthetic (which was formed independently of this production) ultimately compliments *On With the Show*'s strategy of reserving the position of erotic object, or object of bodily display, for white women.[76]

If white female performers in *On With the Show* are "phantom" beings in the sense of bearers of abstractly equivalent exhibition value, then Ethel Waters is also a "phantom sweetheart," though in a very different sense. Because her mobility within the backstage setting is so restricted and because the relationship of her onstage character to the rest of the show's characters is so uncertain, Waters ends up having a kind of spectral presence within the film, vanishing for a long stretch, only to reappear unexpectedly. In one sense, Waters is the star of both shows (*The Phantom Sweetheart* and *On With the Show*). It is she whom everyone has come to see, her song that they hum expectantly. At the same time, Waters appears from and recedes into a state of virtual nonexistence with respect to the rest of the film's action. She is not even present on stage as the rest of the cast reprises her signature song in the final medley, nor does she emerge from backstage to receive the crowd's ovation.

Restricted though it is, Waters's position in the film has the paradoxical effect of making her the film's most autonomous and strong female voice and thus of giving her character a thematic significance in the film that far exceeds her apparently marginal status. Integral to this autonomy, strength of voice, and significance is Waters's exemption from the film's disindividuating economies of exhibition value and racial stereotype and from its voyeuristic gazing. Detached as they are from the backstage drama and *The Phantom Sweetheart*'s crude story, Waters's two numbers constitute a sung mininarrative of African American female self-determination and resistance to male exploitation. Moreover, they serve to highlight access to or control of capital as a crucial precondition for female autonomy in general, prefiguring the surprising conclusion of *On With the Show*'s backstage narrative. Waters's *lack* of involvement in the forms of female image-making addressed above finds a positive equivalent in her character's struggle to keep hold of her fictive capital—a capital located outside of her body as object of erotic display.

Comprising scenes 3 and 10, respectively, of *The Phantom Sweetheart*, Waters's "Am I Blue?" and "Birmingham Bertha" do the most of any of the

Figure 10. Ethel Waters and the Harmony Emperors Quartet perform "Am I Blue?" in *On With the Show* (Warner Bros., 1929).

scenes to preserve the film's show-within-a-show conceit. Both are staged in front of very simple painted backdrops and rely on very static cinematography, which convey the feel of filmed theater. The two numbers describe the trajectory of a woman whose "man," Sam, has left her and gone to Chicago, taking her "diamonds and dough." Accompanied by the Harmony Emperors Quartet, Waters sings her first number in front of a stylized cotton field backdrop, located "down here in Birmingham." She carries a large basket full of cotton, and the male singers gather around similar baskets.

The lyrics of "Am I Blue?" emphasize the loneliness and longing of a woman who "Got up this mornin' along about dawn" and "Without a word of warnin' . . . found he was gone."[77] The song appeals to the listener's sympathy and asks, rhetorically, whether or not her tears are sufficient proof that she is "blue." As "Birmingham Bertha" indicates, however, the character is "only human" in more than just her loneliness. While she loves Sam, he has also absconded with her money and property, indicating that he has deceived her and stolen the fruits of her work. Thus, her appearance in this second number in Chicago—represented by a backdrop picturing the outlines of skyscrapers—indicates her pursuit of Sam both out of love and a desire for restitution and revenge. She demands "an eye for an eye" and claims that "like the police, [she] never release[s] her man."[78]

The economic logic implicit in these numbers is, of course, absurd, indicating another peculiar manifestation of how the film romanticizes southern

Figure 11. Ethel Waters sings "Birmingham Bertha" in *On With the Show* (Warner Bros., 1929).

"plantation" life. While these numbers, taking place in a different space and possibly a different time from the main setting of *The Phantom Sweetheart*, certainly evoke contemporary social and economic issues, they mystify the sorts of exploitation and injustice that underpinned the system of cotton tenant farming and fueled African American migration. Not only does Bertha emerge in Chicago from what she describes as an all-night train trip wearing a fine suit and hat and looking to recover her "diamonds and dough," but she earlier stands in the cotton field wearing a gold pendant, bracelet, and earrings.

Preposterous as these details are in the plantation context, the lyrics of "Birmingham Bertha" suggest that the film might be more aware of the kinds of exploitation and theft of labor involved in this agricultural system than is immediately evident. Bertha sings "We's in Chicago," indicating her and Sam but also suggesting the many thousands of southern African Americans who, by 1929, had made the same train journey she describes. With this collective point of reference in mind, Bertha's intention to take back her property and her injunction, "Treat me fair and I'm on the level," signify, respectively, as a critique of white economic exploitation of African Americans and a plea for social opportunity. There is, she asserts, "no foolin'" this woman, who has "had schoolin'" in fighting for what is rightfully hers.[79]

It is also worth noting that Waters's costumes partake of the film's interest in high fashion. In "Birmingham Bertha" in particular, she wears one of

On With the Show's "many beautiful, new, and unusual creations." She wears a tailored jacket with oversized cuffs and a flowered sash; a two-layered, knee-length crepe skirt; and a tight-fitting, turban-style hat adorned with ostrich feathers. Quite differently, *On With the Show*'s "mammy chorus" typifies the positioning of African American images in the contemporary iconography of consumer culture: frequently used to advertise goods but never recognized as consumers.[80] By contrast, Bertha's costume change intimates to the viewer that she participates in the consumer economy. In light of the contemporary denial of African Americans as consumers by advertisers and the producers of mass-cultural images, this detail further serves to distinguish Bertha as an exceptional film character.[81] In addition to possessing a store of capital, Bertha has purchased glamorous commodities, which, the Hollywood film generally suggests, are the sole privilege of white Americans.

Although the film's segregation of onstage and backstage spaces would seem to preclude any significant white-black collaboration or cultural dialogue between characters, Waters's sung narrative of self-assertion and resistance to expropriation of capital surprisingly anticipates the film's own narrative climax. Given that the timing of Waters's numbers within *The Phantom Sweetheart* is otherwise arbitrary, it is striking that "Birmingham Bertha" is actually sung onstage simultaneously with the unseen backstage episode in which Nita whips Wallace for flirting with Kitty. Just as soon as "Birmingham Bertha" ends, Nita exposes Wallace's philandering to Jimmy and Jerry and explains that she has forced Wallace to surrender his financial control over the show; then her badly beat-up husband makes his final appearance. In the preceding musical number, Bertha has asserted control over Sam by catching up to him in Chicago and physically attacking him; through these means, she recovers her "diamonds and dough." Within the narrative, this scene actually takes the place of Nita's attacking Wallace, and, like this other couple, Bertha and Sam reunite. The details of the lyrics give Bertha a fictive capital—one difficult to imagine in light of her earlier position in the cotton field—and resonate with the film's ongoing discussion of gender and capital in show business.

In the final backstage sequence, Nita's description of her taking off a portion of Wallace's "hide" offers a surprising twist on an earlier figure of speech in the film. When Jerry initially orders Nita to put on her costume and prepare for the performance, she calls him a "slave driver" and asks, "Where's your whip?" When Nita whips Wallace, she does what Kitty earlier hopes to do to him. She makes him her "slave," coercing him to surrender his claim to the money he advanced Jerry, to drop his charges against Dad, and even to give the show an additional $10,000. Although Nita cannot advance her own career through this gesture, she does cede her place to Kitty and thus spares Kitty from having to tread the same path through show business. Kitty will emerge as an immediate star, garnering a significant role without having to "take off her clothes" on- or offstage.

By the same token, Kitty benefits from Wallace's largesse without having to keep up her part of the "racket," which she earlier claims to understand so well. Kitty's earlier proposal to make Wallace her "slave" by seducing him reflects the cultural mythology of the "gold digger," the ambitious but unscrupulous theatrical woman who uses her wiles to extort money from rich male patrons. As Mizejewski explains, this fantasy of female independence and control "masked the actual economic dependency of most women on men," especially women working in the theater.[82] *On With the Show*'s conclusion creates its own fantasy in which Nita, the tough ex-"chorus girl," becomes the production's "angel" by taking control of her now-husband's money. In the show's concluding moments, Kitty thus acquires her own fictive capital by moving straight from the coat room to the center of the stage.

That Waters sings about migration in a stage show that is otherwise locked in the iconography of southern plantation romance must be attributed to her working relationship with the film's white songwriting team, Harry Akst and Grant Clarke. Moreover, it is significant in the context of the film's meditation on women's access to the means of "show business" production that this relationship afforded Waters a significant degree of creative autonomy. In 1925, Akst, working with Sam Lewis and Joe Young, had contracted with Waters to debut in her Plantation Club show their composition "Dinah," a song that became a huge hit both as a recording and on sheet music.[83] According to Waters's autobiography, the songwriting team allowed her and her vaudeville collaborator Pearl Wright to make changes to the original composition, so as to style it in "[her] own way"—slower and less "corny." When Warner Bros. hired Akst (along with Clarke) to write songs for *On With the Show*, he sought out Waters to perform what he hoped would be the "song hit" within the film score.[84]

Waters claims that she and Wright worked on the "lead sheet" to "Am I Blue?" before she presented this version to production manager Darryl Zanuck and that she negotiated her own salary, earning his admiration for "driv[ing] a pretty good bargain."[85] That Akst and Clarke wrote this material with Waters in mind, having earlier collaborated with her in the cabaret setting, points to an extracinematic cultural capital that determines her prominent, if restricted, position in the film.[86] As the person charged with putting across the film's "hit" or theme, Waters is also engaged in a complex performance of self-determination, agency, and mobility, which contributes to the larger cinematic iconography of African American migration examined in the previous chapter. In these respects, Waters's appearance "as herself" in the film becomes more complex, suggesting a kind of autonomy that mitigates or qualifies any marginalizing effects of this casting strategy.

The Only White Woman on the Island

The show business careers of white women in the films discussed in this chapter depend on the cultural privilege entailed by whiteness, although in ironic or ambiguous ways. In entertainment contexts that assume exclusively white audiences, whiteness becomes a crucial precondition for most of the films' diegetic theatrical performers to appear on stage and, by extension, on screen. Yet for women appearing in rigidly gendered and highly sexualized settings, whiteness becomes another "value" to be realized by the shows-in-the-films and the films themselves through bodily display. From the critical perspective offered by Ethel Waters's role, *On With the Show* suggests an even sharper articulation of this idea. In early sound films that foreground "girl" exhibition, whiteness is another form of capital in the "body as object," a prerequisite for a kind of visual exploitation that also entails the body's becoming immobile and interchangeable.

A contemporary melodrama from First National, a subsidiary of Warner Bros., called *Safe in Hell*, offers an interesting test case for *On With the Show*'s suggestion.[87] Though containing scenes of diegetic musical performance, *Safe in Hell* is not a backstage musical, but it does address the same central issues as *On With the Show* in an even more extreme, lurid fashion. The film's protagonist is a poor white woman who actually has been abused and forced into prostitution by a rich white man. Further, the narrative works constantly to illustrate that, lacking any independent financial support herself, the protagonist can find no escape or refuge from this type of exploitation. *Safe in Hell* also echoes films like *On With the Show* and *Gold Diggers of 1933* in being both ostensibly critical of the circumstances impinging on women's freedom and security and complicit in this exploitation within its own visual register. Further, *Safe in Hell* juxtaposes the white protagonist with an African American foil who eludes characterization by "type" and surprisingly models an autonomy and authority that the white protagonist cannot achieve—because rooted in a fictive, nonembodied capital. This African American character is also a musical performer who takes the diegetic stage in a way that, likewise, might not be available to the white protagonist for whom this "stage" is always already a space of quasi-prostitution.

Safe in Hell begins in a New Orleans brothel, where the Madame receives a call and dispatches a young white woman to a posh apartment building. The woman, Gilda (Dorothy Mackail), arrives to encounter Piet (Ralfe Harolde), a man with whom she has had a prior relationship. Piet chides her for having become a prostitute but still expects her to submit to his sexual advances; Gilda refuses, throwing a champagne bottle at him and knocking him out. In the skirmish, a table-mounted cigarette lighter falls over, starting a fire in the room. Gilda runs out of the apartment and later believes, mistakenly, that she has killed Piet and that the building's bellhop has "squealed" on her to the police. As Gilda prepares to flee New Orleans, her boyfriend, Carl (Donald Cook), a sailor, returns from a long voyage.

Gilda explains what has just happened and reveals the details of her past, contradicting the account of her character that Piet gives in the previous scene and helping to explain her fear of Piet. As a young woman with no financial support, Gilda took a job as a servant in Piet's home. Piet coerced her into a sexual relationship and then forced her to remain silent by threatening to reveal their relationship to his wife. Ultimately the wife did discover their relationship and drove Gilda out of the house. As Gilda explains to Carl, she was forced to "make [her] living the only way [she] could," as a prostitute. Although Carl, portrayed as a taciturn and highly religious man, is not fully sympathetic, he agrees to help Gilda escape the police. Concealed in a crate in the hold of his ship, Gilda sets sail for "the only place in the world where they've got no extradition laws," an island Carl begins to describe as "in the Caribbean Sea, just off the coast of," at which point the film conveniently inserts a transition.

As the film's sensationalistic and ironic title indicates, what is supposed to be Gilda's island refuge is, in fact, an intensified, nightmare version of the place from which she has just escaped. She goes to stay in a hotel with a saloon on the first floor, where a group of white men (themselves fugitives from all over the world) while away their days. Upon Gilda's arrival, these men begin to size her up; the fact that she is "the only white woman on the island" elevates her (relative to the largely unseen "native" women in the film) and subjects her to what the film's pressbook euphemistically calls their "indignities." Determined not to work as a prostitute again, Gilda finds herself abandoned in this place with limited funds and no source of income; the men hover around her, waiting for their opportunity to extort sexual access.

As if these perils and "indignities" are not enough, Piet resurfaces on the island. Having escaped from the burning apartment, he, too, is on the run from the law. He explains that his wife foiled the insurance scam that he tried to run following his apparent death. Piet immediately resumes his predations, and, when he tries to force himself on Gilda, she shoots and kills him. In a complex plot twist, Gilda uses a gun that Bruno (Morgan Wallace), the island's jail keeper and executioner, has planted in her room. The most insistent and devious of Gilda's male pursuers, Bruno plants the weapon in order to have a reason to arrest her. Because she has resisted his advances, Bruno seeks to put her in captivity and make her his concubine. When Bruno does arrest Gilda for shooting Piet, the other rogues from the saloon band together, acting as character witnesses at her trial and even, in the case of a former lawyer, taking up her defense. But rather than submit to Bruno's captivity, Gilda confesses to the killing and brings a sentence of death upon herself. In a remarkably grim conclusion, the film shows Gilda being marched down the beach by the prison guards en route to her execution by hanging.

Gilda's foil in the film is Leonie (Nina Mae McKinney), an African American woman also from New Orleans who owns and manages the hotel on the island where Gilda stays. The two women discover their New Orleans connection immediately with Leonie jokingly suggesting that the "climate" must have been "too hot" for her to stay up north. Leonie's knowing manner in this exchange suggests that she may have had her own compelling reasons for leaving New Orleans; in any case, she is financially secure as the owner of the hotel. She works alongside Newcastle (Clarence Muse), the Afro-Caribbean porter in the hotel, who may also be her husband or companion. While the character list for the Huston Branch play from which the film is adapted identifies Newcastle as her "man," the film does not expound on their personal relationship at all, and Leonie entertains and banters with the white fugitives who frequent the hotel's saloon.

Following Gilda's first appearance at the hotel, the men in the saloon pretend to flirt with Leonie as a way of getting information about the new arrival. One of the men counsels patience to the others, commenting, "Gentleman, she's the only white woman on the island. You must at least give the lady time to get settled." But while they claim to accord Gilda the respect due a "lady," they are only interested in her as an embodiment of the social category that makes her accessible as an object of their desire, accessible, specifically, as an object of visual fascination. To be a white woman in a space of otherwise nonwhite femininity means, in this film, to possess a definite exhibition value, an abstract worth realized in public display.

Safe in Hell most significantly overlaps with *On With the Show* and the tradition of the backstage musical in its construction of Gilda's "exhibition value" as a white woman. As a sensational melodrama exploring female victimization, *Safe in Hell* reiterates and reverses some of the backstage musical's main premises. Gilda starts off as a prostitute, occupying the social position that *On With the Show* and contemporary popular representations of the world of show business anxiously link with the "chorus girl." While the opportunity to perform on stage professionally is not available to her, she does consider what it would mean to command the performance space of the saloon and thus to hold the male patrons' attention. Being a white woman in a setting where all other women putatively are off limits to the homogeneous male audience, Gilda has a particular kind of value in her body and subject position. Yet the intensity of the violent and exploitative forces arrayed against her—coupled with her own extreme lack of resources—make this value dubious. And while *Safe in Hell* certainly casts a critical eye on the action of the men who oppress Gilda, it also takes a cue from *On With the Show* in reinforcing the white female character's exploitation as an object of visual fascination at the level of its own cinematography.

In a scene just after Gilda's arrival, the men in the saloon array their chairs in a "baldhead row" to await her first descent of the stairs. Sitting shoulder to shoulder, like theatrical or cinematic spectators, the men position themselves so as to be able to get the best possible view of Gilda's bare legs as she walks across the exposed landing and down the steps, which here become part of the saloon's theatrical space. A pan highlights the men's bored, anxious movements, slumping down in their chairs, eating nuts, and fanning themselves. While this bit of camera work would seem to cast a critical eye on the men's behavior, highlighting their lewdness and cynicism, *Safe in Hell* echoes the backstage musical in giving the viewer privileged, voyeuristic access to women's private space. With the spatial arrangement of the stairs and landing exactly resembling cinematic backstage spaces, Gilda's room at the hotel becomes her dressing room and the saloon floor a theatrical stage. Indeed, just after the scene in which the men watch the staircase, the film uses a camera shot that frames Gilda's legs from just above the knees to the floor to show her undressing.

The inclusion of this shot highlights the complex and contradictory rendering of Gilda's character. She is simultaneously a "fallen woman," a sympathetic victim of male cruelty, and a desirable screen presence for the viewer to enjoy. Interestingly, the film cuts directly from this voyeuristic moment to Leonie's exhibition downstairs as she sings "When It's Sleepy-Time Down South." The contiguity of these two moments in the film suggest an opportunity for Gilda to perform on the saloon's stage and thus to gain some measure of control over the men's attention, which she could parlay, in the fashion alleged of the "chorus girl" or "gold digger," into money or protection.

The material that Leonie sings requires her to align herself with bucolic clichés of southern life. "When It's Sleepy-Time Down South" describes the nostalgic longings of a northern migrant for the "dear old dreamy Southland." Leonie's ambivalent reference to her New Orleans roots and the southerly direction of her own migration complicates her rendering of this lyrical nostalgia. And, for all of the lyrics' references to "darkies crooning" and "mammy fall[ing] on her knees," the film does not seem interested in any significant way in plantation nostalgia. Indeed, the film's production history suggests that this song choice may have been informed more by Clarence Muse's role in the production and by a desire on the part of the filmmakers to alter the direction laid out for the film's music in the earlier script drafts.[88] It is as if the generic plantation song (with its "mammy" iconography) was the logical alternative to the first script's stipulation of hypereroticized "primitivist" and Africanist dance music.

In the position in the narrative occupied by Leonie's song, Huston Branch's original play script offers an orgiastic performance of "primitive African rhythm" by "negro" musicians from the island. Branch's script describes the performance in great detail. The music is a combination of "fox trot" and "jazz," which atavistically conjures "primitive," "African" energy. The musicians appear to be "under the influence of the mabi drug," and, as the music builds to "a gigantic, barbaric climax," two pairs of dancers (a man and a woman and two men) appear and "go through the most voluptuous of sex movements."[89] Leonie's song in the film replaces this overheated rendering of "negro" primitivism and sexual excess with an obviously ersatz image of African American rural timelessness, offering one set of stock representations in place of another.

Moreover, the film eliminates Branch's apparent intention to style Leonie as an object of erotic temptation for other characters in the play/film. The stage direction that introduces Leonie in Branch's original play script refers to her as a "luscious and light colored Negress," and the play refers repeatedly to her flirtations with Bobo, a "native" side character.[90] Such a strategy of framing this character would certainly have been in keeping with McKinney's previous work in Hollywood film. In the African American–cast feature musical *Hallelujah*, she plays a "high-yaller" temptress, a stock "jezebel" figure whose physical appeal is supposed to be linked directly to her skin color. *Hallelujah*'s promotional materials refer to her character, Chick, as "a seductive 'yaller' girl," inviting the implicitly white prospective viewer to indulge in the sort of skin-color fetishization displayed by the film's black male protagonist, Zeke (Daniel Haynes).[91] Moreover, in *Hallelujah*, McKinney's Chick sings and dances for a mixed-gender but exclusively black cabaret audience, making public her extended seduction of Zeke as she seeks to secure his money by offering the prospect of access to her body. Because of *Hallelujah*'s racially exclusive casting, Chick may be presented much more directly as an alluring "dusky belle," according to the type constructed in 1920s black Broadway shows.[92]

Obeying its own taboo on "miscegenation," *Safe in Hell* refuses to suggest any kind of interracial desire. Leonie's white male audience is rapt as she performs, yet the film notably refuses, through cinematography and editing, to frame her as the object of an explicitly desirous gaze. This prosaic framing immediately precedes the camera's entry into Gilda's bedroom (and figurative backstage dressing room), where she listens to a recording of W. C. Handy's "St. Louis Blues," a song that also plays earlier in the scene in the brothel parlor. The film's emphasis on Gilda's interest in music—she earlier plays a few bars of the jazz standard "Darktown Strutters Ball" on a piano—suggests the possibility of her taking Leonie's stage. Even as the particular musical choices that the film uses to characterize Gilda highlight her investment in African American culture, *Safe in Hell* establishes important distinctions between the two women's performances.[93]

Gilda does eventually descend the stairs and join the party in the saloon. She chooses not to perform in the way that Leonie does, but she does begin to ingratiate herself to the men. Despairing that she has not received any word from Carl and unable to sleep, Gilda decides to give up on her policy of shunning the men in the saloon and joins the party. She drinks and smokes with them and begins to establish bonds of friendship with some, later prompting them to intercede on her behalf during the trial. Interestingly, it is Leonie who encourages Gilda to take this step.

In a conversation in Gilda's room, Leonie questions her about why she refuses the advances of the men from the saloon. Gilda's initial response, that the reason is "nothing that you'd understand," is insulting, suggesting that her refusal to debase herself is a matter of her pride and social prestige as a white woman. Leonie responds sharply, saying that while Gilda may be "high-handed" now, she should remember that the "rent's comin' due" and that she will need to turn to one of these men for financial support at some point. Leonie also sympathetically reflects on Gilda's situation, recalling that she has "been fooled by those sailor boys [herself]."[94] While Leonie does not comment further on the identity of "those sailor boys," her choice of words suggests that she has in mind someone in Carl's position, who seems to have abandoned Gilda altogether.

Leonie's experience of such abandonment has occurred previously. At this point, however, the "rent" in question will be "due" to Leonie herself. As the owner of the hotel, she possesses the sort of economic security and independence that persistently eludes Gilda, that makes the island an actual refuge for her, and that allows her to take the stage of the saloon without putting her "body as object" at stake. As is the case in *On With the Show*, the possession of fictive capital here signals or coincides with resistance to erotic exploitation. In early sound films like these two, which foreground the issue of women's reduction to the status of image, such fictive capital accrues to black female characters through complex dialectics of race and gender. These characters, in turn, offer significant glimpses of the sort of independence necessary to alter their counterparts' position in exploitative economies: of what might allow these women to avoid renting their bodies to the men who control the business of showing.

Ethel Waters's and Nina Mae McKinney's roles in *On With the Show* and *Safe in Hell*, respectively, offer crucial precursors for Etta Moten's part in the canonical backstage musical *Gold Diggers of 1933*. As the only African American figure to perform vocally in one of Berkeley's spectacles from this period, and as one of only a few who are not service workers of some sort (porter, bootblack, or maid), Moten likewise acts as a "specialty," with "no part in the plot." Moten carries the two verses of "My Forgotten Man," taking over for one of the show-within-the-show's white stars, Joan Blondell. Although Moten has no role in the narrative before or after this scene, and although she appears in the confined space of an apartment window ledge on the stage set, she participates in shaping the film's anguished cry of Depression-era hardship while also tacitly acknowledging the heroism of African American soldiers in World War I. For all of the song's patriarchal gender politics, it represents a striking and exceptional moment of female public performance where the film's persistent reveling in the fabrication and exhibition of erotic female images subsides. Thus, in the early backstage musical, racial difference from the films' white norm has the paradoxical effect of allowing African American vocal performers to appear on screen as singular individuals, without being subsumed into the abstract-uniform bodies of the films' showgirls.

CHAPTER 4

The Unhomely Plantation

RACIAL PHANTASMAGORIA IN *HALLELUJAH*

In his 1952 memoir, *A Tree Is a Tree*, the white director King Vidor recalls his inspiration for making *Hallelujah*, an all-black-cast feature film that MGM released in 1929: "For several years I had nurtured a secret hope. I wanted to make a film about Negroes, using only Negroes in the cast. The sincerity and fervor of their religious expression intrigued me, as did the honest simplicity of their sexual drives. In many instances the intermingling of these two activities seemed to offer strikingly dramatic content."[1] My purpose in this chapter is to illustrate how *Hallelujah* exceeds and defies this stated intention. I approach *Hallelujah* not as mere racial phantasmagoria, but as a complex, ambiguous film-text; I take this approach despite the film's pervasive tendency to occlude conditions of production within its fictional scenes of labor and despite Vidor's insistence that his own, particular vision of "the Negro" is universally true—a preexisting reality that the film merely documents.[2] Thus, I offer a reading that attends both to the racial and social dynamics of plantation labor and to the film's own conditions of production.

Following the dialectical approach outlined in the introduction, this reading focuses on the range of formal strategies that *Hallelujah* uses to ground African American characters in the diegesis and so to envelope black bodies in a physical space that manifests a sense of stasis. In the film's scenes of nighttime religious worship and Zeke's chase through the swamp, *Hallelujah* creates what Kaja Silverman would call "claustral spaces."[3] Using expressionist lighting techniques and textures of sound in a way that illustrates the film's crucial intertextual relationship with the play and film adaptation of *The Emperor Jones* (United Artists, 1933), *Hallelujah* creates similarly phantasmagoric spaces, aiming to give its characters a bodily hyperpresence within the frame. This hyperpresence connotes vitality and the sort of dynamic energy that Vidor suggests in his comment on the film. Yet such vitality and dynamism are associated in the film with geographic movement and social mobility in a highly ambivalent way. *Hallelujah* is at pains to maintain this "primitive" vitality, against the checks to it that arise from the film's own subject matter, which constantly hints at social barriers, necessitating obviously artificial forward leaps in the narrative. Alternatively, the film's narrative trajectory codes this vitality as the underlying reason for black social immobility.

Like *The Emperor Jones*, this film pairs claustral spaces with a circular plot structure, which contains the protagonist's movements within a trajectory of sameness, extending the work of "interior"-izing blackness to the narrative register. *Hallelujah* uses the racially exclusive casting structure to establish crucial linkages between the main characters and the larger community in order effectively to envelop Zeke and his family's travails in a confining structure. Yet the film's figural rendering of African American "natural" stasis through phantasmagoria also serves to make visible what is otherwise excluded—to inscribe within the film-text a series of fault lines. These fault lines form around issues of sound-image (non-)synchronization, the construction of musical spectacle in the film, and narrative gaps.

The director's comments about *Hallelujah* highlight the degree to which the film is a product of the brief period of cinema-industrial investment in African American performers and popular culture that accompanied the conversion to synchronized-sound production. Associating "the Negro" with musicality and "natural" expressivity, Vidor and a handful of other white industry personnel believed that "Negro talking pictures" were the means of overcoming the limitations that sound technology imposed upon filmmaking—from the immobilized camera, to problems with sound-image synchronization and the intelligibility of dialogue—and thus of realizing the new medium's full aesthetic potential.[4] With respect to all of these maladies, African American musical performance appeared to observers like Vidor to offer a remedy, lending dynamism to the static frame, helping to shore up the illusion of voice-image synchronization, and bringing acoustical "warmth" and "authenticity" to the soundtrack.

In comments that he made in interviews and promotional materials distributed for the film's release, Vidor applied this theory of "Negro" vitality—his belief that African Americans are spontaneously vital and expressive, "strikingly dramatic [movie] content"—to *Hallelujah*'s actors, affirming their superiority to their white counterparts, while also characterizing their performance as something altogether different from acting, conventionally understood. Unlike white sound-film actors, who tend to be "wooden or stolid" before the camera, black actors, according to Vidor, possess "ardor," "vitality," and a "zeal almost religious"; in fact, they lack any "sense of dramatic restraint."[5] "The Negro," Vidor explains, "is one of the greatest actors by nature principally because he really doesn't act at all, but actually feels and experiences the emotions he seeks to portray."[6] In Vidor's romantic racialist conception, blackness equals universal dramatic potential: "You may choose any Negro, at random, and he will probably prove a good actor. The reason is that in their natural, everyday lives, the American Negroes dramatize everything, just as their ancestors did in Africa and as they continue to do through their native rites."[7]

In the film, the "everyday lives" of the main characters, the members of the Johnson family, are dominated by labor—specifically the harvesting of cotton. If, as Vidor claims, all of African American everyday life is already "dramatized," then it would follow that black agricultural work of the kind that the film depicts is also a spontaneous, natural outpouring of corporeal and affective "vitality." Such an ideological formulation appears, indeed, to offer a handle on the film's peculiar depiction of cotton picking. The Johnsons hope to make money by selling their crop, but they do not, it appears, face great economic danger when that money is lost. There are, however, some unsettling details within this representation that the film fails to explain. Why do they live in such a cramped, decrepit cabin? Why do they grow this particular cash crop and not something comestible? Grown in a single-crop economy and on a massive scale, cotton was commercially viable only insofar as the labor costs that went into producing it could be minimized. Following emancipation, this cost reduction took the form of an exploitative tenancy system, in which land was consolidated in the hands of large owners and farmers paid rent on the land they planted in shares of their harvested crop. While certain details in the film evoke this system, no landlords are present, nor is there any overt discourse contextualizing why and how the Johnsons work or explaining the stakes of their working or not working. The Johnsons simply labor contentedly, as if for the spectator's pleasure, even "dramatizing" work, to use Vidor's term, through song and dance—much like the characters in *Hearts in Dixie* (Fox, 1929).

With these unanswered questions in mind, it might be tempting to read *Hallelujah* strictly as a cinematic demonstration of Vidor's romantic racialist ideology of black hypervitality. Indeed, the film's critics to date have, as I show later, pursued this general line of argument. Consequently, I offer an alternative reading of *Hallelujah*, one that focuses on the subtle but decisive presence in the film of an alternative explanation of African American labor—and of its iconic setting, the cotton plantation. While a full historical outline of cotton tenancy is not possible here, it is necessary to highlight a few points that are integral to the alternative explanation that this chapter imagines.

Unable to accumulate the capital necessary to purchase supplies and equipment, the tenant had to rely on a system of furnish and credit. The landlord supplied the tenant with seed, tools, and animals at a cost that would be deducted from the tenant's payment upon settlement—the sale of the harvested cotton. Handling all of the bookkeeping themselves, landlords were able to ensure that tenants "came out either behind or barely even," acquiring inescapable debts in many cases.[8] Because the farmers themselves had no way of earning money until settlement, they had to rely on an equally unfair credit system to sustain their families, buying food from local commissaries or general stores—often run by the landlords—at exorbitant prices. Landlords could assure that tenants had to rely on these commissaries by putting them under contractual obligation to produce only cotton, leaving no room in the field even for a garden plot. For the roughly three million African American cotton tenants working around the time of the film, these conditions produced a state of quasi-slavery or peonage: permanent debt, limited access to courts, and Cotton Belt Jim Crow codes restricted their mobility, making them vulnerable to various kinds of social control and physical violence.[9]

While *Hallelujah* tends toward a mythic presentation of the plantation, it does so by repressing and displacing—that is to say, recognizing by other means—questions of ownership and alienation of labor, power and subjection. The violence of exchange remains hidden but not invisible; it takes the disguised forms of gaps and contradictions in the text. These moments of rupture and the paralogical attempts that the film makes to repair them illustrate *Hallelujah*'s ultimate failure to transform the alienated ground of the plantation into a place of homeliness—to refigure it as a domestic idyll. Interestingly, the memoir in which Vidor details his theory of "Negro" character already manifests this dialectic. Vidor offers a range of patronizing anecdotes regarding his interactions with African Americans in and around Memphis during the production of the film. These anecdotes are meant to be humorous sketches of picturesque, apparently simpleminded "characters"—somewhat like the film at certain points—such as a woman Vidor pays to help choreograph the river baptism scene who cannot tell her right hand from her left.[10] Yet these sketches pivot on questions of exchange, which Vidor handles somewhat anxiously, suggesting either that his "characters" have tried to manipulate him in exchange for more money or that he feels guilty about the bargains he has made. These sketches prove instructive for the reading of the film text, illustrating the distorting traces of the history of production that surround and ultimately mark it.

Racial Phantasmagoria

Two settings best illustrate the audiovisual grounding and enveloping of African American bodies in *Hallelujah*. Not accidentally, these are the two settings in which the religious "fervor" and sexual "drives" that preoccupy Vidor reach their most intense pitch in the film: the nighttime indoor religious worship spaces and the swamp through which Zeke (Daniel Haynes) fatefully chases Hot Shot (William Fountaine) and Chick (Nina Mae McKinney). In the sequences that unfold in these settings, Vidor and his collaborators have used expressionistic cinematographic, lighting, and sound-composition techniques to create a textured image and soundtrack, possessed of a "primitive" vitality. The techniques make these scenes identifiable as "phantasmagoriae," in the sense this term acquired in nineteenth-century English usage.

The phantasmagoria was a "magic lantern ghost show"—the term is a neologism meaning "phantasm assembly"—first mounted by Etienne Gaspard Robertson in Paris in 1799 and widely imitated in Europe and the United States during the nineteenth century. Robertson used a range of innovations in projection (rear projection on diaphanous screens, projections on smoke, a magic lantern mounted on a mobile cart, multiple lanterns, shadow projections) to create an atmosphere of gothic uncanniness, in which images of specters and skeletons materialized and seemed to move toward and away from the audience. Robertson's shows as well as those of several of his imitators often dramatized mythic and legendary scenes of ghostly apparition and played on period interest in communication with spirits (what would later give rise to the "séance").[11] Following the diffusion of this sort of show, the term came into use in literature and philosophy as a general description of any scene or array of figures that appeared to shift or change shape in a way that seemed enchanting, unreal, or gothic.[12] The two scenes from *Hallelujah* are phantasmagoriae in this sense, deriving from but not literally connected to the magic lantern show.

In the scene of Spunk's wake and (even more obviously) in the scene of the jubilee, *Hallelujah* uses high-contrast lighting to create an expressionist play of shadows on the walls of rooms in which an African American communal group has gathered (to mourn and to celebrate the end of a revival, respectively). The lighting in the wake scene doubles the figures of Pappy (Harry Gray) and the mourners beside him; an eye-level shot of the seated and kneeling figures captures their well-defined shadows on the cabin walls as they sway and raise their arms in supplication. The jubilee scene employs these strategies on a larger scale. The composition of a shot used repeatedly in the scene—a high-angle, extreme long shot of the congregation filling the small church—gives the top third of the frame to the blank expanse of the church walls, illuminated in bright pools by the harsh key light. As the only evident source of illumination in the shot, this light cuts across the seated figures at head-height and creates a chiaroscuro effect. When the singing begins in earnest and the worshippers rise, the walls become a kind of screen, reflecting the shadows of their swaying, clapping hands.

With the worshippers' repeated refrain giving continuity to the scene, the camera placements and angles become more extreme. A series of close-ups capture Zeke and Chick's passion (religious ecstasy spilling over into its sexual counterpart) as they face one another, as well as the disapproval of the other members of the Johnson family; hands and arms fill the frame; and an overhead shot captures the bodies of ecstatic individuals collapsed on the floor

Figure 12. The bodily doubling of religious worshippers through shadow in *Hallelujah* (MGM, 1929).

and Chick writhing in Zeke's arms. The soundtrack throughout this scene, dominated by the worshippers' refrain "I belong to that band" and punctuated by ecstatic shouts, typifies *Hallelujah*'s representation of African American religiosity.[13] Further, this singing, intense and layered as it is, provides continuity in the scene, allowing the filmmakers to use a range of camera angles and frequent cutting.

Sound is a diegetic element here that works, like the shadows on the wall, to situate the action of the scene in a stable enclosure. If the shadows double the bodies in the room, visually reinforcing their physical presence and fixating these figures in their interior surroundings, then sound has a comparable enveloping and grounding function here.[14] Sound helps to substantialize the image, giving it a certain vitality and nearly palpable presence. In my reading of this sequence, I agree with Alice Maurice's overall sense that sound and image work together in an unconventionally synchronized way. As Maurice suggests, sound gives a wholeness to the cinematic spectacle—of the sort many early observers thought the talking picture lacked—and it does this, paradoxically, by dispensing with the conventional "moving lips" standard of synchronization: "Once the crowd hysteria takes over [the jubilee sequence] does not feature sound emanating from people's mouths; rather, we hear music and other group sounds—like screaming and wailing—that are not tied to particular identifiable characters."[15]

I question, however, the apparently incompatible conclusions that Maurice draws from her reading of the scene. Maurice argues that this sequence establishes a seamless "marriage" of sound and image, using the preexisting "synesthesia" involved in the idea of the "black voice" (as something both heard and seen) to create an illusionistic sound cinema. At the same time, she stresses that the film progressively moves toward fragmenting the characters' bodies, reducing them to shadows and even "dematerializing" them. In this fashion, Maurice argues, *Hallelujah* creates a kind of "pure cinema" that highlights the ghostly nature of the film medium (the visual sign detached from its referent).[16] In my reading, the shadow is the persistent double of the body, not its replacement—a sign of the film's abiding attempt to link bodies with diegetic space (rather than with the apparatus itself, as Maurice suggests).[17] Hence, it becomes crucial to read the film's representational strategies as bearing the burden of bringing to life its racialist presuppositions. What seem like the most striking, dramatic enactments of *Hallelujah*'s primitivist ideology are always in a sense haunted, accompanied by shadows and ghostly presences of imaginary entities.

In a discussion of how sounds, as "material phenomena," can be used to strengthen the "impact of juxtaposed pictures" (as indexical traces of material phenomena), Siegfried Kracauer cites "asynchronism" as a creative departure from the norm of strict soundtrack-image synchronization. Kracauer highlights the "wonderful swamp sequence of King Vidor's *Hallelujah*" as an example of asynchronism, and the soundtrack-image relationship that he describes is a more extreme version of the one established in the jubilee scene. The swamp sequence, in which Zeke chases and finally strangles Hot Shot, "reverberates with confused sound patterns which impress upon the audience the invisible presence of life in the swamp."[18] The acoustic resonance of the "patterns" on the soundtrack actually imbue the setting with more "life" than can be seen; the image acquires a certain vitality and heightened physical "presence" by virtue of these "confused" sounds. Or, as Kracauer later puts it, this sound-composition strategy "summons the wider material environment from which [the soundtrack] issues."[19]

The swamp sequence has been shot using a very mobile silent film camera (it tracks and pans fluidly and constantly), with a subsequently recorded soundtrack synchronized to the image in postproduction.[20] Perhaps less "confused" than Kracauer remembered them, the "patterns" that make up the sequence's soundtrack consist of the sounds of water moving and splashing as the men stride through it, their labored breathing, and Hot Shot's gasps and groans. The film adorns this acoustic foundation with the occasional shrieks of unseen birds; these birds help conjure the "invisible presence of life in the swamp," while the underlying sounds provide a literal sense of reverberation.

Splashing water and heavy breathing are sounds that appear to echo around the chamber or enclosure that is the swamp. Human and natural sounds are literally harmonized here, in a way that suggests a deeper connection between the characters' bodies and their surroundings.

The channel of water through which the men wade is bordered by massive mangrove trees—"enormous pillars of deeper blackness," to use Eugene O'Neill's apt phrase—which sometimes create confining niches and always suggest a ceiling or canopy. Thus, the physical form of *Hallelujah*'s swamp recalls the island jungle of *The Emperor Jones*, the film as well as the dramatic setting that O'Neill conjured in his original script.[21] Zeke and Hot Shot find themselves enclosed in a "dark" interior. Night-for-night shooting and strong key lights create expressionistic, high-contrast effects, and the foliage often becomes an obstacle blocking the characters' movements—a fact highlighted by the frequent positioning of the camera in front of clusters of trunks that partially obscure their figures. One might say that Dudley Murphy's *The Emperor Jones* film borrows back from *Hallelujah* what Vidor himself borrowed from O'Neill. The descriptions of the swamp that Vidor articulated in his original shooting script clearly echo O'Neill's construction of the play's jungle, both in terms of the setting's physical features and in terms of the racial imagination inscribed therein.

Vidor imagined the swamp placed in earshot of the sawmill where Zeke works prior to this pivotal sequence. Thus, he wanted to use the sawmill's sounds expressionistically, altering them to evoke the changing mood of the scene. Obviously alluding to the soundscape of *The Emperor Jones*, Vidor wrote, "The steady rhythmic bappity-clunk of the sawmill becomes more and more like the beat of an African tom-tom."[22]

Further, Vidor wanted Slickum (as Hot Shot's character was initially called) to suffer the sort of atavistic "regression" to a "primitive" state that O'Neill's Jones does, likewise prompted by Slickum's desperate flight from a terrorizing pursuer. The tearing away of Slickum's/Hot Shot's sophisticated, urban attire thus makes visible his "primitivist" regression: "Invisible hands seem to reach out and rip his fancy clothing as Slickum reels through the briars—the black night seems to suck him down as he sprawls in pools of ooze—untold horrors snap out at him as he narrowly averts snakes and alligators. His veneer of civilization is stripped from him—he is the luckless savage hunted down by a ruthless force. He reverts to his African instincts—he yowls—he screams. He is surrounded by the spirits of the Voodoo as he plunges on with blind, heartbreaking despair."[23] In the shooting script, this savage regression also enthralls the pursuer, Zeke, as he succumbs to the "spirits of Voodoo" and the beat of the "tom-tom." Subsequent drafts of the screenplay simplified this sequence, draining it of many of its more fanciful elements and muting the clear allusions to O'Neill. As constructed in the eventual film, the sequence both clearly shows the traces of its original conception—in the tearing of Hot Shot's clothes and the emphasis on the enveloping "blackness" of night and the swamp's "ooze"—and avoids the kinds of imagery (the alligator) and spirit-play that Murphy uses in his later film.

Although *Hallelujah* stops short of *The Emperor Jones*'s "camera obscura," where "the spirits of Voodoo" come to life through superimposed images and where the character himself becomes a spectator to projected images, it remains faithful to the basic construction of a "dark" or "black" interior that originates with O'Neill. Physical space and human physiology merge—whether in the tom-tom beat that mimics Jones's agitated pulse, or in the breathing and displacement of water that mark Zeke's and Hot Shot's steps. Moreover, sound acts as the medium of this fusion in *Hallelujah*, making audible but also, quite strikingly, visible for the film's viewers an otherwise invisible "life" or vital "force"—the regressive-primitive energy that breaks through civilizing "veneers" to establish the reign of the corporeal ("African instincts"). The jungle/swamp interior enacts the reversal of "race history" in the form of the revelation of the characters' excessive, inescapable embodiment.

In these late sequences, where the very "fervor" and "drives" that the film otherwise indulges become unbound and destructive, *Hallelujah* seeks a total manifestation—visible and audible—of its invisible notions about essential "Negro" character. It stakes this manifestation, interestingly, on a range of striking expressionistic aesthetic strategies, which serve to give an obviously phantasmagoric quality to these sequences. The hyperdiegeticization of black characters unfolds in a spectral theater born out of the recesses of white fantasy.

Having made the connection, however, between expressionism, phantasmagoria, and racial fantasy, I want to turn this line of analysis on the rest of the film—with its comparable realism of style and evident lack of spectral or gothic qualities. I want to apply the term "phantasmagoria" to the more prosaic scenes of labor and song and to the seemingly conventional, linear narrative of the film. By applying this term against the grain—translating it from the discussion of one set of features in the film to another with which it would seem to have little in common—it becomes possible to see how the film tends, throughout, toward the phantasmagoric, if in a slightly more complex sense. As theorized by Adorno, phantasmagoria is an aesthetic strategy that aims at "[the] occultation of production by means of the outward appearance of the product"; insofar as this strategy succeeds, it conveys "the illusion of the absolute reality of the unreal."[24]

Adorno's definition draws on Karl Marx's famous account of the "fetishism" of the commodity in volume 1 of *Capital*: "the commodity-form, and the value-relation of the products of labour within which it appears, have absolutely no connection with the physical nature of the commodity and the material relations arising out of this. It is nothing but the definite social relation between men themselves which assumes here, for them, the fantastic form of a relation between things."[25] "Phantasmagoria"—the popular nineteenth-century "magic lantern ghost show" with which Marx was no doubt familiar—is the critical term through which he names the imaginary but binding relationship "between things" that the commodity form creates. In associating phantasmagoria with the total mystification of labor and the making real of the unreal, Adorno stresses one aspect of Marx's use of the term "phantasmagoric." Yet Marx's word choice also suggests that to call the commodity form phantasmagoric is to look slightly askew at this all-too-familiar "thing," to conjure up the occulted "social relation of people" in the form of spectral-theatrical presences—the thing's uncanny dimension, in other words. Phantasmagoric vision thus insists on the ghosts that are produced in and through the mechanism of reification and on the uncanny "independence" of its products.

This chapter adopts such a double, phantasmagoric vision of *Hallelujah*, moving from the obvious instances of phantasmagoria—the sequences whose use of expressionistic lighting and sound recall this "magical" optical device—to the more subtle instances that the Marxian, materialist usage of this term allows us to see. In this second set of examples, the insistence on seeing phantasmagorically allows us to trace the film's occultation of labor (of social relations of production) up to its limit point, where the ghosts of reification begin to emerge. At this limit point, the more prosaic and "realistic" sections of the film start to look surprisingly similar to the expressionistic jubilee and swamp sequences. The film's illusion of coherence in these sections also depends on complex aesthetic constructions of black immobility.

Uncanny Apparitions

Hallelujah's narrative traces a circle: the concluding shot of the film shows the Johnson family, numbering all eight members, walking away from the camera and toward their cabin, shouldering bags of newly picked cotton. Prior to this concluding shot, the eldest son, Zeke, having been imprisoned for killing Hot Shot in the swamp, is released and journeys back home, receiving a warm welcome from the rest of the family. Upon his arrival, Zeke declares his intention to marry Missy Rose (Victoria Spivey), his adoptive sister, thus fulfilling his mother's original plan. The film tips the viewer off to this plan in an exchange between Missy Rose and Zeke early in the film. Missy Rose chides Zeke, "Why who'd marry you?" To which Zeke responds, "Why you would. What does you think Mammy adopted you for, except so's you could marry me."

By reinforcing this endogamous relationship, the film attempts to close the narrative circle in a very literal way. Not only is the Johnson family restored to its first locale—the family lives away from the cabin during the middle section of the film—but it also seals itself off against the outside world, which has repeatedly threatened its well-being. The family, it seems, will now perpetuate

Figure 13. The Johnsons walk back to their cabin at the end of *Hallelujah* (MGM, 1929).

itself in the same place and through the same members who originally constitute it. By killing off Zeke's temptress, Chick, the film negates at once the possibility of a nonfamilial romantic object and the lure of the city. This final tableau powerfully renders the film's major ideological dynamics. The penumbra that surrounds the cabin signifies the absolute "homeliness" of this locale; the walk up the path through the cotton field underscores the failure of all attempts by the film's characters to migrate elsewhere; and the use of the harvest season to begin and end the film establishes a circular temporality and gives a "natural" charge to the characters' reunion.

This thematic circularity has a very clear formal counterpart. This scene of return is, in fact, identical to a shot that features in *Hallelujah*'s opening sequence. What tips us off to the fact that it is the self-same piece of film is that it too perfectly restores the family to its original state. While this shot includes all eight family members, the next-to-oldest son, Spunk (Everett McGarrity), actually has been killed earlier in the film—just after the first appearance of this shot. The mechanical reproducibility of film enables an absolute restoration of the domestic space; the tableau of the family walking back to the cabin can be staged and shot one time and then duplicated. But in its second appearance, the tableau becomes a haunted one. Reanimated, the deceased son continues to walk among the living.

This ghostly image is uncanny in the strict Freudian sense. It is at once familiar and startling, such that it folds together these normally opposite phenomenological experiences. We have seen the image before, but here it appears out of place, nonsensical. It is an image of the familiar—of "homeliness" (*heimlichkeit*)—yet it brings "to light" what "ought to have remained . . . secret and hidden"—recalling the film's most traumatic image, that of Spunk lying dead. Just as, in Freud's account, what "belong[s] to the house" implies "something withdrawn from the eyes of strangers," this homely tableau gives a glimpse of what should be concealed.[26] More than a mere mistake on the part of the film's editor, this uncanny repetition of shots is a symptom of *Hallelujah*'s failed attempt at narrative closure. Because narrative closure is the formal strategy the film uses to dramatize black self-isolation and endurance, this failure carries significant consequences for our understanding of the film's ideological project.

But what is it about the episode of Spunk's death that would warrant this kind of treatment, this diegetic forgetting, wherein the film rewrites its own plot and brings a character momentarily back to life? To understand the narrative significance of Spunk's death, it is necessary to refer to another crucial Freudian concept: overdetermination. This moment in the text is "a nodal point or junction" that "derives" from more than one motivation: when this moment occurs, it already has begun to perform multiple kinds of figurative work.[27] Spunk dies because Zeke accidentally shoots him after having lost the money that he earned from selling the family's cotton crop. As the film illustrates in its opening sequence, Zeke's job is to gin and sell the cotton in town, before buying essential items for his parents and siblings: a "nice shirt," pants, a dress, a fancy hat, spectacles. Instead, he encounters *femme fatale* Chick, who persuades him to gamble with the money. She wants him to augment the sum, $100, so that they can spend part of it on their own amusement. Chick promptly steers Zeke toward her partner in crime and boyfriend, Hot Shot, who wins the full amount at craps, rolling loaded dice. Enraged, Zeke pulls a knife on Hot Shot, who, in turn, brandishes a pistol. Having scoured the empty streets looking for Zeke, Spunk enters the crowded cabaret in the midst of the melee. In the struggle, the gun is discharged, hitting Spunk, who dies agonizingly in his brother's arms.[28]

This sequence concludes with a double tragedy. Not only has Zeke squandered the family's money—the product of a season's worth of work—but he has also brought his brother home dead. In one striking but extremely brief shot, the film ties these two consequences together. We get a glimpse from Pappy's point of view of Spunk's dead body in the back of the wagon; the body occupies the same place where the cotton was piled upon Spunk and Zeke's departure. This substitution is significant because it illustrates Zeke's failure to substitute crop for commodities in the way he was instructed. By staging Zeke's recital of

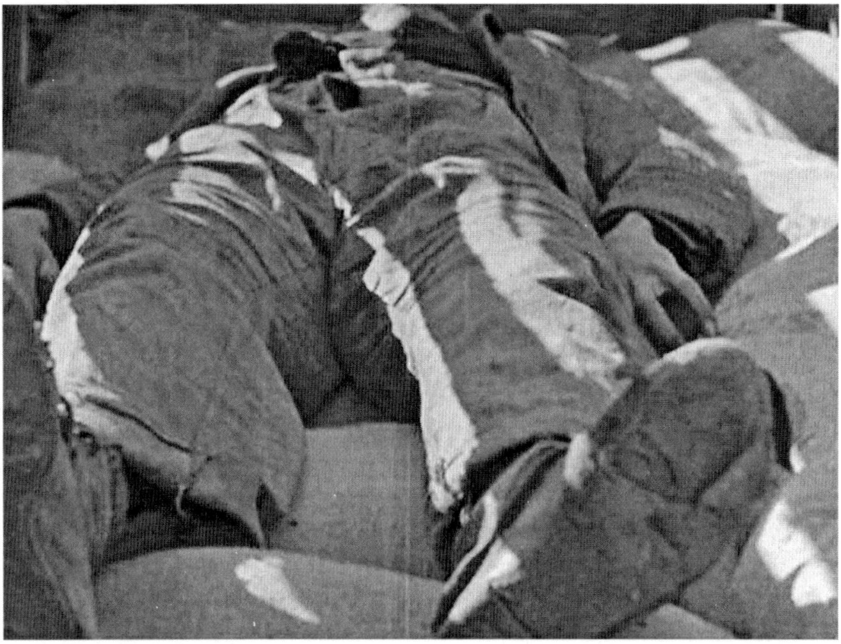

Figure 14. A quick glimpse of Spunk (Everett McGarrity), lying dead in the wagon in *Hallelujah* (MGM, 1929).

the shopping list in the cotton field, the film earlier has allied the bright bolls of cotton that surround the shabbily dressed Johnson family members with the new clothes that they desire. The laborers hold in hand what will eventually replace their tattered clothes—not literally, by being spun into thread and woven into cloth, but symbolically, through the magic, or "transubstantiation," of exchange-value.[29] As if the film does not want us to look upon it for too long, it flashes up the image of Spunk's body ever so briefly; the ragged clothing that dominates the shot makes this another unhomely visual trace.

Telling Not Showing

This remarkable shot notwithstanding, the film, as it unfolds, will consider only the affective and moral consequences of Spunk's death: his death as a cause of deep grief among the family and as a sign of Zeke's irresponsibility and transgression. Overshadowed by the more dramatically interesting scenario of communal mourning and individual repentance, the issue of the family's economic well-being will first drop out of view and then be resolved suddenly and as if by magic. I have described the "issue" of the Johnson family's economic well-being in a deliberately vague way. It is not a question of whether or not the Johnsons will survive, but of whether or not their labor will translate into newer and better material possessions, hence my phrase "economic well-being." (I return later to this mystified treatment of the economic question, which, I argue, is symptomatic of how *Hallelujah* figures the cotton plantation.) Joined by neighbors and friends, the Johnson family mourns Spunk—a process that the film renders through a series of striking musical and gestural tableaux, lit and shot in the expressionist visual style discussed above.

During this sequence, the despondent Zeke remains outside of the cabin, lying face-down at the edge of the cotton field. Pappy, who is also the local parson, comes to console him. Pappy looks up at the sky and professes to see an angel, descending in a "snow-white chariot," wearing "snow-white robes." The viewer catches a glimpse of the luxuriant whiteness Pappy describes in a pair of shots of billowing clouds. The "snow-white chariot" suggests a magnified, surreal version of Zeke and Spunk's cotton-filled wagon. Suddenly inspired, Zeke emerges from his stupor and begins to preach. On his feet, gesturing and intoning charismatically, Zeke picks up the thread of his father's meditation. Zeke quickly draws a crowd. Rapt listeners stream out of the cabin, while others pour into the yard from more distant locations. The film cuts to a series of facial close-ups of the people who have climbed the fence to stand before Zeke. Their transfixed stares during the extempore sermon offer visual proof that the parson's son has discovered his ministerial vocation. Zeke leads his congregation in song, before the film cuts, quite suddenly, to an intertitle: "And Zekiel became a preacher."

Just as he has plunged the family into utter destitution, by squandering the cotton money, Zeke delivers it, single-handedly, from its economic worries. This time the substitution of tattered clothes for fine ones does occur, instantaneously and almost by magic. Following the intertitle, the Johnsons reappear wearing new suits and dresses; only the laconic, less-than-revealing text links these two disparate states of affairs. It is as if Spunk's death inspires Zeke with the spiritual and oratorical raw materials he needs to go into a new business. The intertitle marks the absence of the intervening process of production, compensation, and exchange—a narrative "fault line." It further allows the film to assert the family's comfortable existence via an authoritative, but disembodied, narrative voice—speaking, no less, through a vestigial silent-film device. Following the concrete and visceral cinematic event of Spunk's murder, communal mourning shifts Hallelujah onto a different narrative track from the one on which it commences.

I use this metaphor purposely to evoke the film's use of the railroad to put its narrative in motion again. The family's home is now a set of train cars; the cabin and surrounding cotton field have, for the time being, been left behind. Focusing on Zeke's use of train imagery in his sermon and the ensuing revival, Paula Massood has argued that *Hallelujah* uses trains as symbols of otherworldly redemption, rather than of the this-worldly "promised land" of the northern city. Yet I would argue that the appearance of this train in the mise-en-scène, which ferries the newly prosperous Johnsons into town, complicates this point slightly. Here trains are an agent of geographical and social mobility for the characters.[30]

The episode of Spunk's death is overdetermined because it enables this complicated narrative relay. Through its placement in the back of the wagon, Spunk's rag-shrouded corpse is metonymically linked to the crop and to the trauma of financial loss. At the same time, the magnitude of his loss allows the film to begin to shift focus from this more complex, historically fraught financial crisis to matters of private feeling. Thus, Spunk's death participates in the work of forgetting that leads to the restoration of the familial idyll at the end of the film, even before the fratricide is itself forgotten. What makes the ultimate forgetting of Spunk's death and the loss of the crop possible is the massive narrative shift signaled by "And Zekiel became a preacher." I have repeatedly stressed the significance of "the economic" or "financial question." But why is this issue so significant that it would require this complex, ambivalent response in the text—conjured in the displaced form of Spunk's body but just as quickly cancelled out by the film's narrator-system? To answer this question, we need to take one step further back in our reading, all the way to *Hallelujah*'s opening sequence.

An Effort to Picturize Conditions

Hallelujah's opening montage consists of panoramas and close-up shots of African American laborers picking cotton in a vast field and carrying and emptying filled sacks and baskets. From the final shot of the montage, the film cuts to a shot that establishes the Johnsons in what looks to be a smaller cotton field, bordered by trees. The "economic question" toward which this chapter has been gesturing depends wholly on what we believe the Johnsons' financial status to be. Clearly this opening sequence raises more questions than it answers in its strategy of locating the Johnsons in social and spatio-temporal terms. Do they own their land and thus the crops that they grow on it? Or are they tenant farmers, renting their plot of land in exchange for a share of their crop? Have they bought supplies, seed, or other staples on credit? These questions become particularly pressing once Zeke loses the crop money. Depending on the Johnsons' status, that episode might carry additional ramifications. What will happen to them now? Will they be able to support themselves? Will they be in debt or punished for failing to fulfill their obligations? Will they be kicked off their land or face legal or extralegal retribution from creditors or lien holders?[31]

While the family's tattered clothing in the opening scene highlights the urgent necessity of new pants and dresses, the scene glosses over other, equally pressing needs. We might single out *nourishment* in particular. If the family depends on a single, seasonally harvested crop for its income, then other provisions should factor into its purchases. Why do foodstuffs not make it onto Zeke's shopping list? Are we to believe that Zeke will exhaust the money from the sale of the things that he enumerates on his list? If not, what else will he buy in town with the $100?[32] Even as this question remains crucially pending, the family eats its dinner, in the next scene, off of what appears to be fine china. This surprising detail of mise-en-scène very nicely crystallizes the material paradox in which *Hallelujah*'s narrative of economic aspiration is caught at the outset. The dishes hide, as it were, in plain sight the question of where the food that they contain comes from, while the unexpected bit of finery reassures the viewer of the Johnsons' security by bringing fine commodities into the family's apparent purview. It is the family's hope for better goods, but not their physical survival, that Zeke must guarantee.

As to the issue of the Johnsons' economic independence, it is helpful to consider a phrase that appears in an illustrated promotional pamphlet that the MGM studio sold at theaters during the film's initial release. The booklet's initial synopsis of *Hallelujah* identifies the film's setting as "the little Johnson plantation," a chimerical construction that succinctly demonstrates how the film intends the spectator to understand the Johnsons' situation.[33] "The little Johnson plantation" turns the paradigmatic site of historical white ownership, enslavement, and exploitation into the proprietary locale of poor African American farmers themselves. Having excluded white authority figures from the scenario, the film can reinvent the plantation as a mythic space of quaint subsistence. As W.E.B. Du Bois pointed out in his review of the film in *The Crisis*, "white folk are carefully omitted [from the film], although it strains the imagination to see a cotton gin or convict gang without a swaggering white boss."[34] The viewer's imagination is also put to the test in trying to discern the relationship between the main characters and the large groups of cotton pickers that appear in the opening shots.

Hallelujah cuts directly from the shots of large-group labor to the first scene of the Johnson family by themselves in a smaller field. The film does nothing else to locate the second space in relation to the first, or to posit a definite connection between the two groups. Are we to assume that the family is a subgroup of the larger one, engaged in the same tasks? If so, why do the Johnsons carry the large baskets of cotton back to their cabin and take the crop to market themselves? This transition joining the two sets of shots signals an important diegetic "fault line."

Hallelujah's field scenes were shot on location at a massive cotton plantation in Wilson, Arkansas, a town named for its "owner," Robert E. Lee Wilson, who ran some of the largest farms in the South (in addition to railroads,

Figure 15. Plantation workers in Wilson, Arkansas, line up to weigh the cotton that they have picked in the opening montage of *Hallelujah* (MGM, 1929).

banks, and general stores). The individuals in the shots are African American cotton-croppers—probably wage-workers and tenants both—employed by Wilson. In order to shoot these and other locations, the film's cast and crew traveled by train from New York to Memphis and surrounding locales in the Mississippi valley. In the shots taken on the Wilson plantation, the dozens of anonymous pickers line up to have their cotton weighed, before it is dumped into a single wagon. The balance upon which each worker hangs his or her canvas bag is a decisive marker of tenant farming or day labor. It belongs to a specific bookkeeping practice, where an overseer measures and records each picker's daily production for the final settlement (in the case of tenants) or the payment of wages (in the case of day workers).[35] That we catch a brief glimpse of this measuring device serves definitively to introduce the historical subject of share-cropping into the film; yet its presence does not, by itself, clarify the issue of the Johnsons' relationship to their land and crop, the relationship between the film's cotton fields being so indeterminate. Because of the remarkable cinematic afterlife of these cotton-field shots, it is even possible to conceive of another strategy for locating fictional characters in relation to the Wilson plantation workers, thus bringing *Hallelujah*'s (dis-)locating strategy into relief.

Figure 16. Production still showing King Vidor, the crew of *Hallelujah* (MGM, 1929), and field-workers shooting on location in Wilson, Arkansas. Courtesy of the Academy of Motion Picture Arts and Sciences.

Several of the shots that comprise *Hallelujah*'s opening montage reappear at the beginning of *Cabin in the Cotton* (Warner Bros., 1932), a film that, as its "Foreword" informs the viewer, is "concerned with an effort to picturize [the] conditions" of landlord-tenant relations on southern cotton farms. In order to "picturize" these conditions, *Cabin in the Cotton* turns to *Hallelujah*. First, *Cabin in the Cotton* borrows *Hallelujah*'s field and cotton gin footage as the backdrop for the scrolling text of the "Foreword." The earlier footage reappears in *Cabin in the Cotton* initially as visual evidence for that film's claims about the impoverishment of share-croppers, unfair credit practices, and the problems of the one-crop system. Second, *Cabin in the Cotton* goes on to use one of the group panoramas in a process shot, which represents this film's only scene of actual cotton picking. The image from *Hallelujah* has been projected onto a screen at the back of the set, while the actors who play the principal tenant characters mimic picking cotton in the foreground. If *Hallelujah*'s editing spatially removes the Johnson family from the Wilson plantation setting, then *Cabin in the Cotton*'s kinetic mise-en-scène seeks to collapse this distance. The film strains to include its characters in the same physical setting. It adds an imaginary foreground to that setting, where professional actors mirror the actions of twice-filmed "extras."[36]

Swaggering White Bosses

Since Du Bois, *Hallelujah*'s critics have chosen, by and large, to accept the film's construction of "the little Johnson plantation" at face value, setting aside the incongruities that it contains, while condemning the film for its mythic tendencies. At the most basic level of synopsis, critics have tended to characterize the Johnsons in general terms. They are "a poor black family," "poor farmers," or "Southern, rural . . . blacks," who work "in the cotton fields."[37] The lack of concrete determination becomes evidence, in the quotation from Arthur Knight's *Disintegrating the Musical*, of the film's ideological project. Knight suggests that, by naturalizing black labor and presenting a pseudo-organic ("timeless") link between bodies and the land, *Hallelujah*, like other black-cast Hollywood musicals, situates African Americans outside of history and in the realm of myth. While this suggestion is understandable, it dispenses too quickly with the analytical problem posed by the opening scenes. Such a hasty move risks reducing *Hallelujah*'s strange, disorienting cotton fields to "the cotton field" in the sense of a stereotyped, all-too-familiar symbolic locale, an example of what Knight calls the "white controlled and concocted . . . institutional settings" of the rural-folk "cycle" of black-cast musicals.[38]

Here Knight echoes the boldest and most interesting reading of *Hallelujah* to date, that of James Snead, who, using a striking analogy to Faulkner, indicts the film for its mystification of social history:

> One of the prime codes surrounding blacks on screen, then—one much at variance with the narrative codes that mandate potential mobility for other screen characters—is an almost metaphysical stasis. The black—particularly the black woman—is seen as eternal, unchanging, unchangeable. (Recall Faulkner's appendix to *The Sound and the Fury*: "They endured.") The code of stasis arises in order to justify blacks' continuing economic disadvantage. Throughout the history of Hollywood cinema, in films from King Vidor's 1929 *Hallelujah!* through Steven Spielberg's 1985 *The Color Purple*, blacks' character is sealed off from the history into which whites have trapped them. . . . The only explanation can be an enduring "black nature" that no historical tragedy or intervention has ever or could ever have been responsible for.[39]

Snead's argument takes Du Bois's wry observation about the implications of a fantastical, all-black agricultural economy to its logical extreme. In his view, the film simply seals off black characters in a permanent state of economic weakness—as a matter of natural law.

Although Snead's treatment of *Hallelujah* is limited to this general comment, it bears certain similarities to the discussion of the film's circular narrative offered above. Indeed, Snead's notion of endurance is helpful in articulating the film's prevailing ideological project: to render the family as a self-enclosed and -sustaining unit, organically rooted in the rural space.[40] That said, it is crucial to highlight how such an ideological project fails to produce a coherent dramatic image—to highlight the network of traces that interfere with the film's movement toward closure. Not only does the heretofore dominant critical approach give too much credit to the film's powers of mystification, but it also produces readings that simplify the film, setting aside its most interesting representational subtleties. I stress this second tendency because *Hallelujah*'s multiple narrative impasses and magical detours have gone totally uncommented on in extant critical writing on the film; it is as if such formal features have been invisible or at least illegible.

Hallelujah's opening scene in the cotton field is a case in point of the need for readings that more closely describe the film's material structures and less readily force it to conform to familiar templates. In the opening shots of group labor, a row of African American agricultural workers in a vast field pick cotton by hand, bending over to reach the bolls and depositing the locks in long sacks worn about the neck. They sing as they work, or, more precisely, they appear to sing. An offscreen choir actually performs a medley of songs, including the first verse of Stephen Foster's "Old Folks at Home." The film expects the spectator to forget about the spatial disparity between the scenes of vocal and pictorial production, accepting that the workers are the ones who sing, despite visual evidence to the contrary.

Contemporary commentators Knight and Richard Barrios have aptly noted the incongruity between the ambience of the Foster song and the difficult labor of cotton picking. In making this observation, however, they accept the phantom vocal production as actual, identifying the laborers themselves as the singers. Papering over the significant diegetic "fault line" of asynchronism, critics have helped complete the phantasmagoria in this sequence. Discussing the musical selections in *Hallelujah*, Barrios describes "an early shot of cotton-pickers *singing* 'Old Folks at Home.'"[41] In order to condemn this opening scene as a "painful" instance of racial stereotype, Barrios revises what is seen and heard in it, completing the work of synchronization for the film. Knight echoes Barrios in a caption he includes next to a frame enlargement from the cotton-field montage; the caption reads: "The black community singing and laboring in the opening of *Hallelujah*." Making a similar argument about the inappropriateness of the song, Knight states that it is the Johnson family who "performs" the Foster tune.[42]

The technical challenge of unifying sound and image in *Hallelujah*'s cotton-field montage is intimately linked to the film's ideological project. Not simply a matter of formal illusion, cinematic synchronization is the figurative vehicle through which the film attempts to generate a semblance of *thematic* unity between what is seen and what is heard. *Hallelujah* uses the aural to prepare the image to be interpreted; the sentimental tonality of a song like "Old Folks at Home" inflects the way in which the spectator receives the visual signifiers, preparing him or her to attribute certain symbolic connotations to the image. "Old Folks at Home" is one of Stephen Foster's "Plantation Melodies" (published in the 1840s); in it, the singer, a stock persona from the antebellum blackface minstrel show, finds himself estranged from the plantation, longing for return and reunion with his familiars.[43] The desire of the lyric "I" to return to "the old plantation" conjures the kind of homeliness that the film, as I have argued, tries to associate with the Johnsons' cabin in the cotton.

To keep open the gap between voice and image in my account of the film's opening sequence is to remain mindful of the alternative vision of "the plantation" that the film includes in the opening shots and thus to name these phantasmagoriae as such. After directing the film's chorus, the African American composer Eva Jessye wrote a remarkable series of five articles for the *Baltimore Afro-American*, which ran during the summer of 1930 and detailed *Hallelujah*'s production.[44] In the third installment of "The Truth About 'Hallelujah,'" Jessye describes the cast and crew's arrival in Wilson, Arkansas, focusing on the socioeconomic dynamics of the plantation and surrounding town and noting the discomfort experienced by many of the African American members of the cast and creative team—some of whom were traveling through the South for the first time:

> For the off shots in the opening scene of "Hallelujah" we went to Wilson, Arkansas, a little town that we were told is owned and run by a white man after whom the town is named. The scenes were taken in a field belonging to Wilson, who, it was said, owns some 20,000 acres of cotton and conducts experiments to improve the grade of cotton on an immense scale.
>
> One did not have to stay in Wilson long to know the relationship between the whites and Negroes in the little one-man town. Many of the residents turned out to see the making of the picture, and the whites congregated along the edge of the field behind the cameras. . . . As for the New York delegation [the film's African American actors, singers, and musicians], they went quietly about their business, paying no attention whatever to the onlookers, for they realized that one word or glance could have precipitated serious trouble.
>
> One colored man drove up in a fine automobile and was introduced to the group. It developed that he "stood in" with the boss of the town, to be exact, it was said that he had the one "joint" run for Negroes in the community. Needless to say, it was owned by the white man, who, rumor had it, paid his cotton pickers twenty-five cents more on the hundred [lbs. picked] than others. There was method in his madness for he promptly got it back in the long run through the amusement place.

> The Negro proudly displayed for our admiring gaze a gold pencil studded with diamonds, which he stated cost $350. His watch, specially made, had the hours marked with diamonds and cost $1,250. We noted no such prosperity among the other Negro inhabitants.[45]

In another anecdote, Jessye recalls the cast's earlier experience of shooting the cotton gin scene on a farm in Mississippi. The "notoriously hard-boiled white man" who ran the farm objected to King Vidor's "calm" and "solicitou[s]" treatment of his actors and became enraged, insulting Daniel Haynes and Everett McGarrity (the actors who played Zeke and Spunk, respectively) with racial epithets.[46] Here is Du Bois's "swaggering white [cotton gin] boss," never appearing in the film frame, but standing behind the camera during production, attempting to interpellate the film's cast of black New Yorkers into the same Jim Crow social position occupied by the plantation workers.

The black nightclub manager that Jessye describes appears to feature in a couple of the trove of production stills (many of them really preproduction research photographs) from *Hallelujah* preserved in the Margaret Herrick Library's Core Collection. An African American man in a three-piece suit (one quite different from the sport suits worn by the California-based production staff) and driving gloves stands atop the platform used for shooting the cotton-field scenes, gesturing and speaking authoritatively to the either exhausted or bored black "extras" clustered around him. The narrative that Jessye offers about this individual provides a glimpse into the larger economic machinery of cotton tenancy, resonating in an interesting way with the film's own cabaret scene (in which Zeke gambles away the crop money).

In light of Jessye's comments, this money, the too-tidy sum of $100, can be seen in a different light. This vague economic placeholder is reflective of the film's phantasmagoric strategy (in the Marxian-Adornian sense). It allows the film to depict one kind of exchange process (the farming of cotton on shares) as another (the simple exchange of the Johnsons' labor for cash, then a set of commodities). Lest it seem as though I am holding the film to an artificial standard of logical consistency, note that, in his original shooting script, Vidor clearly began to consider the questions that I pose here.

In constructing the cotton gin scene, Vidor begins to leave the racial fantasy realm he has constructed for his characters in order to recognize that cotton-cropping involves particular modes of exchange and relations of production. Striking an expert's pose, he offers some intriguing, if nebulous comments on the process of ginning and sale: "The cost of the ginning is usually met by the by-product of cotton seed which the gin keeps in payment." And he crafts a dialogue between Zeke, Spunk, and a "broker" of unspecified race (could this be Du Bois's "swaggering white boss"?), in which the men briefly haggle over price, bandying around seemingly random two-digit figures (dollar values?).

Figure 17. Production still from *Hallelujah* (MGM, 1929) evidently showing the night-club manager described by Eva Jessye in her "The Truth About *Hallelujah* Series." Courtesy of the Academy of Motion Picture Arts and Sciences.

Yet Vidor also notes in the script that the "detail of buying and selling the cotton [will have] to be determined by actual process on location."[47] Through subsequent drafts and in the eventual film, however, this scene becomes shorter and less detailed (there is no mention of any two-digit figures) and altogether eliminates the "broker."

The film's abandonment of Vidor's proposed research project is striking and suggests that the "actual process" Vidor observed on location proved incompatible with his romantic racialist conceptions or with his sense of what he might be able to represent in a Hollywood studio. In the film, instead of negotiating price, Zeke sings a song with a group of itinerant musicians, while Spunk transfers the cotton into the gin. Thus, the strains of Irving Berlin's "Waiting at the End of the Road"—whose lyrics actually contain romantic images of white cotton fields—even substitute for the sound of the gin machinery, and a montage of black laborers acquires the same ostensibly pleasing aesthetic charge that the opening "Old Folks at Home" sequence carries.

All of this further illustrates why Spunk's death, the narrative event that registers and also makes it possible to forget Zeke's loss of the money, is overdetermined. Instigated by his attraction to Chick, Zeke's folly may be the result of the sexual "drives" that the film both romanticizes and shows to be disruptive. But if the film allows Zeke's religious "fervor" initially to offset this excessive sexual desire and keep the character on a continuum of "primitive" vitality, then his economic success as a preacher highlights the threat of *too much* stasis in the film. Spunk's dead body raises the specter of the material underpinnings of cotton tenancy, requiring that the film use a kind of *deus ex machina* to keep the plot moving forward. In the reconstructed domestic idyll that closes the film, the phantasmagoria of this plot device becomes apparent, insofar as Spunk is visible as a ghost (as the unreal made real, a visual sign without a referent).

Interestingly, the same sort of magical plot-advancing device is required after Zeke kills Hot Shot (another effect of his supposedly unbounded sexual desire). Zeke is imprisoned, and *Hallelujah* includes a brief scene of him breaking rocks on a chain gang. Then, all of the sudden, an intertitle appears declaring "Probation." We then see Zeke traveling home via train and on foot, leading to the Johnson family reunion and the walk back to the warm glow of the cabin. Once again, the excessive outpouring of "Negro" vitality—rendered through expressionistic phantasmagoria—creates a situation of social stasis or entrapment that is sufficiently extreme that it must be canceled out through a more subtle form of phantasmagoric representation: the magic plot device of the intertitle that restores the family. One could draw a parallel between the consequences of Zeke being imprisoned for murder as an African American man in the South and the consequences of the family's loss of money from the sale of the crop. In both cases, the film chooses to ignore these consequences and restore the kind of blithe, romantic racialist tone that pervades the film; it is not by chance that Du Bois highlighted the phantom presence of the "swaggering white boss" around the two scenes of cotton ginning and the chain gang, specifically.[48]

Thus, there is a crucial way in which Zeke returns to the cabin, like Spunk, as a ghost, making an impossible/unreal walk with the rest of his family. He has been subjected to a kind of figurative death, a social death perhaps, from which he should not, logically, be able to return—or at least not in a way that would restore him to full presence in the family circle. The viewer wonders what precisely "probation" could mean in this context. Through the machinations of racial fantasy (Zeke's regression to primitive savagery in the swamp), the film places its protagonist in a situation of immobility that threatens to break the envelope of the racially exclusive diegesis, to raise issues of social and legal power and subjection.

That the film finally chooses the fully restored family unit—locked in a repeating cycle of "natural" endurance and continuity—highlights its investment in the myth of stasis that Snead so eloquently describes. Yet this circular narrative, a paradigmatic structure of black diegetic grounding and enclosure within the archive of "Negro talking pictures," is not undisturbed or seamless. The ghosts of Spunk and Zeke haunt this idyllic space, reading as uncanny or unhomely traces distorting the homely scene. What Adorno calls the "illusion of the . . . reality of the unreal" thus does not become "absolute"; the phantasmagoria at work here remains legible in its authentic sense as haunted.

In a remarkable moment in the archive of *Hallelujah*'s initial reception, one of the film's earliest African American critics insisted on resisting the film's passage into hopeless phantasmagoria. His response throws into relief the ideological stakes of the film's representation of African American vitality and work.[49] In his extended account of *Hallelujah*'s premier at the Lafayette Theater in Harlem, Romeo Dougherty, dramatic editor of the *New York Amsterdam News*, describes African American audience members focusing on individual scenes in a way that detaches those scenes from the film's general mood and narrative trajectory, highlighting their affective complexity and celebrating the subtle performances of the actors Daniel Haynes and Fanny Belle DeKnight (who plays Mammy).

Dougherty suggests that he and other viewers in the Lafayette have observed Haynes's performance as Zeke with a kind of double vision, noting the film's attempt to give an aura of mirth to the sale of the cotton, while also claiming that another tonality is visible in the scene: "Despite the happy vein in which Zeke rolled his cotton bales for which he drew the magnificent sum of one hundred dollars we saw the tragedy that still exists to a great extent in certain sections of the South—that tragedy of the toil of black men and women making rich their overlords." Zeke's work is not a simple manifestation of intrinsic "vitality," but registers, for this African American audience, as undercompensated "toil." By making reference to the struggle between tenants and "overlords," Dougherty's *Hallelujah* works on a second melodramatic register—beyond *Hallelujah*'s overt treatment of Zeke's sexual temptation, religious conversion, and crime of passion—raising moral questions about economic exploitation. Anticipating the materialist language of *Cabin in the Cotton*'s "Foreword"—itself a textual commentary on *Hallelujah*'s cotton-field scenes—Dougherty alludes broadly to "those conditions depicted on screen," which Zeke's plight illustrates; thus, Dougherty asserts the visibility of the economic register in the film and identifies this depiction as the focal point of his fellow audience-members' engagement with the film.[50]

For the African American audience for whom Dougherty speaks, this second "tragedy" more powerfully defines the experience of watching the film. Dougherty claims that a complex, layered tableau like this one provokes tears among many viewers gathered in the Lafayette. These tears, Dougherty suggests, were invisible to the white journalists in attendance at the Harlem premier, who noted, in their comments on black audience response, only hilarious laughter. Employing a "reprint strategy" with a venerable history in African American cinema journalism, Dougherty has included one of these white accounts, James Gow's *New York World* piece, on his own entertainment page.[51]

According to Gow's account, the Lafayette audience responds to the film with a unified outpouring of laugher—laughter that is not motivated by any specific incident in the film: "They laughed. It was gorgeous, rich laughter. At a given point in the film the laughter cracked out like a shot, spontaneously. It was husky-voiced laughter from deep throats—'belly laughter,' if you will—but it was not the 'belly laughter' with which an audience responds to doubtful jests in a musical revue. The laughter of this Harlem audience depended little upon the immediate situation, little upon the individual line of dialogue."[52] As if applying Vidor's romantic racialist conception of black expressive vitality to *Hallelujah*'s own audience, Gow revels in the corporeal and vocal excess of the audience. The viewers in the theater simply mirror the characters on screen in their elemental "Negro" outpouring of excessive affect.

Framing his piece as an implicit response to this patronizing depiction of the Lafayette audience, Dougherty establishes a different affective relay between black audience members and *Hallelujah*'s characters—one that explicitly rejects the imagery of expressive vitality. Dougherty's juxtaposition of texts illustrates the stakes that accompany his critical task of detaching the film from the pervasive racial imagery of bodily and affective excess. His tragic vision of the film offers a powerful alternative to the one dictated, on the one hand, by Vidor's treatment of "Negro" acting and everyday life and, on the other hand, by Gow's dismissive, farcical rendering of black spectatorship. Remarkably, Dougherty marshals the film itself as evidence against such racialist ideology. The otherwise occluded traces of the relations of production underlying tenant farming become visible in the seemingly "happy" scene at the cotton gin.

CHAPTER 5

Blackness without African Americans

CHECK AND DOUBLE CHECK AND THE DIALECTICS OF CINEMATIC BLACKFACE

In 1930, RKO's top-grossing film was *Check and Double Check*, a feature adapted from the country's most popular radio program, *Amos 'n' Andy*. Airing in six fifteen-minute installments each week on NBC's Blue network, *Amos 'n' Andy* was a comic serial about two poor black men, recently migrated from the rural South, trying to succeed in Harlem. Voiced by white performers Freeman Gosden (Amos) and Charles Correll (Andy), the characters were peculiar by-products of the blackface minstrel show. While Gosden and Correll fashioned their "blackvoice" technique while working in theatrical minstrelsy, the medium of radio enabled them to suppress the visual dimension of blackface. By contrast, the sound-film version of *Amos 'n' Andy* reunites "blackvoice" with blackface. In *Check and Double Check*, Gosden and Correll act the roles in greasepaint.[1] Perhaps more strikingly, *Check and Double Check* invents a group of socially mobile white characters whose interactions drive the narrative of the film. These white characters are in Amos and Andy's film; yet as parodic doubles of the familiar characters, the former serve to enframe the latter. Being, as its title suggests, a double film, *Check and Double Check* uses the white narrative to envelop the black narrative, grounding the latter in a space of extreme diegetic interiority and thereby highlighting the relative social immobility of its black characters.

Moreover, the film is at pains to keep these groups of characters separate within the diegetic space and within the individual frame and to do so without evoking the institutional structures that sustain white privilege or without overtly referring to historical "checks" on African American movement. A preproduction report published in the trade magazine *Exhibitors Herald-World* asserts that the RKO studio wanted scrupulously "to avoid offending Southern exhibitors and audiences" by depicting interracial "familiarities." This news item attributes the studio's concern to southern audience backlash following a "picture released some time ago" in which "two Negro impersonators slapped Caucasians on the back." While the explanation offered is extremely vague, the piece suggests that RKO's contract with the actors stipulates that their part in the film will be limited and, perhaps, that they must obey a certain decorum around their white counterparts during shooting: "No stills released by RKO show Negroes and Caucasians together. Furthermore, there is only one scene in the picture in which members of the two races mingle. The famous radio team only tip their hats."[2] The fact that the piece does not refer to Gosden and Correll by name but treats Amos and Andy as if they were real people oddly makes them into "Negroes"; the extreme Jim Crow sensitivity of the imagined white southern audience makes real the performers' act of racial cross-dressing. Even as African American "impersonators," their "untoward familiarities" with white figures on screen threaten, mimetically, to give "Negro audiences 'big ideas' in regard to the relationship between the two races."[3]

Begging the question of why the studio would bother to pair a group of white characters who have no prior role in the radio show with Amos and Andy in the first place, this report brings into relief the driving contradictions of *Check and Double Check*. The two plot lines must have some relation to each other, yet they must be clearly "separate." The "famous radio team" is the main attraction for the film's audience, yet the iconic, visual dimension of cinema makes them "Negroes" in a more threatening way, such that their characters must be stripped of any "big ideas" of their own. Amos and Andy are "Negro" characters, and yet the film remains haunted by the "primal scene" of blackface masquerade. The characters are rigidly separated according to Jim Crow norms, and yet the underlying issue of racial ambiguity and transformation tends to recall the resemblances between characters, white and black. Moments of mirroring and uncanny doubling—the surprising "familiarities" that the producers wish would remain hidden—unsettle the film's basic assertion of racial separateness and independence. In its formal structures—its narrative organization, shifting mise-en-scène, and handling of diegetic spectacle—*Check and Double Check* is a spatio-temporal elaboration of these contradictions. As such, the film lends itself to a dialectical reading practice; its formal structures both give body to an ideology of African American social immobility and produce obvious "fault lines" within this ideology. In turn, these fault lines offer glimpses of an obscured or disavowed social subtext surrounding African American migration.

By including "black" characters played both by African American actors and by white actors in blackface in the same scene, *Check and Double Check* departs significantly from the dominant strategy whereby early sound-era films incorporate blackface. In films like *The Jazz Singer* (Warner Bros., 1927), *Kid Millions* (United Artists, 1934), and *Swing Time* (RKO, 1936), stars Al Jolson, Eddie Cantor, and Fred Astaire, respectively, play characters who are themselves performers and who use blackface to entertain. As such, these films show the act of blacking up—what Michael Rogin calls the "primal scene" of the "blackface musical"—making masquerade itself a spectacle.[4] In contrast to these films, *Big Boy*, one of Jolson's Warner Bros. musical comedies, handles blackface quite differently, seemingly making it a more useful point of comparison for *Check and Double Check*. Released in 1930 as well, *Big Boy* also presents the viewer with a "black" leading character played by a white performer in blackface who emerges on the scene already in burnt cork and remains that way for the duration of the film—almost. Using a sort of reverse transformation scene, the film restores Jolson to his "white" self in the climactic moment, thus recasting the narrative as an extended fantasy of masquerade. Although *Check and Double Check* engages in no such disavowal, forcing us to move past the scene of blacking up as the primary guide for interpreting the role of blackface in the film, this scene is by no means irrelevant here.

Check and Double Check represses the scene of blacking up; in so doing, the film stages a return of the repressed "story" of expropriation and exploitation—the underlying network of sociohistorical relations—that makes the fantasy of white self-making through masquerade possible. The second repression paradoxically highlights and reverses an earlier one: check and double check. It is possible to characterize the unique situation of blackface in *Check and Double Check* by pointing to the crucial mirror scene that it offers as an alternative to the blackface musical's scene of blacking up: the scene of facing between black characters (played by blacked-up white actors) and white characters (also played by white actors). In contrast to the scene of blacking up, the scene of facing poses the question of African American desire and evokes the white demand for recognition, framing the dynamics of racial intersubjectivity in a much more complex, unstable dialectical relationship.

This chapter proposes an appositely *double* vision of the blackface mask. On the one hand, it accepts the film's basic representational wager, approaching Amos and Andy as diegetically "black" characters. On the other hand, it recursively considers the role of the burnt cork mask—as just one element in a complex texture of visual and narrative signifiers—in constructing this blackness. If this partial acceptance of blackface as a means of black characterization seems perverse, then it must be pointed out how *Check and Double Check* illustrates that, where Hollywood film is concerned, the racial legibility of characters does not immediately follow from the profilmic social status of performers' bodies. During the shooting of their scenes for *Check and Double Check*, two musicians in Duke Ellington's band, Barney Bigard and Juan Tizol, were forced to wear skin-darkening makeup—so as to avoid any suggestion that the band was "mixed," not "all-colored." In a brilliant reading of this self-defeating strategy, the *Baltimore Afro-American*, a major black news-weekly, printed a picture of the band with the following caption attached: "Members of the famed Jungle Band of Duke Ellington must use burnt cork over their complexions when working in their forthcoming picture with Amos 'n' Andy. The blackface comedy team felt that 'being colored' was not enough, with the result that the ruling was made."[5]

Check: A fabric woven or printed with such a pattern [as on a chess board]

Check and Double Check attempts to establish substantive linkages between two plot lines, whose very distinctiveness rests on the unbridgeable divide between the social settings in which they take place: the postmigration African American ghetto and the upper-class white countryside. The film addresses this difficulty by constructing a prior relationship between Amos, Andy, and the main white character, Richard Williams (Charles Morton), which it locates in a temporal moment antecedent to the beginning of the narrative. Amos and Andy worked for Richard's father in Georgia before they migrated north. Because Amos and Andy's eventual encounter with Richard unfolds like a reunion between estranged brothers, the accidental events that bring the plots into collision acquire a providential, foreordained quality. The shared back-story establishes a bond between the three men sufficiently powerful to make them mutual participants in each other's affairs; at the same time, *Check and Double Check* locates that relationship in a physical and symbolic locale that has been lost, the southern plantation. As if compelled to disavow the very linkage on which it depends for its own internal coherence, the film treats the social divisions that mark its present time and place in a wholly matter-of-fact manner. *Check and Double Check* envisions relations across the color line only retrospectively or nostalgically.

The first semblance of a connection between *Check and Double Check*'s two plots occurs in the opening sequence, where the film localizes Amos and Andy on the same urban landscape as Mr. and Mrs. Blair (Irene Rich and Edward Martindel), Richard's hosts in New York. Tracking across a block of immobile traffic, the camera takes the viewer forward from the Blairs' gleaming, chauffeured sedan to the cause of the jam, Amos and Andy's stalled jalopy. While Amos and Andy remain invisible to the Blairs, the film suggests, at this early moment, a latent interrelation between the two racial and class groups. Treating his partner like a servant, Andy enacts a parodic repetition of the Blair couple's leisured impatience. As "president" of the operation, Andy sits in the car, the "Fresh Air Taxicab Company of America Incorpulated," and exhorts Amos, who works under the hood.

At the beginning of *Check and Double Check*, Amos, Andy, and their decrepit vehicle cause the Blairs to miss Richard's arrival at Penn Station. The film's conclusion replays this scene, while reversing its outcome; Amos and Andy become the very agents of the Williams-Blair familial reunion. Upon Richard's eventual arrival, he and the Blairs' daughter, Jean (Sue Carol), who were childhood playmates when her family lived in Georgia, fall in love almost immediately. Jean is pursued, at the same time, by Ralph Crawford (Ralf Harolde), whom she refuses to marry. Richard's father, who was "a great friend" of Mr. Blair, has recently passed away, leaving "the family in difficulty"; the son has come to New York in order to "trade" some property, which will ameliorate their financial straits. The goal of economic security acquires added urgency in light of Richard's burgeoning romance with Jean, and Richard makes it clear to Mr. Blair that finding the deed he is looking for will "enable [him] to stay north."[6] In the end, Amos and Andy come into possession of the deed and return it to Richard. After a manic race to Penn Station, with Amos driving the suddenly agile taxi at full speed, the pair catch Richard just before he boards the return train for Georgia.

In *Check and Double Check*, the shared memory of the patriarchal, southern plantation brings together white and black characters in the North. While the film never visually represents this idyll, the characters evoke it through spoken testimony about their past relations with the now-deceased patriarch. When Amos and Andy encounter Richard, shared reminiscence serves an ideological purpose; the visual dynamics of "facing," of mirroring and recognition, around which the scene is structured, give plastic form to sentimental, affective bonds that seem to nullify class and race distinctions. Amos and Andy's subsequent encounters with Richard (and with Ralph) replay the drama of facing, which, however, never regains its initial transformative power. In each subsequent reiteration, the fraternal relation deteriorates further, even as Amos's and Andy's lives become (through the film's bizarre narrative machinations) more elaborately intertwined with Richard's search for the lost deed. The social divisions that mark its contemporary urban setting make it impossible for *Check and Double Check* to preserve the nostalgia-driven relation between Amos, Andy, and Richard.

Moreover, the film takes a gothic turn when Amos and Andy visit the "haunted" old Williams house in Harlem; there they establish a counternarrative of historical violence and enslavement that undermines the film's dominant ideology. By unmasking the operations of racial fantasy in *Check and Double Check*, the gothic set-piece makes legible the contradictions that riddle the film's twin migration stories. In its two failed attempts to establish a new basis for the three main characters' future ties to one another, the film provides complex allegories of race, labor, and consumption.

Just as the film begins to explore these dynamics, however, it exposes a deeper contradiction. *Check and Double Check* highlights its own paradoxical position with respect to these histories of exchange and compensation by drawing the spectator's attention to the expropriating relations of production on which it depends—as a film about African Americans that employs white actors. Once the trace of this metanarrative of blackface mimicry comes into view, the film grinds to a halt. Unable to proceed any further, *Check and Double Check* collapses under the weight of the multiple historical strata that it contains—not the least of which is minstrelsy itself.[7]

Check: To diversify or vary with a different colour or shade; to variegate, mottle

In his tour de force analysis of *The Jazz Singer*, Michael Rogin identifies the film as one of four "race movies" that "provide the scaffolding for American film history." Rogin frames his reading of *The Jazz Singer* by juxtaposing it with two of the other three "race movies" that prominently feature blackface performance. In its "identification with suffering blacks," *The Jazz Singer*, Rogin states, resembles Edwin S. Porter's 1903 version of *Uncle Tom's Cabin* but contrasts sharply with D. W. Griffith's *The Birth of a Nation*, which espouses "race hatred."[8] *The Jazz Singer* differs from both of these films, however, in its use of blackface: "whereas [*Uncle Tom's Cabin* and *The Birth of a Nation*] apply burnt cork unselfconsciously, *The Jazz Singer* makes blackface its subject."[9] In his study of race and American movie musicals, *Disintegrating the Musical: Black Performance and American Musical Film*, Arthur Knight has paired Rogin's suggestive term "unselfconscious" with its implied opposite, "self-conscious," to offer a two-part schema for distinguishing cinematic "uses" of blackface.[10] Going back to Rogin's use of "unselfconscious," it becomes clear, however, that the term does not offer a sufficiently solid foundation for the kind of critical framework that Knight imagines. The adjective "unselfconscious," like the opposing adjective from which it derives, does not seem to refer to any specific consciousness.[11]

One can assume that, in this film-critical context, "self-conscious" does not carry its popular-psychological meaning of "shy" or "socially awkward." What then does it mean to label the deployment of blackface in a film "self-conscious" or "unselfconscious"? Who or what is the "self" aware or unaware of the masquerade? The film-text itself, understood metaphorically as a kind of "consciousness"? The spectator according to classical film theory? A particular viewer? Moreover, of what, precisely, does this "self" remain aware or unaware? Of the material presence of burnt cork in the mise-en-scène? Of the fact of cross-racial casting? Of the social and historical issues bound up in blackface performance? Rogin's and Knight's discourses do not suggest clear answers to any of these questions, and it appears that "self-consciousness," in the precise phenomenological sense, is not what is ultimately at issue in their descriptions.

In using the two adjectives, Knight attempts to work out generally valid descriptions of two different strategies of introducing blackface into the film diegesis. He distinguishes between films that show the "transformation" to blackface and films that do not.[12] Certainly, Knight makes a viable, heuristic distinction between two *filmic situations*, one that can be applied usefully to a range of specific examples insofar as one remains consistent and rigorous in using his terms, while acknowledging the complex ways in which these two situations may be paired in individual films. Knight allows us to see that, in the one situation, white performers in blackface play diegetically "black" characters. In the other, white actors playing diegetically "white" characters don blackface in a key narrative episode (an episode depicted or at least referred to in the narrative discourse) and become "black" in a circumscribed setting, either in the context of a stage performance or in an attempt momentarily to deceive a social audience.

Beyond making this basic distinction, however, Knight gestures at a more broadly theoretical but less convincing opposition between two modes of representation. Here "unselfconscious" means something like "realist" representation—Knight offers "dramatic, impersonating, and illusionist" as synonyms—while "self-conscious" means something like "theatrical" representation.[13] These terms, however, lend themselves more to aesthetic value judgments than to a sharply theorized account of the uses of cinematic blackface. In Rogin's work on blackface, issues of desire, recognition, labor, dependence, power, and subjection are paramount, in a way that makes the Hegelian sense of "self-consciousness"—as opposed to the vague senses described above—seem like a useful starting point for such an account.

In the commentary accompanying his translation of the famous lord and bondsman passage from Hegel's *Phenomenology of Spirit*, Alexandre Kojève offers the provocative identity, "Man is Self-Consciousness." According to Kojève's gloss, Hegel means that an individual (an "I") gains his essential being as "man" (a state of existence above the mere "animal" level) at the point at which it achieves "self-consciousness," channeling its desire "toward something that goes beyond the given reality."[14] For Hegel, this "something" is, perforce, the desire of another human being (a "non-I"). Thus, Hegelian self-consciousness emerges ("comes to light" in Kojève's wording) at the moment at which the subject risks his animal life to satisfy his human desire in a struggle for recognition.[15] In this struggle, the subject seeks to make the other surrender to his will, recognizing him without being recognized in turn; this unequal relationship, the relationship of master and slave, represents, for Hegel, the "fundamental" social grouping.[16]

The Hegelian master-slave relationship momentarily freezes the former adversaries in "unequal and opposed" states of consciousness. The master represents "autonomous Consciousness," or essential "Being-for-itself," while the slave represents "dependent Consciousness"—consciousness that exists for another—because he "has accepted the life granted him by another."[17] But because it is mediated by the consciousness of one who has yielded his desire, the master's "autonomous consciousness" remains crucially compromised, ironically dependent on the being of an entity that is "for him an animal or a thing"—and not, finally, another human self-consciousness capable of "worthy" recognition.[18] Hegel's discussion of the master's ensuing "alienation" introduces the possibility of a radical reversal. What appeared as total independence and autonomy reveals itself to be total dependence, and these revealed realities prefigure a total reversal of positions.[19] In his idle enjoyment of the fruits of the slave's work, the master becomes aware that he lacks essential being, while the slave becomes aware of the transformative potential of his work. Paradoxically, the possibility of fulfilled being-for-self—true existence as "man," true "self-consciousness"—is revealed to lie at the end of the traumatic passage through slavery.[20]

With this (admittedly hasty) summary in place, it becomes possible to read Michael Rogin's discussion of intrafilmic blackface masquerade as a static, nondialectical version of Hegel's relationship of master and slave—a relationship without the possibility of alienation leading to reversibility. Whiteness depends, in Rogin's account, on some reference to blackness, but the dynamics of reciprocity and reversibility that animate the Hegelian dialectic are missing from it. On the one hand, the white subject understands himself as "master" over the black "slave," but *without* first demanding or seeking the latter's "recognition." On the other hand, the black subject's self-consciousness and desire for recognition never bear upon the two figures' relationship.

In Rogin's reading, the white performer-character defines his or her whiteness in and through a temporary identification with blackness, which serves, paradoxically, to reinforce a sense of distinction. According to the ideology of American self-fashioning, the white performer-character becomes a national subject by putting on and then taking off the identity of a fixed, subordinate social group. Rather than demystifying the blackface mask, films that show the "primal scene" of the blackface musical, the scene of "the performer blacking up," present blackness as a substance that can be manipulated by the white subject. At the same time, such films conceal the network of historical-social relations in which white expropriation of black culture—including their own exclusions of African American performers—becomes possible. Thus, the blackface mask functions, according to Rogin, like a fetish. At the same time, the very scene that defines what could be called "self-conscious" blackface actually ends up obscuring the underlying social struggle between racialized adversaries to attain self-consciousness (in the Hegelian sense).[21]

Translating Rogin's claims into the Hegelian vocabulary, it might be said that in films that show the act of a white performer blacking up, blackness is inherently being-for-another; this simulated struggle for recognition obviates all questions of African American desire. Moreover, the white subject's "master" status is reflexively determined but demands no reciprocity in recognition. In fact, the white subject seems to demand no recognition at all; it is as if racial difference is enough to assure "being-for-self." In this respect, Rogin echoes a claim that Frantz Fanon makes in his reading of Hegel in *Black Skin, White Masks*, the work from which Rogin borrows his title. Fanon concludes that the history of colonialism and New World slavery, where recognition becomes intertwined with racial difference, does not illustrate the form of struggle between master and servant that Hegel imagines: "For Hegel there is reciprocity; here the master laughs at the consciousness of the slave. What he wants from the slave is not recognition but work."[22] For Rogin, the white American subject of blackface entertainment wants not only work (in the form of cultural innovation) but also the serviceable and manipulatable symbolic properties of blackness. These properties become available during the scene of blacking up in the mirror, which seems to occur after the underlying social struggle has been permanently resolved, making blackness (through the burnt cork mask) in some vague sense a fetish. I wonder if this particular account of blackface as fetishism might not serve to exacerbate the erasure of historical struggles that Rogin critiques. While there is not sufficient room here to consider the implications of this irony for films that showcase the act of blacking up, my goal in this chapter is to give an account of cinematic blackface that interrupts this erasure, that excavates the signs of interracial struggles (with their attendant reciprocity and reversibility) and insistently poses the question of African American desire (in the Hegelian phenomenological sense).

"Self-consciousness" and "fetish" are useful terms in distinguishing the filmic situation of blackface in *Check and Double Check* from the one that typifies blackface musicals like *The Jazz Singer*. Whereas Rogin might consider *Check and Double Check* a case of "unselfconscious" blackface and films in the latter category "self-conscious," it is the *Amos 'n' Andy* film that actually makes the struggle for self-conscious, realized existence (in Hegel's sense) between racialized adversaries its driving force, while at the same time positioning blackness as a fetish—and in a much more theoretically precise and productive sense. The salient difference between *Check and Double Check* and a film like *The Jazz Singer* is that, in the former, the scene of applying burnt cork has been repressed or disavowed, in the sense of being distanced from conscious representation. This scene has not been erased or wiped out completely, in the sense of having no bearing on the film; indeed, I show that it remains very much on the film's mind. Rather, it has been repressed, according to the classic Freudian account of fetishistic disavowal. As such, this scene becomes a metonymy for agonistic, power- and economic-exchange–based social relationships across the color line—for the very idea that institutional racism, segregation, and exploitation constitute an American color line in the first place.

In this sense, the film becomes a series of racialist fetish objects that work to help the spectator—the representative of the white audience that is its intended addressee—maintain his or her beliefs against the return of "unwelcome" knowledge. This knowledge has to do both with the white privilege of the actors who play black characters (their masquerade) and with the actual instability and sustaining violence of Jim Crow society; the film's fetishes aim to secure and sustain the spectator's shaky beliefs in both the main characters' "blackness" and in fixed, nonagonistic race relations against the return of these "unwelcome" forms of knowledge.

Freud uses "repression" and "disavowal" in an overtly visual, spectatorial sense in his paper on "fetishism"—a key theoretical concept for Rogin—making them amenable to a discussion of representations of self-consciousness. To repress or disavow is simply to hold a scene at a distance from consciousness, not to wipe it out completely—to "scotomize" it in Freud's suggestive optical metaphor.[23] An obvious analogy exists between the scene of blacking up and the "unwelcome perception"—the perception of the mother's lack of a phallus—that, Freud argues, it is the fetish's role to keep at bay. For a film that attempts to generate black characters out of white actors in burnt cork, the scene of masquerade cannot appear on screen, in order to sustain the spectator's belief (which he or she knows better than to accept) in the film's fictional gambit. Freud introduces his argument about the fetish by explicitly rejecting the argument that the memory-image of the "lost" phallus is scotomized—"entirely wiped out, so that the result is the same as when a visual impression falls on the blind spot in the retina"—but repressed or disavowed.[24] For Freud, the fetish separates perception and belief, the image and its interpretation, by acting as a substitute point of anchorage for the "interest which was formerly directed to [the fetish's] predecessor [that is, the woman's phallus]," making possible new forms of dramatic play and storytelling in service of the initial belief.[25]

This account of fetishism, however, differs sharply from the one that Rogin offers, where the display of the act of blacking up helps secure blackface's function as fetish. Rogin is right to suggest that the blackface musical's scene of blacking up generally disavows the complex "story" of "historical crimes [that are] embedded in [blackface's] invidious distinction" of "white over black." However, his underlying claim that "the fetish is a story masquerading as an object" seems more closely related to the Marxian notion of commodity fetishism than it does to Freud's concept, where stories are precisely what make it possible for the fetish to act as a viable substitute. Indeed, Rogin's discussion tends to conflate these two theoretical discourses, without taking into account significant distinctions between them.[26] What is remarkable about the situation of blackface in *Check and Double Check* is how other elements of narrative and spectacle in the film "inherit the interest" that the spectator might have attached to the visual fact of masquerade; in concealing (but not "scotomizing") the scene of blacking up, the film obsessively narrates stories about similarities and differences between "white" and "black." It must find strategies beyond mere visual imitation to persuade the spectator that its main characters belong to the latter category, while, at the same time, avoiding any suggestion that the experience of being "black" is defined by "white" historical crimes.

Perhaps because it must divert the "interest" attaching to the "unwelcome" knowledge of blackface artifice to so many other facets of the film text, *Check and Double Check* ultimately foregrounds the crucial moments of the Hegelian dialectic that are effaced in the scenario that Rogin describes. In this film, blackface performance becomes a marker of the "master's" anxieties about recognition and the attendant reversibility of power relations—the struggle for self-consciousness is being evoked, in other words, through this complex, fetishistic operation. It is possible to illustrate the distinction between how *Check and Double Check* handles blackface and how a film like *The Jazz Singer* does by contrasting the former's paradigmatic scene of "facing" with the latter's blacking-up scene. By "scene of facing," I mean quite literally a scene in which white and black characters stand face-to-face, engaging in a specular encounter within a social field defined by racial difference.[27] Like the scene of blacking up in *The Jazz Singer*, the scene of facing in *Check and Double Check* is the primary spectacular means through which the film negotiates the Hegelian themes of desire, recognition, and self-consciousness—and can be understood, much more precisely, as a dramatic fetish object. These scenes explicitly evoke benevolent, noninvidious white–African American relationships, while always hinting at a disavowed story of exploitation.

Check: To come into collision with . . . Obs.

Until Amos and Andy appear at the Blair house to drop off members of Ellington's band, *Check and Double Check*'s two plot lines unfold in strictly separate, parallel fashion. The film prefigures Amos and Andy's meeting with Richard through a series of allusions to the elder Mr. Williams. In a scene that precedes Richard's discussion with Mr. Blair about his father's estate, Amos mentions a "Mr. Williams" from Georgia. Arguing with Andy over the cab company's finances, Amos, who is prone to bouts of profound nostalgia for the pair's southern birthplace, expresses ambivalence about life in Harlem: "You know we ain't got no money. We ain't no better off now than we was when we worked for Mr. Williams down in Georgia." His statement establishes not only that the move north has been an economic failure but also that it has brought out the worst in his partner: "Ever since we've been up here in New York, all you've been doin' is puttin' on the dog. Sometimes I wish I *was* back down in Georgia." Amos contrasts the self-aggrandizing Andy with Mr. Williams, whom he calls "a friend that is a friend."

Amos and Andy's dialogue with Richard reflects their mutual surprise in encountering the son of their former boss. In the reaction shot that follows the shot of Richard hailing the other two, Amos's expression conveys pleasurable disbelief: "Mr. Richard," he says, "that ain't really you, is it?" The three construct a relation of facing or mutual recognition by channeling shared memories of the plantation and of Richard Sr. Indeed, the original story by Burt Kalmar and Harry Ruby preserved in the RKO story files calls this "the recognition scene."[28] Richard has not seen Amos and Andy since they migrated from the South: "You know boys, I often wondered what became of you after you left Georgia." After explaining that they are in business for themselves, Amos and Andy cite their frequent discussions about Georgia. Suddenly overcome with nostalgia, Andy pronounces, "That was the best home we ever had." Amos affirms this notion, stating, "You all certainly was good to us down there. Your papa treated us just like we was his own children." With the camera trained on Richard's face during Amos's soliloquy, we see the former's expression grow increasingly grave with each mention of the father. After Amos states his intention to reestablish contact by writing Mr. Williams a letter, Richard informs the two men that his father has recently died.

At this point, the film defines Amos and Andy's past strictly in terms of their relationship with the Williams family. They have no evident familial past of their own, and it as if their *de facto* parent-child relationship with Mr. Williams provides the sole affective support of their existence at present. With tears in their eyes, both Amos and Andy express their sympathies to Richard, illustrating a rare moment of agreement between the two habitually bickering characters. The very memory of the idyllic space of the Williams home, presided over by the benevolent patriarch, unites them and temporarily suspends their usual hierarchical relationship. The memory of Richard Sr. not only restores the bond between Amos and Andy but also diminishes the sense of displacement that characterizes postmigration life for them, assuaging their displacement with the memory of *homeliness*. Thus, Amos is able to recall Mr. Williams's parting words to him and Andy as a kind of promise of perpetual security and assistance in a time of need—even after their physical displacement from Georgia. Amos says, "Your dad was the best friend we ever had; ever since we worked for him. He raised us and we loved him. And when we was telling him goodbye, he said to us . . . : 'Boys, if . . . you ever need anything or if anything ever go wrong, remember that you can always write home.' And he made us feel like we had a home. And I know that if he didn't have but one loaf of bread, he would give us half of it." By sharing tears, the three men try to stave off the awful loss of the familial sanctuary, the memory of which is sufficiently strong that it can, by being talked about in such a moment as this, appear to live on. That is to say that Amos and Andy seem able at this point in the film to restore a lost brotherly bond with Richard.

The power of the family idyll as it is conjured in this scene lies in its ability to suspend the racial divide that structures the film's social topography. The imaginary brothers are able to face and recognize one another, even in a territory that is relatively alien for all three, because they do so under the watch of the absent father.[29] The recalled scene of the initial command or covenant acts as a template for this and for all of the subsequent specular, facing episodes depicted in the film. The eucharistic image of Mr. Williams's last loaf of bread suggests that "covenant" is an appropriate description of his guarantee to Amos and Andy. In the present scene, the younger Williams "descendents" play at the benevolent relations of recognition, mastery, and dependency established in the earlier scene or scenes of facing that they recall. Fittingly, Amos and Andy proffer their assistance to "Mr. Richard" during his stay in New York. For his part, Richard promises them that he will try and "get in touch" with them soon.

The phantom presence of Mr. Williams makes this specular play possible. By entering the scene in the form of a voice that makes promises, the father guarantees the three sons' continued bond, enabling them to act beyond the constraints of the racial divide. But just as the film signals this possible transcendence of the color line, it must negate the possibility of interracial community in its own present-tense setting. According to the logic of the *Exhibitors Herald-World* report, the racial logic of Hollywood in 1930 demands that the characters never touch; indeed, even their "getting in touch" is difficult to depict. Where in New York could this interaction take place? What would be its setting or purpose? Under Mr. Williams's gaze, cross-racial intersubjectivity is possible. However, because none of the written or vocal traces through which he is conjured can restore him to full presence, the venue in which these forms might subsequently be repeated already has vanished from view.

Check: A Means to ensure accuracy, correctness, security from fraud . . .

Amos and Andy's encounter with Richard occurs just before they convene with their lodge, the Mystic Knights of the Sea, another *fraternal* group whose mission is to commemorate the death of a father figure. Again, repetition and doubling shape the narrative at every moment. The scene of Amos and Andy receiving their orders from the Kingfish (Russ Powell), while the rest of the assembly looks on, replays, precisely, the scene at the Blairs' where an attentive audience approaches the stage to applaud the Ellington band; the meeting even concludes, symmetrically, with a musical performance (the lodge members' rendition of "Nobody Knows But de Lord"). The lodge's ritual also necessitates going to "the old Williams house" to look for a piece of paper. Although the pair's quest to commemorate the death of the Founder of the lodge mirrors Richard's search for his father's document, the stakes of the former are much less clear. Unlike Mr. Williams, the Founder of the Mystic Knights of the Sea has left no contractual signature. Whereas the text of the lost Williams paper clarifies property ownership, the phrase written each year on the Founder's note is purely self-reflexive, significant only in the context of an obscure game of remembrance—a statement, as we will see, about repetition, to be rewritten repetitively. In spite of these clear differences, the film confuses and conflates the two documents, exchanging the one for the other.

The ritual to commemorate the Founder is arcane indeed, consisting of a series of arbitrary and unexplained gestures that the Kingfish presents as a coherent narrative. He explains it as follows: "This special meetin' comes once a year, in honor of the Founder of this great lodge, who was lost at sea while doing night-watch duty. So brothers, once a year, on this night, two of the members have to do night-watch duty in the old, vacant house, so as to prove that they has the courage of the Founder and be worthy of this great organization, the Mystic Knights of the Sea." Beyond this hazy outline, we do not learn anything more about the life and death of the Founder, about when, where, or in what capacity he was "at sea"; nor does the Kingfish shed any light on the symbolic relevance of the night-watch duty.[30] Through the drawing of lots, the "great honor" of representing the lodge falls on Brothers Amos and Andy. The Kingfish begins to explain the instructions for the night watch to them, which are, as befits "the most important secret of the lodge," exceedingly abstruse. The linkage between the historical personage of the Founder and "the old, vacant house" is, as far as the viewer can tell, an artificial one. Because popular legend calls it a "haunted house," it offers a theater for testing the bravery of the lodge members who enter it.

The "haunted house" ritual gives the film's title a specific internal point of reference, without initially illuminating the significance of this phrase. It is only when the "check and double check" paper is found and then lost again that the phrase begins to acquire a thematic resonance. As the Kingfish explains, a Brother Jackson, the "caretaker of the old Williams home," will open the door for Amos and Andy at midnight, precisely—"exactly the same hour the Founder was lost at sea"—and let them out after one hour, provided that they have accomplished a specific task. While they are in the house, Amos and Andy are to "find a piece of paper that was left there by the two brothers last year, marked with the words 'check and double check'; then leave a paper, marked in the same way, for the brothers to find next year." Finally, they must bring the paper found in the house back to the lodge for inspection. Complicating their task is the fact that, at the same time as Amos and Andy have entered the old

Williams house (through the basement), Ralph (Richard's romantic rival) and his henchman have arrived and forced entry through the front door.[31]

When the Kingfish finally names the "old vacant house" in question, Amos and Andy exhibit a shock of recognition, which, however, has an unexpected cause. They gasp when they are told it is the old *Williams* house but not because of the obvious connotations of the name itself. Their shock has only to do with the fact that they have been asked to enter what they regard as a "haunted house." The film gives no indication that they associate the house with the Williams family, despite their crucially important membership in it and their very recent reunion with Richard. Why, the viewer wonders, do they not make this connection? Only when Amos and Andy end up with the missing deed and find the inscription, "Richard Williams, Sr.," do they realize that it has some significance for their relationship to Richard.[32] Even then, this second surprise does not cause them to reflect on the uncanny appearance of the Williams estate *in their own neighborhood*. The film's treatment of the Williams family's Harlem outpost is paradoxical. Amos and Andy look upon the house with utter horror, while never addressing its relevance to their lost bond with the family; yet they react calmly to the revelation of the "important" paper, linking it immediately with the son, whom *they have just encountered by happenstance after years of total separation*. Why is Grandfather Williams's house in Harlem, of all places? How do we go about mapping the film's bizarre social geography?

Check and Double Check's Harlem is what Slavoj Žižek has termed an "extimate field": "a field whose innermost center meets its radical exterior." As in Žižek's description, the film "reveals . . . traces of the traumatic 'repressed' past" by establishing an uncanny, subterranean link between sociohistorical spaces that should be radically separate. The "other" space of the southern plantation-manor is thus reinscribed "at the very heart" of the northern, post-migration African American metropolis.[33] Ultimately, the gothic old Williams house is the place where the traumatic/repressed past of slavery returns.

Prior to the scene inside the house, the Williams name signifies in the film a pastoral idyll whose associations are precisely the opposite of the dynamics visible in the Harlem house. The Williams estate appears to be the only potentially sustaining, remunerative locus of work and community for Amos and Andy. The earlier mise-en-scène of facing serves to hold the film's two plots together in a tenuous suspension. Intertwined in a very loose way, these two plots continuously mirror one another, as if the film has temporalized the scene of facing, turning it into the structuring principle of the narrative. The spectral presence of Mr. Williams holds the two plots together in this suspension, and the uncanny appearance of the Williams's domestic interior in the "haunted house" scene attenuates his mediating authority. Here the film excavates another history of cross-racial relations: one that emphasizes difference, rather than fraternity, and violence, rather than benevolence. Fittingly, the "haunted house" scene turns on an aggressive scene of black-white facing. From this point forward, the film's reenactments of the scene of benevolent facing will be frustrated by visible obstacles. *Check and Double Check* will promise a final reunion between Richard and Amos and Andy but will reveal any such reunion to be impossible.

While the scene inside the house begins in a comedic mode, its underlying gothicism gradually rises to the surface. The parallel activities of the two pairs of men, searching the different floors, appear to corroborate the legends about the old house; making floorboards creek and knocking things over in the dark, each pair frightens the other repeatedly. Amos and Andy manage to compose themselves enough to locate the "check and double check" paper, tacked to the wall next to a mantelpiece. Eager to return to the lodge, the men realize that they do not have any paper with which to duplicate the document for the following year's night-watch team. Rifling through a nearby desk to find a suitable piece of paper, they happen, of course, to find the missing Williams deed. The film uses a close-up of the paper to convey the dramatic irony. On the side that faces away from Andy, it clearly reads "Deed," in large, black-letter type.

With Amos and Andy's discovery of the deed, the film's tone changes abruptly and unexpectedly. While Amos searches his pockets for his customary pencil stub, he and Andy hear the other men approaching and set off for the basement. In his haste, Andy puts the deed in his left-hand pocket, already having the Mystic Knights' paper in his right. The villains catch up to Amos and Andy as they struggle to force open the locked basement door. Demanding the piece of paper, one draws a gun, while the other shines his flashlight into their faces.

This climactic tableau is shot through with violence and fear. Amos and Andy cower in the glare of the flashlight, with their backs to the door and hands raised to the ceiling. Sedimented in this tableau—in the specific manner of its staging and shooting—are a series of cultural and historical traces, which are legible against the grain of the film's overt discourse of the plantation. When the other men bar their exit, Amos and Andy assume the postures of captured fugitives, frozen in the glare of a searchlight. While in the scene at the train station the film will implicitly criminalize Amos and Andy a second time, here the crucial metaphor is not the prison but the fugitive slave. The setting links the black characters' experience of the gothic return of the repressed with the act of sifting through the textual traces of white property ownership—of ransacking the master's desk. Chronology is important here. Considering Richard's age and the date of the film, the grandfather, the father of Richard Sr., who is supposed to have owned the house, would have been of the immediate antebellum generation.

This unwitting excavation of the slave past momentarily interrupts the film's dominant representation of Amos and Andy's ancestral connection with earlier generations of the Williams family. While the ill-tempered Ralph is an obvious foil for the innocent, sincere Richard, the film suggests a subterranean connection between the two figures: they are doubles. The scene that introduces Richard and initiates his antagonism with Ralph contains an argument about the most effective way to treat a horse.[34] Against Ralph's regime of physical aggression and punishment, Richard argues for gentle care and guidance: "I don't think you ought to take it out on the horse . . . you'll get more out of him if you're gentle with him." An utterly gratuitous episode, the argument introduces the two men as opposite sides of the same masterly coin, anticipating the eventual return of (or to) the plantation—where Amos and Andy, quite tellingly, encounter Ralph and not Richard.[35] By intimidating Amos and Andy, Ralph manages to secure the piece of paper that he assumes to be the deed.

Because each pair is unaware of the other's reason for being in the old Williams house, each pair assumes that there is only one piece of paper in play. Amos attempts to bargain with the villains and insists upon keeping the paper. Only after further threats does Andy comply with Ralph's demand, reaching into his right-side pocket. To the careful viewer who has followed the paths of the two purloined letters, it is clear that the thieves have been duped—or have duped themselves. Indeed, in the car on the way back to the suburbs, the ironic twist and the full significance of the title are revealed. Reading aloud in disbelief from the page, Ralph finds "check and double check": the very direction he has failed to heed. By failing to consider the existence of another paper and thus seeing no need to "check" with care, Ralph has departed the house empty-handed. That the slogan only becomes meaningful when Ralph reads it points to the first of two perplexing, paralogical moments in this section of the film. Impossible explanations suggest themselves. It is as if the "check and double check" slogan has no significance in the context of the lodge's own ritual. Or it is as if the Mystic Knights of the Sea invented and staged the entire elaborate ritual with the sole purpose of duping Ralph. The text becomes specifically meaningful only in light of a complex series of events that its writer(s) could not have predicted.

The sequence that follows, in which Amos and Andy finally recognize the deed for what it is and make a deliberate effort to restore it to Richard's hands, offers a parallel moment of logical difficulty. A more detailed synopsis is in order, as some of this sequence's developments even contradict earlier events and their implications. By having Andy pull the remaining piece of paper out of his pocket, the film mirrors Ralph's moment of shock. Andy initially assumes it to be the one belonging to the lodge, before discovering that it is, in fact, the deed. Making the two scenes mirror one another in such a comprehensive way, the film verges on the impossible. The confrontation between Amos, Andy, and the two thieves is predicated on the shared (but incorrect) assumption that there is a *single* paper of any importance. As Ralph's reaction makes clear, he and his partner deceive themselves by assuming that Amos and Andy are agents working for Richard. While the two white men remain unaware that a second paper exists, Amos and Andy manage to preserve the deed because they know nothing about it. Logically, the ironic moment of recognition marked by "check and double check" should occur for Andy, too. After all, why would Andy think that he had given away the deed, which seems to him—because he does not yet know that such a deed exists—to be a meaningless scrap of paper? Recall that in the encounter with Ralph, Amos has only the "check and double check" paper in mind when the extortion is taking place. Nevertheless, Andy expresses surprise when, moments later, he relates to Amos the sequence of events (whereby he gave away the paper he meant to keep). Indeed, Andy looks at the paper, producing it from the left-side pocket, and only then realizes that it does not say "check and double check." Why are Andy and Amos not already aware that they have failed the lodge's test by giving up the evidence of their "night-watch duty"? Has Andy forgotten what just occurred in the old Williams house?[36]

These are unanswerable questions, which, like the confusion posed by "check and double check," point in the direction of an explanation of one of the film's most peculiar aspects. Amos and Andy are always double agents, working for Mr. Williams and his son, even (especially?) when they believe themselves to be acting on their own behalf (and/or on behalf of the lodge). Here is the logic of white enframing and black confinement to a white-governed inner narrative at its most blatant.[37]

As Amos and Andy begin to contemplate the consequences of their failure in the Mystic Knights' ritual, the fate of the deed appears to be in jeopardy. Absentmindedly, Andy scans the document, already lying in the trash can. Spelling out the letters, he misrecognizes the word "deed," as "dead": "That spells 'dead.' Someone's dead." After realizing Andy's mistake, Amos jogs himself out of his sad reveries and seizes the paper, reading from the contract's legal language. He exclaims, "Look here, Andy: 'Richard Williams, S r [read as individual letters].' That thing looks important to me. There's 'Richard Williams.' We better not mess with that thing. We better call Mr. Richard." Again, no surprise surrounds the reappearance of the Williams patronymic; the two men link this "Mr. Williams" with their friend and take the care of his document very seriously—even though Richard has told them nothing of the existence of the deed, nor of his plan to go to the old house to locate it. Thus, it would seem to follow that, in an echo of Rogin's stalled dialectic of blackface, their labor and autonomous "story" are fully contained by and subsumed within the Williams family's story of success and mobility. The manner in which their intercession on behalf of Richard Jr.'s romantic and financial interests plays out does not, however, support this conclusion. The gothic climax in the old Williams house marks the point at which Amos and Andy begin to fall out of the white characters' purview and vice versa, the point at which the tenuously linked narratives begin to separate again. Amos and Andy's final plight is comparatively abject; yet as the two plots begin to disentangle themselves, they achieve something like a state of narrative autonomy. Moreover, the film effectively negates the image of white-black fraternity that it has so carefully fostered.

Check: Any person or thing that . . . acts as a stop or restraint

Appropriately, *Check and Double Check* has two endings. First, there is the final facing tableau with Richard and Amos and Andy in Penn Station, which the film abandons in midscene, fading out just as Andy begins his breathless explanation of the recovery of the deed. Second, following an intertitle stating "Several Days Later," the film returns to Amos and Andy's taxi office for a brief narrative coda that revisits and glosses the events at the train station, while again disengaging their story-line from Richard's in a decisive way. The first "ending" occurs when Amos and Andy consummate their offer of service to Mr. Richard—without his having sought it out. Having gleaned the importance of the deed, Amos and Andy attempt to locate Richard, rushing in the taxi to Penn Station in order to stop him before he returns to Georgia. The ensuing scene replays the encounter at the Blair house, but with the spatial positions reversed. Amos and Andy shout Richard's name from the top of the stairs leading to the train platform; he hears their cries and steps off the train just as it begins to move. Unable to come closer because the gate separating the platform from the rest of the station has been closed, they transact the entire exchange—the relay of the deed plus Andy's interrupted monologue—through a set of vertical bars.

The interaction across the iron bars marks the one and only instance where the three men "get in touch" after Richard's initial promise. That the train platform scene is a deliberate repetition of the reunion at the Blair house is evident in the way that it revolves around spoken references to the dead father and his own spoken and written traces. The generally stiff Richard is relatively effusive in his gratitude to Amos and Andy, emphasizing that the deed "means everything" to him and eagerly inquiring into where they found it. However triumphant the conversation may sound, the physical constraints that frame the scene make it an exceedingly ironic instance of being "in touch." In this climactic episode, racial division clearly marks the limit of brotherly reunion. The bars emblematize the social limitations placed on the black characters' mobility and the obstacles to social interaction across the color line within modern urban space (as opposed to the Georgia of their minds).[38] As a narrative resolution to the complex, chiastic plot structure, the repetition of the facing tableau is a partial and unsatisfying one. By interrupting or barring

Figure 18. Publicity still from *Check and Double Check* (RKO, 1930) showing Amos and Andy being separated from Richard at Penn Station. Courtesy of the Academy of Motion Picture Arts and Sciences.

the very harmonizing movement of the facing scene, the film's first attempt at formal self-enclosure shows the imaginary space of the southern agrarian idyll to be receding from view.

Fittingly, the film spares Amos and Andy the difficult, if not impossible task of explaining to Richard how the deed came into their possession—a relevant issue given his surprise upon seeing them again. Although this explanation offers *Check and Double Check* another means to sketch out the relationship between the Williams family and Amos and Andy, the particulars of the gothic scene in the old house (and of the "extimacy" of the southern plantation to their Harlem home) are perhaps too disturbing to the film's dominant ideology to be mentioned again. The scene at Penn Station closes with Andy beginning to respond to Richard's questions: "You see, Mr. Richard, me and Amos belong to a lodge and every year we have to go out to a house to find a piece of paper . . ."—at which point the shot fades out. Andy's explanation is halting and labored, as though he himself is waiting to be rescued by the fade-out and thus spared this impossible task. At the moment at which we begin to imagine what the rest of Andy's explanation would sound like—his unfolding of the relation between the lodge and the old house—we are able to sense the decisive imprint of *Check and Double Check*'s political unconscious upon its narrative surface. The film offers a compromise solution to the problem of making sense of its own climax by gagging Andy, while instructing the viewer to infer that the missing explanation continues offscreen. The editing makes us think that we already know what he will say and that, because we have seen the series of events unfold, any further commentary would be redundant. In fact, because the presentation of these events was so confusing, it would be most helpful.

One shot in this sequence briefly introduces another black figure—who, like Amos and Andy, works in the city's transportation economy—and positions him in relation to the three other men. As Richard steps off the train, he shouts for the redcap to follow him back onto the platform; the camera lingers over the latter—portrayed, like Amos and Andy, by a white actor in blackface—for a surprisingly long time. Occupying the middle of the frame, the redcap stands still, holding Richard's bags, his back to the train as it pulls away. Given that it occurs in a sequence that foregrounds intradiegetic-looking relations more than any other in the film, the shot of the redcap occupies a strange place in the montage. The redcap faces the camera, whose position bears no clear relation to those of the other characters. While the sequence employs crude point-of-view shots to represent Amos and Andy's downward gaze at the track and platform below, the redcap is shot at the same height and from close range. Further, because it coincides with Richard's rushing the stairs, the shot represents a lull in the scene's forward momentum and a digression away from its focal point of suspense; the redcap is, perhaps, the person at whom he would have been looking had he not headed off in Amos and Andy's direction. Engaged in an impersonal, strictly commercial service relationship with Richard, the redcap represents, moreover, Amos and Andy's present and future within contemporary urban space, the image that, in their desire to salvage the imaginary-familial ("familiar") relationship to the Williamses, they cannot yet recognize or "face." Here Amos and Andy's professional identity as transportation-service workers in the metropolis is crucial. Consider how closely their several outings in the film shadow Richard's comings and goings: Richard is always about to become their next fare.

Check: To accept or hand over (an article) in return for a check . . .

The film returns the viewer to Amos and Andy's world, just as Richard's romantic plot has achieved implicit resolution. Richard does not appear again after receiving the deed, and Jean has made her exit well before this moment in the film. This return to the taxi company office represents the film's second and actual ending. Through their own labor and perseverance, Amos and

Andy have managed to restore the integrity of the Williams estate. Yet there is nothing in the train station scene to indicate that they will have any reward or compensation to show for their efforts. By emerging from their secret mission with the Williams deed, instead of the document required for the lodge ritual, Amos and Andy have earned the scorn of their brothers; having missed their date with Madame Queen and Ruby Taylor during the confusion, Amos and Andy appear, further, to have sabotaged their own romantic relationships.[39] Across the temporal divide marked by the "Several Days Later" intertitle, the excitement of the train platform has dissipated completely; the scene in the cab company office finds the protagonists defeated, taking stock of their bleak situation—much as they have done in the opening scene, prior to Richard's reappearance. As in *Hallelujah* (MGM, 1929), the vestigial silent-film device of the intertitle serves to momentarily restart a narrative that has stalled (like the taxi) around the too-bleak social prospects of the black protagonists.

Their misery is interrupted, if not finally alleviated, by the arrival of a package from Richard. It is a piece of the Williams-Blair wedding cake, accompanied by a note reading: "Dear boys, we want you to have a part of our wedding cake. We'll never forget you for the happiness you have brought us, and as soon as we return from our honeymoon, we will get in touch with you." Admiring the layers of pristine white cake, swaddled in paper wrapping that almost glows, Amos and Andy fail to see how it can alleviate their present pitiful condition and confess to having "no appetite" at all. Not having been informed of the details of Richard's financial-romantic predicament, they would have no way of connecting the wedding cake and the fact of his marriage to their own heroic efforts on his behalf; indeed, Amos's response suggests that Richard's marriage comes as an unexpected event.

Although Amos and Andy are pleased for Richard, they are left only to note the absolute disparity between his fate and their own; with a sense of finality, Andy adds, "Well Amos, it looks like everybody's happy but us." Just as he has pronounced this verdict, the scene delivers another affective reversal. The telephone rings with Madame Queen and Ruby Taylor calling to say that they "done heard all about it" (in Amos's paraphrase) and are no longer upset. Hence, the arrival of the wedding cake becomes timely indeed; Andy instructs Amos to tell the women that they are coming to visit, bearing a surprise. Echoing their swift action with the deed, Amos and Andy wrap up the cake and head out into the street. However dramatic their reversal of fortune might seem (Amos: "Everything is all right now"), it is equally short-lived. Having insisted on carrying the cake, Andy drops it when he is startled by the horn of an approaching truck, leaving it to be crushed beneath the wheels.

The cake episode maintains the tenuous interconnection between the two plots, while at the same time illustrating that the twain shall not meet. Answering the question of what Amos and Andy have to show for their aid to Richard, the cake itself provides an ambivalent reference to the two earlier scenes of reunion between estranged "brothers." By sending food, Richard enacts the transcendental moment of familial harmony, but only in a diminished, almost parodic form. The cake recalls Richard Sr.'s promised "last loaf of bread," but here it proves to offer no nourishment or use to Amos and Andy. Richard Jr. seems to say, "Let them eat cake." Moreover, the note defers again Richard's earlier promise to "get in touch" with Amos and Andy in New York—itself a diminished reiteration of his father's guarantee of home and sustenance—beyond the temporal limit of the film's narrative. In the off-screen action that precedes the scene, the consumption of the cake has played a symbolic role in the ritual feast of reconstituting and regenerating the Williams family. By sending part of it to Amos and Andy, Richard seeks to include them ostensibly in the ritual, even as the mode of the cake's delivery—via an anonymous courier—draws attention to their distance from it. It is tempting to read the cake as a kind of effigy for Richard—a grotesquely white mask sent to represent Richard in absentia in a final scene of facing. In this final attempt to imitate the father—someone physically absent who can be conjured through recited linguistic traces—Richard in fact brings the mise-en-scène of benevolent facing to an end.

Thus the piece of wedding cake functions as a fetish in a recognizably Freudian way. As a token through which the loss of the familial idyll can be disavowed, the cake acquires ("inherits," in Freud's suggestive formulation) the metaphysical associations that had been carried by the father's promises to provide in times of need. These associations manifest themselves in the form of the object's visual appearance: the "luminous shine" (Freud) that solicits Amos and Andy's (and the viewer's) gaze.[40] At the same time, the fetish object's very transformed appearance elicits an aversive response, which acknowledges a necessary abandonment of belief in the idyll itself. Here we must not limit our reading to the contrast between the cake and the loaf of bread, but instead consider the entire scene of the former's delivery as a surrogate for the familial-idyllic facing scene. The defining feature of the cake episode is that it attempts to paper over, while ultimately highlighting, the fact that Richard himself has not come to visit, much less invited Amos and Andy to the wedding. Like the barred gate at the train station, the cake and its accompanying text ultimately signify distance within the very performance of unfettered emotional exchange.

The aversive component of Amos and Andy's response to the gift manifests itself in a peculiar and subtle way, which, however, puts it beyond the reach of the Freudian analytic of the fetish. Having sampled the frosting but declared themselves without appetite, Amos and Andy have a flash of insight. Realizing that they can utilize it as a token of romantic reconciliation, they discover the wedding cake's true hidden value. Disengaging it from the symbolic tableau in which the cake first appears, Amos and Andy choose instead to treat it negatively, as a disguised form of monetary compensation. "Something pretty" and "good to eat," the cake is an otherwise inaccessible commodity, which they recognize will confer social prestige upon them as its bearers. Amos and Andy finally seize upon the exchange value of the object, the "social relation" of production that appears phantasmagorically to be contained in the cake's very substance; it becomes a commodity-fetish in the sense that Marx describes.[41]

Amos and Andy's momentary reappropriation of the gift marks a decisive turn in the film. At this moment, the two are jogged out of their stasis, acting skillfully and resourcefully in their own interests. Their own desire—in no way regulated by Richard's—prompts transformative work on the "raw material" provided by Richard. By incorporating a prop from Richard's marriage comedy plot into their own romantic scenario, they seek to duplicate its successful resolution. In other words, Amos and Andy wager on restoring the symmetry between the two stories—this time to their advantage—through a gesture of calculated imitation, a reversal.[42] While Amos and Andy are supposed to cement their bond with Richard through admiring glances at the cake, accompanied by outpourings of gratitude and nostalgia, they instead appropriate the cake (as a signifier of Richard's social privilege) and discard the old master-servant idyll. At this moment in the film, Amos and Andy are interested strictly in bonding with black women, not white men. It is in this context of emerging narrative autonomy that the destruction of the cake becomes significant. The film seems here to disallow Amos and Andy's wager, or to punish them for attempting to turn the tables on Richard.

Check: To stop (a person) from receiving a part of his wages as a fine or penalty . . . Obs.

There remains one scene of facing/mirroring about which I have yet to say anything and which has material precedence over all of the others in *Check and Double Check*: the act of blackface masquerade itself. While organizing its complex dual plot structure around episodes of interracial harmony and alienation, the film already has generated its black characters out of blackface's ("primal") scene of facing, which here unfolds off-screen. Recall the earlier discussion of this scene through Michael Rogin's work and the Hegelian rhetoric of recognition. The scene of blacking up involves an implicit reference to a strictly regulated notion of blackness, always already available for white usage. To what degree does this originary scene of facing, which occurs here only in preproduction, leave its mark within the diegetic world of the film? Does it simply serve to establish a kind of visual illusion? Or, does it have other effects?

The scene of blacking up, as I have analyzed it here, works off of the principle that James Snead calls "exclusionary emulation": "the principle whereby the power and trappings of black culture are [imitated] while at the same time their black originators are segregated away and kept at a distance."[43] Through "exclusionary emulation," the white performer seeks to appropriate the affective and libidinal potentialities that blackness appears to symbolize—charisma, comedic license, irrationality, sexual power—situating "blackness" within the ensemble of white subjectivity. Imitation and the play with "identity" serve to reaffirm and naturalize historical white power, by, as Rogin has argued, turning racial difference into a fetish and excluding African American performers from the scene of American entertainment. Because the white performer must be able to occupy the site of blackness in a manner that can sustain this fantasy of racial difference, emulation becomes necessarily exclusionary.[44] In Snead's suggestive Hegelian formulation, the marginalization of African American subjects entails that they appear to exist "not . . . for themselves, but mainly for others, and more precisely, *for whites*."[45]

In the wake of contemporary theoretical understandings of blackface minstrelsy, one cannot fail to be struck by the constellation of ideas and images that comprises *Check and Double Check*'s final scene. Much like earlier avatars of the blackface minstrel show, and much like King Vidor's reminiscences about *Hallelujah*, the concluding scene of *Check and Double Check* fixates on themes of lending/borrowing and sale/compensation. What is at issue here is Amos and Andy's labor on behalf of Richard as compared to his compensatory gesture.[46] Moreover, the scene figuratively evokes blackface masquerade by dramatizing the ability of images to migrate between bodies—the cake as Richard's mask; Amos and Andy's giving voice to that mask by reading Richard's letter; their attempt to don this mask of luxury. Taken together, these traces suggest that the scene of blacking up is by no means irrelevant to the film-text. Nor has it been "scotomized"; rather, it is a disavowed tableau that, nonetheless, haunts the film's attempt to resolve Amos and Andy's relationship to Richard.

In its final sequence, *Check and Double Check*'s narrative converges upon the crucial, although invisible, scene of facing that undergirds the film. The specular event of racial masquerade itself resurfaces as a contradictory element in the film's composite treatment of the question of Amos and Andy's desire. While weaving its principal thematics into the narrative texture, the film replays the drama of blackface in inverted form, suggesting a parodic reworking of Snead's paradigm. "Exclusionary emulation" is precisely the operation that Amos and Andy perform with respect to Richard and his confectionery mask. By capitalizing upon his gift, they effectively detach his image from its relational context—in an effort to appropriate its suprasensible qualities. Or, by altering Snead's terms slightly, one might say that in the final scene, the power and trappings of white culture are imitated while at the same time its white guardian is relegated to the domain of memory. If Amos and Andy's treatment of Richard's gift is a displaced echo of minstrelsy's expropriating mode, then the accident that interrupts the cake's new trajectory evokes the materiality of blackface itself.

Breaking off Amos and Andy's narrative agency suddenly and unexpectedly, the truck carries with it—literally into the frame from an invisible, exterior point—the occluded, framing episode. As the instrument that violently crosses out and smears over the white mask, the tire tread puts the cake into virtual blackface, translating it into the dilapidated, crumbling state of all things in Amos and Andy's surroundings.[47] Here the film points to its underlying structural contradiction. *Check and Double Check* cannot critique white dependence on and undercompensation of black labor (Richard's ultimate treatment of Amos and Andy) at the same time as it visually evokes the tableau of blackface theft. In this way, the already fetishized cake is forced to support one layer too many. At the moment at which these two stories-masquerading-as-objects begin to share the same frame, the cake is reduced to a distorted mess on the pavement.

Combining the filmic narrative's relations across the color line with cinematic blackface's founding gesture of racial cross-dressing, *Check and Double Check* concludes with an almost inscrutable tableau of facing. Despite its complexity, this fractured allegory of production may offer the most comprehensive explanation of the film's interwoven, simultaneously diverging and converging, double plot. Invented for the radio, Amos and Andy, the poor, African American migrant characters, brought Freeman Gosden and Charles Correll fame and fortune and enabled them to live in a manner that might be rendered on screen as the world of Richard and Ralph. In *Check and Double Check*, the celebrities (the "famous radio team") and their abject alter egos ("Negroes") share the stage. This bizarre encounter takes the form of an attempt to reconcile the contradictory movement whereby the representability of the latter in popular culture is the condition of possibility for the former's social ascension.

A cryptic item in the Chicago section of *Motion Picture News* highlights this convergence. The anonymous writer describes Gosden and Correll's appearance upon their return to the city (where the radio show originated), following "a three months Hollywood interlude" to make the film: "[Gosden and Correll] alighted from their train looking like a couple of undergraduates from an investment broker's office. Light tan hats with that Prince of Wales brim, darker tan suits of Wilshire Boulevard cut, and tan camel's hair top coats blended with tan faces and shoes to complete an ensemble that left any one unaccustomed to the street garb of the West Coast professional with a decidedly dark brown taste in his mental mouth." "Vastly changed" since leaving Chicago, the radio comedians look prosperous and hale, their several pieces of tan clothing complementing their "tanned" skin. But while these clothes signify "professional" success in their original, Hollywood setting, they seem to leave the writer's imagined Chicago observer confused, seeing (tasting?) the men, instead, as "dark brown." The odd trope of the "mental mouth" perhaps recalls the radio show's synesthetic play (the idea of authentic "black voice") and the pleasurable confusion it fostered for listeners over the performers' racial identities. In any case, it renders Gosden and Correll figuratively black at the precise moment at which they might be seen as most white (as looking like Ivy Leaguers or investment bankers), turning them into Amos and Andy even as they appear off set in "street garb." Indeed, the writer occupies the position of the imagined, perplexed observer, alternately calling the performers by their real names and by the names of their characters.[48] *Check and Double Check* is an allegory of this convergence of contradictory social images. Its narrative attempts to resolve this contradiction, but, in the process, dredges up the very histories of race that make revising that story, and by extension, the story of blackface, impossible.

Conclusion

"THE REQUIRED NEGRO MOTIF" AFTER THE TRANSITION TO SOUND

Having established a reputation in Hollywood for his highly atmospheric pictorial style, Austrian émigré director Josef von Sternberg met the arrival of synchronized-sound technology with more than the usual trepidation. Whereas other artists working in the studio system saw an imperfect, challenging apparatus that could be mastered over time, von Sternberg saw an alien technology with no obvious cinematic function. Because the microphone, unlike the camera, had no "viewpoint," it could merely "reproduce" sound.[1] At best, the microphone enabled the filmmaker to include a redundant layer of information in the film. At worst, it confined the camera by forcing the filmmaker to photograph sound sources, stripping the visual register of its own expressive qualities—or, in von Sternberg's ironic locution, "silencing" the camera.[2] In another, more striking formulation, von Sternberg would even blame the phenomenon of sound itself (rather than the recording instrument) for this loss of expressive power. Because "sound throws no shadows," von Sternberg holds, it cannot be blended into the "entire chiaroscuro" that is the cinematic artifact.[3] Von Sternberg's first talking picture, *Thunderbolt* (Paramount, 1929), is an attempt to convert sound into an element of cinematic chiaroscuro, which reflects both his contempt for the synchronized-sound apparatus and his provocatively synesthetic understanding of acoustics.

Treating synchronized sound not as an aesthetic obstacle but as an occasion for expressive uses of both camera and microphone, *Thunderbolt* explores themes and situations rehearsed in von Sternberg's silent gangster film, *Underworld* (Paramount, 1927). Refusing to adhere strictly to the "moving lips" standard for managing sound-image relations, von Sternberg uses high-contrast lighting and pervasive camera movement to impose a conceptual and psychological point of view on the film's story materials and to generate the greatest possible "pictorial . . . impact" from them.[4] In order to achieve a similar point of view and impact in the acoustic register, von Sternberg builds a soundtrack out of multiple layers of speech, song, and ambient noises, while also using frequent voice-offs and peculiar sound bridges. Given both the racial dynamics of Hollywood's transition to sound and von Sternberg's own racial imagination, *Thunderbolt* not surprisingly turns to African American performance as its primary vehicle for these innovations in sound cinema. The film couples the wider studio interest in promoting ostensibly "exotic" Harlem culture as a production feature with von Sternberg's declared interest in the "expressive countenance and vibrant voice of the Negro."[5]

Like Dudley Murphy and King Vidor, von Sternberg is a white director for whom the "Negro voice," with its presumed expressive intensity and ability to evoke bodily presence, enables strategic uses of "asynchronism," while African American performance seems to fit easily with a highly stylized and atmospheric visual expressionism. Recalling the jubilee sequence of *Hallelujah* (MGM, 1929) and Fredi's deathbed sequence in *Black and Tan* (RKO, 1929), *Thunderbolt* doubles African American figures with their own shadows, using the latter to establish presence without including an actual body in the frame. Because of von Sternberg's view of cinema as chiaroscuro, *Thunderbolt*, however, pushes this tendency a step further. According a privileged role to African American acoustic and vocal production (and to other noise-making objects coded as "black"), in the context of a film primarily about white characters, *Thunderbolt* establishes a more radical identification of African Americans with "shadows." It suggests that "Negro" bodies and voices more readily "throw shadows" and, in turn, yield themselves to von Sternberg's expressionist poetics.

Of course, it is possible to read this identification as a romantic racialist gesture and as one more of von Sternberg's strategies to "eradicate the traces of [his] labor" in his films.[6] The appearance of a natural fit that he (like Murphy and Vidor) establishes between African American performance and cinematic shadow-play is the effect of a deliberate process of cinematic composition rather than an expression of any preexisting physiological or cultural difference. Fusing expressionist visual and acoustic composition with African American cabaret performance and spiritual singing in a very self-conscious way, *Thunderbolt* provides an extreme but also highly representative case of what I have called the black acoustic or black vocal object. Further, *Thunderbolt* typifies the ambiguity that attaches to the black vocal object in this period. Depending on the degree to which a given film marshals surrounding historical context, this object registers either African American stasis or social movement—and often some tense combination of the two—and may or may not amount to anything more than a highly codified or stereotyped African American screen image. Moreover, *Thunderbolt* points ahead to some of the more durable cinematic conventions that emerge from experiments in representing African American performance carried out by directors like von Sternberg, Murphy, and Vidor.

Von Sternberg's cinema is almost always characterized by a dense, highly modeled, synthetic texture. One need only think here of the veils, louvers, lattices, feathers, and shadow patterns that he arrays around and in front of Marlene Dietrich's figure in films like *Morocco* (Paramount, 1930) and *The Devil Is a Woman* (Paramount, 1935). Whether or not von Sternberg succeeds in suffusing the image (or the soundtrack) with the mystical, elusive concepts that he claims drive his filmmaking, he creates layered tableaux that, while obviously stylized and flat, possess a certain intense, tangible quality—what Lotte Eisner calls "depth without depth."[7]

Early in *Thunderbolt*, the white characters Ritzie (Fay Wray) and her ex-boyfriend, wanted criminal Jim Laing, aka Thunderbolt (George Bancroft), arrange a clandestine meeting at The Black Cat nightclub. The lengthy nightclub scene serves an important narrative purpose. In this scene, Ritzie articulates her love for Bob Morgan (Richard Arlen) and pleads with Thunderbolt to leave them alone. The police raid the club, but Thunderbolt manages to elude capture.[8] This scene also provides an extended display of the sorts of visual and acoustic texturing that defines von Sternberg's expressionist poetics. Using a "black and tan" cabaret—a cabaret in an African American neighborhood featuring black entertainment and a racially mixed clientele—as his setting, von Sternberg attempts to make sound "throw shadows." During the establishing shots of the club, we hear simultaneously the sound of the band, the laughter of the mostly African American patrons, and the stuttering of the African American maitre d'. Having established this dense and somewhat strident soundscape, where distinct noises compete for the viewer's attention, the film uses an extended tracking shot to follow Thunderbolt as he enters the club and descends the stairs, revealing an equally dense and multifaceted mise-en-scène.

Over the course of the scene, the camera will focus alternately on the entertainment on stage, on Ritzie and Thunderbolt's conversation, and on other patrons (who gossip about Thunderbolt's crimes and legendary strength). But the sounds audible during this shot will not necessarily depend on what is being shown; or, more to the point, the noises introduced on the soundtrack will not dictate the introduction of visible sources. The two "tracks" unfold more or less in parallel, working together but making no effort to offer proof of their synchronization. For instance, people seated out of frame gossip about Thunderbolt during the tracking shot. In a later shot of two men telling tall tales about Thunderbolt's exploits, one is very noticeably obscured behind a pillar supporting the ceiling. When Thunderbolt fights with another white patron, comments by other patrons are audible as a voice-off. Later, one of the stage performer's blues lyrics adds counterpoint to the scene of Thunderbolt leaving the club.

This singer is heard more than she is seen, and, when the film does visually register her presence, it tends to do so by including her looming shadow in the frame. A bright, directed light projects her shadow onto the wall and stairway leading to the door; when Thunderbolt exits this door, he physically passes through her shadow. In a surprising acknowledgment of interracial desire, the film includes a medium close-up of Thunderbolt pausing at the exit to gaze desirously at the performer, who sings what an early script draft calls "one of those hot daddy blues."[9] The strategy of doubling this singer's body with her shadow or silhouette serves to add texture to the mise-en-scène of the room, while also giving her a surplus diegetic grounding. These shots typify the early sound-era visual construction of what I have termed the black vocal object.

Following the racial logic of early sound cinema, the presence of African Americans as producers of sound—the blues singer, Curtis Mosby and His Blue Blowers (the band accompanying her), and the gossiping patrons—enables significant departures from the requirements of "moving lips" convention.[10] These "black sounds" carry with them an implied embodiment or physical presence that makes the demonstration of their sources less necessary. *Thunderbolt* signals this logic by reducing the blues singer to a shadow on the wall. She is present, if only indirectly, in certain shots where her singing features prominently. Given von Sternberg's interest in chiaroscuro and carefully textured surfaces, her voice also "throws a shadow" in the sense of adding an element of acoustic dimensionality, helping to give a concrete presence to the psychological dynamics that define the scene.

In other words, von Sternberg has attempted to use sound expressionistically, carefully layering and blending sounds to evoke particular associations. More than simply relaying information through speech or direct musical cues, the soundscape of The Black Cat conveys the sense of simmering tension prompted by Thunderbolt's arrival and the atmosphere of vice and sexual license that typify this underworld hideout. For instance, the murmuring of the crowd above the sound of the music figurally conveys the tension. At the same time, the particular rhythm played by Mosby's band—to which a group of light-skinned African American chorines, costumed like Fredi in *Black and Tan*, perform an energetic dance—is the kind of "staccato jazz" held by the film's pressbook to appeal to white "sensation-seeking Broadwayites." This music represents what the pressbook calls "the heart-beats of southern plantations to metropolitan civilization."[11] While violence, sexual desire, and "primitive" sensation are associations conventionally carried by African American culture in this period, von Sternberg and his sound engineers have put these associations to a particular end—that of developing Thunderbolt's character and milieu.

This strategy of developing Thunderbolt's character continues in the film's lengthy death-row section. Like The Black Cat, the cellblock is a racially mixed space in which African American musical performance serves to establish atmosphere and to express the affective undertones of the dramatic situation. During this section of the film, a black inmate, whom a guard tells us has a "special dispensation from the warden" to leave his cell, frequently plays piano and sings spirituals like "Roll Jordan, Roll." Although the film visually establishes the singer and piano player's presence, the other men listen from their cells without being able to see him.[12] In a film-historical moment in which practices of non-diegetic soundtrack music have not been codified, the spirituals provide a kind of "score" for these scenes. More strikingly, the inmate's body casts a shadow on the other men, becoming a part of the overall chiaroscuro that envelops them. Here chiaroscuro has a very literal application. Due to the high-contrast lighting used to construct the mise-en-scène, the prisoners' bodies are often crisscrossed by shadows of the ubiquitous bars. More evocative than realistic, this visually and acoustically textured space provides the setting for Thunderbolt's rise in moral stature, as he faces the ultimate punishment for his crimes. Hence the anguish and sorrow conveyed by the spirituals become part of *Thunderbolt*'s projection of the main character's interiority throughout this portion of the film. Here again, visual texture coincides with the projection of an African American body onto the walls that define the diegetic space (as an enclosure), in a way that highlights the black inmate's grounding or object quality.

The dense synthetic texture visible (and audible) in *Thunderbolt* and in von Sternberg's later work emerges from the representational paradox that defines his filmmaking. Von Sternberg's expressionism is an art that seeks to directly substantialize or incarnate some kind of "idea" that is more or less abstract and ineffable.[13] This task requires an initial derealization of the objects that make up the profilmic space. From props and costumes to the actors' very bodies, all of these objects must be emptied of their prosaic meaning or severed from their conventional contexts. Following this emptying, these objects may more fully incarnate the concepts and states of mind sought by the director—his "viewpoint" and/or that of a specific character. This sense of personal vision is crucial to von Sternberg, who considers the director "a man who writes with a motion picture camera," and also begins to explain his veritable obsession with shadow and chiaroscuro.[14]

For a filmmaker who eschews true abstraction and nonrepresentational techniques but works with a more or less realist mise-en-scène (centered around human actors and fairly conventional narratives), this project becomes fraught with paradox. The profilmic material proves obviously resistant to von Sternberg's control, inhibiting his ability to directly "paint with light." As Gaylyn Studlar has astutely shown, von Sternberg's films necessarily reference "nature" despite their attempts to become totally artificial, to use signs self-referentially, and to generate highly idiosyncratic conceptual and psychological meanings. The films "clear" the filmic space "of the elements of actuality" only to "re-admit" these elements in an attenuated way; in fact, the "actuality" of these elements may, paradoxically, become legible as a result of the initial strategy of "clearance." Studlar understands von Sternberg as working in an unconventionally iconic register, in which signs are revealed to be simultaneously real and not real—recognizable as belonging to everyday actuality and seeming to belong only to a constructed, imaginary world.[15]

In its use of African American musical performance for evocative and quasi-symbolic purposes, *Thunderbolt* offers an interesting example of this dynamic paradox at the heart of von Sternberg's work. The presence of the inmate who sings and plays the piano is not obviously motivated by the setting or the plot surrounding Thunderbolt's impending execution. As profilmic objects, the spirituals and this musician's performance of them are radically decontextualized, detached from conventional semiotic points of reference. Similarly, the nightclub singer's performance becomes gradually disembodied, so that it may become a signifier of Thunderbolt's interiority—a part of his fantasy life as rendered visible by the film's mise-en-scène.

Interestingly, however, *Thunderbolt* seems anxious about the manipulability of profilmic objects, specifically where "black" acoustic objects are concerned. The gratuitous way in which the film develops a series of "black cat" signifiers, underlining their "pliable" qualities, suggests an allegorical reflection by the film on its own expressionist techniques.[16] This reflection, in turn, puts into relief those features of *Thunderbolt*'s treatment of "black" sound sources that are not subsumed into von Sternberg's "entire chiaroscuro." Albeit in a much more subtle way than some of the cases examined in this book, *Thunderbolt* develops strategies of diegetic grounding and objectification that take on a dual aspect, appearing, from a critical point of view, like rather shaky structures of containment.

Thunderbolt opens with the image of an actual black cat. In the first shot, the camera pans to follow this animal walking past the feet of couples on park benches in amorous embraces. Although the cat does not itself make a sound in this shot, it seems to usher the acoustic register into the film frame, acting as a metonymy for the novel medium. As the cat crosses the park, we begin to hear bells in the distance, muffled dialogue, and the sound of shoes on gravel. The film again correlates the figure of the black cat with novel sound production in setting up the "black and tan" cabaret scene. In an establishing shot of the club's sign, the film reveals its name to be The Black Cat, a signifier which now acquires a hackneyed racial connotation. Then, during the prison sequence, Thunderbolt has in his cell a toy ostensibly for the dog he is allowed to keep with him: the rubber likeness of a black cat's head that emits an eerie cry when squeezed. Plotting to strike Bob with a fatal blow, Thunderbolt exercises his legendary right fist by squeezing the toy. Hence the toy is audible in several shots, and the film lingers over it in one extreme close-up.

This curious chain of "black cat" signifiers helps to provide an esoteric organizing structure for the film. Interesting deployments of sound-film technology are marked by this trope, conventionally a sign of bad luck, which serves to underscore *Thunderbolt*'s use of sound to create a "shadowy" mood. This chain also encompasses African American performance, which represents the privileged (though not the only such) form of sound production. The most unusual instance of the trope, the squeeze toy, emphasizes the idea of pliability—the ability to produce a plaintive sound on command. As an otherwise gratuitous object, the squeeze toy can, perhaps, be read as a symbol of von Sternberg's desire to make sound "throw shadows"—to be strategically available for the purposes of building tone and expressing character interiority. (Thunderbolt channels his anger into the toy, but its cry suggests the sort of expression of pain that he will let out only in the last moments of the film.) As a profilmic object, it is more or less emptied of its prosaic meaning—what is a dog toy doing in a jail cell?—in order to be made available for this use. Alluding to the putative capacity to "throw shadows," this black cat becomes a metonymy for all acoustic objects in the film, including African American performance.

Despite or perhaps as a result of *Thunderbolt*'s attempts to rework "black" signs (visual and acoustic) in the service of expressionist representation, the film begins to point out how this profilmic material resists total manipulation. In The Black Cat cabaret sequence, the film presents a social texture that is not simply reducible to the expressionist texture of evocative chiaroscuro, revealing a tension between the film's desire to create a completely artificial space and its engagement with messier "elements of actuality." Over the course of the scene, the viewer encounters African Americans not only as musical performers but also as the consumers of this musical performance, interacting with white people in a mixed if not completely egalitarian social space and having disposable income and leisure time. Treating social mixing and African American consumption frankly, this section of *Thunderbolt* registers, however partially and inadequately, the sort of demographic change associated with African American mass migration. The studio pressbook's comment about the link between "southern plantations" and "metropolitan civilization" casts this change according to a condescending, primitivist formula. Nevertheless, the interest evinced here (on the part of the Paramount studio and the director alike) in depicting Harlem on screen registers an abiding curiosity about what is a new facet of social "actuality."

The pressbook notes that, in the growing African American neighborhood based around the Central Avenue district, Los Angeles has "its own miniature Harlem" and that the studio was able to find not merely "Negro types" but even "scores of Negroes who really have lived in Harlem."[17] This account (which is presented as a quotation from von Sternberg himself) even makes a fetish of a certain kind of authenticity. At the same time, it does cast Harlem (and by extension Los Angeles's Central Avenue district) as a distinctive social space that is interesting but also somewhat foreign to the people making the film, who here confess some desire to preserve this sense of foreignness on screen—over and against the film's need to make "black" objects fully compliant with specific semiotic ends.

Migration, Sound, and Visual Form in Early Black Independent Sound Films

Despite the bold predictions of enthusiasts like Paramount's Monte Brice, "Negro films" were a relatively minor Hollywood phenomenon, yielding no "deluge" of like movies and never becoming an established, durable genre in their own right.[18] The studios would continue to produce African American–cast musical features in the vein of *Hallelujah* and *Hearts in Dixie* (Fox, 1929), but only sporadically; the first subsequent such film, *The Green Pastures*, was released by Warner Bros. in 1936. The industry's talk about a "fad" or "vogue" for African American performance makes this outcome predictable, perhaps; by definition, fads demand that their objects rapidly fall out of fashion or become obsolete.[19] Due to the imprecise nature of existing mechanisms of audience research, shifts in what Brice called "public taste" were, furthermore, highly speculative. But whether or not the "Negro film" vogue had truly run its course by 1930 or 1931, industry talk about such audience interest—or even a discrete category of films warranting this name—had ceased.

At the same time, the sorts of transformative dramatic roles—roles that would go beyond the boundaries of the song-and-dance tradition, which commentators like Locke and Brown thought might follow novel African American characters like *Hearts in Dixie*'s Chincapin—did not materialize. Nor did the sorts of peculiar mirror-image representations of African American and white narratives (as seen in films like *On With the Show* [Warner Bros., 1929], *Safe in Hell* [First National, 1931], and *Check and Double Check* [RKO, 1930]) become common. With the exception of a more socially conscious film like *Imitation of Life* (Universal, 1934), African American actors continued in the 1930s to play the sorts of stereotyped "bit" roles from which the "experiment" in "Negro talking pictures" had seemed to offer relief. The coveted "place in the studios" that observers like Floyd Covington espoused for these actors thus seemed to disappear just as soon as—or even before—it was established. As early as 1933, the *Baltimore Afro-American* would look back nostalgically to the excitement of 1929, wondering, "Will 'The Emperor Jones' Restore Our Lost Place in the Movies?"[20]

Yet in spite of this sense that "Negro films" were a failed experiment, African American entertainment would persist as a Hollywood production feature in a variety of forms for the duration of the classical or studio era. But in what ways does the presentation of African American musical performance in Hollywood films after the transitional period follow or diverge from the course traced by early sound films? More immediately, how do the films produced after 1931 by the reorganized race cinema companies resemble or part ways with Hollywood's African American films in their presentation of musical performance? To what degree do sound race films offer an alternative "place" for African American cinematic representation?

As Thomas Cripps has demonstrated, African American independent or race cinema, like many independent cinemas, was given a "dual shock" by the transition to sound and the onset of the Great Depression, virtually halting production during the transitional years.[21] With sound-recording technology making film production much more expensive and technically demanding, African American filmmakers and entrepreneurs who had forged a viable silent race cinema were forced temporarily or permanently out of business in the late 1920s. African American auteur Oscar Micheaux and some members of the Lincoln Motion Picture Company managed by 1930 to reenter the motion picture game, by securing white capital backing.[22] At the same time, white-owned and -operated independent or "poverty row" companies (like Sack Amusements, mentioned below) largely filled the void left by the defunct companies with low-budget, Hollywood-style genre films for African Americans, yielding a talking "race cinema" that "would deserve the name only because of the players and audiences."[23]

The sound race cinema takes up the task of grappling with African American migration and changes in the racial dynamics of American society following World War I. In a sense, the race cinema can be said to *reclaim* this task, insofar as it already defined the most significant race films of the 1920s: Oscar Micheaux's *Within Our Gates* (1920) and *Symbol of the Unconquered* (1920) and the Colored Players Film Corporation's *Scar of Shame* (1927). As compared to the products of the Hollywood studios, race films offer a much more straightforward treatment of these sociohistorical developments. Whereas Hollywood's "Negro films" operate under an imperative not to appear to have what one commentator called "a mission or a problem to solve," race films are more or less free to take up specific positions on pressing black social and political questions. Made specifically for distribution to African American audiences and, in some cases, scripted and directed by African American artists, race films adopt an informed, engaged stance toward issues of migration and social mobility, as well as differences between rural and urban spaces. Race films often contextualize their characters and dramatic action in terms of these issues, assuming a certain level of audience familiarity.[24]

The first race films made with synchronized sound, though not musicals in generic terms, provide a showcase for African American musical performance. In these instances of musical spectacle, race films reflect the legacy of the Hollywood cinema's construction of black performance as an entertainment "bonus." The sorts of Harlem-centered performance—orchestral jazz, precision and acrobatic tap dancing, the Lew Leslie–style chorus line—featured in these films resemble the fare that the Hollywood studios sought to market to white "Broadway" sophisticates. And, although race films represent the Harlem cabaret as an exclusively African American setting, avoiding its "black and tan" counterpart, they tend to code it as a space of luxury, hedonism, and (sometimes problematic) cultural pleasure. At the same time, however, the way that race films contextualize and narrate this space and the kinds of spectacle showcased within it distinguish them very clearly from their Hollywood counterparts. In these race films, the Harlem cabaret is an extension of a complex, dynamic black urban milieu, which is represented neither as a threat to the racial-social order nor as an exotic territory to be colonized by white pleasure seekers.

Thus, as Arthur Knight has demonstrated, race films featuring sound can be usefully positioned in relation to Hollywood products through Houston Baker's dialectic of the mastery of form and the deformation of mastery. Rather than seeing race films as failed imitations of their Hollywood predecessors, Knight argues, it is imperative to recognize the ways in which they mimic the narrative and visual strategies of Hollywood films, in an attempt to "master" them.[25] In Baker's dialectic, this kind of formal imitation brings with it a subtle attempt to "deform" the ideological "mastery" historically associated with it—the pervasive will to disparage African Americans through mass-cultural representations.[26] Films like *The Exile* (Micheaux, 1931) and *The Black King* (Sack Amusements, 1932) intermittently adhere to the conventions of Hollywood narrative films as codified by the early 1930s, in terms of characterization (melodramatic positioning of good and malevolent figures), plotting (emphasis on mystery and detection, creation of suspense), and incorporation of sound (adherence to the "moving lips" standard of synchronization).

At the same time, they weave these conventions into a cinematic tapestry that is highly idiosyncratic, often featuring nonnormative practices of cinematography, editing, acting, and mise-en-scène. Because of limited production resources (equipment like lights, lenses, and film stock, as well as the time required for intricate camera setups) and the aesthetic preferences of the filmmakers, the sorts of expressionist visual flourishes seen in a film like *Thunderbolt* are rare, if not nonexistent, in these films. Their overall visual style is heterogeneous, and the profilmic worlds they establish are less carefully controlled or manipulated than those of a studio auteur like von Sternberg (or King Vidor or Alan Crosland, for that matter). Sound race films' heterogeneous style accompanies their dialogic or multivoiced narrative discourse, which actively "deforms" the existing master discourses of race in Jim Crow society.

Micheaux's first sound films take an ambivalent approach to the social and political aspects of their subject matter. On the one hand, *The Exile* frankly treats migration and its causes.[27] The opening titles of *The Exile* frame the film as a narrative about "Negroes" in Chicago just after the close of the First World

War, highlighting the role of war-related industrial jobs in spurring the migration that has transformed the city's South Side and satirizing the resultant flight of whites "frightened and terrified by the sight of a—seemingly endless stream of Negroes."

On the other hand, *The Exile* moralistically indicts what Micheaux sees as the culture of easy money and status seeking that afflicts African American urban life. *The Exile* initially presents main character Edith Duval (Eunice Brooks) as a former maid who has ascended to the position of "an ambitious 'social leader,'" representing, it would seem, the possibilities of socioeconomic advancement available in the postmigration South Side. Through the gossip of a couple of aristocratic-looking women playing cards in one of Edith's salons, however, the film recontextualizes her character as a denizen of the underworld, who once ran a "notorious row house" (a place of gambling and bootlegging) and is now putting on airs. Although Edith has become one of the South Side's most important "hostesses" and aspires to turn her mansion—abandoned by a rich white family in their flight from the neighborhood—into a "social club" of great quality, she will, one of the gossips predicts, return to her old rackets and end up running another "dive." Indeed, the film later reveals their prediction to be accurate, at least in part. Edith is confronted by Jango (Carl Mahon), an ambitious African student who has come to Chicago to train as a doctor or lawyer. Instead of earning his degree, Jango has spent money, drunk liquor, and become addicted to "reefers," all at Edith's "dive." After Edith dismisses Jango's accusation that she has ruined him, a complicated series of events culminates with his fatally shooting her. A newspaper headline announces, "'Queen' of Chicago's Negro Underworld Slain!" and the film implicitly blames Edith for her own demise, though it gives her the opportunity to justify her chosen life of crime.

Based on this example, it is clear that Micheaux's treatment of the geography, economics, and culture of migration is circumscribed within his ongoing critique of the desire for status and easy money that, in his view, vitiate contemporary urban society. Micheaux's novels and films routinely espouse a doctrine of individual self-making through the gradual accumulation of land and property in agricultural settings as a remedy for social problems facing African Americans. Based on the autobiographical figure at the center of Micheaux's 1912 novel *The Conquest*, *The Exile*'s Jean Baptiste most clearly exemplifies this interesting combination of Washingtonian uplift ideals and frontier mythology.[28] Jean Baptiste spurns Edith's vision of social advancement in the urban culture of the South Side; instead, he goes to South Dakota, where he becomes a prosperous farmer and meets a woman who adheres to the Victorian morals and gender norms that he professes.

In spite of such overarching critiques of urban life, Micheaux tends to exploit its cultural manifestations for diverting spectacle. Although *The Exile* stigmatizes Edith's mansion as a site of illegal gambling and drinking, it features scenes of the kinds of musical performance staged there, scenes that are, strictly speaking, excessive to the requirements of the narrative. In one of these scenes, a group of ten light-skinned chorines perform a synchronized tap routine. In their costuming and in the cinematography that Micheaux uses, the film clearly recalls Murphy's *Black and Tan*. The women execute high kicks while holding their skirts, yielding a "crotch shot" of the sort that characterizes female bodily spectacle in Hollywood musicals.[29] Here, as in later Micheaux sound films like *The Girl from Chicago* (1932), a certain indulgence in African American cabaret performance at the level of audiovisual spectacle coincides with an overtly critical narrative of urban life.

A film produced by Sack Amusements, *The Black King*, demonstrates a similar political ambivalence. In fact, the film seems deliberately ambiguous in how it represents the project of its central figure, a Baptist minister who launches an organization for black social empowerment, superficially resembling Marcus Garvey's United Negro Improvement Association (UNIA).[30] The film's narrative trajectory works to unmask the minister and self-styled black emperor, Charcoal Johnson (A. B. DeComathiere), as a fraud; the film tends to mock both his misuse of language and the ignorance of his victims. Because the exposure of Johnson's misdeeds requires him and his followers to return to the town in Mississippi where they are from, the film's narrative enforces the idea of the southern plantation—where the congregants from Jones's church are said to work—as a natural "home" for African Americans. The sympathetic black characters who work to foil Johnson align themselves, in fact, with the white judge (Bud Pollard) in the town "way down South" where they live. Unlike Doc Shelby in *Hearts in Dixie*, who actually supports Chincapin's journey north, this judge stands for the established racial order, sending the sheriff to apprehend the departing black townspeople. The film here recalls the more conservative brand of southern-centric racial ideology of some Hollywood films, containing the threat of African American migration, both actual—Johnson and his followers journey to Tulsa, Oklahoma; Chicago; and finally Harlem—and proposed—as in Johnson's plan for a "back to Africa" movement.

For all of its overt hostility toward the idea of a charismatic black leader in the mold of Garvey, *The Black King* nevertheless devotes great time and attention to Johnson's political program and his group's quasi-martial displays. Johnson offers forceful critiques of white racism and makes a strong case for the need for African American self-governance, despite the occasionally parodic quality of his way of speaking and his outlandish promises (that great riches await in Africa). Although Jones's detractors, Sug (Knolly Mitchell) most notably, level strong (and finally persuasive) charges that he is a womanizer and a confidence man, they end up allying themselves with white power; by contrast, Johnson can seem both charismatic and compelling, if occasionally pompous and ridiculous. So, *The Black King* leaves some doubt as to the true significance of its main character: Is he just a harmless buffoon, or a dangerous charlatan? Could he be a political leader with legitimate ideas who is simply brought down by his moral corruption? How seriously is the viewer to take Johnson's movement and the underlying issues that it addresses? Is he a threat to the Jim Crow social order?

As *Variety*'s review indicates, *The Black King*'s tone is wildly uneven, "wavering between seriousness and burlesque." "Sometimes it is difficult to determine whether the action is intended as serious or whether as comedy," the reviewer writes, settling on the term "quasi-comedy" for the film.[31] The terms "seriousness" and "burlesque" nicely characterize the film's treatment of African American social mobility, oscillating between overt critique and indulgence at the levels of oratory and visual pageantry. It is as if the film offers these contending representations so as to be able to satisfy different social audiences; the critique of Jones's "back to Africa" movement insulates the film against white charges of radical propaganda, while the film offers a platform for antiracist critique that would be legible to informed African American viewers.[32]

Alongside the "deformation of mastery" that *The Black King* executes through its coupling of a serious treatment of black political organization and geographic movement with a mocking, comedic one, the film offers an interesting case of the "mastery of form." The opening titles unfold over a visual backdrop of shadows of raised arms and hands, with a choral rendition of "Wade in the Water" providing the soundtrack. One critic in the black press, John Louis Clarke, characterized this opening as the "moan[ing] of a weird chant" by an "unseen" chorus, "while waving hands and bending figures are shadowed on the screen." Opening with the kinds of silhouettes of black bodies in ecstatic religious celebration codified in earlier Hollywood offerings, *The Black King* aligns itself at the outset with films like *Hallelujah* and *Black and Tan*. The deployment of the "black vocal object" serves initially to place this film within a particular trajectory of black representation in sound cinema, signaling the film's attempt to master an established Hollywood form. Clarke saw the film as deliberately using "the required Negro motif" in order to "[recall] previous Negro pictures and plays," calling this strategy "hackneyed."[33]

Yet this strategy proves to be something of a decoy. Following the initial scenes inside and in front of the Rise and Shine Baptist Church, *The Black King* entirely eschews the "hackneyed" and "required Negro motif" of chiaroscuro coupled with "weird chant." Instead, the film derives cinematic spectacle from tightly framed shots of Johnson's followers in uniform marching in formation. In a few shots, characters march directly toward the camera until their faces are seen in extreme close-up.[34] In these extensive sequences, the film offers viewers a chance to indulge in a spectacle of disciplined black motion, symbolizing political organization and radical self-refashioning through geographic movement—and offsetting the film's satirical depiction of black incompetence (in Johnson's mangled speech, for example). This form of spectacle ultimately contrasts with the Hollywood-derived "Negro motif" that Clarke highlights. Here the film shifts from a strategy of extreme diegetic grounding, a strategy conventionally used to symbolize physical immobility, to one of impressive movement within the frame—monumentalized bodies moving toward a "promised land."

The Studio Musical and the "Frozen" Image of Black Performance

During the transitional period, African American performance acquires a privileged status as a Hollywood production feature, however contradictory and ideologically fraught. Once the studios resolve the technical problems initially confounding the sound-recording apparatus, African American performance appears to lose this status. The "tempering" of the soundtrack and the "integration" of sound into the filmic diegesis, at the same time, problematizes the African American screen presence, making what had once seemed like an asset a decided liability.

Crucially, black musical performance comes into the American cinema during the transitional period as one "novelty" among many, the most prominent of which was recorded sound itself. Donald Crafton explains: "When the transition began, sound was treated by the studios as a bonus, something dispensed to add value to a film or program. Audiences seemed to respond favorably, regardless of the quality or content. It may also be that there was a tendency to think of movie sound as a new kind of electrical appliance; audiences were drawn to see what science had wrought. They were curious, and producers gave them what they wanted: sound tracks which spiced up traditional films by injecting music, noises, and perhaps an added reel or two of talking."[35] As Robert Spadoni's work illustrates, however, sound, for all of its appealing novelty for early audiences, often confronted them with "unforeseen side effects."[36]

The presence of recorded sound in the cinema seemed for many early viewers to subtract from film experience, draining the image of its "lifelike" quality and rendering it two-dimensional, mechanical, or even ghostly. By diminishing human "presence" or shrinking the actor's "personality," sound could make viewers aware of the obvious but easily ignored fact that the medium was "colorless" and "flat."[37] Given the conception of sound as an add-on or bonus, this subtractive "side effect" is highly ironic; sound should, theoretically, add to the "presence" or "personality" of the body on screen. Alice Maurice's work on period discourses of "the black voice" (and on period conceptions of embodied African American performance) suggests that the studios saw African American performance as a dual novelty. Said to record with greater "warmth" and "fidelity," this mythic voice was thus employed experimentally to ward off potentially "uncanny," denaturing effects, remedying the deficient novelty of the apparatus itself and creating a more integral sound-film body.[38]

As Crafton explains, following "Hollywood's standardization of techniques and establishment of storytelling conventions that balanced voice and music," sound looses its status as a novelty: "When all films had dialogue, the term *talkie* lost its descriptive power."[39] By the 1930–1931 season, the studios no longer see sound as a "bonus" feature; rather, they begin to control sound by "integrating" it into productions that use classical narrative techniques. Moreover, technological advances allow filmmakers to create a soundtrack that is "tempered" or "modulated."[40] Sound no longer draws attention to itself as a novelty, and, by the same token, the audiences, whose initial misgivings about the talkies the studios tried to heed, have become fully habituated to sound in the cinema.[41]

When the "talking picture" loses its novelty and specificity as an aesthetic form, the privileged additive function accorded to the figure of "the Negro"—visible in the period conjunction "Negro talking pictures"—diminishes. Having settled on a particular "marriage of sight and sound" (Maurice's term) as its standard, the industry leaves room for articulations of "the black voice" only in very restrictive contexts. Knight's work on the history of black performance in the film musical indicates that the dynamics of sound-image "integration" intertwine paradoxically with the social equivalent of this term after the early sound period. Discussing the interplay between three different "senses" of "integration"—film-industrial, formal, and racial-social—Knight's historical narrative suggests that increasing efforts at achieving integration in the first two senses coincides with rigid opposition to it in the final sense.[42] Knight notes that the film industry's ongoing effort to expand its audiences through this vertical integration—"the efforts of Hollywood film studios to rationalize, control and expand the production and consumption of movies"—directly conflicted with the historical realities of sociocultural segregation, which the studios tended to accommodate, even against their own financial interests.[43]

Knight's second "sense" of integration deals with the emergence of the genre of the "integrated" theatrical and film musical, "pattern[ed upon] commensurability, coherence, and appropriateness of story or drama and the music" and an extension, in a sense, of early efforts to "temper" the soundtrack. Apropos of the two Otto Preminger–directed, African American–cast films, *Carmen Jones* (Twentieth Century-Fox, 1954) and *Porgy and Bess* (Columbia, 1959), Knight notes ironically that the "integrated musical relied on an explicit social-racial segregation"; even in the 1950s the studios resist any suggestion of "integration" in Knight's third, social, sense.[44] During the tumultuous period that produced "Negro talking pictures," African American performers are used to shore up certain deficiencies within the aesthetic structure of the film and the sensory array of cinematic experience, but they cannot be "integrated" into the films as characters in mixed-race diegetic worlds. And, by an odd chiasmus, the demand for different kinds of formal integration creates a resistance to any suggestion of social integration on screen; African American musical performance can be included—and even be given a privileged place—within the Hollywood cinema but only insofar as this inclusion reads as a form of setting apart. This inclusion, which I have theorized in this book as a form of valuation, coincides precisely with an enforcement of difference at the level of the filmic structure and diegesis.

Hence, it is not surprising that African American performance becomes a permanent, though secondary production feature of the Hollywood film musical, the musical being the genre that provides a refuge for the now marginal tradition of aesthetic "superabundance." As the subcategory of classical narrative cinema that permits the accumulation of disparate, novel entertainment features, the film musical makes available a permanent "place" for African American performers while also allowing questions of integration (in the social sense) to be bracketed off. Specific ways of presenting African American performance that arise during the transition to sound become frozen in place as subgeneric conventions. These conventions, it is crucial to note, are by no means fully codified within early sound-era "Negro films"; nor should they be seen as an inevitable film-historical development, whereby the studios maintain the racial status quo in Hollywood and appease a racially conservative "mass" audience. This study has attempted to illustrate the possible alternative paths that arise during this transitional period and to highlight the uncertainty attending to the earliest "experiments" in "Negro films."

Once these conventions are more or less codified, however, it is not surprising that the studios primarily feature African American performance in a series of limited formats, all of which have obvious precursors in the transitional period. The studios sporadically produce African American–cast feature musicals for another quarter century (*The Green Pastures*, followed by *Cabin in the Sky* [MGM, 1942] and *Stormy Weather* [Twentieth Century-Fox, 1943], then the two Preminger films), while releasing African American–cast shorts in greater number and with more consistency. Likewise, in the late 1930s and early 1940s, several white-cast film musicals include discrete scenes of black performance. These musical set pieces feature African American dancers (like the Nicholas Brothers and the Berry Brothers), singers (like Lena Horne), or musicians (like Louis Armstrong) playing "themselves" rather than dramatic characters. Presented as spectacles for intradiegetic audiences, these set pieces are thus doubly isolated from the rest of the narrative. The convention of the black musical set piece builds on the sort of simultaneous inclusion and setting apart (and arguably exacerbates the latter dynamic) that characterizes the handling of the cabaret scene in *Thunderbolt*, Ethel Waters's performances in

On With the Show and, in a more complicated sense, Duke Ellington and his orchestra's presence in *Check and Double Check.*

Within these subgenres of the film musical, a specific set of strategies for presenting the African American vocal and kinesthetic performance, which originate in the early sound period, also become conventional, though by no means universal. In several notable cases, 1930s and 1940s musicals featuring African American performers mimic the striking expressionist visual accompaniment of an imagined "black vocal object" typified by a film like *Thunderbolt.* Thus, the constellation of techniques like chiaroscuro lighting and the framing of iconic tableaux with African American performance construed in romantic racialist terms becomes a stylistic hallmark of the American film musical well after the initial "Negro film" movement. Interestingly, this hallmark tends to appear in settings where plot events, characters, actors, or even musical themes first seen in the films examined in this book are also present.

Surveying these later examples, the dialectical tension that, I have argued, animates early sound-era "Negro films" appears to have dissipated. By dialectical tension, I mean the movement whereby the films both reflect the valuation as commodity of certain forms of cultural blackness witnessed by late-1920s mass culture and yield "exorbitant" representational moments. In the films central to this study, strategies of black objectification and excessive diegetic grounding become legible as forced attempts to contain African American movement and to screen off pressing socioeconomic questions. Through the distorting strain that these film-texts exert in order to contain and/or screen off, they end up registering such pressures in interesting ways. As a result, it becomes possible to chart the force of historical upheavals that are overtly unrepresentable—not as contexts in the usual sense but as contradictions that erupt within the films. Hence, *Hollywood's African American Films* has employed a method focused on establishing historical points of reference as they distort and trouble these films, using the concept of the "fault line," and, in turn, on developing dialectical readings of specific filmic structures. This method has less purchase on later moments of African American musical performance in Hollywood movies because they lack the dialectical tension created by the strain of historical containment—even as they mimic their earlier counterparts on the level of expressionist spectacle.

The distorting points of reference yielding "fault lines" in early "Negro films" seem not to be in play in later films, as if the films' basic premises have allowed them to bypass any kind of disruptive historical material. In later musical films, period settings and fantasy structures distance the treatment of African American social life, making these films more self-contained or seamless; the conventions charted in the preceding discussion of *Thunderbolt* start to function in these films in a kind of self-referential system. Thus, the aesthetic strategies described above serve primarily to convey the sense of

Figure 19. Petunia (Ethel Waters) praying for Joe's recovery in *Cabin in the Sky* (MGM, 1942).

another "freezing of an image" (to use Daniel Leab's description of 1920s silent film representations of African Americans), instead of pointing, dialectically, to a repressed or unconscious social stratum in the film.

Consider, for example, the scenes in *Cabin in the Sky* that immediately follow Joe's (Eddie Anderson) stabbing during a craps game at the saloon—an episode that brings to mind Spunk's untimely death in *Hallelujah*. The mise-en-scène of the cabin where Joe lies recovering from his wound is characterized by low-key, high-contrast lighting, which compliments a range of different dramatic moods. As Petunia (Ethel Waters) kneels and prays for Joe's recovery, the camera frames her in a close-up, her face brightly illuminated but ringed by shadow, creating a melancholy effect. When the servants of the devil come to carry Joe away, *Cabin in the Sky* exploits these lighting effects to create an atmosphere of menace, using low-angle shots to emphasize their looming silhouettes on the wall. Then, when Joe returns to consciousness, during Pentunia's first rendition of her theme song, "Happiness Is a Thing Called Joe," her relief and happiness contrast with the "gloomy" cabin (as the lyrics describe it). It is worth noting here that the songs chosen for Waters's Petunia faintly echo her sequence of "Am I Blue?" and "Birmingham Bertha" from *On With the Show*. Like the first of these songs, "Happiness" draws on Waters's talents as a singer of slow ballads; its lyrics fuse romantic love with lamentation. When Petunia enters Jim Henry's Paradise to try to win the now wealthy Joe back, she performs "Honey in the Honeycomb" with a bravado and sense of demanding her due that recalls "Birmingham Bertha." Interestingly, she dances in the ensuing production number with John "Bubbles" Sublett (aka Angelus Babe), Sam from *On With the Show*.

Sublett's own vocal and dance performance of "Shine" channels the expressionist nightclub ambience created in *Thunderbolt*'s The Black Cat sequence. To the sound of the Duke Ellington Orchestra's driving percussion, he dances up a set of stairs into a thicket of shadow arms swaying on the wall (cast by the patrons below), before exiting the room. Again the 1942 film equates black sounds and gestures with the trope of the shadow. In its essentialist guise as rhythmic energy, blackness is here figured as hyperpresent.

Cabin in the Sky earlier evokes *Yamekraw*'s (Warner Bros., 1930) tableaux of pastoral harmony. As Joe and Petunia sing the title song, a crowd of people—the members of the "folk" community—gather around her at the base of a large tree in the center of the frame. The camera zooms out slowly to reveal a picturesque arrangement in which the actors' bodies virtually meld into the landscape. Some of them sway slowly in time to the music, their movement mimicking that of the smaller trees behind them, blown by the breeze. Several members of this ensemble appear to sing, indicating a diegetic source for the choral harmonies that well up behind Waters's vocals and form a "sonorous envelope" around the characters, further evoking their physical linkage to the mise-en-scène. This tradition of iconic tableaux also runs through *The Green Pastures*, which, in a more epic fashion, tends to situate African American bodies against stylized pastoral landscapes, using low-angle shots and situating the characters at ascending heights (moving toward the center of the frame) to create depth without depth. Such shots give the characters a monumental presence, while a layered soundtrack of nondiegetic singing helps establish a connection between them and their surroundings.

These conventions of iconic tableaux and chiaroscuro receive perhaps their most striking rendition in the expressionist tour de force that accompanies Paul Robeson's singing of "Old Man River" in *Show Boat* (MGM, 1936). As Robeson's character, Joe, sings the famous Jerome Kern tune, the film dispenses with spatial and temporal continuity—this is the only occasion during which such a break occurs—dissolving into a series of shots that act as self-contained vignettes: Joe laboring, kneeling on the ground in supplication, leaving a saloon, and standing in jail. Combining simplified backdrops and sets with high-contrast lighting and the full array of expressionist cinematographic gestures—extreme low and high angles, Dutch angles—these shots give graphic, embodied expression to the pain and hardship described in the song lyrics. Robeson's performance is nonnaturalistic, a set of stylized gestures helping to underscore the physical and emotional intensity of the scenes, and the group shots featuring other black men working contain arrays

Figure 20. John "Bubbles" Sublett dancing among shadows in *Cabin in the Sky* (MGM, 1942).

of figures in geometric patterns. The kinds of work represented have some connection to the historical vicissitudes of African American life in the South around the turn of the twentieth century. For instance, Robeson and the other men are shown carrying heavy bales of cotton on their backs and hoeing rows in a cotton field. But in the "Old Man River" montage, these vicissitudes are exploited for their symbolic value, recast as expressions of an essential racial plight, given iconic form in what is an extended African American set piece in a mostly white-cast film.

In these moments from *Show Boat*, *The Green Pastures*, and *Cabin in the Sky*, we see aesthetic manifestations of the particular way of valuing African American performance that emerged during the transition to sound. These are constructions of black vocal or acoustic objects in which sound and image work together to convey a sense of embodied presence, ostensibly evoking certain notions about African American existence and experience. In this respect, they show that a set of representational strategies that came about in "Negro talking pictures" has been codified and institutionalized. At the same time, these particular 1930s and 1940s films suggest that such representational strategies lose the unsettled, ambiguous quality they possess in the cases examined in *Hollywood's African American Films*. Moreover, this loss occurs because the contexts surrounding the films' way of valuing African American performance have changed.

As a result of the ways in which these films use period settings (*Show Boat*) or complex fantasy structures (*The Green Pastures* and *Cabin in the Sky*) to frame and motivate African American performance, they lack the sort of outside points of reference that can make such performances exorbitant, in the sense traced through the preceding chapters: not contained within a predetermined track. Moments at which an unprogrammed and unanticipated value accrues to African American performance are rare, if not nonexistent in these films. The settings of these films offer little opportunity for them to register (even in a mode of disavowal) pressing questions of racial-social change in the way that early sound-era "Negro films" do, thus making their characters and narrative situations more coherent, not fractured by the same contradictions. Despite working in subgenres, borrowing performers and kinds of material, and using representational strategies rooted in the transitional period, these films make no reference to the kinds of hard-to-represent historical tensions needed to make an exorbitant value manifest or to enable complex, dialectical interpretations.

Both *The Green Pastures* and *Cabin in the Sky* use textual "Forewords" to present their contents as illustrations of African American "folk" beliefs. Further, both films establish ostensibly contemporary settings that are already heavily lacquered with myth, only to shift over the course of their narratives to several levels of fantastical regress. The children's Sunday school in *The Green Pastures* gives way to a fantastic all-black heaven, which gives way to a series of retellings of Old Testament stories in which the situations and characters are blended with signifiers from contemporary African American culture. Most of the action of *Cabin in the Sky*, following Joe's wounding in the saloon, is later reframed as Joe's fever dream, including segments of the plot in which Petunia seems to exist as a completely independent character. Whereas a film like *Hearts in Dixie* aims at a similar framing of its material through the spoken prologue, it breaks the frame by introducing the subtext of African American migration. Thus, Chincapin's story is crucially not recontained in a mythic circle like that of Joe, who must realize that everything he wants or needs exists right at home in the titular cabin. Nor does the film seem to be at such great pains as *Hallelujah* to complete this circle; *Cabin in the Sky* does not present the kinds of economic complexities that would require such narrative violence as wrought in the earlier film in order to be canceled out.

As Knight points out, the 1936 film version of *Show Boat* "makes several opportunities to comment directly on racist inequalities, particular of opportunity and labor"; at the same time, it tends to squander these opportunities, diminishing what is the obviously, even "astonishingly political" substance of the original novel and stage production.[45] The distancing effects of the film's period setting, coupled with its tendency to cast African American existence as essentially hyperaffective, allow *Show Boat* to present "black" music as existing primarily for white consumption and strategic appropriation. I put "black" in quotation marks here because, as Knight illustrates, the African American characters sing only songs composed by the stage show's white composers, Jerome Kern, Oscar Hammerstein, and P. G. Wodehouse. These songs draw on certain African American musical traditions but allow for only "one compositional voice" for black characters; thus, the putatively "black" affects that white characters pleasurably put on through their performance of music originated by African American characters are, in an ironic way, white affects.[46] African American characters in *Show Boat* get sealed in what James Baldwin called a diegetic "vacuum" insofar as they are cast as figures existing out of time in a quasi-natural realm of heightened feeling.[47] Further, the film's ironclad assumption that blackness exists for white consumption serves to seal this racial vacuum.

This assumption can be observed by comparing how the Kern music works in *Show Boat* with how the Johnson-arranged spirituals and hymns work in the earlier *The Emperor Jones* (United Artists, 1933). In the case of the Kern music, there are no relevant contemporary sociohistorical points of reference to be excavated; the period setting and the narrative trajectory of whiteness too effectively distance the film's action from such points of reference. As Knight points out, *Show Boat*'s African American characters should (according to the source material) carry "social baggage" into the film. Yet the narrative easily casts aside this baggage, progressively fixating on Magnolia's (Irene Dunne) romantic and career plots, such that it never really exerts any visible effect on the narrative or diegesis.[48]

This kind of "baggage"—contemporary sociohistorical points of reference—starts to come into play in Hollywood film musicals again during the World War II era. Making the textual construction of black screen characters more fluid, these musicals recall the unsettled dynamics of early sound-era "Negro films." During 1942–1943, two major pressures combine to force this change: the efforts of African American civic groups to combat racial discrimination in the studio system and another mass migration driven by the demands of wartime industrial production. For instance, *Stormy Weather* attempts to celebrate the historical "contribution" of black performers to the history of American entertainment, thus framing its protagonist (Bill Robinson) as a war veteran and national icon. At the same time, the film confronts—however ambiguously and evasively—the African American urban youth culture of the period, making allusions to the socially volatile symbol of the "zoot suit." In a slightly more complicated case, *Panama Hattie* (MGM, 1942) introduces a provocative black Atlantic cultural framework for scenes featuring African American performers (Lena Horne and the Berry Brothers) attempting to broadcast official, government-sanctioned messages about the "Good Neighbor Policy" in U.S.–Latin American relations.

While film scholars have duly acknowledged changes in the industrial and racial-social organization of the studios during World War II and recognized the importance of *Stormy Weather*'s particular turn to the African American urban milieu, they have generally treated the preceding period (going back to the inception of sound) as a unified historical bloc. As I have argued, this tendency has led scholars to posit a too consistent and static "black screen image" stretching across a spectrum of films and shifts in industrial dynamics. And, more important, it has contributed to a dominant narrative that, during the pre–World War II period, the Hollywood studios managed simply and successfully to refuse any acknowledgment of African American history. Paula Massood has recently offered a forceful assertion along these lines: "Although African American literary production echoed the complexity of the tensions attending the massive population shifts in the early part of the century, Hollywood films from 1929 to 1943 utterly failed to recognize the sociopolitical changes in the American landscape."[49] One of my main goals in this book has been to challenge this verdict, by amending the concept of "recognition" that it assumes and developing an adequate method of film-textual analysis for charting the often negative, anxious manifestations of this recognition.

To excavate these moments of recognition is in no way to credit the studio system with a more progressive racial politics—to find new "positive images" surrounding migration and other "sociopolitical changes in the American landscape." But it is to attune our critical discussions to the ways in which such changes—instigated by specific performances of African American historical agency—irresistibly challenge the existing apparatuses of mass culture. And it is to make newly legible those uneven, contradictory features of transitional film-texts, which, I have tried to demonstrate, are plentiful: to make what are ultimately the most striking features of these films yield their exorbitant value for the project of film history.

Notes

INTRODUCTION

1. James Gow, "Harlem First Night," *New York Amsterdam News*, 28 August 1929. The *New York Amsterdam News* reprinted this article from the *New York World*, 25 August 1929.

2. *Hallelujah* opened in New York on 20 August 1929, with a unique dual premier: at the Embassy, a Times Square movie palace, at 46th and Broadway, and the Lafayette, at 132nd and 7th. While some African Americans in Harlem applauded the early arrival of "the much talked about picture with its colored stars" to the Lafayette, others interpreted this move as an effort by MGM to "keep Negroes away from the Broadway showing of the picture." A plan to picket the Lafayette was floated briefly at a public meeting held by a group of vaudeville actors "calling themselves the Negro Artists' Protective Association." Over the course of the meeting, it became clear that this group was most concerned with the threat that synchronized-sound films posed to live performers working in Harlem theaters and that their main goal was to gain leverage over Frank Schiffman, the white manager of the Lafayette. As this goal became clear, public interest in the plan to picket the Lafayette waned. One journalist present at the meeting proposed that the suspicion of a Jim Crow exhibition policy would best be tested by "go[ing] to Broadway . . . and having secured evidence that segregation existed [making] an appeal to the Civil Rights Law." "Negro Artists in Protest Meeting," *New York Amsterdam News*, 21 August 1929. While applauding the willingness of the African American vaudeville performers to organize and air their grievances publicly, the editor of the *New York Amsterdam News* dismissed their allegations of Jim Crow around the *Hallelujah* premiere as opportunistic. "The Negro Actor's Association," *New York Amsterdam News*, 21 August 1929.

Suspicions of a deliberate Jim Crow policy grew again when the Embassy box office denied tickets to several African American patrons. Three men filed suit against the ownership under the New York State Civil Rights Law, and their stories were circulated in African American papers in New York, Chicago, and Pittsburgh. See J. Finley Wilson, "Jim-Crow Charges Hit 'Hallelujah' in Court Actions," *New York Amsterdam News*, 28 August 1929; J. Winston Harrington, "Harlem Folks Claim Jim Crow Move in

Hallelujah Showing," *Chicago Defender*, 24 August 1929; and Anna Everett, *Returning the Gaze: A Genealogy of Black Film Criticism, 1909–1949* (Durham, N.C.: Duke University Press, 2001), 176–177.

3. *The Greenwood Encyclopedia of African American Civil Rights: From Emancipation to the Twenty-first Century*, s.v. "Oscar Stanton DePriest"; *The Encyclopedia of Chicago*, s.v. "Oscar DePriest."

4. James Grossman, *Land of Hope: Chicago, Black Southerners, and the Great Migration* (Chicago: University of Chicago Press, 1989), 3–4, 19. See also Milton Sernett, *Bound for the Promised Land: African American Religion and the Great Migration* (Durham, N.C.: Duke University Press, 1997), 57–86.

5. *Greenwood Encyclopedia of African American Civil Rights*, s.v. "Oscar Stanton DePriest." DePriest's family participated in the 1879 "Kansas Fever Exodus," a movement of roughly 6,000 African Americans from the lower Mississippi Valley to Kansas. Seeking to become independent landholders, the "Exodusters," as these migrants were known, were motivated by millenarian religious longings and a desire to escape the violence and oppression of white southern "redemption." See Nell Irvin Painter, *Exodusters: Black Migration to Kansas After Reconstruction* (New York: W. W. Norton, 1986), 184–201.

6. Grossman, *Land of Hope*, 130.

7. "Congressman DePriest Speaks Highly of the Great Movietone 'Hallelujah,'" *California Eagle*, 8 November 1929.

8. The photograph appears under the caption "DePriest Congratulates King Vidor," *New York Amsterdam News*, 23 October 1929. The timing of and caption accompanying the *New York Amsterdam News* photograph appear to date DePriest's visit to MGM to after the film's release: "He Paid a Visit to the Metro-Goldwyn-Mayer Studio to Personally Thank King Vidor for Having Made and Produced the Picture." According to Thomas Cripps, DePriest was invited "to the studio during production," ostensibly in exchange for public praise of *Hallelujah*. Thomas Cripps, *Slow Fade to Black: The Negro in American Film, 1900–1942*, 2nd ed. (Oxford: Oxford University Press, 1993), 250–251. Given that Cripps does not mention a subsequent visit, it seems possible that the *New York Amsterdam News* photograph predates *Hallelujah*'s release.

9. "Congressman DePriest," 1.

10. Daniel Haynes, "What 'Hallelujah' Means to the Negro Race," *Chicago Defender*, 27 February 1929. (Haynes's column also appeared in the 15 February 1929 issue of the *California Eagle*.) I discuss important industry terms like "atmosphere" and "bits" in chapter 2.

11. Ibid.

12. Ibid.

13. Ibid. Haynes's costar Harry Gray also used the idea of "paving the way" for future African American actors in a contemporary interview. See Ruby Berkley Goodwin, "Philosopher or Movie Actor? Both!" *Pittsburgh Courier*, 15 June 1929.

14. "The Value of the Talkies," *Pittsburgh Courier*, 6 July 1929.

15. Ibid.

16. "Movies Open New Field to Actors of Our Group," *Chicago Defender*, 3 May 1930.

17. Geraldyn Dismond, "The Negro Actor and the American Movies," *Close Up* 5, no. 2 (1929): 91.

18. Ibid.

19. Ibid.

20. "The Negro in Motion Pictures," in *The Negro Yearbook: An Annual Encyclopedia of the Negro, 1931–1932*, ed. Monroe C. Work, 465–466 (Tuskegee, Ala.: Tuskegee Institute, 1931).

21. Dismond, "Negro Actor," 95–96.

22. Ibid.

23. Space constraints prevent me from including in this book a suitable discussion of the Christie-Cohen films, four of which are extant: *The Melancholy Dame* (1929), *Music Hath Harms* (1929), *The Framing of the Shrew* (1929), and *Oft in the Silly Night* (1929). Because of their static, dialogue-heavy style and their tightly codified fictional milieu—rooted in Cohen's popular *Saturday Evening Post* stories and the southern-regionalist, "dialect" fiction tradition—these films lend themselves somewhat less well to the kind of analysis developed in the following chapters. Nevertheless, they are noteworthy as early instances of white "talking picture" producers' interest in African American–cast films and for the involvement of African American actor, director, writer, and entrepreneur Spencer Williams in their production. Williams appeared in the four films mentioned above, as well as writing dialogue for them and serving as an assistant director. Donald Bogle asserts that Williams assisted in the casting for Christie and had prior experience at the studio as a sound technician. Donald Bogle, *Bright Boulevards, Bold Dreams: The Story of Black Hollywood* (New York: Random House, 2005), 86–87. Williams also appears to have directed and acted in an independently produced sound short, *Tenderfeet* (1928), prior to his work with the Christie studio; I have been unable to locate a copy of this film. See "Tender Feet," *California Eagle*, 27 July 1928.

24. See Michael Rogin, *Blackface, White Noise: Jewish Immigrants in the Hollywood Melting Pot* (Berkeley: University of California Press, 1996).

25. Donald Crafton, *The Talkies: American Cinema's Transition to Sound, 1926–1931*, History of the American Cinema, vol. 4 (New York: Charles Scribner's Sons, 1997), 4–5; David Bordwell, "The Introduction of Sound," in David Bordwell, Janet Staiger, and Kristin Thompson, *The Classical Hollywood Cinema: Film Style and Mode of Production to 1960* (New York: Columbia University Press, 1985), 298–308.

26. Daniel Leab, *From Sambo to Superspade: The Black Experience in Motion Pictures* (Boston: Houghton Mifflin, 1975), 83–84.

27. Ibid., 117.

28. Cripps, *Slow Fade to Black*, 219, 262.

29. Ibid., 236. See also Mark Reid, *Redefining Black Film* (Berkeley: University of California Press, 1993), 15.

30. According to the *Oxford English Dictionary*, 2d ed., "exorbitance" refers first to a "divergence or aberration from the prescribed or ordinary track" or "path" and only later takes on its dominant contemporary meaning of "extravagance" of price.

31. Ryan Jay Friedman, "'A Moving-Picture of Democracy': President Obama and African American Film History Beyond the Mirror Screen," forthcoming in *Quarterly Review of Film & Video*. In this article, I examine the reemergence of the Mirror Screen understanding of cinema in recent responses by critics and bloggers to Barack Obama's election. These critics and bloggers argue that African American presidents in movies and on television deserve substantial "credit" for making Obama's candidacy and eventual election possible, creating an imaginary role that a real person could then fill.

32. Vachel Lindsay, *The Art of the Moving Picture* (New York: Macmillan, 1915).

33. Ibid., 65. See also Gerald Stanley Lee, *Crowds: A Moving-Picture of Democracy* (New York: Doubleday, Page, 1913), 273.

34. Lindsay, *Art*, 238.

35. On the history of the democracy of consumers, see Stuart Ewen, *Captains of Consciousness: Advertising and the Social Roots of the Consumer Culture* (New York: McGraw-Hill, 1976), 27, 91–94; and Roland Marchand, *Advertising the American Dream: Making Way for Modernity, 1920–1940* (Berkeley: University of California Press, 1985), 63–64.

36. Will Hays, *See and Hear: A Brief History of the Motion Picture and the Development of Sound* (New York: Motion Picture Producers and Distributors of America, 1929), 3. Crucial to my reading of Hays's *See and Hear* is Jared Gardner's interpretation of Paramount's silent epics of the 1920s as allegories of cinema's nationally unifying function. I am particularly indebted to Gardner in my thinking about tropes of exodus and about the screen as a way of dissolving divisions between individuals. Jared Gardner, "Covered Wagons and Decalogues: Paramount's Myths of Origins," *Yale Journal of Criticism* 13, no. 2 (2000): 361–389.

37. Hays, *See and Hear*, 3–4.

38. See Friedman, "Moving-Picture."

39. Hays, *See and Hear*, 3–4.

40. Robert E. Weems, *Desegregating the Dollar: African American Consumerism in the Twentieth Century* (New York: NYU Press, 1998), 1–2.

41. Hays, *See and Hear*, 3.

42. Will Hays, "Supervision from Within," in *The Story of the Films, as Told by the Leaders of the Industry to the Students of the Graduate School of Business Administration*, ed. Joseph P. Kennedy, 29–54 (Chicago: A. W. Shaw, 1927). See also "Hoover Will Follow Coolidge Policy of Non-Interference," *Exhibitors Herald and Moving Picture World*, 24 November 1928, 25.

43. Lary May, *Screening Out the Past: The Birth of Mass Culture and the Motion Picture Industry* (New York: Oxford University Press, 1980).

44. Charles Eckert, "The Carole Lombard in Macy's Window," in *Movies and Mass Culture*, ed. John Belton, 95–118 (New Brunswick, N.J.: Rutgers University Press, 1996). See also Mary Ann Doane, "The Economy of Desire: The Commodity Form in/of the Cinema," in Belton, *Movies and Mass Culture*, 119–134; and Jeanne Allen, "The Film Viewer as Consumer," *Quarterly Review of Film Studies* 5, no. 4 (Fall 1980): 481–491.

45. Eckert, "Carole Lombard," 101–113. For a detailed discussion of one specific product tie-up campaign, see Jane Gaines, "The *Queen Christina* Tie-Ups: Convergence of Show Window and Screen," *Quarterly Review of Film & Video* 11, no. 1 (1989): 35–60.

46. On Hollywood stars as idols of consumption, see May, *Screening Out the Past*, 189–199; on DeMille's consumer aesthetic, see ibid., 200–236. For a study that examines DeMille's commodified mise-en-scène and reads his "Jazz Age" comedies in terms of their "intertextual" connections with period advertising, see Sumiko Higashi's superb *Cecil B. DeMille and American Culture: The Silent Era* (Berkeley: University of California Press, 1994), 142–178.

47. Max Horkheimer and Theodor W. Adorno, *Dialectic of Enlightenment: Philosophical Fragments*, ed. Gunzelin Schmid Noerr, trans. Edmund Jephcott (Stanford, Calif.: Stanford University Press, 2002), 94–98.

48. Ibid., 131. See also Theodor W. Adorno, "On Jazz," trans. Jamie Owen Daniel, *Discourse* 12, no. 1 (Fall–Winter 1989–1990): 48.

49. Adorno, "On Jazz," 47–49.

50. Ibid.

51. Lloyd Lewis, "The Deluxe Picture Palace," *New Republic*, 27 March 1929, reprinted in Stephen J. Ross, ed., *Movies and American Society* (Oxford: Blackwell, 2002) 91.

52. Lizabeth Cohen, *Making a New Deal: Industrial Workers in Chicago, 1919–1939* (Cambridge: Cambridge University Press, 1990), 125. The quoted phrases in Cohen's parentheses are from the Balaban & Katz manual.

53. Ibid., 413n.96. On evidence of discrimination in Chicago movie palaces during the 1920s, see also St. Clair Drake and Horace R. Cayton, *Black Metropolis: A Study of Negro Life in a Northern City* (New York: Harcourt, Brace, 1945), 102; and Mary Carbine, "'The Finest Outside the Loop': Motion Picture Exhibition in Chicago's Black Metropolis, 1905–1928," *Camera Obscura* 23 (1990): 18–19. On Balaban & Katz's policies, see also Douglas Gomery, *Shared Pleasures: A History of Movie Presentation in the United States* (Madison: University of Wisconsin Press, 1992), 50. On the history of movie theater segregation more broadly, see Eric Ledell Smith, introduction to *African American Theater Buildings: An Illustrated Historical Directory, 1900–1955* (Jefferson, N.C.: McFarland, 2003), 1–7; Jacqueline Najuma Stewart, *Migrating to the Movies: Cinema and Black Urban Modernity* (Berkeley: University of California Press, 2005), 101; and Gregory Waller, *Main Street Amusements: Movies and Commercial Entertainment in a Southern City, 1896–1930* (Washington, D.C.: Smithsonian, 1995), 161–179.

54. "Negro Wins Suit vs. Tivoli Theatre," *Variety*, 18 February 1925, 24.

55. Karl Marx, *Capital: A Critique of Political Economy*, vol. 1, trans. Ben Fowkes (New York: Vintage, 1977), 163–167.

56. Leab, *Sambo*, 41–57.

57. Cripps, *Slow Fade to Black*, 115–149.

58. Ibid., 119.

59. "What we want" and "where we are going" are crucial phrases from Gerald Stanley Lee's discussion of mass self-representation through mechanically reproduced culture in *Crowds*.

60. "From Harlem to Hollywood," *Chicago Defender*, 15 December 1928. "From Harlem to Hollywood" was a report on a visit to the set of *Hallelujah*, written by the Hearst syndicate's white gossip columnist Louella Parsons; it appeared in the *Defender* without Parson's byline. Comparing the MGM soundstage to "a real down South plantation," Parsons characterizes the film's African American cast in the same patronizing terms as King Vidor himself did during the production and in subsequent reflections (see chapter 4). She waxes over "this emotional race," describes the "thrill" that white people get from hearing the performers' "soft chanting music," and claims that the lead actors cannot be "rehearse[d] too much" lest they succumb to the "nerve strain" of such fervent expression. Interestingly, an Associated Negro Press writer filed a critique of Parson's "gush," quoting her piece at length, while refuting her descriptions point by point and highlighting why specific word choices and tropes are offensive to African Americans. See "Will 'Hallelujah' Be Slap at Race Pride, Is Query," *Pittsburgh Courier*, 15 December 1928.

61. Carme Manuel, "A Ghost in the Expressionist Jungle of O'Neill's *The Emperor Jones*," *African American Review* 39, nos. 1–2 (2005): 73–74.

62. Eugene O'Neill, *The Emperor Jones*, in *Three Plays by Eugene O'Neill* (New York: Modern Library, 1937), 27.

63. Manuel, "Ghost," 75.

64. Ibid., 72–75. See also Lotte Eisner, *The Haunted Screen: Expressionism in the German Cinema and the Influence of Max Reinhardt* (Berkeley: University of California Press, 1973), 141.

65. Manuel, "Ghost," 75, 83n.19.

66. Siegfried Kracauer, *From Caligari to Hitler: A Psychological History of the German Film* (Princeton, N.J.: Princeton University Press, 1947), 75.

67. David Pan has illustrated how, in the context of its original articulation in early-twentieth-century German art and philosophy, the concept of expressionism was intertwined with an abiding concern with "primitive mental life," particularly the mental life of non-European peoples deemed "savage" or "uncivilized." See David Pan, *Primitive Renaissance: Rethinking German Expressionism* (Lincoln: University of Nebraska Press, 2001), 83–97.

68. Quoted in Susan Delson, *Dudley Murphy: Hollywood Wild Card* (Minneapolis: University of Minnesota Press, 2006), 131. This book's cover image is a good example of Murphy's attempt to create expressionist "mood and fantasy" in *Black and Tan*.

69. See the stage directions throughout scene 3 of O'Neill, *Emperor Jones*, 33–36. See also Manuel, "Ghost," 76.

70. Kaja Silverman, *The Acoustic Mirror: The Female Voice in Psychoanalysis and the Cinema* (Bloomington: Indiana University Press, 1988), 54.

71. Ibid., 45.

72. Ibid.

73. James Snead's tragically interrupted project of constructing a semiotics of black screen representation is crucial to my thinking here, especially his move to locate the strategy of "omission" (the fact of African American absence from the screen) on a continuum with other strategies of diegetic inscription that render black characters "other." See James Snead, *White Screens/Black Images: Hollywood from the Dark Side*, ed. Colin MacCabe and Cornel West, 4–7 (New York: Routledge, 1994).

74. Sigmund Freud, "Negation," in *The Standard Edition of the Complete Psychological Works of Sigmund Freud*, vol. 19, ed. and trans. James Strachey et al., 234–239 (London: Hogarth Press, 1964).

75. As James Baldwin noted, apropos of a later "Negro talking picture," *Carmen Jones* (Twentieth Century–Fox, 1954), at such moments we catch glimpses of the films that Hollywood "was studiously *not* making"—the phantom films, which, being disavowed, shape or even "control" each film. James Baldwin, "*Carmen Jones*: The Dark Is Light Enough," in *James Baldwin: Collected Essays* (New York: Library of America, 1998), 36. I explore this aspect of Baldwin's dialectical reading strategy in my article "'Enough Force to Shatter the Tale to Fragments': Ethics and Textual Analysis in James Baldwin's Film Theory," *English Literary History* 77, no. 2 (Summer 2010): 385–411.

76. The congregation in the film sings a portion of "Oh, I Want Two Wings" before the film cuts to the first series of shots in Jones's room. When he enters the church, Robeson sings the verses, and the congregation sings the refrains of "Now Let Me Fly." They begin singing "Same Train" just before the film dissolves to a shot of Jones's departing train. "Oh, I Want Two Wings" and "Now Let Me Fly" appear in a collection that J. Rosamond Johnson edited and arranged. See J. Rosamond Johnson, *Rolling*

Along in Song: A Chronological Survey of American Negro Music (New York: Viking, 1937), 31–33, 81–82. Johnson classifies "Oh, I Want Two Wings" as a "Ring Shout" and "Now Let Me Fly" as a "Jubilee" song. "Same Train" appears in the second collection of spirituals that James Weldon Johnson edited; Rosamond Johnson did the musical arrangements for these collections. See James Weldon Johnson and J. Rosamond Johnson, eds., *The Second Book of Negro Spirituals* (New York: Viking, 1926), 60–62.

CHAPTER 1 — "BLACK BECAME THE FAD"

1. "Dorothy Mckail Is 'Blues' Enthusiast," in *Safe in Hell* pressbook, 6, United Artists Collection, Warner Bros. Pressbooks, Wisconsin Center for Theater and Film Research (hereafter cited as Pressbooks, WCTFR).

2. *Safe in Hell* pressbook, 10–11, Pressbooks, WCTFR.

3. "Negro Who Did 'Porgy' on Broadway Stage Coming in Film" and "Colored Actor Who Created 'Porgy' Is in 'Safe in Hell,'" *Safe in Hell* pressbook, 5, 8, Pressbooks, WCTFR.

4. This text appears alongside several production stills in an announcement of *Hallelujah*'s Broadway premier, "Salvation with Lots o' Music," *Exhibitors Herald-World*, 24 August 1929. "Audien" is a neologism that this publication briefly used as a substitute for "talkie" or "talking picture," terms the editors deemed inelegant and sought to replace.

5. "Inside Stuff—Pictures," *Variety*, 19 December 1928, 41. See also "Colored Show Field," *Variety*, 2 January 1929, 22; "Harlem Going West," *Variety*, 10 April 1929, 1; and "Colored People in Many Short Talkers," *Variety*, 8 May 1929, 23.

6. "Race Films Making Hit," *Pittsburgh Courier*, 7 September 1929. For further examples of African American press stories on African American–cast films as a fad, on talkies in production, and on emergent African American talkie stars, see "King Vidor to Film Race Movie," *Chicago Defender*, 13 October 1928; "King Vidor Finds His Most Interesting Type Working for Amsterdam News," *New York Amsterdam News*, 17 October 1928; Dave Peyton, "The Musical Bunch," *Chicago Defender*, 27 October 1928; "Movietone Opportunity Knocks for Negro Artists," *New York Amsterdam News*, 12 December 1928; "From Harlem to Hollywood," *Chicago Defender*, 15 December 1928; Maurice Dancer, "Colored Films All the Rage," *Pittsburgh Courier*, 29 December 1928; "Vidor Hopes Film Will Vie with Best," *New York Amsterdam News*, 16 January 1929; "'Hallelujah's' Star,' *Chicago Defender*, 9 February 1929; Maurice Dancer, "'Talkies' Are Boon to Race Actors; Competition Keener," *Pittsburgh Courier*, 23 February 1929; Maurice Dancer, "Webb's Harlem Stompers, Sterling Manhattan Band, to Play in 'Dew Drop In,'" *Pittsburgh Courier*, 23 March 1929; "A Good Week for Colored Actors and Extras," *New York Amsterdam News*, 22 May 1929; "King Vidor's Fondest Dream Is Realized by Clever Work of Performers in Hallelujah," *Chicago Defender*, 8 June 1929; Ruby Berkley Goodwin, "From 'Blackbird' Chorine to 'Talkie' Star," *Pittsburgh Courier*, 8 June 1929; "Sets Himself Quite a Task," *New York Amsterdam News*, 19 June 1929; "Value of the Talkies"; "Race Films Making Hit," *Pittsburgh Courier*, 7 September 1929; Harry Levette, "Gossip of the Movie Lots," *New York Amsterdam News*, 25 September 1929; "1930 Gives Ample Promise of Being a Banner Year for Negro Screen Players," *California Eagle*, 10 January 1930; "Movies Open New Field"; "California Movie Studios Employ Host of Performers," *Chicago Defender*, 16 August 1930; Harry Levette, "Big Season Ahead Viewed for Extras on Hollywood Lots," *Chicago Defender*, 27 September

1930; Harry Levette, "Screen Extras Are Victims of Questionable Booking Agents," *Chicago Defender*, 25 October 1930.

7. Richard Maltby, "Sticks, Hicks, and Flaps: Classical Hollywood's Generic Conception of Its Audiences," in *Identifying Hollywood's Audiences: Cultural Identity and the Movies*, ed. Melvyn Stokes and Richard Maltby, 26 (London: BFI, 1999).

8. The fifth "major," RKO, effectively began in 1929 as a sound-film production company. Douglas Gomery, *The Coming of Sound: A History* (New York: Routledge, 2005), 88–99; Crafton, *Talkies*, 1–18.

9. Crafton, *Talkies*, 14.

10. Dismond, "Negro Actor," 90–97.

11. Harry Alan Potamkin, "The Aframerican Cinema," *Close Up* 5, no. 2 (1929): 108. A novel by the white author DuBose Heyward, *Porgy* was first published in 1925; DuBose and Dorothy Heyward adapted it into a play, which was produced on Broadway in 1927. George Gershwin's "folk opera" *Porgy and Bess*—for which DuBose Heyward wrote the libretto—premiered in 1935. See David Krasner, *A Beautiful Pageant: African American Theatre, Drama, and Performance in the Harlem Renaissance, 1910–1927* (New York: Palgrave Macmillan, 2002), 226.

12. Potamkin, "Aframerican Cinema," 109.

13. Alice Maurice, "'Cinema at Its Source': Synchronizing Race and Sound in the Early Talkies," *Camera Obscura* 17, no. 49 (2002): 36; Crafton, *Talkies*, 230–232.

14. Crafton, *Talkies*, 81. On the range of audience responses to film voices, see ibid., 445–479; and Robert Spadoni, *Uncanny Bodies: The Coming of Sound Film and the Origins of the Horror Genre* (Berkeley: University of California Press, 2007), 6, 11–13.

15. Maurice, "Cinema at Its Source," 36; Crafton, *Talkies*, 76–77; Spadoni, *Uncanny Bodies*, 14–16.

16. See Kenneth MacPherson, "As Is," *Close Up* 5, no. 2 (1929): 87; and Robert Benchley, review of *Hearts in Dixie*, *Opportunity: A Journal of Negro Life* 7, no. 4 (1929): 122–123.

17. Benchley, review of *Hearts in Dixie*, 122.

18. Ibid.

19. Frank Davis, "Fox's 'Hearts in Dixie' Is 100% Entertainment," *Sound Waves*, 1 February 1929, 1, 9. My thanks to Jenny Romero for directing me to this publication in the Periodicals Collection at the Margaret Herrick Library, Academy of Motion Picture Arts and Sciences (AMPAS).

20. Maurice, "Cinema," 32, 44–45.

21. An Insider, "Motion Pictures; The Producers; Exhibitor and the Negro Actor," *California Eagle*, 9 August 1929.

22. Goodwin, "'Blackbird' Chorine." See also Floyd Calvin, "'Talkies' May Help Negro Artists!" *Pittsburgh Courier*, 15 September 1928; Elmer Anderson Carter, "Of Negro Motion Pictures," *Close Up* 5, no. 2 (1929): 118–122.

23. Maurice, "Cinema," 32–33, 46–47.

24. Benchley's comment about African American actors' "timing" in the delivery of lines is particularly suggestive here.

25. "The Negro in Motion Pictures," 465–466.

26. See David Levering Lewis, *When Harlem Was in Vogue* (New York: Vintage, 1982), 207, 214. Dismond edited the *Tattler* from 1928 to 1931; between 1925 and 1928 she also published regular columns in the *New York Amsterdam News*, *Pittsburgh Courier*,

Chicago Bee, and *Baltimore Afro-American*. On her career, see *The Harlem Renaissance: A Historical Dictionary for the Era*, s.v. "Dismond, Geraldyn."

27. Quoted in Lewis, *Harlem*, 98.

28. Lewis, *Harlem*, 98–106. On Van Vechten as Harlem "guide," see ibid., 182. See also Ann Douglas, *Terrible Honesty: Mongrel Manhattan in the 1920s* (New York: Farrar, Straus, and Giroux, 1995), 81, 287–292; and Bruce Kellner, *Carl Van Vechten and the Irreverent Decades* (Norman: University of Oklahoma Press, 1968), 195–223.

29. Kellner, *Carl Van Vechten*, 195, 198; Lewis, *Harlem*, 105–106, 164; Jervis Anderson, *This Was Harlem: A Cultural Portrait, 1900–1950* (New York: Farrar, Straus and Giroux, 1982), 168–178. See also the newspaper and magazine articles reprinted in Allon Schoener, ed., *Harlem on My Mind: Cultural Capital of Black America, 1900–1968* (New York: Delta, 1979), 81–85. For an indication of how thoroughly these slumming accounts shaped the mass-cultural representation of Harlem, see John B. Kennedy, "So This Is Harlem!" *Collier's*, 28 October 1933, 22, 50–52; and Helene Margaret, "The Negro Fad," *Forum and Century* 87, no. 1 (January 1932): 39–43.

30. Rudolph Fisher, "The Caucasian Storms Harlem" (1927), in *Double-Take: A Revisionist Harlem Renaissance Anthology*, ed. Venetria K. Patterson and Maria Honey, 96 (New Brunswick, N.J.: Rutgers University Press, 2001).

31. Ibid.

32. Nella Larsen, *Passing*, in *The Complete Fiction of Nella Larsen*, ed. Charles R. Larson, 229 (New York: Anchor, 2001).

33. Nicholas Evans, "'Racial Cross-Dressing' in the Jazz Age: Cultural Therapy and Its Discontents in Cabaret Nightlife," in *Hop on Pop: The Politics and Pleasures of Popular Culture*, ed. Henry Jenkins, Tara McPherson, and Jane Shattuc, 389 (Durham, N.C.: Duke University Press, 2002). The cost ranges that Evans cites are suggestive, but not fully contextualized or interpreted relative to the Harlem cabaret scene. Frederick Bond makes the interesting but still anecdotally based claim that "[Harlem nightclub] entertainment is very expensive to the average working man of small salary" in *The Negro and the Drama* (Washington, D.C.: Associated Publishers, 1940), 154–155.

34. For an extensive list of such clubs, from which "Negroes find themselves crowded out and even segregated," see Wallace Thurman, "Negro Life in New York's Harlem: A Lively Picture of a Popular and Interesting Section," in *The Collected Writings of Wallace Thurman: A Harlem Renaissance Reader*, ed. Amritjit Singh and Daniel M. Scott III, 47 (New Brunswick, N.J.: Rutgers University Press, 2003).

35. "Black Belt's Nightlife," *Variety*, 16 October 1929, 12. For further information on the number and types of nightclubs in Harlem during this period, see Arnold Shaw, *The Jazz Age: Popular Music in the 1920s* (New York: Oxford University Press, 1987), 59; and Lewis A. Erenberg, *Steppin' Out: New York Nightlife and the Transformation of American Culture, 1890–1930* (Westport, Conn.: Greenwood Press, 1981), 254–259. On the parallel phenomenon of white cultural tourism on Chicago's South Side—specifically in the area along State Street between 26th and 39th streets, known by African Americans as "the Stroll," see William Howland Kenney, *Chicago Jazz: A Cultural History, 1904–1930* (New York: Oxford University Press, 1993), 15–26.

36. "Black Belt's," 1.

37. Ibid., 12.

38. Maltby, "Sticks," 26. For an account of this "unifying social function," see Hays, "Supervision from Within," 51–53.

39. Maltby, "Sticks," 23–26.

40. Ibid.

41. Ibid., 25.

42. Ibid., 27–28.

43. Ibid., 24–25. See also Mae D. Huettig, "The Motion Picture Industry Today" (1944), in *The American Film Industry*, rev. ed., ed. Tino Balio, 288–292 (Madison: University of Wisconsin Press, 1985).

44. Maltby, "Sticks," 24–25.

45. Ibid., 25, 32–34.

46. Ibid.

47. The reviews often make specific recommendations to exhibitors for the successful "exploitation" of the films that they might rent; in this respect, the trade magazines have a similar function to studio pressbooks like the one discussed above.

48. For useful background on Hollywood conceptions of female audiences in this period and of concomitant arguments for their relative dominance, see Melvyn Stokes, "Female Audiences of the 1920s and Early 1930s," in Stokes and Maltby, *Identifying Hollywood's Audiences*, 42–60.

49. Maltby, "Sticks," 34. Earlier in the 1920s, the term "flapper" had a slightly different frame of reference in American cinema culture, referring not to female white-collar workers but to younger, high school– and college-age women. In this prior context, the use of the term also presupposed certain tastes and cultural sensibilities; the term's associations with younger-generation rebellion and "Jazz Age" rejection of conventional gender and sexual decorum were, however, more explicitly in play here than in the later discourse that Maltby examines. On early 1920s flapper characters and audiences, see Sara Ross, "The Hollywood Flapper and the Culture of Media Consumption," in *Hollywood Goes Shopping*, ed. David Desser and Garth S. Jowett, 57–81 (Minneapolis: University of Minnesota Press, 2000).

50. Maltby, "Sticks," 34.

51. Ibid., 32.

52. Ibid., 29.

53. On the wiring of theaters for sound, see Gomery, *Coming of Sound*, 91–99. Gomery offers a striking statistic: "Over 76 percent of [first-run] theaters [owned by the major studios] had been wired by the end of 1928, compared to only 5 percent of all theaters in the United States." Ibid., 92. *Variety*'s review of *The Jazz Singer* (12 October 1927), a film distributed in synchronized-sound and silent versions, offers a useful illustration of how disparities in access to wired theaters helped to solidify audience typologies held by the studios' distribution arms.

54. Maltby, "Sticks," 30.

55. Ibid., 30–31. These exhibitors began to complain that the films were increasingly offensive, particularly to the child audiences on which they relied for business. In tone and substance, the objections raised by small-town exhibitors anticipate the critiques of Hollywood movies that would lead to the passage of the Production Code in 1934. See Thomas Doherty, *Pre-Code Hollywood: Sex, Immorality, and Insurrection in American Cinema, 1930–1934* (New York: Columbia University Press, 1999), 319–336; and Richard Maltby, "'Baby Face' or How Joe Breen Made Barbara Stanwyck Atone for Causing the Wall Street Crash," in *The Studio System*, ed. Janet Staiger, 251–278 (New Brunswick, N.J.: Rutgers University Press, 1995).

56. Steven Ross, *Working-Class Hollywood: Silent Film and the Shaping of Class in America* (Princeton, N.J.: Princeton University Press, 1998), 178. See also May, *Screening Out the Past*, 201. During this period, women joined the expanding white-collar sector in large numbers, especially in lower-paying clerical and service positions, operating small machines in office settings and staffing sales counters.

57. C. Wright Mills, *White Collar: The American Middle Classes* (Oxford: Oxford University Press, 1951), 76; Ross, *Working-Class Hollywood*, 179–180. My understanding of these shifting notions of class has been informed by Siegfried Kracauer's "anthropological" study, *The Salaried Masses: Duty and Distraction in Weimar Germany* (1930), trans. Quintin Hoare (London: Verso, 1998).

58. The very trope "white collar" highlights how clothing confers prestige. These workers were able to wear "street clothes," rather than uniforms, to work and were even rewarded professionally for their skillful manipulation of fashion and other commodities required to convey an appealing "personality," such as grooming and hygiene products. Thus, the white-collar workers were, in effect, the paradigmatic subjects of the new consumer economy. Mills, *White Collar*, 182–188.

Interestingly, the conversion to sound led some commentators to note that the cinema itself was becoming a more white-collar industry, the new technology requiring its own "armies" of "brain workers" to run smoothly. Maurice quotes a 1930 *Photoplay* magazine article, "How Talkies Are Made," which describes camera operators and electricians as being elevated to "white collar job[s]" in the "new order" of production. Maurice, "Cinema at Its Source," 41.

59. Ross, *Working-Class Hollywood*, 180.

60. Mills, *White Collar*, 248–249.

61. While these magazines did not review all of the same films and discussed shorts less consistently, combined they published at least one review of each of the features on which this study focuses. *Exhibitors Herald-World* began to use this title only in January 1929. Following the 1927 merger of two trade magazines, the publication had been called *Exhibitors Herald and Motion Picture World*.

62. Freddie Schader, review of *Hearts in Dixie*, *Motion Picture News* 39, no. 9 (2 March 1929).

63. Eugene O'Neill's name appears in several of the arguments that Maltby cites both for and against the industry's embrace of "highbrows" between 1929 and 1933; "O'Neillish" functions as a metonymy for the tastes of legitimate theatergoers, the kind of "class" trade that appreciates sophisticated dialogue and artistic innovation.

64. Review of *Hearts in Dixie*, *Variety*, 6 March 1929, 15. The writer's allusion is apt in light of the fact that DuBose Heyward, author of *Porgy*, later wrote the screenplay for the film *The Emperor Jones*. On Heyward's role in *The Emperor Jones* film, see Lary May, *The Big Tomorrow: Hollywood and the Politics of the American Way* (Chicago: University of Chicago Press, 2000), 69–70.

65. Wilbur Morse Jr., "Universal's 'Hearts in Dixie' Wins; Character Study of Negroes," *Exhibitors Herald-World*, 16 March 1929, 46; T. O. Service, review of *Hearts in Dixie*, *Exhibitors Herald-World*, 25 May 1929, 49.

66. Review of *Hearts in Dixie*, *Variety*, 15.

67. Ibid. Like the piece in *Motion Picture News*, this review sees the film as best suited to "the art theaters"; yet it notes that these theaters are not yet "wired" for sound. According to Gomery, "art theaters" in the 1920s were a subset of a small circuit of

theaters (mostly in the Northeast) showing European films. With very limited success, these theaters, unlike those that attracted neighborhood audiences with national ties to particular European cinemas, sought an audience of cinephiles interested in aesthetically challenging films. See Gomery, *Coming of Sound*, 173–180.

68. Review of *Black and Tan*, *Variety*, 6 November 1929, 19.

69. Ibid.

70. Review of *Hallelujah*, *Harrison's Reports*, 31 August 1929, 138.

71. Freddie Schader, review of *Hallelujah*, *Motion Picture News* 40, no. 8 (24 August 1929): 735.

72. Ibid. Written by two white dramatists, *Lulu Belle* billed itself as a "melodrama of Harlem Street Life." The original 1926 David Belasco production featured "a cast of 100 blacks and 15 whites," with white performers in blackface or brownface playing the four main "Negro" roles. Leonore Ulric, a white actress, played the part of Lulu Belle, a "mulatto" character who, in many ways, is a model for *Hallelujah*'s "high yella" temptress, Chick. Edward Sheldon and Charles MacArthur, *Lulu Belle*, in *The Stage Works of Charles MacArthur*, ed. Arthur Dorlag and John Irvine, 15–75 (Tallahassee: Florida State University Foundation, 1974); and Lewis, *Harlem*, 164.

73. Schader, review of *Hallelujah*, 735.

74. Review of *Hallelujah* (1), *Variety*, 28 August 1929, 23.

75. Ibid., 31. The word "sticks" actually appears in the preceding summary of the three reviews; a synonym for "hinterlands," "sticks" is another key term in trade press discourse, forming a binary with "big city."

76. Review of *Hallelujah* (2), *Variety*, 28 August 1929, 22.

77. Ibid.

78. Ibid.

79. The prefatory blurb explicitly identifies the other two reviewers as "male" but does not identify them by name.

80. Review of *Hearts in Dixie*, *Variety*, 21.

81. Ruth Morris, review of *Hallelujah*, *Variety*, 28 August 1929, 21.

82. Ibid. Morris's word choice—"should *not* be worn" (emphasis mine)—is either a mistake or a subtle jab directed at female viewers whose senses of fashion are informed by movies.

83. Ibid.

84. Ibid. According to William Kenney, the phrase "black and tan" "stemmed from a slang expression used after the Civil War to describe the Republican factions that included both blacks and whites." In the 1920s, the phrase routinely was applied to cabarets with racially mixed clientele. Kenney, *Chicago*, 16.

Morris had expressed an intermittent interest in black entertainment and white practices of Harlem "slumming" in her recurring column on *Variety*'s "Women's Page." See, for example, her enthusiastic account of taking in the "entertainment" offered by black performers and white audience members alike at a series of Harlem clubs. Ruth Morris, "Uncommon Chatter," *Variety*, 10 April 1929, 46. Here Morris clearly depicts this kind of entertainment consumption as a marker of status distinction.

85. Morris, review of *Hallelujah*, 22.

86. Review of *Thunderbolt*, *Variety*, 26 June 1929, 22.

87. "Highlights," *Thunderbolt* pressbook, 1, Paramount Press Sheets Collection, Margaret Herrick Library, AMPAS (hereafter cited as Paramount Press Sheets, AMPAS).

88. "Sights and Sounds of the largest Negro city in the world . . ." *Thunderbolt* pressbook, 2, Paramount Press Sheets, AMPAS.

89. Morris, review of *Hallelujah*, 22.

90. Ibid. Morris's reference to Covarrubias is quite apt as the artist illustrated a promotional pamphlet for *Hallelujah*, which MGM sold at theaters showing the film. See "Metro-Goldwyn-Mayer Presents 'Hallelujah,' a King Vidor Production . . ." (New York: Pace Press, 1929), Special Collections, Northwestern University Library. For other examples of Covarrubias's illustrations, see Lewis, *Harlem*. On Covarrubias's attraction to Harlem nightlife, see Anderson, *This Was Harlem*, 140.

91. D. F., "Jazz Heaven," *Exhibitors Herald-World*, 9 November 1929, 50. The magazine reviewed *Black and Tan* in the context of a description of the premiere of *Jazz Heaven*, a white-cast RKO film on whose program it was exhibited in at least one New York theater. Both *Exhibitors Herald-World* and *Variety* noted that *Jazz Heaven* might be a more fitting title for the Murphy short, the feature containing no music recognizable as jazz.

92. Ibid.

93. Review of *Yamekraw*, *Variety*, 30 April 1930, 17. The review incorrectly spells the film's title as "Yamekrow." In the above quotation, "Murnau" refers to the innovative German director F. W. Murnau, who came to Hollywood to work for Fox in 1927. I discuss the influence of German expressionist cinema on *Yamekraw* further in the next chapter.

94. Ibid.

95. Freddie Schader, review of *St. Louis Blues*, *Motion Picture News* 40, no. 9 (31 August 1929): 794.

96. In the reviews of the two African American–cast features, the fact that scenes of suggestive dancing are presented within a larger southern, quasi-pastoral context seems to insulate these films against the kind of worries about censorship in evidence here. See, for instance, the assurances in the first *Variety* review of *Hallelujah* that all "lovemaking" is depicted in a "clean" way. Likewise, even as it condemned *St. Louis Blues*, *Motion Picture News* predicted mass-audience appeal for *Hearts in Dixie* on the basis of its "sympathetic," universally inoffensive representation of African Americans as a group. This is a film that "lacks any trace of offense to white or black," acceptable to the former, the reviewer suggests, because it represents southern African Americans as content, superstitious, and picturesque. Morse, "Universal's 'Hearts in Dixie,'" 46. In other words, *Hearts in Dixie* conforms to the widely held ideology of the "typical southland." (Why such a representation would not give offense to African American viewers, the reviewer does not specify.) Schader's *Motion Picture News* review also predicts that those in the South will like *Hallelujah*.

97. Review of *On With the Show*, *Motion Picture News* 39, no. 21 (25 May 1929): 1785; T. O. Service, review of *On With the Show*, *Exhibitors Herald-World*, 17 August 1929, 79.

98. Review of *On With the Show*, *Variety*, 5 June 1929, 15. As is often the case in these reviews, the reviewer's own discussion of cinematic technique leads him or her, somewhat snobbishly, to attribute "class" interest to the film. The logic here is that the same technical accomplishments that the discerning critic has been provoked to mention will be lost on the "mass" audience, which is, by nature, unable to appreciate films on a formal level.

99. Ibid.

100. I take up this question in chapter 3.

101. Morris, review of *Hallelujah*, 22.

102. Review of *Check and Double Check*, *Variety*, 8 October 1930, 22.

103. Bill Crouch, review of *Check and Double Check*, *Motion Picture News* 41, no. 40 (4 October 1930): 52.

104. Maltby, "Sticks," 31.

105. Ernest A. Rovelstad, "Get Children Back to Theater, Plunkett Tells RKO Sales Force," *Exhibitors Herald-World*, 24 May 1930, 23.

106. At least one film fan magazine highlighted the glamorous side of the movie. *Motion Picture* featured a one-page photo spread on Sue Carol (who plays Jean Blair) under the caption, "Chic and Double Chic": "That's what they nearly called the *Amos 'n' Andy* hit, all because Sue Carol was in it. For when this girl makes a picture, she's there twice over." "Chic and Double Chic," *Motion Picture* 40, no. 6 (January 1931): 75.

107. Review of *Check and Double Check*, *Variety*. *Motion Picture News*'s Crouch also reduces the white story to "background for [Amos and Andy's] comedy" (52). The white "love interest and climax is not nearly so important to the picture as the comedy" for the *Exhibitors Herald-World* reviewer (4 October 1930, 25).

108. In chapter 5, I offer an extended close reading of the complex, uncanny narrative of *Check and Double Check*, exploring the significance of this antecedent connection to the film's treatment of African American migration.

109. Crouch, review of *Check and Double Check*, 52. The *Check and Double Check* review in *Exhibitors Herald-World* makes the identical claim (25).

110. Review of *Hallelujah*, *Harrison's Reports*, 138.

111. Morse, "Universal's 'Hearts in Dixie'" 56; Review of *Hallelujah* (2), *Variety*, 22.

112. Thomas Cripps, "The Myth of the Southern Box Office: A Factor in Racial Stereotyping in American Movies, 1920–1940," in *The Black Experience in America: Selected Essays*, ed. James C. Curtis and Lewis L. Gould, 116–144 (Austin: University of Texas Press, 1970).

113. I deal with this aspect of *Check and Double Check*'s production history in chapter 5. On the production of *Hallelujah*, see King Vidor, *A Tree Is a Tree* (New York: Harcourt, Brace, 1952), 175–176; Bob Thomas, *Thalberg: Life and Legend* (New York: Doubleday, 1969), 162–163; and Judith Weisenfeld, *Hollywood Be Thy Name: African American Religion in American Film, 1929–1949* (Berkeley: University of California Press, 2008), 19–20. For an interesting case of a studio bowing to perceived southern tastes, see *Variety*'s review of Al Jolson's *Big Boy*, 17 September 1930, 21, 30.

114. Cripps, "Myth," 121–124.

115. Aaronson, review of *The Emperor Jones*, *Motion Picture Herald*, 23 September 1933, 33.

116. Review of *The Emperor Jones*, *Variety*, 26 September 1933, 15.

117. The only other references to African American theaters and exhibitors (and, by extension, audiences) that I have encountered in the trades during this period come in a pair of *Variety* reviews of black-cast films made by independent producers, *Harlem Is Heaven* (Lincoln Motion Picture Company, 1932) and *The Black King* (Sack Amusements, 1932). These reviews speak enthusiastically about the two films' chances for success in race movie houses and recognize the existence of large numbers of "colored film fans." While noting the technical flaws of these two low-budget productions, the reviewers disparage these same fans by claiming that "for the colored trade the technical

side will not matter." The reviewer of *Harlem Is Heaven* argues that the film, possessing great novelty, might appeal to other audiences as well; he or she makes the bold but vague claim that "theaters are now generally welcoming anything off the beaten track." Review of *Harlem Is Heaven*, *Variety*, 7 June 1932, 20; and review of *The Black King*, *Variety*, 19 July 1932, 25.

118. Review of *Hearts in Dixie*, *Variety*, 15.

119. Schader, review of *Hearts in Dixie*.

120. Review of *Hearts in Dixie*, *Variety*, 15.

121. Review of *The Emperor Jones*, *Variety*, 15.

122. Ibid. Given that Eugene O'Neill wrote the play on which the film is based, the reference is apt though redundant. The *Exhibitors Herald-World* reviewer concurs with the *Variety* assessment, stressing, in particular, that the film will not be suitable for children. Aaronson, review of *The Emperor Jones*, 33.

123. Review of *The Emperor Jones*, *Variety*, 15.

124. Ibid.

CHAPTER 2 — "THE NEGRO INVADES HOLLYWOOD"

1. On the history of the black-cast musical subgenre, see Arthur Knight, *Disintegrating the Musical: Black Performance and American Musical Film* (Durham, N.C.: Duke University Press, 2002), 123–168.

2. *Hearts in Dixie* (unpublished continuity script, 26 February 1929), 46, Box 496, Collection of Motion Picture Scripts, Performing Arts Special Collections, University of California, Los Angeles (UCLA).

3. Quoted in Knight, *Disintegrating the Musical*, 134–135.

4. Silverman, 54.

5. See MacPherson, "As Is," 87; and Benchley, review of *Hearts in Dixie*, 122–123.

6. Silverman, *Acoustic Mirror*, 45, 54.

7. The films that I discuss in chapters 4 and 5, *Hallelujah* and *Check and Double Check*, respectively, make subtextual migration references through enigmatic images of blocked mobility for African American characters—patterns of frustrated movement. Migration references help to make legible a kind of latent or unconscious stratum in these films' historical visions: histories of oppression and exploitation that begin to surface in and around their considerations of when, why, and how black individuals relocate themselves.

8. Alain Locke, "The New Negro," in *The New Negro*, ed. Alain Locke, 5 (1925; repr., New York: Simon & Schuster, 1997).

9. Ibid., 3.

10. Ibid., 5.

11. See Grossman, *Land of Hope*, 2–9. See also Drake and Cayton, *Black Metropolis*, 58–97; and Louise Venable Kennedy, *The Negro Peasant Turns Cityward: Effects of Recent Migrations to Northern Centers* (New York: Columbia University Press, 1930), 23–57.

12. Locke, "New Negro," 6.

13. Grossman, *Land of Hope*, 14.

14. Locke, "New Negro," 6.

15. Ibid. "Pushes" and "pulls" are Grossman's terms. See his discussion of "macro-" and "micro-historical causes" in *Land of Hope*, 14–18. Grossman stresses that to cite

"causes" for migration is different than to identify individuals' "motivations." Grossman's detailed case studies of actual historical migrant narratives delve into this latter, more elusive realm.

16. Locke, "New Negro," 3.

17. Ibid., 5.

18. Ibid., 5–6.

19. Amiri Baraka (LeRoi Jones), *Blues People: Negro Music in White America* (New York: William Morrow, 1999), 96.

20. Locke, "New Negro," 6.

21. Ibid., 7.

22. The phrases cited in this paragraph come from Locke's foreword to *New Negro*, xxv.

23. Floyd C. Covington, "The Negro Invades Hollywood," *Opportunity: A Journal of Negro Life* 7, no. 4 (1929): 111. At the time of Covington's writing, *Hearts in Dixie* had just been released, while *Hallelujah* was still in production.

24. Gilbert Osofsky, *Harlem: The Making of a Ghetto; Negro New York, 1890–1930* (New York: Harper & Row, 1963), 105–110. See also Evans, "'Racial Cross-Dressing,'" 392–393; Anderson, *This Was Harlem*, 59; and James Weldon Johnson, "Harlem: The Culture Capital," in Locke, *New Negro*, 304.

25. A slightly earlier piece in *Variety*, indeed, correlated the demand for "colored talent" in talking pictures with a labor migration to Los Angeles. Describing the city's bourgeoning Central Avenue neighborhood as "a nucleus for a second Harlem district," the writer of this piece highlighted Paramount's call for extras to cast in a cabaret scene of an unnamed film (most likely *Thunderbolt*) and asserted that a number of "ex-Harlem night club entertainers . . . had migrated here for the film." "Harlem Going West," *Variety*, 10 April 1929, 1. For more on the discussion of the links between Harlem (as a historical community and an idea) and *Thunderbolt*'s construction of an interracial cabaret, see the conclusion.

26. The anonymous writer of an important contemporaneous *Negro Yearbook* entry on "The Negro in Motion Pictures" appears to pick up on Covington's rhetoric, underlining the connection between sound film and the racial transformation of "Filmland": "The introduction of sound has made many changes in the motion picture business. One of the most interesting of these changes has been the opening of filmdom to the Negro race. Negroes had been in pictures, but their position had been a very obscure one. Today the Negro has an important place in filmland." Work, *The Negro Yearbook*, 465.

27. Krasner, *Beautiful Pageant*, 11, 131–163.

28. Covington, "Negro," 111.

29. Ibid. On the history of Central Casting, see Tino Balio, "Part III: A Mature Oligopoly, 1930–1948," in Balio, *American Film Industry*, 271–273. On Charles Butler's role as the "black agent" for the Central Casting Corporation, see Cripps, *Slow Fade to Black*, 103–104.

30. "Negro Finds Talker Voice," *Sound Waves*, 1 March 1929, 5.

31. Covington, "Negro," 112–113, 131. Production records for Paramount's *Thunderbolt* (1929) offer an instructive case study of the trend that Covington describes. According to initial cost estimates, "colored" extras in the Harlem cabaret scene were to receive $10.00/day for their work, while their white counterparts in the same scene

were to receive \$7.50/day. Cost Estimates, *Thunderbolt*, Box 197, Folder 1, Paramount Pictures Production Records, Margaret Herrick Library, AMPAS. *Variety*'s survey of trends in extra casting in 1928 confirms Covington's assertion of a heightened demand for "colored extras" and demonstrates that the majority of these performers were hired at the \$7.50/day pay rate. The magazine's comprehensive averages for daily wages, however, show white extras receiving slightly more overall than African American extras (\$8.94/day versus \$8.22/day).

32. Covington, "Negro," 111.

33. Ibid.

34. Ibid., 112. While Covington does not comment further on the contractual status of "bit" players, it seems likely that these actors also would have been registered with Central Casting.

35. Ibid., 111. Although Covington does not specify what constitutes a star, his comments imply a conventional understanding: an actor under long-term contract with an individual studio who plays leading roles and receives primary billing. Covington's rhetoric of "distinctive" personalities also suggests the ways in which the star's roles are tied into his or her singular screen presence. Along these lines, John Ellis usefully defines a star as "a performer in a particular medium whose figure enters into subsidiary forms of circulation, and then feeds back into future performances." John Ellis, "Stars as a Cinematic Phenomenon," in *Film Theory and Criticism*, 6th ed., ed. Leo Braudy and Marshall Cohen, 598 (Oxford: Oxford University Press, 2004).

36. Covington, "Negro," 113. The notion of "the Negro as atmosphere" figures prominently in several other contemporary treatments of black film history by African American writers. Both Geraldyn Dismond and Elmer A. Carter (the then editor of *Opportunity*) invoke this trope in their important contributions to the 1929 black film issue of *Close Up*. See Dismond, "Negro Actor," 93; and Carter, "Of Negro Motion Pictures," 118. In "What 'Hallelujah' Means to the Negro Race," actor Daniel Haynes also uses the term "atmosphere" to describe Hollywood's casting of African Americans before sound. "Atmosphere" was an industry term of art. Warner Bros. Daily Production and Progress Reports from this period use "atmosphere" as a heading to group actors contracted for a given production, underneath character actors (who are identified by name) and "bits." Daily Production and Progress Reports, *Safe in Hell* Box, Warner Bros. Archives, University of Southern California.

37. Covington, "Negro," 113.

38. Covington closes with the grand statement, "the success of these pictures shall erect the foundation of the Negro's permanent place in the cinematographic industry in California." Covington, "Negro," 131.

39. Ibid., 113.

40. See Locke's description of "a new figure on the national canvas and a new force in the foreground of affairs," in his foreword to *New Negro*, xxv.

41. Covington, "Negro," 131.

42. Harold Cruse, *The Crisis of the Negro Intellectual* (1967; repr., New York: New York Review of Books, 2005), 37–38.

43. As one of the group of intellectuals whom Cruse critiques, Covington was not unaware of the barriers to black self-expression inherent in the Hollywood studio system, backed as it was by white corporate capital and even more rigidly segregated behind the camera than in front of it. In the essay, he expresses a hope that such

production-sector jobs will be forthcoming for African Americans, pointing to the work of Harold Garrison on *Hallelujah*. Garrison was nominally a bootblack at MGM who received assistant director credit for the film. According to Judith Weisenfeld, his "role seems to have been to act as an intermediary between [white director King] Vidor and the large numbers of local extras engaged on location and perhaps to oversee the travel of the lead cast members on Jim Crow railroad cars to the location shoot in Memphis, Tennessee." Weisenfeld, *Hollywood Be Thy Name*, 21. As Weisenfeld also stresses, the African American playwright Ransom Rideout contributed additional dialogue for the film, whose story was conceived by Vidor and embellished by a white screenwriter, Wanda Tuchock.

44. Covington, "Negro," 113.

45. Alain Locke and Sterling Brown, "Folk Values in a New Medium," in *Folk-Say: A Regional Miscellany*, vol. 2, ed. B. A. Blotkin, 340–345 (Norman: University of Oklahoma Press, 1930).

46. David Bordwell and Kristin Thompson, *Film Art: An Introduction*, 8th ed. (Boston: McGraw-Hill, 2008), 94–96.

47. Ibid.

48. Stephen Ross has demonstrated that fantasies of consumption and social mobility are the dominant source of film narrative in this period in *Working-Class Hollywood*, 173–211.

49. Locke and Brown, "Folk Values," 341. The writers spell the character's name "Chinquapin," the correct spelling of the variety of chestnut for which the character, indeed, appears to be named. Because the extant screenplay drafts render the name "Chincapin," however, I have opted for this spelling throughout the chapter.

50. The film's critical reception history reflects a pervasive confusion about when it is supposed to be set. In a program written for the catalog for the Museum of Modern Art's 1971 series "The Roots of the American Musical Film," Miles Kreuger states that the film is "set in an impoverished Negro cotton community in the South during some undetermined time after the Civil War." Miles Kreuger, "The Roots of the Musical Film," *Hearts in Dixie* clipping file, Celeste Bartos International Film Study Center, Museum of Modern Art. Reviewing a black film retrospective featuring *Hearts in Dixie*, a 1988 *Los Angeles Times* article calls the film "a Civil War comic-drama" and compares it to *Roots* for its depiction of a family laboring under the "peculiar institution." Charles A. Johnson, "A Young Perspective on Two Old Black Movies," *Los Angeles Times*, 13 March 1988, *Hearts in Dixie*, Clipping File, AMPAS.

51. Paula Massood, *Black City Cinema: African American Urban Experiences in Film* (Philadelphia: Temple University Press, 2003), 14–15.

52. Ibid., 14, 36.

53. Walter Weems, "Hearts in Dixie" (unpublished story, 23 October 1928), scene 17, Produced Scripts, Twentieth Century–Fox Collection, Performing Arts Special Collections, UCLA (hereafter cited as Fox Scripts, UCLA). In the Paul Sloane and A. H. Van Buren scenario, this conversation has been pared down, with Nappus still associating ignorance with slavery but no longer identifying his land as a bequest of his former master. (In the finished film, the land that Nappus sells to fund Chincapin's trip has no particular provenance.) An odd direction in this early draft identifies the film's setting as 1870, indicating that, while "there was no tap-dancing in 1870," the ensuing dance sequence calls for this style. Sloane and Van Buren, *Hearts in Dixie*

(unpublished scenario from the story by Walter Weems, November 1928), Scene 27, Fox Scripts, UCLA.

54. Weems, "Hearts in Dixie," Scene 17, Fox Scripts, UCLA.

55. Chloe and Truelove do not appear as characters in the original story, which begins by announcing Chincapin's immanent departure. Nappus's motivation here is strictly to give his son the educational opportunities he never had. Weems, "Hearts in Dixie," Fox Scripts, UCLA. The events surrounding Chloe's and Truelove's illness and death—which become the impetus for Nappus's sending Chincapin away—appear for the first time in the Sloane and Van Buren scenario. *Hearts in Dixie*, Fox Scripts, UCLA.

56. Valerie Lee, *Granny Midwives and Black Women Writers: Double-Dutched Readings* (New York: Routledge, 1996), 1–12.

57. Ibid., 12.

58. Georgia Douglas Johnson, *Plumes*, in *The Plays of Georgia Douglas Johnson*, ed. Judith Stephens, 75–76 (Urbana: University of Illinois Press, 2006).

59. Lee stresses this point in her reading of the play. Lee, *Granny*, 11. I thank Valerie Lee for drawing my attention to this connection between *Plumes* and *Hearts in Dixie* and for prompting me to think about the ways in which the film both relates to and differs from representations of traditional healers in texts by African American women writers like Johnson and Alice Walker.

60. Johnson, *Plumes*, 81–82.

61. Lee, *Granny*, 37.

62. Locke, "New Negro," 7.

63. The film's early admirers noted this particular exploration of black performance as pure cinematic spectacle. See Potamkin, "Aframerican Cinema," 108; see also Maurice, "'Cinema at Its Source,'" 31–71.

64. See Cripps, *Slow Fade to Black*, 262.

65. For a critical analysis of these commentaries, see Friedman, "'Moving-Picture of Democracy.'"

66. Because Waters's character is not named in the film, I will refer to the character by the actress's name.

67. Waters's other son, Henry (played by the adult actor Edgar Connor), returns to the offscreen site of the scuffle to confront Sinbad Johnson, and Waters encourages him "to kick [the other boy] on the shins for [her.]" She rather cryptically declares, "I'll sure be glad when they rid the neighborhood of such as him."

Rufus's frosting mask is doubly significant in the context of this film's self-conscious emphasis on appetite and stereotyped foodstuffs and references to blackface minstrelsy. This episode echoes the climactic scene of *Check and Double Check* in which Amos and Andy smash the white-frosted piece of Richard's wedding cake. See my detailed reading of this scene in chapter 5.

68. Richard Wright, "The Ethics of Living Jim Crow: An Autobiographical Sketch," in Federal Writers' Project, *American Stuff: An Anthology of Prose & Verse by Members of the Federal Writers' Project*, 39–52 (New York: Viking, 1937).

69. The word "line" has a particularly strong resonance in the discourse of postmigration patterns of racial segregation. Fearing black "invasion" of certain neighborhoods, white property owners' associations and realtors banded together to draw boundary lines along certain streets, hoping to preserve all-white enclaves. On such practices in

Harlem, see Osofsky, *Harlem*, 108; and Johnson, "Harlem," 303–304. On the South Side of Chicago, see Drake and Cayton, *Black Metropolis*, 195–213.

70. Jabari Asim, *What Obama Means . . . For Our Culture, Our Politics, Our Future* (New York: William Morrow, 2009), 79.

71. Ibid., 79–80.

72. Ibid., 80. During the Senate sequence, Waters acts as the interlocutor in the conventional first section of the minstrel show, fielding questions and making jokes with a chorus that tellingly includes a "Senator Bones." On the dramatic conventions of blackface minstrelsy, see Robert Toll, *Blacking Up: The Minstrel Show in Nineteenth-Century America* (Oxford: Oxford University Press, 1974), 51–54.

73. See *The Encyclopedia of Popular Music*, 4th ed., s.v. "Mack Gordon."

74. Jeffrey Melnick, *A Right to Sing the Blues: African Americans, Jews, and American Popular Song* (Cambridge, Mass.: Harvard University Press, 1999), 52–55.

75. Ibid., 60–80.

76. Ibid., 50–52. See also Jeffrey Melnick, "Tin Pan Alley and the Black-Jewish Nation," in *American Popular Music: New Approaches to the Twentieth Century*, ed. Rachel Rubin and Jeffrey Melnick, 29–45 (Amherst: University of Massachusetts Press, 2001).

77. See Locke, foreword to *New Negro*, xxv.

78. For a fuller analysis of costume symbolism and Waters's introduction as "star" in *On With the Show*, see the next chapter.

79. She further describes the song's plural subject as being "ready to take charge of any so-and-so": "Don't stop for law nor traffic when we're raring to go."

80. Massood, *Black City Cinema*, 67.

81. In one instance, the actors on screen act as a de facto chorus, appearing to sing one of the vocal refrains. In another, the film uses instrumental effects (the squawks of a muted trumpet) to suggest diegetic sounds (the cries of a baby).

82. Paul Oliver, Max Harrison, and William Bolcom, *The New Grove Gospel, Blues, and Jazz* (New York: W. W. Norton, 1986), 256. See also Samuel Charters and Leonard Kundstadt, *Jazz: A History of the New York Scene* (New York: Doubleday, 1962), 276.

83. A Johnson solo performance of *Yamekraw*, recorded around 1944, appears on the 1996 Smithsonian Folkways compact disc *The Original James P. Johnson: 1942–1945* (Piano Solos). Because I viewed *Yamekraw* in an archival setting, I have not been able to conduct a thorough comparison of the film's arrangements and Johnson's in the Smithsonian Folkways recording.

84. For example, the chorus sings about a character "sighing, crying, dying to get to Dixieland"—a bit of nonsense given that the character in question is already in the town of Yamekraw (which the lyrics also identify as "way down in Dixieland").

85. Johnson's "rhapsody was intended as a musical sketch of the Negro section of Savannah, Georgia." Charters and Kunstadt, *Jazz*, 276.

86. Eisner, *Haunted Screen*, 21–25.

87. Ibid., 31.

88. Ibid., 141. By using light as a "space-forming factor" and adding extreme camera angles, filmmakers, Eisner explains, may convey "an obliqueness which projects [figures] out of the screen and makes them . . . tangible, three-dimensional." Ibid., 104.

89. While the film's opening titles do not list credits for performers, the lead male performer is identifiable as the tap dancer Jimmy Mordecai. Because his character is not named, I will refer to him as Mordecai.

90. On the use of distorting mirrors in expressionist films, see Eisner, *Haunted Screen*, 20–21.

CHAPTER 3 — ON (WITH THE) SHOW

1. Richard Dyer, "Entertainment and Utopia," in *Only Entertainment*, 2nd ed. (London: Routledge, 2002), 26.

2. On the film's handling of the mythic figure of the "gold digger," see Pamela Robertson, "Feminist Camp in *Gold Diggers of 1933*," in *Hollywood Musicals: The Film Reader*, ed. Steven Cohan, 129–142 (London: Routledge, 2002).

3. Lucy Fischer, "The Image of Woman as Image: The Optical Politics of *Dames*," *Film Quarterly* 30, no. 1 (Autumn 1976): 2–11. Laura Mulvey articulates the idea of female "to-be-looked-at-ness" in classical Hollywood cinema in her famous "Visual Pleasure and Narrative Cinema," in *Visual and Other Pleasures* (Bloomington: Indiana University Press, 1989), 19.

4. Fischer, "Image," 10.

5. Quoted in ibid.

6. The two female members of The Four Covans, whom I discuss below, offer a complex variation on this general rule.

7. Robyn Wiegman identifies this filmic convention of pairing glamorous white female characters and African American maids as a strategy for "the cultural elevation and adornment of white womanhood" in "Black Bodies/American Commodities: Gender, Race, and the Bourgeois Ideal in Contemporary Film," in *Unspeakable Images: Ethnicity and the American Cinema*, ed. Lester D. Friedman, 313 (Urbana: University of Illinois Press, 1991).

8. In a sense, *On With the Show* bridges the two "vogues" or film cycles noted by Paramount's Monte Brice in the long passage quoted early in chapter 1. It has elements both of "pictures dealing with the show business" and "Negro pictures."

9. Although the film's promotional materials bill Louise Fazenda as one of *On With the Show*'s stars and although her character, Sarah Fogarty, features prominently in several backstage sequences, her only role in *The Phantom Sweetheart* is to provide an "offstage laugh" at a critical time in the show. In "Shoestring," the original undated play from which *On With the Show* is adapted, Sarah Fogarty is an aspiring actress whom the producer of *The Dream Song* (the model for *The Phantom Sweetheart*) hires to do the laugh from offstage in place of the actress playing the "phantom" woman onstage. The play explains that this laugh is extremely important, as a "seductive" sign of sexual temptation or "promise" for the young, engaged man and that the actress playing the role is unable to produce the sound required to make that significance clear. "Shoestring" builds a rather cryptic discussion of the limits of appropriate erotic suggestion around this point in the narrative. The finished film eliminates any explanation of why Nita cannot do the laugh herself but stresses that it is very important: Sarah receives mention in the show's reviews for the quality of her laugh. Humphrey W. Pearson, "Shoestring" (unpublished play, n.d.), Box 297, Folder 5, United Artists Collection, Warner Bros. Scripts, Wisconsin Center for Theater and Film Research (hereafter cited as Scripts, WCTFR).

10. Once again, the earlier material adapted in subsequent screenplay drafts offers some insight into an enigmatic point in the film. In the play "Shoestring," all of the action takes place backstage; the reader learns of the content of *The Dream Song*

through Jerry's quick synopsis of the musical comedy to Bloom. Trying to delay Bloom from reclaiming his props and sets, Jerry explains that the film centers on a "New York boy" who goes to visit his grandfather in Georgia. At a masked ball, this boy meets a young woman with whom he "shares an hour of love"—a phrase that, the dialogue suggests, may mean a sexual liaison. Back in New York, the protagonist falls in love with and becomes engaged to "a society girl." Unable to forget the "Dream Song Girl," he returns south on a hunting trip, at which point he hears her laughter and begins to pursue her. By eliminating any mention of the prior relationship between the two characters, the film leaves the young man without any apparent motivation for his sudden interest in the "Phantom Sweetheart" (formerly the "Dream Song Girl"). Pearson, "Shoestring," Scripts, WCTFR.

11. Performing mostly in New York and Los Angeles in the late 1920s, The Four Covans were a groundbreaking tap group that combined jazz, speed, precision, and acrobatic styles. The group was composed of husband and wife Willie and Florence Covan, along with Dewey Covan (Willie's brother) and his wife (whose name I have not been able to determine). Marshall Stearns and Jean Stearns, *Jazz Dance: The Story of American Vernacular Dance* (New York: Macmillan, 1968), 268–270.

12. Massood, *Black City Cinema*, 14–15. See also my discussion of *Hallelujah* in the next chapter.

13. Richard Haines, *Technicolor Movies: The History of Dye Transfer Printing* (Jefferson, N.C.: McFarland, 1993), 4–7.

14. Ibid., 8–13.

15. Ibid., 17–23. See also Scott Higgins, *Harnessing the Technicolor Rainbow: Color Design in the 1930s* (Austin: University of Texas Press, 2007), 3–4, 23–24. On Warner Bros.' investment in color filmmaking in the early sound era, see Crafton, *Talkies*, 196–198.

16. Crafton, *Talkies*, 76–87.

17. Ibid., 279–280.

18. Martin Rubin, *Showstoppers: Busby Berkeley and the Tradition of Spectacle* (New York: Columbia University Press, 1993), 14–19.

19. "'On With the Show' First 100% Natural Color, Talking, Singing, Dancing Vitaphone Picture," *On With the Show* pressbook, 3, Pressbooks, WCTFR. Only black-and-white prints of the film survive.

20. "'On With the Show' Is Coming as First All Talking, Color Film," *On With the Show* pressbook, 3, Pressbooks, WCTFR.

21. "'On With the Show' First 100% Natural Color, Talking, Singing, Dancing Vitaphone Picture," *On With the Show* pressbook, 3, Pressbooks, WCTFR.

22. "'On With the Show' Vitaphone's First Color Song Film," *On With the Show* pressbook, 3, Pressbooks, WCTFR.

23. "Beauty Chorus of 100 in Vitaphone's First Color-Film," *On With the Show* pressbook, 3, Pressbooks, WCTFR; "Play Within a Play in Signing, Natural Color, 'On With the Show,'" *On With the Show* pressbook, 4, Pressbooks, WCTFR; "'On With the Show' Is Coming as First All Talking, Color Film."

24. "Thirty-eight Mikes Record 'On With the Show' First 100% Natural Color, Talking, Singing, Dancing Vitafilm," 4, *On With the Show* pressbook, 3, Pressbooks, WCTFR.

25. Review of *On With the Show*, *Motion Picture News*, 1785.

26. Review of *On With the Show, Variety*, 15. *The Desert Song* (Warner Bros., 1929) was a Vitaphone adaptation of a Broadway musical with some Technicolor sequences.

27. See, for example, the cluster of stories grouped together under the extravagant headline, "Girls! Girls! Girls! Girls! Girls! Melody! Mirth! Dancing Feet! Riot of Rainbow Glory!, *On With the Show* pressbook, 4, Pressbooks, WCTFR.

28. Maurice, "'Cinema at Its Source,'" 31–32, 51.

29. Ibid.

30. James Baldwin, *The Devil Finds Work*, in *James Baldwin: Collected Essays* (New York: Library of America, 1998), 554.

31. I draw here on Dyer's theory of cinematic whiteness, as articulated in Richard Dyer, *White* (London: Routledge, 1997), 1–4.

32. Review of *On With the Show, Variety*, 15. The *On With the Show* reviewer's language suggests that he or she sees Waters's appearance as an attractive aspect of the film for the young, urban, white-collar workers often labeled "class" or "Broadway" audiences and as a potential liability for "mass" or "Main Street" audiences (the intolerant "southern box office" in particular).

33. While Sublett's role in the film is uncredited, the pressbook identifies him by the odd stage name "Angelus Babe." The great pioneer of "rhythm tap," Sublett is better known by the stage name John Bubbles, which he used in his famous collaborations with Ford Lee Washington, "Buck" of the duo "Buck and Bubbles." See Stearns and Stearns, *Jazz Dance*, 212–219; see also Jacqui Malone, *Steppin' on the Blues: The Visible Rhythms of African American Dance* (Urbana: University of Illinois Press, 1996), 79.

34. "'Angelus Babe' Is Darktown Wow," *On With the Show* pressbook, 8, Pressbooks, WCTFR.

35. "Harmony Emperors' Quartet Heard in 'On With the Show,'" *On With the Show* pressbook, 8, Pressbooks, WCTFR.

36. "'On With the Show' Vitaphone's First Color Song Film," *On With the Show* pressbook, 3, Pressbooks, WCTFR.

37. Linda Mizejewski, *Ziegfeld Girl: Image and Icon in Culture and Cinema* (Durham, N.C.: Duke University Press, 1999), 11. Mizejewski's study highlights the importance of exhibition and display to early-twentieth-century consumer capitalism generally and theater specifically. Hence, I borrow the loaded phrase "on show," which recurs frequently in *Ziegfeld Girl*, for the title of this chapter.

38. Walter Benjamin, "The Work of Art in the Age of Mechanical Reproduction," in *Illuminations*, ed. Hannah Arendt, trans. Harry Zohn, 224–226 (New York: Schocken, 1968). See also Giorgio Agamben, *Profanations*, trans. Jeff Fort (New York: Zone Books, 2007), 90.

39. Mizejewski, *Ziegfeld Girl*, 90.

40. Ibid., 16.

41. Ibid., 89–91.

42. On the importance of product "tie-ups" in the marketing of early sound films, see my introduction and chapter 1.

43. "Women's Wear Tie-Up," *On With the Show* pressbook, 15, Pressbooks, WCTFR.

44. Mizejewski explains that Ziegfeld and his collaborators developed a particular choreography of modeling, including a slow, stately "Ziegfeld Walk" that his "showgirls" would perform in revue numbers in which they would make a "parade downstage . . . usually a procession down a staircase." Mizejewski, *Ziegfeld Girl*, 97–98. On

Ziegfeld's attempts to imitate the "shop window of life" in his productions, see ibid., 101. Another of the *On With the Show* tie-up ideas suggests that theater owners stage a "show girl drill," hiring a trained female vaudeville performer to lead "some local girls" in choreographed group movements, and staging this spectacle in "the public square, park or bandstand—even in the lobby of [a] theater. "Show Girl Drill," *On With the Show* pressbook, 15, Pressbooks, WCTFR.

45. Mizejewski, *Ziegfeld Girl*, 109–120.

46. Ibid., 101–102.

47. Ibid., 121.

48. On Leslie, see Shaw, *Jazz Age*, 61.

49. At least three of the African American performers in *On With the Show* appeared before or after in Leslie productions: Ethel Waters, John William Sublett (both in *Blackbirds of 1930*), and Willie Covan (*Dixie to Broadway*, 1924). Malone, *Steppin' on the Blues*, 76–79.

50. Mizejewski, *Ziegfeld Girl*, 125.

51. Susan Courtney, *Hollywood Fantasies of Miscegenation: Spectacular Narratives of Gender and Race, 1903–1967* (Princeton, N.J.: Princeton University Press, 2005), 113.

52. Ibid., 103, 113. Courtney notes that in the Production Code, the wording of the "miscegenation clause" is identical, except for the change of the plural "relationships" to the singular "relationship"; she concludes that this change was arbitrary or accidental. Ibid., 115.

53. Ibid., 105–107.

54. See, for example, Courtney's discussion of the PCA discussions of the various script drafts of the 1934 *Imitation of Life* (Warner Bros.). Ibid., 145. The PCA censors were anxious initially about the "suggestion [that] is omnipresent" of miscegenation via Peola's character despite the lack of an "active portrayal of miscegenation." Ibid.

55. Ibid., 106–107.

56. The first blatant challenges to the Hollywood taboo on "miscegenation" (as pertains to sexual relationships between African American women and white men) do not occur until Dorothy Dandridge's roles in films like *Island in the Sun* (Twentieth Century–Fox, 1957) and *Tamango* (1958). See Marguerite Rippy, "Commodity, Tragedy, Desire: Female Sexuality and Blackness in the Iconography of Dorothy Dandridge," in *Classic Hollywood, Classic Whiteness*, ed. Daniel Bernardi, 178–209 (Minneapolis: University of Minnesota Press, 2001); and Karen Alexander, "Fatal Beauties: Black Women in Hollywood," in *Stardom: Industry of Desire*, ed. Christine Gledhill, 45–54 (London: Routledge, 1991).

57. Susan Delson, *Dudley Murphy: Hollywood Wild Card* (Minneapolis: University of Minnesota Press, 2006), 85–86. After developing the "Photophone" sound-on-film system for synchronized-sound filmmaking, the Radio Corporation of America (RCA) formed RKO Radio Pictures in 1928 by purchasing two smaller studios, Pathé and FBO (where Murphy was under contract), as well as the Keith-Albee-Orpheum chain of converted vaudeville theaters. See Crafton, *Talkies*, 160–164.

58. Delson, *Dudley Murphy*, 86–99, 129–132.

59. The book's cover image is a production still from this scene.

60. This technique recalls the early cinematic practice of the "repeated action edit," which predates the "parallel editing" (or "cross-cutting") that became conventional with D. W. Griffith's Biograph films of the early teens. Tom Gunning uses an example

from the early Thomas Edison Corporation film *The Life of an American Fireman* (1903) to illustrate this concept. The film represents a fire rescue scene two times in its entirety, first by a camera positioned inside the bedroom inhabited by the mother and child that the firefighters want to reach and then by a camera positioned outside of the burning house. Tom Gunning, *D. W. Griffith and the Origins of American Narrative Film* (Urbana: University of Illinois Press, 1991), 96–97.

The appearance of a repeated action edit in an early sound-era musical film points both to the unsettled nature of editing conventions during the transition—in which highly innovative and sometimes unsuccessful attempts to achieve spectacular effects with the new equipment are common—and to the reemergence of what Gunning would call an "attractions"-based cinema during this period—in which spectacle can take precedence over narrative continuity. See Tom Gunning, "The Cinema of Attraction: Early Film, Its Spectator and the Avant-Garde," *Wide Angle* 8, nos. 3–4 (1986): 63–70.

61. Murphy had likely developed the "faceted, beveled lenses" that he used to create this effect doing research in the Dartmouth College physics department during August 1921. Murphy had used similar lenses in his pioneering collaboration on the avant-garde film *Ballet mécanique* (1924). See William Moritz, "Americans in Paris: Man Ray and Dudley Murphy," in *Lovers of Cinema: The First American Film Avant-Garde, 1919–1945*, ed. Jan-Christopher Horak, 122, 130 (Madison: University of Wisconsin Press, 1995); and Delson, *Dudley Murphy*, 24, 53.

62. See Nadine Walls, "'110 Per Cent Woman': The Crotch Shot in the Hollywood Musical," *Screen* 42, no. 4 (Summer 2001): 121–141. Delson claims that Murphy employs an "approach" to creating "near-abstract visual sequences that engage the sheer pleasure of gazing at the screen," which "would reach its apogee with Busby Berkeley's string of three 1933 hits—*Footlight Parade*, *Gold Diggers of 1933*, and *42nd Street*." See Delson, *Dudley Murphy*, 94–95.

63. Lewis, *Harlem*, 208–211; Malone, *Steppin' on the Blues*, 88. Murphy also featured a slightly more extensive chorus of light-skinned African American women in *The Emperor Jones* (United Artists, 1933).

64. On the demographics and fantasy life of interracial cabarets, see chapter 1.

65. Mulvey, "Visual Pleasure," 19–20.

66. A detail from the film's mise-en-scène underlines this use of women's bodies as repetitive, fungible motifs: the decoration on the stage curtain includes abstracted nude female forms.

67. There is one brief, comedic instance of male substitution in the effort to keep the stage show going. Bert (Otto Hoffman), the actor playing a white valet with a brief speaking role in the show, falls ill, and Jerry, the producer, has to take the stage in his place.

68. Pearson, "Shoestring," 78, Scripts, WCTFR. In the film, Nita does use the phrase "So, I took off my clothes" to joke about an earlier decision to go back into show business.

69. Irving Lewis Allen, *The City in Slang: New York Life and Popular Speech* (Oxford: Oxford University Press, 1993), 174.

70. "As Skirts Lengthen, Baldheads Exit from Front Row," *On With the Show* pressbook, 10, Pressbooks, WCTFR.

71. The later Warner Bros. backstage musical *Gold Diggers of 1933* reproduces this shot almost exactly.

72. *42nd Street* features its own version of this shot.

73. Pearson, "Shoestring," 27, Scripts, WCTFR.

74. Robert Lord, "Broadway or Bust" (unpublished final screenplay, 1929), n.p., Box 297, Folder 7, Scripts, WCTFR.

75. Over time, Waters's career significantly intersects with the two poles of black female mass-cultural representation that Wiegman and Mizejewski discuss: the hyperexoticized and hypereroticized black chorine and the extremely desexualized mammy figure. While Waters is perhaps best known for her more sentimentalized, matronly roles in films like *Tales of Manhattan* (Twentieth Century–Fox, 1942), *Cabin in the Sky* (MGM, 1943), and *Pinky* (Twentieth Century–Fox, 1949), she earlier rose to prominence as a vaudeville and cabaret performer by virtue of her skills as a blues singer who could also dance the "shimmy"—a staple of hypereroticized black female performance in the 1920s. In her autobiography, Waters notes the erotic associations of this "quivering" and "wriggling" dance movement, while making interesting claims about how her own performance of it managed to avoid any association with vulgarity. Ethel Waters and Charles Samuels, *His Eye Is on the Sparrow* (New York: Bantam Books, 1952), 110, 131.

76. Despite being a mixed-sex group, The Four Covans ultimately function like the five-man precision tap ensemble in *Black and Tan*. Stearns and Stearns note that one of their signature routines was "a tricky regimental drill to 'Parade of the Wooden Soldier' in which they danced together as one man." Stearns and Stearns, *Jazz Dance*, 269.

77. Quotation from the text of the first verse as it appears in the *On With the Show* pressbook, 8, Pressbooks, WCTFR.

78. At the end of the number Sam does emerge on stage; he and Bertha begin to fight but end up dancing together.

79. The title to this section of the chapter comes from a photo caption in the pressbook, which draws on this lyric.

80. Roland Marchand's work makes clear that American print advertisements in the 1920s and 1930s never featured African American figures as the fictional consumers in their "social tableaux," but only in secondary roles as smiling service figures: porters, janitors, and maids, and, in certain well-known cases (Aunt Jemima, the Gold Dust Twins), as advertising trademarks. Marchand, *Advertising the American Dream*, 193, 202. See also Weems, *Desegregating the Dollar*, 1–2; Paul K. Edwards, *The Southern Urban Negro as a Consumer* (New York: Prentice-Hall, 1932), 196–251; and Lauren Berlant, "National Brands/National Bodies: *Imitation of Life*," in *Comparative American Identities: Race, Sex, and Nationality in the Modern Text*, ed. Hortense J. Spillers, 36 (New York: Routledge, 1991).

81. Wiegman's work illustrates that such a claim about the significance of a representation of an African American woman as consumer must be carefully contextualized. Within a matter of a few decades, she points out, the Hollywood cinema and American mass culture at large would begin using images of black female consumers to efface historical struggles and to fashion a myth of American freedom and equality. In this mythic conception, "equal access to the commodity world" represents the imagined fulfillment of demands for equal rights; the woman who consumes with impunity has "made it." See Wiegman, "Black Bodies," 308–313.

82. Mizejewski, *Ziegfeld Girl*, 74.

83. Phillip Furia, *The Poets of Tin Pan Alley: A History of America's Great Lyricists* (New York: Oxford University Press, 1990), 244–262.

84. Perhaps reflecting the emergence of the "Negro film" fad, Waters's entrance into the production was relatively late. See *Variety* magazine's 27 February 1929 notice, "On With the Show," 72. Her part, listed only as "Plantation Singer" on the "Characters" list of the final screenplay draft, is completely undefined; even then, this draft does not mention her numbers at all. Lord, "Broadway or Bust."

85. Waters and Samuels, *His Eye*, 245.

86. See Melnick's superb *A Right to Sing the Blues*, which contextualizes collaborations between black cabaret and recording artists like Waters and white Jewish American songwriters like Akst and Harold Arlen.

87. In 1928, Warner Bros.' chief financial officer, Waddill Catchings, engineered the acquisition of the Stanley theater chain (which dominated the mid-Atlantic region) and its controlling interest in First National (including a valuable studio facility in Burbank, California). According to Douglas Gomery, First National "existed in name only" following this merger, as part of a "public relations move" meant to maintain an apparent distinction between it and Warner Bros. Gomery, *Coming of Sound*, 115–118; Crafton, *Talkies*, 193–195.

88. "When It's Sleepy Time Down South" became one of Louis Armstrong's signature tunes, after he recorded it in April 1931. While Clarence Muse himself is credited conventionally as one of the song's writers, James Lincoln Collier, one of Armstrong's biographers, claims that the song "was written by two New Orleans Creoles, Leon and Otis René, who had emigrated to Southern California" and met Armstrong in Pasadena. James Lincoln Collier, *Louis Armstrong: An American Genius* (New York: Oxford University Press, 1983), 245.

89. Branch, "Safe in Hell" (unpublished play, 1930), 39–42, Scripts, WCTFR.

90. Ibid., 5–6.

91. Advertisement for *Hallelujah*, *Motion Picture News* 39, no. 28 (29 June 1929).

92. Indeed, the film punctuates Chick's cabaret performance with a close-up of her dancing legs. See Maurice, "Cinema at Its Source," 56.

93. Recall my discussion of First National's marketing of *Safe in Hell* at the beginning of chapter 1. The studio emphasized the film's investment in black popular music as mediated through the tastes of the glamorous white star.

94. Following this exchange, the two women carry out a sympathetic, if one-sided, relationship. At one point they embrace, and when Leonie sees Gilda after she receives her death sentence, she weeps. Leonie and Gilda's relationship illustrates another radical transformation of the story's racial politics that occurs over the course of the script revisions. In Branch's original play, Gilda is a virulent racist who is aghast at the prospect of having to stay at a "nigger joint." In the play, Gilda has extensive conversations with Carl about the blackness of the islanders and insists that characters like Leonie obey a kind of southern, Jim Crow etiquette in their dealings with her. She lashes out at Leonie at one point, insulting her moral virtue. Branch, "Safe in Hell," 10–11, 43, Scripts, WCTFR.

CHAPTER 4 — THE UNHOMELY PLANTATION

1. Vidor, *Tree*, 175.

2. My use of the term "phantasmagoria" derives from Theodor Adorno's two-part definition: "[the] occultation of production by means of the outward appearance of the product" and "the illusion of the absolute reality of the unreal." Theodor W. Adorno, *In Search of Wagner*, trans. Rodney Livingstone (London: NLB, 1981), 85, 90.

3. Silverman, *Acoustic Mirror,* 45.

4. See chapter 1. On the cultural association of African Americans with musical performance as a generative force in the cinema, see also Knight, *Disintegrating the Musical,* 1–7.

5. Quoted in "Metro-Goldwyn-Mayer Presents 'Hallelujah.'"

6. Quoted in Covington, "Negro," 113.

7. Quoted in "Metro-Goldwyn-Mayer Presents 'Hallelujah.'" See also "King Vidor's Fondest Dream"; and "Emotional Temperament of Negro Actors Is Phenomenal—King Vidor," *Pittsburgh Courier,* 28 January 1929.

8. James Grossman, "A Chance to Make Good: 1900–1929," in *To Make Our World Anew: A History of African Americans,* ed. Robin D. G. Kelley and Earl Lewis, 346–352 (New York: Oxford University Press, 2000).

9. Charles S. Johnson, Edwin Embree, and W. W. Alexander, *The Collapse of Cotton Tenancy* (Chapel Hill: University of North Carolina Press, 1935), 1–33.

10. Vidor, *Tree,* 177–180.

11. X. Theodore Barber, "Phantasmagorical Wonders: The Magic Lantern Ghost Show in Nineteenth-Century America," *Film History* 3, no. 2 (1989): 73–86.

12. See Barber's discussion of Nathaniel Hawthorne's frequent use of "phantasmagoria" in his novels. Ibid., 84.

13. Judith Weisenfeld offers invaluable background on the film's musical selections and compositions, as overseen by Eva Jessye, in *Hollywood Be Thy Name,* 38–42.

14. Once Chick runs out, the film cuts several times to an extreme long shot of the church, which highlights the sense of containment and the association of black bodies with the confining interior. The open door of the church is brightly illuminated, and, as a line of people pass through this doorway, a parallel shadow procession is visible directly above them.

15. Maurice, "'Cinema at Its Source,'" 60, 62.

16. Ibid., 34, 60–62.

17. Maurice describes a total identification or "merging" of black bodies and the apparatus in a way that is in tension with her use of Silverman's *The Acoustic Mirror* to theorize black bodily diegeticization. Ibid., 46.

In Silverman's analogous theory of sexual differentiation, female restriction to diegesis links male characters to the apparatus. To pursue this analogy further, one would have to understand, against Maurice's suggestion, the apparatus as governed by a white authority that is only a phantom presence in this African American–cast film. (See my reading of the film's narrative discourse below.) I insist on pushing Silverman's analogy further than does Maurice in this case in order to point out the finally fantastical, illusory nature of the "black voice" synesthesia and the claims of privileged access to the apparatus that it underwrites.

18. Siegfried Kracauer, *Theory of Film: The Redemption of Physical Reality* (1960; repr., Princeton, N.J.: Princeton University Press, 1997), 130.

19. Ibid., 145.

20. On Vidor's use of silent film–making techniques in this and other outdoor-location scenes, see Weisenfeld, *Hollywood Be Thy Name,* 30–31; and Vidor, *Tree,* 180–183.

21. See in particular the stage directions to scene 2. O'Neill, *Emperor Jones,* 27.

22. King Vidor, *Hallelujah* (Shooting Script), 124, *American Film Scripts Online* (AFSO), http://www.alexanderstreet4.com.proxy.lib.ohio-state.edu/cgi-bin/asp/afso/

getvolume.pl?FS000870-5. What AFSO calls the Shooting Script is the first draft of the *Hallelujah* script. "Story by King Vidor / Continuity by Wanda Tuchock," 15 September 1928, Box 12041248, Folder 34, Turner/MGM Scripts Collection, Margaret Herrick Library, AMPAS.

Vidor's symbolic sound device (the sawmill-"tom-tom"), of course, anticipates his use of a water pump to evoke a heartbeat in the equally atavistic, naturalist swamp of *Ruby Gentry* (Twentieth Century–Fox, 1952).

23. Vidor, *Hallelujah* (Shooting Script), 124.

24. Adorno, *In Search*, 85, 90.

25. Marx, *Capital*, vol. 1, 165. The word "fantastic" in this translation might also be rendered as "phantasmagoric"; the ensuing lines describe a "misty realm" in which imaginary figures "appear . . . endowed with a life of their own." See Walter Benjamin, "Paris, the Capital of the Nineteenth Century," in *The Arcades Project*, trans. Howard Eiland and Kevin McLaughlin (Cambridge, Mass.: Belknap/Harvard, 1999), 7.

26. Sigmund Freud, "The Uncanny," in Strachey et al., *Standard Edition of the Complete Psychological Works of Sigmund Freud*, vol. 17, 220–225. I am indebted here to Jacques Derrida's commentary on Freud in *Specters of Marx: The State of the Debt, the Work of Mourning, and the New International*, trans. Peggy Kamuf (New York: Routledge, 1994), 145.

27. Sigmund Freud, *Jokes and Their Relation to the Unconscious*, trans. James Strachey (New York: W. W. Norton, 1963), 163.

28. As Paula Massood persuasively demonstrates, the film construes the urban setting as an immediate moral threat for the rural characters. Massood, *Black City Cinema*, 20–22.

29. "Transubstantiation" is Marx's term for the liberation of exchange value from the body of the commodity that occurs at the moment of purchase—its conversion into a monetary equivalent. See W. F. Haug, *Critique of Commodity Aesthetics: Appearance, Sexuality and Advertising*, trans. Robert Bock (Minneapolis: University of Minnesota Press, 1986), 23. For a discussion of "transubstantiation" in *Hallelujah*, albeit from a different perspective, see Rick Altman, *The American Film Musical* (Bloomington: Indiana University Press, 1987), 294.

30. Massood, *Black City Cinema*, 20–22. Likewise, the brief shot in the final montage of Zeke riding on top of a boxcar as he journeys home from prison is slightly more complex than Massood's reading suggests. Massood argues that the rural idyll becomes the "promised land" in the film, as opposed to the urban setting, which, she claims, historically (but against the grain of the film) was a sort of "promised land" for rural migrants. As I argue throughout this chapter, *Hallelujah*'s rural idyll—back to which Zeke travels by train (and by other means) at the end of the film—is all too worldly to be a "promised land" in any logically transformative, redemptive sense. The film, thus, is fractured internally, rendered almost incoherent by the contradictory move of portraying the cotton field and cabin (the already existent) as a "promised land."

31. These questions derive from my research into the history of African American sharecropping in the South during the early twentieth century. See Johnson, Embree, and Alexander, *Collapse*; Grossman, "Chance"; Donald Crichton Alexander, *The Arkansas Plantation, 1920–1942* (New Haven, Conn.: Yale University Press, 1943); Donald Holley, *The Second Great Emancipation: The Mechanical Cotton Picker, Black Migration, and How They Shaped the Modern South* (Fayetteville: University

of Arkansas Press, 2000); T. J. Woofter, *Landlord and Tenant on the Cotton Plantation*, U.S. Works Progress Administration Research Monograph 5 (Washington, D.C.: Works Progress Administration, 1936); Charles S. Johnson, *The Negro in American Civilization: A Study of Negro Life and Race Relations in the Light of Social Research* (New York: Henry Holt, 1930), 117–131; Howard Kester, *Revolt among the Sharecroppers* (New York: Covici-Friede, 1936); and Richard Bardolph's source material on "The Crop Lien System" in *The Civil Rights Record: Black Americans and the Law, 1849–1970* (New York: Thomas Y. Crowell, 1970), 41–44.

32. As Zeke and Spunk ride away in the wagon, Mammy (Fanny Belle DeKnight) shouts directions, which might address this omission in part: "Don't forget the flour and the paper."

33. "Metro-Goldwyn-Mayer Presents 'Hallelujah.'"

34. See W.E.B. Du Bois, "Dramatis Personae," *The Crisis* 36, no. 10 (1929): 355.

35. See Holley, *Second Great Emancipation*, 5–10.

36. All of the actors in this scene are white; moreover, none of the main tenant characters are black. While black farmers fit into a pair of key scenes dealing with credit and payment, they disappear from view during the climactic disputes with the landlord.

37. These quotations are from (in order) Maurice, "Cinema at Its Source," 55; Altman, *American Film*, 292–296; and Knight, *Disintegrating the Musical*, 133, 138. Thomas Cripps takes the provocative step of deeming them "cotton tenant[s]" in *Slow Fade to Black*, 248; and Weisenfeld calls the Johnsons "a large family of sharecroppers" in *Hollywood Be Thy Name*, 20. In using these terms, however, these writers gloss over the basic ambiguity in the film's premises. Discourse around the DVD release of *Hallelujah* suggests that the general and specific labels are viewed as interchangeable. While the synopsis offered on the back of the DVD case calls Zeke "a poor cotton farmer," reviewers tend to be bolder in referring to him as a "sharecropper." See, for example, Dave Kehr, "Critic's Choice: New DVD's," *New York Times*, 10 January 2006.

38. Knight, *Disintegrating the Musical*, 133.

39. Snead, *White Screens/Black Images*, 3.

40. Snead's "code of stasis" is similar to the "idyllic chronotope" that Massood, following Bakhtin, detects in black-cast musicals with rural southern settings. Yet *Hallelujah*'s urban setting (and use of contemporary signifiers like Chick's clothing and automobiles) tends to mitigate against the obfuscating effects of what Massood calls the "iconography of a rural, preindustrial southern agricultural economy." As a result, I am hesitant to see the film as presenting a coherent or closed idyllic space and time. See Massood, *Black City Cinema*, 14–15.

41. Richard Barrios, *A Song in the Dark: The Birth of the Musical Film* (Oxford: Oxford University Press, 1995), 314, emphasis mine.

42. Knight, *Disintegrating the Musical*, 138.

43. On the rise of "sentimentalized images of plantation life" in early minstrelsy, see Eric Lott, *Love and Theft: Blackface Minstrelsy and the American Working Class* (Oxford: Oxford University Press, 1993), 171–173.

44. Born in Kansas, Jessye was also an important composer of what Weisenfeld calls "religious dramas and oratorios." She published books of poetry and her arrangements of African American spirituals, in addition to teaching music, directing professional choirs, and working in the theater in Baltimore and New York City. Weisenfeld, *Hollywood Be Thy Name*, 251n.20.

45. Eva Jessye, "The Truth About 'Hallelujah' [Part 3]," *Baltimore Afro-American*, 19 July 1930. My research on Robert E. Lee Wilson's enterprise confirms the basic details that Jessye offers. See Jeannie M. Whayne, "Robert E. Lee Wilson and the Making of a Post-Civil War Plantation," in *The Southern Elite and Social Change: Chapters in Honor of Willard B. Gatewood, Jr.*, ed. Randy Finley and Tomas A. DeBlack, 95–117 (Fayetteville: University of Arkansas Press, 2002).

46. Eva Jessye, "The Truth About 'Hallelujah' [Part 2]," *Baltimore Afro-American*, 12 July 1930.

47. Vidor, *Hallelujah* (Shooting Script), 37–39. Weisenfeld points out that, because of his unusual arrangement with MGM executives, "to defer receiving his salary in order to defray the film's production expenses, in exchange . . . [for] a percentage of the film's profits," Vidor was able "to exercise a large measure of control over all phases of production." Weisenfeld, *Hollywood Be Thy Name*, 20.

48. Again, it is instructive to trace the evolution of this scene through the drafts of the screenplay. Vidor originally conceived of a lengthy chain gang sequence in which Zeke and a group of African American convicts are put to work sandbagging a "weak spot" in a levee bordering a flooded river. One night, as the shackled convicts sleep, the levee breaks; a guard (a white man?) frees Zeke from the "master chain," sparing him from drowning but fleeing before he is able to free the other convicts from the rising water. Zeke takes action, catching up to the guard, who is drowning (possibly fatally), and seizing the keys. He frees several of the other prisoners, bringing them to safety on high ground. Filled with the same inspiration as after Spunk's death, Zeke leads the others in prayer, at which point the waters stop rising. (Vidor's directions leave open the question of whether "faith" actually has saved them.) Zeke then is free simply to go home, although the script never addresses the fact that he is a fugitive. Vidor, *Hallelujah* (Shooting Script), 126–141.

While it would be difficult to say which of the two narrative strategies is ultimately more improbable—the Shooting Script's flood and escape or the simple assertion of "Probation" for a convicted murderer—Vidor's original rendering of the scene suggests his tacit recognition of the difficulties of restoring Zeke into the bosom of his family following the climactic, O'Neill-inspired scene of atavistic regression.

49. Having followed the film's production with great anticipation, black newspapers like the *Baltimore Afro-American*, *Chicago Defender*, and *New York Amsterdam News* published a wide range of professional reviews (some of which comment on audience behavior) and letters from readers (many of which make reference to community "talk" about the film). This remarkably extensive archive documents a tradition of skeptical, even oppositional response and a vigorous black public-sphere debate. A full survey of this archive is beyond the scope of the present chapter. Arthur Knight explores the range of reader letters that appeared in the *Chicago Defender* in *Disintegrating the Musical*, 140–144. See also Weisenfeld's survey of published responses in *Hollywood Be Thy Name*, 45–51.

50. Romeo L. Dougherty, "'Hallelujah' Film Continues to Draw," *New York Amsterdam News*, 28 August 1929.

51. Anna Everett has discussed this strategy, whereby black film critics position their pieces next to reprinted texts by white writers, commenting on them more or less explicitly. Examining two instances where Lester Walton, who edited the *New York Age*'s entertainment page during the second decade of the twentieth century, employed

this strategy, demonstrates its rhetorical efficacy: it "permits the internal contradictions of opposing arguments to be self-disclosed, thereby bolstering [the responding writer's] own contestation of specific points at issue." Everett, *Returning the Gaze*, 19–35.

52. Gow, "Harlem First Night." Illustrating the peculiar interest in black film spectatorship that *Hallelujah* elicited among white journalists, Mark Vance offered an almost identical account of the Lafayette audience's laughter in *Variety*. While mentioning other forms of viewer affect, Vance's extensive piece asserts that the African American members of the audience universally and constantly let out "gales of laughter that swept the Lafayette up and down." He further charges that these "gales" were often ill-timed, discounting the possibility of derisive laughter—a gesture of ridicule directed toward *Hallelujah*'s representations of African American life. As the title of his report indicates, Vance uncritically presupposes the audience's enjoyment of the film in its entirety, while also using his own sense of what should or should not be funny in the film to judge the timing of their laughter. Mark Vance, "Harlem, the Black Belt, Laughed in Wrong Spots—Likes 'Hallelujah,'" *Variety*, 28 August 1929, 5, 27.

CHAPTER 5 — BLACKNESS WITHOUT AFRICAN AMERICANS

1. Melvin Patrick Ely, *The Adventures of Amos 'n' Andy: A Social History of an American Phenomenon*, 2nd ed. (Charlottesville: University of Virginia Press, 2001), 26–46.

2. "Color Issue Finessed in Amos 'n' Andy Contract," *Exhibitors Herald-World*, 20 September 1930, 41.

3. Ibid. The *Motion Picture News* review of *Check and Double Check* highlights the relative separateness of the groups of characters in the film, noting that the "two classes" appear in only one scene together "and then with no familiarity." Crouch, review of *Check and Double Check*, 52. This description is not precisely true: Amos and Andy interact with Richard again in the train station, with Ralph and his accomplice in the haunted house, and with the white chauffeur who delivers the cake at the end of the film.

4. Rogin, *Blackface, White Noise*, 182.

5. "They Must Black Up for Part in Movies," *Baltimore Afro-American*, 9 August 1930. I have adapted the following section headings from the entries for "check" in the *Oxford English Dictionary*, 2nd ed.

6. The most definite information we get about the "property issue" comes in this conversation between Richard and Mr. Blair. Richard offers an update on the progress of his mission: "It's about that property I've been trying to clear. This morning I learned that the deed was never recorded, but I have an idea." Although it is hard to square this explanation with Jean's earlier description of the reasons for Richard's visit, it appears that the transfer of part of the father's estate to the son is being held up by the missing document. The deed surfaces in the end, but no fuller explanation of its significance is given, nor is any further mention made of the rest of the Williams family. Richard's "idea" is to go to the "old Williams house" in Harlem, his grandfather's long-vacant former residence ("many years ago, when that part of New York was considered way uptown"); the deed corresponds, it seems, to that property, although the specifics are frustratingly vague.

7. Because *Check and Double Check* may be unfamiliar to many readers, I have integrated sections of plot synopsis into the analysis of the film that follows. The crucial events that follow the opening sequence described above are these. The film's two story lines become intertwined when Amos and Andy secure the job of driving a Harlem jazz band (the Duke Ellington Orchestra) in their taxi, to perform at Jean Blair's birthday

party. Amos and Andy encounter Richard Williams outside of the Blair mansion, where they struggle to change a flat tire on the cab. The trio's unexpected reunion elicits shared joy, nostalgia, and finally sadness, as Richard informs the other two of his father's recent death. Returning to Harlem, Amos and Andy attend the meeting of their fraternal lodge, the Mystic Knights of the Sea. There they are chosen to participate in the lodge's most important ritual, which commemorates the death of its founder. The ritual requires them to stand "night-watch" in the reputedly haunted "old Williams house." The section of the chapter that deals with the ensuing gothic set piece in the old house will describe in detail its convoluted, almost illogical structure.

8. Rogin's fourth "race movie" is *Gone With the Wind* (Selznick, 1939). Rogin uses the term "race movie" unconventionally and somewhat against the grain to indicate mainstream or Hollywood films that thematize issues of race rather than independent films produced for African American audiences. See my discussion of this term in the conclusion.

9. Rogin, *Blackface*, 73, 79.

10. Knight, *Disintegrating the Musical*, 50.

11. Reflected in what follows, my thinking about the vagaries of the terms "self-conscious" and "unselfconscious" has benefited immensely from Jacqueline Stewart's nuanced, theoretically subtle discussion of the complex "and/or" logic of black representation in preclassical films. Stewart, *Migrating to the Movies*, 53–55, 57–58, 63–64.

12. Knight, *Disintegrating the Musical*, 50.

13. Ibid. I draw the terms "realism" and "theatricality" from Stewart's account. She illustrates that such a distinction might represent a dead-end when applied to the study of American film blackface. Stewart, *Migrating to the Movies*, 53.

14. Alexandre Kojève, *Introduction to the Reading of Hegel: Lectures on the Phenomenology of Spirit*, ed. Allan Bloom, trans. James H. Nicholas Jr. (Ithaca, N.Y.: Cornell University Press, 1980), 3. While the English edition of Kojève uses capital letters for crucial Hegelian abstract concepts like "Desire" and "Self-Consciousness," I have adopted the more conventional practice of using lowercase spellings, thus following the model of Hegel's English translator, A. V. Miller. That said, I use the terms "master" and "slave" (which appear in Kojève's commentaries) in place of the more antiquated "lord" and "bondsman" (which appear in Miller's Hegel translation). I also follow the exclusively masculine language of "man" used in these texts, a proper historicization and critique being beyond the scope of the present discussion.

15. Ibid., 7.

16. Ibid., 8–9. G.W.F. Hegel, *Phenomenology of Spirit*, trans. A. V. Miller (Oxford: Oxford University Press, 1977), 114–115.

17. Kojève, *Introduction*, 16. See Hegel, *Phenomenology*, 115.

18. Kojève, *Introduction*, 19. See Hegel, *Phenomenology*, 116.

19. Hegel, *Phenomenology*, 116–117.

20. Ibid., 118–119.

21. Rogin, *Blackface*, 103–105, 182–183.

22. Frantz Fanon, *Black Skin, White Masks*, trans. Charles Lam Markmann (New York: Grove Press, 1967), 220.

23. Sigmund Freud, "Fetishism," in Strachey et al., *Standard Edition of the Complete Psychological Works of Sigmund Freud*, vol. 11, 153–154.

24. Ibid., 152–154.

25. Ibid., 154.

26. Rogin, *Blackface*, 182–183.

27. In using the term "facing," I mean to make a general allusion to Kimberly Benston's concept of the "facing scene," which has crucially informed my thinking about race and intrafilmic specular relations. Kimberly Benston, "Facing Tradition: Revisionary Scenes in African American Literature," *PMLA* 105, no. 1 (1990): 98–109.

28. Burt Kalmar and Harry Ruby, "Check and Double Check" (unpublished story, n.d.), 10, Box 116S, RKO Scripts, Performing Arts Special Collections, UCLA (hereafter cited as RKO Scripts, UCLA).

29. One might add that, although the front yard of the Blair house is an unfamiliar site, it serves to evoke the (missing) Williams plantation. It is the only rural, quasi-pastoral space physically depicted in the film, and the Blairs themselves are migrated southerners. Inquiring at first whether Amos and Andy "work for Mr. Blair," Richard seems to sense this symmetry.

30. Amazingly, the lodge ritual was conceived in these vague terms in the original story, persisting through all subsequent drafts of the screenplay.

31. During the discussion about the estate at Jean's party, Ralph, sitting on the veranda just outside the room, overhears Richard's plan. He connives to go to the old Williams house that night and intercept the document before Richard can get there the following day.

32. The conversation between Richard and Amos and Andy at the Blair house does not address the "property issue." Even when they hand the deed over to Richard, they appear to know nothing of its import.

33. Slavoj Žižek, *Enjoy Your Symptom! Jacques Lacan in Hollywood and Out*, rev. ed. (New York: Routledge, 2001), 131–132. The journey that Ralph, his sister, and their unnamed partner make to Harlem further illustrates the film's convoluted social geography. It reverses the conventional trajectory of white "slumming." With the representatives of Harlem nightlife—Duke Ellington's Cotton Club band—relocated to the suburbs in *Check and Double Check*, the white sophisticates' outing to the city actually takes them away from the scene of "exotic" jazz.

34. Ralph, who has been riding with Jean, walks the horses back to the stable. By the side of the road, he encounters Richard, who asks for directions. As Richard's taxi departs, the horse scares, prompting Ralph's violent punishment.

35. The horse scene includes a shot of Richard cringing as Ralph whips the animal with his riding crop (offscreen), the noises of the blows audible to the viewer.

36. If the viewer assumes that Andy has "forgotten," then it becomes possible to read his action as faithfully executing the lodge's unacknowledged intention of duping Ralph—as hypothesized by the impossible, conspiratorial reading of the ritual offered above.

37. One trade-press review of *Check and Double Check* nicely captures this weirdness by stating that Amos and Andy become "an indispensable quotient in the solution of the plot" after their initial encounter with Richard. Review of *Check and Double Check*, *Exhibitors Herald-World*, 4 October 1930, 29.

38. Acting as a typological repetition of the Williams plantation in Georgia, the secluded Blair mansion is a safe space for the three men to interact. The urban public space of the train platform is not, necessitating the symbolic prison bars.

39. As on the radio show, the women exist in the film only as Amos and Andy's (inaudible) interlocutors during telephone conversations.

40. See Freud, "Fetishism," 154.

41. Marx, *Capital*, vol. 1, 163–167.

42. In Kalmar and Ruby's original story, Amos and Andy successfully carry the cake across the street. This happy ending calls for the two couples to be shown eating the cake "by silhouette through the frosted window of Madame Queen's beauty shop." Kalmar and Ruby, "Check and Double Check," 31, RKO Scripts, UCLA. Given the film's handling of frosting and the blackface mask, the "frosted" window and silhouette devices are suggestive tropes in their own right. The finished film's succinct, ironic ending evolves through a series of more complicated situations sketched out in ensuing drafts of the script. In two subsequent drafts, Amos and Andy propose to take the women to the country for a picnic, and the story ends with them all in the taxi on "a lonely country road." The taxi backfires and "stops dead in its tracts [*sic*]." Kalmar and Ruby, Check and Double Check ("Final Script"), 167, RKO Scripts, UCLA. While this ending produces frustration and disappointment, the cake survives.

43. Snead, *White Screens/Black Images*, 60.

44. I draw throughout this section on Tania Modleski's work. Modleski theorizes the ways in which "male power frequently works to efface female subjectivity by occupying the site of femininity." Tania Modleski, *Feminism Without Women: Culture and Criticism in a "Postfeminist" Age* (New York: Routledge, 1991), 7. Snead's "exclusionary emulation" describes a paradox of racialization that parallels Modleski's "feminism/'femininity' without women": blackness without African Americans. See also Rogin, *Blackface*, 34.

45. Snead, *White Screens/Black Images*, 58. See also Fanon's discussions of the ideology of "Negro" labor as "gift" in *Black Skin, White Masks*, 49–50.

46. Lott has discussed these central minstrel-show themes in *Love and Theft*, 55–62.

47. In an earlier scene not discussed here, Amos and Andy attempt to change a flat tire on the taxi. In this scene, the film establishes a metonymic linkage between car tires and Amos's and Andy's bodies—their taxi company is not simply "incorporated," after all, but "incorpulated"—which helps to illuminate the final sequence. By destroying the cake in this way, the film bypasses what would be the seemingly more conventional comedic pratfall: one of the characters falling into the cake, or somehow ending up with it on his face (like the young Rufus in *Rufus Jones for President*). In her brilliant analysis of *Singin' in the Rain*, Carol Clover reads the episode in which Kathy Selden (Debbie Reynolds) hits Lina Lamont (Jean Hagen) in the face with a white-frosted cake as one of the film's many veiled jokes about blackface; see "Dancin' in the Rain," *Critical Inquiry* 21 (1995): 722–747.

48. "Sartorial Amos and Andy Refuse to Taxicab Home," *Motion Picture News* 41, no. 40 (4 October 1930): 49. The writer even describes "Mrs. Gosden" and "Mrs. Correll" following behind Amos and Andy, respectively, playing with the taboo image of an interracial couple.

CONCLUSION

1. Josef von Sternberg, *Fun in a Chinese Laundry* (New York: Macmillan, 1965), 218–219, 321.

2. Ibid., 320–321. In von Sternberg's account, the camera and the microphone exist in a "congenital . . . contradict[ion]," a sort of zero-sum relation in which satisfying the demands of the one forces the filmmaker to neglect the demands of the other.

In broadly theoretical terms, he asserts that the camera is an instrument for creative distortion (which, for him, is the essence of art), while the microphone is a "primitive reproductive" instrument (verisimilitude being the antithesis of art).

3. Ibid., 108, 321. The phrase "sound throws no shadows" comes from Béla Balázs, *Theory of the Film: Character and Growth of a New Art*, trans. Edith Bone (London: Dennis Dobson, 1952), 213.

4. Von Sternberg, *Fun*, 166. The idea of "moving lips" synchronization as making the image "redundant" comes from Rick Altman's provocative "Moving Lips: Cinema as Ventriloquism," *Yale French Studies* 60, no. 6 (1980): 67–79.

5. Von Sternberg, *Fun*, 297. Von Sternberg mobilizes these same tropes in the infamous "Hot Voodoo" number of *Blonde Venus* (Paramount, 1932). See Snead, *White Screens/Black Images*, 71.

6. Von Sternberg, *Fun*, 53.

7. Eisner, *Haunted Screen*, 141.

8. *Thunderbolt* begins by establishing the reformed Ritzie's relationship with Bob, a hardworking bank clerk. Although Ritzie lives with Bob and his mother and plans to marry Bob, she is unable to escape her ties to the criminal underworld. The police detain her to question her about Thunderbolt's whereabouts, and her reputation causes Bob to lose his job at the bank. After failing to persuade Thunderbolt that she is through with him and the life of crime (during the nightclub scene), Ritzie sets a trap by arranging a meeting with Thunderbolt. After Thunderbolt is arrested and sentenced to be executed for past crimes, the remainder of the film unfolds almost entirely in a gloomy death-row setting. From his cell, Thunderbolt plots to have Bob framed for murder, so that Bob will be incarcerated in the same cellblock. Then he will lure Bob to his cell door, administering a fatal punch through the bars with his legendary right fist (the reason for his nickname). Luring Bob back to the bank under false pretenses, Thunderbolt's men stage a robbery and shoot a guard, planting the gun on Bob before the police arrive. After learning that Ritzie and Bob were romantically involved even before she knew Thunderbolt and feeling some remorse for his actions, Thunderbolt eventually decides not to carry out his revenge plot. He confesses to the frame-up, gives his approval to Ritzie and Bob's marriage, and goes stoically to the electric chair at the end of the film.

9. Jules Furthman and Charles Furthman, "Thunderbolt" ("tentative silent script," n.d.), 12, Box 7, Folder 11, Jules Furthman Collection, Margaret Herrick Library, AMPAS.

10. Mosby's Blue Blowers were a Los Angeles–based jazz orchestra that also provided music for all of the African American–cast Christie-Cohen comedy shorts, most notably *Music Hath Harms* (1929). On Mosby's career as a bandleader and theater owner, see Marshal Royal's oral history in Clora Bryant et al. eds., *Central Avenue Sounds: Jazz in Los Angeles* (Berkeley: University of California Press, 1998), 33.

11. "Sights and Sounds of the largest Negro city in the world . . ." *Thunderbolt* pressbook, 2, Paramount Press Sheets, AMPAS.

12. This portion of the film actually thematizes hearing without seeing. For instance, when a "new guy" comes to the cellblock, the inmates in opposite cells (who are able to see him) try to describe his face to the men in adjacent cells (who are not).

13. Von Sternberg sees cinema as communicating "an indefinable element" or "precious essence" not intrinsically "visible in the substance that [is] represented" via the camera. Von Sternberg, *Fun*, 292–293.

14. Ibid., 25.

15. Gaylyn Studlar, *In the Realm of Pleasure: Von Sternberg, Dietrich, and the Masochistic Aesthetic* (New York: Columbia University Press, 1988), 92–94.

16. "Pliable" is von Sternberg's term for the condition that all representational elements must attain in order to be useful to the artist. See von Sternberg, *Fun*, 219.

17. "Sights and Sounds of the largest Negro City in the World . . ."

18. "Race Films Making Hit," *Pittsburgh Courier*, 7 September 1929.

19. Cultural historians like David Levering Lewis have dated the end of the Harlem Renaissance itself—of which this filmic "Negro vogue" was a complicated secondary manifestation—to 1932, its supporting institutions (magazines, publishers, civic organizations, theaters, nightclubs) crippled by the economic effects of the Great Depression and the concomitant rise of Left politics. Lewis, *Harlem*, 282–307.

20. Ralph Matthews, "Will 'The Emperor Jones' Restore Our Lost Place in the Movies?" *Baltimore Afro-American*, 23 September 1933.

21. "Race cinema" refers to a cluster of small producers (some run by or at least employing African American behind-camera artists) making films for African American urban audiences featuring all or largely African American casts. Like the phrase "race records" (sound recordings of African American musicians marketed to African American consumers), "race cinema" draws on the use of "the Race" (often capitalized, even in its adjectival form) typical in early-twentieth-century black press and civic discourse: to project an ideal and socially uplifted African American community and to indicate self-naming. Black newspapers used the phrase "race movie" to describe Hollywood productions like *Hallelujah*, a confusion of terms that has led critics like Cripps to conclude that black-press enthusiasm for Hollywood's African American films helped curtail audience interest in black independent cinema. See, for example, "King Vidor to Film Race Movie," *Chicago Defender*, 13 October 1928; and "Race Films Making Hit," *Pittsburgh Courier*, 7 September 1929. See also Cripps, *Slow Fade to Black*, 236.

22. Micheaux struck a production deal with Frank Schiffman, a white theater magnate (whose company owned Harlem film and vaudeville theaters like the Apollo and the Lafayette). The first result of this collaboration was *The Exile*; see "Micheaux to Produce New Film," *Chicago Defender*, 10 January 1931. See also Reid, *Redefining Black Film*, 15–18.

23. Cripps, *Slow Fade to Black*, 323–326.

24. My understanding of silent race films, Micheaux's work in particular, is crucially informed by Stewart's *Migrating to the Movies*, 202–244.

25. Knight usefully argues against the tendency of earlier film historians to privilege silent race films (Micheaux's especially) and neglect their sound counterparts in *Disintegrating the Musical*, 169. See also Jane Gaines, *Fire & Desire: Mixed-Race Movies in the Silent Era* (Chicago: University of Chicago Press), 7–9.

26. Knight, *Disintegrating the Musical*, 187.

27. Although space constraints prevent me from discussing other examples, I want to stress that other films from this period in Micheaux's oeuvre, like *The Girl from Chicago* (1932), contain the same basic dialectic of representation that I trace through *The Exile*.

28. J. Ronald Green's account of the Washingtonian ethos and critique of illegitimate enterprise in *The Exile* has been helpful to my reading. See J. Ronald Green, *With a*

Crooked Stick: The Films of Oscar Micheaux (Bloomington: Indiana University Press, 2004), 126–128, 130–133.

29. See Walls, "'110 Per Cent Woman.'"

30. The main character's actions and costuming also nod in the direction of O'Neill's *The Emperor Jones*.

31. Review, *The Black King*, *Variety*, 19 July 1932, 25.

32. Judith Weisenfeld's work on *The Black King*'s production history is extremely suggestive here. She explains that *The Black King* began as "a play by the Trinidadian immigrant writer, director, and composer Donald Heywood . . . based on Garvey's life." After the play's apparent failure on Broadway, Heywood "became involved with the white producer and director Bud Pollard" (who also plays the judge in the film), working on the film's dialogue. One wonders if this collaboration is, at least in part, responsible for the film's ideological ambiguities: the combination of a complex, multifaceted depiction of black social and political ambitions coupled with heavy-handed mockery and containment of such ambitions. Weisenfeld, *Hollywood Be Thy Name*, 137–138.

33. Quoted in ibid., 144.

34. As Weisenfeld stresses, the film also crosscuts between staged shots of the Johnson movement's members and "what appears to be newsreel footage of a UNIA parade to invoke the visual power of the organization's marches." Ibid., 141.

35. Crafton, *Talkies*, 268.

36. Spadoni, *Uncanny Bodies*, 17.

37. Ibid., 12–19. While such "unforeseen side effects" jeopardized the medium's claim to realism, they were not always, Spadoni stresses, negative, from the studios' point of view. As another form of novelty, these effects could be exploited for the audience's pleasure, as in the case of the "uncanny bodies" that the directors of early horror films created, using offscreen and nonsynchronous sounds to make animate bodies seem inanimate, and vice versa.

38. Maurice, "'Cinema at Its Source,'" 32–33.

39. Crafton, *Talkies*, 269.

40. Ibid., 355–362.

41. Spadoni, *Uncanny Bodies*, 18–19.

42. Knight, *Disintegrating the Musical*, 8–17.

43. Ibid., 8.

44. Ibid., 13–16.

45. Knight, *Disintegrating the Musical*, 22.

46. Ibid.

47. Baldwin, *Devil Finds Work*, 554.

48. Knight, *Disintegrating the Musical*, 22.

49. Massood, *Black City Cinema*, 14.

Index

About the Author

RYAN JAY FRIEDMAN is an assistant professor in the Department of English and the Program in Film Studies at The Ohio State University. He received his Ph.D. from Northwestern University and has published articles on race and American film and literature in *Quarterly Review of Film & Video*, *English Literary History*, and *Arizona Quarterly*.